Daily

Guideposts,

1994

Guideposts®

Carmel, New York 10512

ACKNOWLEDGMENTS

All Scripture quotations, unless otherwise noted, are from *The King James Version of the Bible*.

Scripture quotations marked (RSV) are from the *Revised Standard Version of the Bible*. Copyright © 1946, 1952, 1971 by the Division of Christian Education of the National Council of Churches of Christ in the U.S.A. and are used by permission.

Scripture quotations marked (NRSV) are from the *New Revised Standard Version Bible*, copyright © 1989, by the Division of Christian Education of the National Council of the Churches of Christ in the U.S.A. Published by Thomas Nelson, Inc., Nashville, TN 37214.

Scripture quotations marked (TLB) are from *The Living Bible*, © 1971. Used by permission of Tyndale House Publishers, Inc., Wheaton, IL 60189. All rights reserved.

Scripture quotations marked (NIV) are from the *Holy Bible, New International Version*. Copyright © 1973, 1978, 1984 International Bible Society. Used by permission of Zondervan Bible Publishers.

Scripture quotations marked (NAS) are from the *New American Standard Bible*, © 1960, 1962, 1963, 1968, 1971, 1972, 1973, 1975, 1977 by The Lockman Foundation. Used by permission.

Scripture quotations marked (GNB) are from the *Good News Bible, the Bible in Today's English Version*. Copyright © American Bible Society, 1966, 1971, 1976.

Scripture quotations marked (NKJV) are from *The New King James Version of the Bible*. Copyright © 1979, 1980, 1982 by Thomas Nelson, Inc., Publishers.

"Gifts of the Season," which appears on the calendar page of each month, was written by Marilyn Morgan Helleberg.

"Prayer Can Change Your Life" series, which appears in the beginning of each month, is adapted from *Prayer Can Change Your Life* by Dr. William R. Parker and Elaine St. Johns. Copyright © 1957, by Simon & Schuster, New York, NY 10020. Used by permission.

Charles Swindoll, taken from January 1992 Insight for Living letter referred to in the February 2 devotional. Copyright © 1993, Insight for Living, Anaheim, CA 92806. All rights are reserved. Used with permission.

Quote from "Birches" referred to in the February 14 devotional and quote from "The Death of the Hired Man" referred to in the March 5 devotional are from *The Poetry of Robert Frost* edited by Edward Connery Lathem. Copyright © 1958 by Robert Frost. Copyright © 1967 by Lesley Frost Ballantine. Reprinted by permission of Henry Holt and Company, Inc.

"A Busy Mother's Prayer" by Hazen G. Werner from *A Pocket Prayer Book*. Copyright © 1941 by General Board of Evangelism. Copyright © renewed, 1969, by The Upper Room. Used by permission.

When You Can't Come Back by Dave & Jan Dravecky referred to in the May 10 devotional. Copyright © 1992 by Dave & Jan Dravecky. Used by permission of Zondervan Publishing House.

"Handling Grief," which appears in the May 17 devotional, is reprinted with permission from *Kicking Your Stress Habits* by Donald A. Tubesing. Whole Person Associates, Inc., 210 W. Michigan, Duluth, MN 55802.

"Prayer enlarges the heart until it is capable of containing God's gift of Himself," which appears in the May 24 devotional, Mother M. Teresa M.C., Missionaries of Charity. Reprinted with permission.

Quote by Eugenia Price from *Just As I Am* referred to in the May 29 devotional, copyright © 1968 by Eugenia Price. Reprinted by permission of Harper Collins, New York, NY. All rights reserved.

"Deliver Me from Spinach" cartoon by John Brundige. Reprinted with permission.

Quotes from *Alphabet of Who You Are in Christ*, copyright 1991 by Sylvia Gunter, Prayer Portions, The Father's Business.

If Two Shall Agree by Carey & Pamela Moore referred to in the December 5 devotional, Chosen Books, a division of Baker Book House. Copyright © 1992, Chosen Books, Grand Rapids, MI. Used by permission.

Morning Has Broken by Eleanor Farjeon. Reprinted by permission of Harold Ober Associates, Incorporated. Copyright © 1957 by Eleanor Farjeon.

Photo of David P. Jacobsen by Daniel Ray appears on page 369. Used by permission.

Designed and Illustrated by Holly Johnson
Indexed by Patricia Woodruff
Printed in the United States of America

Table of Contents

TABLE OF CONTENTS

Introduction

And all things, whatsoever ye shall ask in prayer, believing, ye shall receive.
—Matthew 21:22

Welcome to *Daily Guideposts, 1994*.

Our aim, as always in *Daily Guideposts*, is to help you draw closer to God every day of the new year. And what better way to carry our devotion to God into our day than through prayer, the act of communicating with God. "Pray without ceasing," we are commanded in I Thessalonians 5:17. So in this, our eighteenth edition, we celebrate *the power of prayer*.

Prayer has been called the mightiest force in the world. Because we pray *to God*, there are amazing promises connected to the call to pray. "Ask, and it shall be given you," Jesus promises in Matthew 7:7. "You are My friends if you do whatever I command you," He says in John 15:14, 16 (NKJV), and "whatever you ask the Father in My name He may give you." Even more incredible, God says in Isaiah 65:24, "Before they call, I will answer; and while they are yet speaking, I will hear." Our needs and concerns are being heard and met by God before we can even put them into words.

These are just a few of the promises that await your discovery throughout the year with *Daily Guideposts, 1994*. Each chapter opens with *Gifts of the Season*, a three-line verse followed by a prayer to help you turn your spirit toward God for the month. *Quiet Time*, monthly bonus prayers, are scattered throughout the book to remind you to pause and draw close to God. The *Prayer Diary* at the end of each month is a place to record briefly your thoughts after each day's reading, and includes a special box for your monthly prayer requests.

Many of your favorite writers are here to greet you in 1994, including Fred Bauer, Marilyn Morgan Helleberg, Marion Bond West and Scott Walker. There are also some new folks, like Dolphus Weary, a lay minister from Mendenhall, Mississippi, and our special guest David Jacobsen from Bear Valley, California, who writes of his difficult days in captivity as a hostage in Lebanon in the series *Faith: Your Daily Survival Kit*. Occasional visitors make *House Guest* calls and include Bonnie Lukes, Ellen Secrest and Timothy Sledge, the college-age son of Linda Ching Sledge, who appears with his mother in a special week-long, end-of-summer series, *A Season of Change: When a Child Leaves Home*.

Six other special series await you in 1994: Pam Kidd starts each month with the powerful promise that *Prayer Can Change Your Life*, based on the famous 1957 classic book of the same title by Dr. William R. Parker and Elaine St. Johns. Learn with Pam how honest prayer transformed her life by taking her from depression and fear to joy and hope. In *Practicing the Power of Prayer*, various writers share their special prayer techniques throughout the year, and invite you to try them out.

During Holy Week, we will be *Listening to Jesus' Answers*. Eric Fellman uncovers the hidden meanings behind the answers Jesus gives to questions He was asked during His eventful last week, and shows how they are the keys to new life. As summer begins, Daniel Schantz's series *Finding the Joy in Living* invites us to learn from an unlikely source—the Book of Ecclesiastes—how to enjoy all that God has blessed us with. Elizabeth Sherrill's *Waiting: The Hardest Part of Prayer* takes us through the difficult in-between times of prayer when we're waiting for God's answers, and teaches how we can learn to trust God, no matter what. Finally, our year closes with Advent and Phyllis Hobe's *How Shall We Adore Him?*, where we learn about the meaning of adoration during this joyous season of anticipating and celebrating Jesus' birth.

Then there are all the other extras you've come to expect: the *Scripture Bookmark*; four specially designed *Prayer Postcards*, this year with church scenes; *A Gathering of Friends*, the biography section, where your writer-friends tell you about themselves, their activities of the past year, and especially what prayer means to them; and our three-part index *The Reader's Guide*.

Daily Guideposts, 1994, is chock-full of good things for you to experience in this new year—and all are meant to draw you closer to God and to remind you of His great and powerful gift, *prayer*.

May God bless you throughout this year. May His grace and love abound and grow within you as you grow in love and devotion, and make prayer your heartfelt practice during 1994.   —The Editors

January

S	M	T	W	T	F	S
						1
2	3	4	5	6	7	8
9	10	11	12	13	14	15
16	17	18	19	20	21	22
23	24	25	26	27	28	29
30	31					

GIFTS OF THE SEASON

The Snow

This newborn year, a
slate of freshly fallen snow
awaits my footprints.

*Creator God, guide my steps through the coming months,
that the path I make may conform to Your will.*

1   PRAYER CAN CHANGE YOUR LIFE
SAT   Practice Honesty

Lord, teach us to pray....   —Luke 11:1

I was knee-deep in the bleakest January I had ever known. We had just spent our first Christmas without my brother David. His divorce had divided our extended family, and he thought it kinder to stay away. My widowed mother was terribly hurt by the family crisis and was inconsolable. And Keri, our fifteen-year-old daughter, was protesting the death from a brain tumor of her favorite young cousin Justin by turning on God, friends and family.

Trying to recover from this shattering time, I was dusting my husband David's study when a book fell from the bookcase. Catching it before it hit the floor, I found its title daring me: *Prayer Can Change Your Life*. Could this be a sign? After this emotionally draining time, I longed for a new year of strength and serenity.

As I opened the book and began reading, I learned that within this classic volume, written by Dr. William R. Parker and Elaine St. Johns in 1957, was the revolutionary story of an unusual scientific experiment that proved that prayer does bring positive results. What emerged from these experiments was "prayer therapy," specific prayer techniques that could be used by individuals or small groups with astounding success. The book came with this promise: *Follow the book's direction and make every prayer you pray a practice in honesty, and your life will change for the better.*

I vowed to give prayer therapy a try. I gathered a group of my dearest friends together and we followed the strategies in *Prayer Can Change Your Life*. All six of us — Nancy, Gloria, Martha Kay, Diane, Pam P. and I — committed ourselves to meeting every Thursday at noon for the coming year, as we struggled to pray honestly, and learned to relinquish control of all our troubles and trust them to God. Did we see a change in our lives because of prayer? Well, that's what I want to tell you about during this coming year.

On the first day of each month in 1994, I will share some of my life-changes with you. I will try to show you how prayer helped me face my problems, brought me peace and sometimes offered surprises that could only be called miracles. Indeed, the book that almost fell on my head was a sign that pointed the way for me — and now points the way for you — to a life changed through prayer.

Lord, teach me to pray.   —Pam Kidd

Editor's Note: The book that changed Pam Kidd's life, Prayer Can Change Your Life *by Dr. William R. Parker and Elaine St. Johns, can also change your life during 1994. If you would like to order this Christian classic, please write to: Prayer Can Change Your Life, Guideposts Associates, Inc., P.O. Box 569, Brewster, NY 10509.*

$\frac{2}{SUN}$　*But let a man examine himself....*　　—I Corinthians 11:28

I woke up early this Sunday morning to the first snowstorm of the season, which had covered the dead-brown fields below our house with a pure white blanket of fluffy flakes. After we got home from church, I hastily changed my clothes, strapped on my cross-country skis and took off for a quick jaunt across the pristine snow. Soon I came upon some fresh animal tracks and made two discoveries: I found where the red foxes had dug their winter den (now I could watch them closely all winter!); I realized that our own dog had wandered much too close to the busy highway while we were at church (that's the end of her unlimited freedom!). Tracks are *revealing*, I decided, and then I noticed my own obvious tracks in the snow.

What if I left tracks wherever I went? I thought back to my morning at church where my tracks would reveal that I made a beeline to the exact same pew I always choose (even though I've vowed to start moving around). During the coffee hour, I zoomed straight across the room, seeking familiar faces (even though I passed several strangers standing alone). And, finally, I made a detour to avoid shaking the minister's hand on the way out (I was in a hurry).

As I turned my skis toward home, I noticed that the falling snow was already covering my tracks, reminding me that God graciously covers my errant tracks — after my self-examination and confession.

Maybe I need to make a daily habit of reviewing my track record, snow or no snow.

Thank You, Jesus, for covering my tracks.　　—Carol Kuykendall

$\frac{3}{MON}$　*Put off your old nature...and be renewed in the spirit....*
　　　　　—Ephesians 4:22–23 (RSV)

For the past two years, I've spent New Year's Day in Pasadena,

California, watching the Tournament of Roses Parade. It's an exciting morning, but by ten o'clock the parade is over. The spectators pack up their thermoses and blankets, and the marching bands and float builders begin to celebrate a job well done. Seems ironic that while most of us are thinking about a new beginning, these folks are celebrating the successful ending of many months of hard work.

It makes me think about fresh starts in the new year. I usually put a lot of pressure on myself to post my New Year's pledge on the refrigerator and get started right away: "Read the Bible every day"; "Lose ten pounds"; "Watch less television." I fear that if I don't make a fresh start now, I'll have blown it. *But who says New Year's Day is my one big chance to start anew?* Maybe New Year's resolution traditionalists think so, but certainly not God.

Thankfully, God gives me 365 opportunities, and reminders, to start again. For instance, if I haven't begun an exercise program by February, then watching the graceful athletes of the Winter Olympics will remind me to get in gear. When my son Ross starts kindergarten in September, I can rededicate myself to turning off the TV and reading with him. And if I've slipped up on my Bible reading, I'll be prodded to start again on National Bible Sunday in November. In a sense, every day is New Year's Day with God.

Lord, hear my earnest prayers for renewal and change throughout this year, and give me the strength and courage to follow them through.   —Gina Bridgeman

---

$\frac{4}{TUES}$ *For the commandment is a lamp and the teaching a light....*   —Proverbs 6:23 (RSV)

Not long ago, one of our staff arrived at the office chuckling. "What's so funny?" I asked.

"Several people on the train this morning were asking the conductor where he had been for the past few days," the staff member replied.

"'Oh,' said the conductor, 'I've been to *rules* class. The railroad makes us take it once a year, so they can teach us everything we need to know about working on the railroad!'

"Well, we all laughed at the preposterousness of the idea of learning everything you need to know about work in a once-a-year class. And then one of the commuters spoke up: 'Wouldn't it be nice if they had a rules class for life!' Imagine that!"

I began to think about this idea of a "rules class for life," and it occurred to me that Norman and I do have one, and we've followed it all our lives. It's the Bible. All we have ever needed for knowing how to live and to love is found in its pages. It contains the Golden Rule, the Lord's Prayer, the Twenty-third Psalm, Jesus' Sermon on the Mount, Paul's great treatise on love in I Corinthians 13, and much more.

Perhaps you feel the need for a rules class today. Why not reach for God's Word and find, as David did, "a lamp to my feet and a light to my path" (Psalm 119:105, RSV).

Lord, the world seems a more difficult place to understand as each day passes. Let Your Word show me the way today.
                                                    — Ruth Stafford Peale

---

5
WED
What things soever ye desire, when ye pray, believe that ye receive them, and ye shall have them.   — Mark 11:24

You probably won't be surprised to learn that my barber does a lot of talking. He fancies himself a philosopher, and sometimes I believe he is. At least, it seemed so to me at my last haircut when with the first snip of the scissors he said, "I live out of the future."

"What does that mean?" I asked courageously, knowing full well that I was in for an onslaught.

"Some people live in the past," he began, "some in the present and not enough know to live out of the future. I'm not going to worry about the past — it's done and gone. And the present? Look!" He waved his scissors in the air. I looked. "It's here, it's gone, it's here again." He went back to snipping.

"But the future...*ah-h-h*," he sighed. "There's a lot of it waiting out there and all I have to do is decide what part of it I want." He went on to tell me how a long time ago when his kids were little, he "lived" with them as one by one they graduated from college. "Now I'm doing the same with my grandkids. Right this minute, I *see* them with their diplomas."

I was getting the drift, but he forged on, giving me a list of things he was enjoying that hadn't happened yet. To him, this was something larger than hope. It was reality. "No sir, we can't go back to the past," he repeated. "But we can live *up* to the future. We can make it happen."

"So how do people start living your way?" I asked.

"Simple," he said. "Pray. Thank God. He's got it all laid out for you."

The philosopher got a bigger tip than usual that day. Who knows, maybe he'll add it to his grandkids' college fund.

Right now, Lord, I'm thanking You for all the good things You have in store for me in the year ahead.   —Van Varner

6
THURS

HOUSE GUEST

Arise, shine; for thy light is come, and the glory of the Lord is risen upon thee.   —Isaiah 60:1

I sit in the living room in the early morning quiet this first week of January. The children are back in school; my husband is at work. Tonight we'll take down the Christmas tree, wrap up the ornaments and pack everything away until next year. This was a whirlwind holiday for us; we moved here three weeks ago and by some miracle managed to survive both the move and the Christmas festivities. Now I wonder what this new year in this new town will be like for us.

Sipping my coffee, I thumb through last Sunday's church bulletin and read an article by our pastor about the feast of the Epiphany. It seems it was an ancient custom of the church to bless homes on this significant day by inscribing the initials of the three wise men — Gaspar, Melchior and Balthazar — over the main entrance of the home. The pastor further suggested that members of the congregation might wish to continue this unique tradition.

What a special way to start our first year in this house, I think, and five minutes later have the ladder out of the garage and on the front porch. Balancing on the aluminum steps I scrawl $G + M + B$ and the present year with a piece of chalk on the wood frame over the door. To complete the blessing, we'll all say the following prayer later at dinner:

> God, our Father, we ask You to visit this home.
> Chase far away from it all the snares of the enemy.
> Send Your holy angels to live with us and keep us at peace.
> May Your blessings be always with us.
> We ask this through Christ our Lord. Amen.

"Welcome to our home," I whisper as I put away the ladder. I step out and receive the new year with a peaceful heart.

Draw me close to You, Father, as the Star drew the wise men to Your side.   —Ellen Secrest

Quiet Time

O gracious and holy Father,
give us wisdom to perceive Thee,
intelligence to understand Thee,
diligence to seek Thee,
patience to wait for Thee,
eyes to behold Thee,
a heart to meditate upon Thee,
and a life to proclaim Thee;
through the power of the Spirit
of Jesus Christ our Lord.
                    — *Benedict of Nursia*

7
FRI
*When the multitudes saw it [the healing], they marveled,
and glorified God....*   — Matthew 9:8

Once I asked a friend of mine who was a physician how he came to choose that profession. "Did you have scientific inclinations as a child?" I wanted to know. "Were there doctors in your family?"

"No," he said, "but I remember very well the moment when I made that decision. I was a youngster on a remote Kansas farm. In winter, the snows lay deep and often the roads were blocked. One terrible winter day, my younger sister became very ill. She had a high fever and became delirious. My parents were beside themselves. How to get the doctor — that was the problem.

"A neighbor volunteered to try to get through the drifts to the doctor's office, which finally he did. The doctor, in turn, struggled through the snow to our house. He found his patient desperately ill. He sat with my sister for nearly twenty-four hours. I remember the fear, the anxiety, the terrible concern. No one slept.

"Finally when morning came," my friend continued, "the doctor got up from beside my little sister. I was crouched behind a chair, because I didn't really understand all that was going on. My father and mother were standing there, almost hopeless, when the doctor walked over to them. I shall never forget it. He put one hand on my mother's shoulder, the other on my father's, and he said, 'I am happy to tell you that by the grace of God your little daughter has passed the crisis and will get well.'

"I was looking at my parents," my friend said. "Never in all my life have I seen such blinding happiness. Tears rolled down their cheeks. They threw their arms around each other and sobbed. And in that moment I knew I had to be a doctor. I wanted to be able to do and say things that would put happiness like that on human faces."

Regardless of profession, what better motivation can any of us have as we walk through life? Make that your goal, and watch the happiness that you cause come flooding back to you.

Dear Lord, keep us ever mindful that it is giving that makes us able to receive.   — Norman Vincent Peale

---

$\frac{8}{SAT}$ *O give thanks to the Lord, for he is good, for his steadfast love endures for ever.*   — Psalm 136:1 (RSV)

All healthy families have their squabbles. That is part of being human. We had such a flare-up today.

This afternoon I took my two sons to the mall to return a coat that did not fit. While making the exchange, one of my sons — I will not say which — saw an athletic warm-up suit he felt he could not live without. Remembering the mound of Christmas presents he had just received and realizing that it is going to be June before I finish paying off the Christmas bills, I told him no.

Well, he pitched a fit. "I've been wanting that suit for a year! If I don't get it, my athletic career will come to a screeching halt!" Finally, worn down and near the end of my patience, I walked with him to a bench where we had a nose-to-nose talk.

I knew that he had fifty dollars of his own Christmas money stuffed in his pocket, and I decided it was time he learned a financial lesson. "I'll pay for half of the suit if you'll pay for the other half," I told him.

"Pay twenty dollars!" he exploded. "Dad, you've got to be kidding! That's my money!" He sulked off down the mall, leaving me hurt and angry.

Driving home, I was seething. *This kid thinks he can have anything he wants. He doesn't appreciate a thing... has no idea how much his mother and I sacrifice... has no comprehension of the value of money... is absolutely ungrateful.* With stern parental rectitude, I summed up my reactions —

sounding a whole lot like my own father: *He's got a lot of growing up to do.*

Somewhere between the mall and home, however, God shook me awake. He seemed to say, "Scott, your attitude is not a whole lot different from your son's. No matter how much I give you, you always want more. Seldom do you really gush with thanksgiving. You, too, often think that everything should be given to you exactly when and how you want it, without your working for it. Come on, Scott, look at your own attitude. After all, you're forty-two years old!"

Well, thanks to my young son, and a nose-to-nose talk with my heavenly Father, I got a glimpse of myself. My son and I must grow up together, learning to handle money responsibly, and to be grateful. And when I showed my son this devotional, he commented, "I like it."

Dear God, I come to You as a little child. Forgive my immaturity and receive my prayers of gratitude. Amen.   — Scott Walker

---

$\frac{9}{SUN}$ *Sing psalms and hymns and spiritual songs with thankfulness in your hearts to God.*   — Colossians 3:16 (RSV)

Recently, I heard a radio interview that helped me understand a mystery.

Why does the same experience affect people in such different ways? Why did Corrie ten Boom emerge with vibrant faith from a Nazi concentration camp that left others shattered? Why did job layoffs at their firm last year plunge one friend into inertia, another into action?

The interview was with a pianist and composer who'd gotten his start accompanying silent films in movie theaters. "That must have required great attention," the interviewer commented. "You must have followed the action frame by frame to reflect in the music what the audience was seeing on the screen."

"Yes," William Parry agreed, "but it also worked the other way. The music I played affected what moviegoers saw."

He remembered one Charlie Chaplin film, with its trademark blend of humor and pathos, where he could underscore a scene either way. "If I played bright, bouncy tunes, the audience would roar with laughter. But if I accompanied the very same scene with mournful music, handkerchiefs would come out all over the theater."

This got me wondering, *Do we go through life itself, each hearing our own background music?* For some brisk and stirring, for others in a minor key. For one full of dissonance, for another melodic and harmonious.

And if I cannot change the events of my life, could I learn to change the music to which they are set?

Give me a hymn of praise, Father, for Your presence in all that occurs today.
                                                              — Elizabeth Sherrill

---

10 *Besides being wise, the Teacher also taught the people*
MON *knowledge, weighing and studying and arranging many*
       proverbs.   — Ecclesiastes 12:9 (NRSV)

When I was in high school, I was infatuated with science and soon found myself seriously considering a career in medicine. I looked to my teachers of biology and chemistry and physics to fill my head full of the stuff that I needed to make my way in the world. But one of my teachers — not in the sciences — found my head too full. Mrs. Siegel weighed and studied and decided that some of my proverbs needed re-arranging and unstuffing.

She was my senior English teacher for an advanced placement college course. One day, she threw out a challenge to me right in class. "Why are you going to college?" she asked.

"To become a doctor," was my confident reply.

"Wrong!" she lamented. "Try again."

"To learn how to become a doctor?" I proposed in a more tentative tone.

"No. You haven't gotten it yet. I had hoped you would go to college to learn how *to become a human being who happens to be a doctor.*"

I've forgotten the names of those other fine teachers, and most of the facts that filled my head. It is Mrs. Siegel I remember, the woman who taught me that reading, writing, public speaking are tools of life for us all. Only when I succeed in being a human being can I be the doctor that my patients need me to be. I think that is true for all of us, whatever career we choose.

I praise You, God, for wise instruction and wise instructors, precious gifts from You to me.
                                                              — Diane Komp

11
TUES
...*Forgetting those things which are behind....*
— Philippians 3:13

In 1994, I'd like to be a better person than I have been this past year, and to help me achieve this goal I've formed a spiritual alphabet. I'm resolved to memorize and practice my ABC's:

Anger makes me unattractive. Overcome it (Psalm 37:8, TLB).

Be forgiving. I want my sins forgiven, don't I? (Luke 6:37).

Count my blessings; name them one by one (Proverbs 10:22, NAS).

Delete negatives from my mind and conversation (Philippians 4:8).

Eat wisely, exercise regularly. My body is the temple of the Holy Ghost (I Corinthians 6:19–20, TLB).

Find a place of service and then be a faithful servant (Matthew 25:21).

Go the second mile (Philippians 3:14).

Hide God's Word in my heart. It will keep me from sinning (Psalm 119:11).

Imitate Jesus (John 13:35).

Judge not (Matthew 7:1).

Know the truth. It will set me free (John 8:32).

Live by the Golden Rule (Matthew 7:12).

Make a joyful noise unto the Lord (Psalm 66:1–2).

Never spend time or effort trying to even the score (Matthew 5:39–42).

Owe no one anything but love, appreciation, forgiveness (Romans 13:8).

Pray about everything (Philippians 4:6, TLB).

Quench not the spirit (I Thessalonians 5:19).

Respect all human life. We are made in God's image (Genesis 1:27).

Start to keep a prayer journal (I John 5:13).

Tell someone you love that you love them; tell them again (Romans 5:5).

Up with praise, down with criticism (Matthew 7:3–4).

Visit a shut-in (Matthew 25:36).

"Whosoever" in God's Word means me! Take it personally (John 3:16).

"X-cell" in saying, "I'm sorry" (Luke 17:3, TLB).

Yesterday is gone — enjoy today. It may be all I have (Psalm 118:24).

Zero in on my spiritual ABC's. Make them priority this year (Matthew 6:33).

*Dear Lord, help me to be disciplined in learning to love You —
from A to Z.*   — Dorothy Shellenberger

12 *The Heavens are telling the glory of God....Without a*
WED *sound or word, silent in the skies, their message reaches*
out to all the world....   —Psalm 19:1, 3–4 (TLB)

This winter, I splurged and bought myself a mechanical indoor walking track. While I'd prefer to exercise out-of-doors, the below-zero wind-chills often keep me inside.

One day, as I was walking on the treadmill's belt, I noticed the lettering on the motor: "6 hp motivational fitness track." *Motivational* fitness track? I laughed at its presumption. What made it think it was motivational? But I realized, as I approached my second mile on the thing, that it was right. How could I *not* be motivated? So little effort was required of me. Its very presence reminded me of my need to exercise, and a "portable" walking path was right here near the comfort of my wood stove.

By the time I'd finished my second mile, I'd thought of lots of other "silent motivators," too. Like the cross on top of the church I passed on my way to the grocery store, which helped remind me of the need for what my pastor called "weekday religion." Or the simple act of witnessing a hymn book passed to a newcomer in church, which inspired me to be more aware of strangers in our congregation. Even the chill of the season prompted me to recall with awe that God had provided for His smallest furry and feathered creatures.

I'm walking more on my track these days—and pondering the fact that sometimes a silent witness can be the most powerful motivator of all.

Open my heart, Father, to Your silent motivators all around me
that remind me to seek Your presence. Amen. —Mary Lou Carney

13 *How can a man be born when he is old?...*   —John 3:4
THURS

My dear Grandchild,

I know that you are very comfortable there in your mother's womb, lulled by her heartbeat and warmed by her love. But it's not a good place to live forever. It's dark in there, and you're upside down, and you've never been out to play.

Come February, your tranquil world will be disturbed by the pangs of birth, and you will be asked to leave the place you call home. But don't be afraid. Loving arms are waiting to receive you. Wonderful things have been planned to welcome you to life. Things like rattles and rocking chairs, blocks to stack and crayons to smear over clean white paper. You'll get to taste some sweet things like strained beets and applesauce, and later on, pizza and chocolate and popcorn.

There's much to learn here in this world, like how to crawl and how to walk and how to fall. Then comes swimming and biking and basketball and skating and mopeding. This life is full of strange and curious wonders, like Ninja Turtles and Batman, robots and trampolines, bubble gum and Green Slime.

So much to see and do! More than you could ever imagine! So don't be afraid to leave your safe little world. Comfort isn't all it's cracked up to be. I've gotten much too comfortable myself. And in anticipating your joyous arrival, you remind me: *I, too, need to be born — again, and again, and again.*

With love, your Grandpa-to-be.

Lord, give me the childlike trust of a newborn to let go of the old, and be renewed every day by Your love.   — Daniel Schantz

---

14
FRI
Be ye not stiffnecked...but yield yourselves unto the Lord....   — II Chronicles 30:8

"Chris, the bathtub faucet is leaking again," my wife Roe said to me one morning.

I had been battling that leak for four months. First, I thought it was the cold water line. I replaced the washers and the stem. *Drip. Drip. Drip.*

Then I replaced the hot water line's washer and stem. *Drip. Drip. Drip.*

I drove to the plumbing store, and they suspected my handles were worn so they sold me new handles. I screwed them in place, washed the tub, closed the lights for the night. *Drip. Drip. Drip.*

"That's it!" I announced to Roe after she pointed out that, yes, the leak still wasn't fixed. "I'm calling the plumber." Two days and ninety dollars later, the leak stopped.

I have a hard time with failure. I want to believe I can handle everything by myself and that I don't need anyone's help. But sometimes my best efforts aren't enough and I have to accept that *I can't do it all.* Then I can turn to One Who can make things right.

Is there some problem that's been wearing you down and you can't seem to let go of it? A problem or relationship that you've been stubbornly struggling with that you refuse to be defeated by? Listen to one who's been there: It's okay to let it go. Not everyone can fix all the leaking drips in life. And isn't it good that we have a gracious Lord Who loves us and to Whom we can surrender and say, "I can't do it all. Help me, God, with my problem."

Lord, remind me when I'm trying too hard to be "Superman" that I don't have to carry everything on my shoulders. You are there and so are Your angels, ready to help me.

—Christopher de Vinck

15
_{SAT} *And so you became a model....* —I Thessalonians 1:7 (NIV)

I thought I knew a lot about Dr. Martin Luther King, Jr. I have heard his stirring "I Have A Dream" speech and have read of his fighting for equal rights and the end of segregation. I know that he is considered not just an American civil rights leader, but an international one, for hundreds of schools have been named after him. I know there is a street named for him in Oakland, California, close to where I live. And when I was in the Netherlands, I saw that there was a park named for him in Amsterdam, too.

With all I learned about him, I was surprised when I read that when he was born he was named "Michael." His name was not changed to Martin Luther until he was five years old and about to start school. That's when his father Michael Luther King changed both his own name to Martin Luther King, Sr., and the name of his son to Martin Luther King, Jr., in honor of the Protestant reformer.

It seems fitting that on this day, Martin Luther King, Jr.'s birthday, we can consider those who have been role models in our own lives. Perhaps a favorite teacher? Or a relative you could turn to when you were at a rocky passage in your life? Or perhaps there was a public figure— such as Martin Luther King, Jr.—whose moral courage and persistence inspired you to keep trying for a goal that seemed unreachable. If possible, why not write that person a letter today, briefly explaining his or her role in your life. And then consider your own life in light of this question: *What's there in my life that could be a model for others?*

God, thank You for creating spiritual and moral leaders. Let me act as if I were a leader to someone else—perhaps I am.

—Linda Neukrug

16 *O Lord, thou hast searched me, and known me.*
SUN   —Psalm 139:1

The other day I was listening to some songs out of the 1940s, and one of them was the plaintive World War II hit "Now Is the Hour." Remember? If you're over fifty you probably do. Then it came to me: *That's the same melody used for the glorious old hymn "Search Me, O God."*

> *Search me, O God, and know my heart today*
> *Try me, O Savior, know my thoughts I pray*
> *See if there be some wicked way in me*
> *Cleanse me from every sin and set me free.*

A little research revealed that the music has been traced to the Maori people of New Zealand, and the lyrics to writer Edwin Orr. I don't know if the Maori owe the tune to some other culture or not, but I do know that Mr. Orr borrowed liberally from a poet named David. Compare the hymn to that famous king's prayer in Psalm 139:23, 24.

The point? Only to observe that the past is always prologue to the present. That what we are and do and say today has roots in other people, times and places. Though we may think our trials and tests unique, we have much the same physical and spiritual needs as our forebears—certainly the same dependence upon God's mercy and grace to sustain us, which He has promised to do even when we fall short of His high calling. That's why this old hymn is such an appropriate and appealing prayer, today and every day of our lives.

> *Yes, search us, O God, and know our hearts today,*
> *Try us, test us, cleanse us and help us find our way.*
>   —Fred Bauer

17 *"I am with you always, even to the end of the age."*
MON   —Matthew 28:20 (NAS)

Losing is hard. In the last ten seconds of our semifinal game, the basketball team I coach had gone from being one point ahead to losing by one point. From screaming with excitement to dejected silence. Some, including my son Jon, had tears in their eyes.

I called them all together, saying a quick, silent prayer for guidance. Then I said, "Boys, losing doesn't make you losers. Acting beaten can make you a loser. Hold your heads up, be proud we played such a close game today. Remember that we were the only ones who believed we could get this far, and that makes us all winners."

Nobody burst into a cheer, but the tears dried up. Then the youngest and smallest player said, "Mr. Fellman, are you going to come back and coach next year?"

"Sure, Neal," I replied.

"Great!" said Neal.

Besides making me feel good, his comment sparked a thought. It meant a lot to the boys that I was there when we were winning, but it also was important to be around for the losing.

I guess that's why God makes so many promises to be with us in "the valley of the shadow of death" or "even to the end of the world." He knows losing is hard and that life has many losses. He also plans to be there all the time.

Are you facing a setback today? Has a sudden unexpected event, like the opposing team's scoring in the last ten seconds, turned a great joy into despair? Remember, losing doesn't make you a loser, and remember, too, that our "Coach" never quits on us.

Lord, help me face losses with grace and with the confidence that they are only temporary and that You are beside me, turning setbacks into comebacks.
— Eric Fellman

18
TUES

Blessed be the Lord: for he hath showed me his marvelous kindness....
— Psalm 31:21

I've always been sensitive, my feelings easily hurt. Things that might not bother a lot of people could make me cry and often spoil the day: a boss bawls you out; a cab driver is rude; a husband scolds; a neighbor or friend or your own child says something cutting. Stung though you may be, don't take it out on someone else. I've found that the best way to get over an unexpected hurt is to try to cancel it by comforting somebody else.

Life is usually prompt in giving us the chance. One day, still seething and suffering from a sharp remark from one of my children, I was seated on a bus next to a small, shabby man staring fixedly out the window and struggling not to cry. As he turned and groped for a handkerchief, I found myself saying, "I'm so sorry. Is there anything I can do to help you?"

"No, thanks, ma'am," he said, producing a picture from his worn wallet. It was of a pretty little girl. "We lost her yesterday," he said, eager to talk about it. "I'm going down now to pick out the flowers."

In our few blocks' ride across the city, we shared his pride in her, and his great loss. We touched upon the mystery of being born at all, of being parents, of the brevity and beauty of life upon this earth, and the joy of sharing it with someone we loved, even for a little while. We spoke of the wonderful comfort of faith and the promises of Jesus. How He bade the children to come unto Him, for theirs "is the kingdom of God" (Mark 10:14).

When we parted, I knew the man's heart was lighter. He was actually smiling. "This has meant a lot to me, ma'am. I'm going to tell my wife some of the things we said."

"You made me feel better, too," I told him. It was as if some vital balance had been struck between that which is hurtful and that which is healing. My day was no longer spoiled, and his had been brightened. And isn't that what really counts? That the good, the kind, the encouraging things we do for one another can equal and even surpass the pain we all inflict sometimes, and sometimes suffer.

Dear Lord, please give me the strength to heal hurt feelings. And guard me against hurting anyone else.   — Marjorie Holmes

19 *I pray thee, say me not nay....*   — I Kings 2:20
WED

Years ago, during a church committee meeting I attended, our group was brainstorming a new project. Suggestions were flowing freely, but for some unexplainable reason I was finding fault with all of them. "We'll never get enough people," or "That won't work because...," or "There isn't enough room" were some of my replies. I certainly didn't intend to put down every idea. In fact, I thought I was being helpful.

Then one of the members spoke up. "Okay, Ellie," Alice said with a smile and a kindly voice, "you've responded negatively to almost every suggestion that's been made. Now do you have any *positive* ideas to contribute?"

Embarrassed, I had to admit that I didn't.

Since that day, I've always been grateful to Alice, not just for her honesty, but because it helped me change my behavior. Now when I'm in a

meeting or in a conversation with friends and I feel myself getting critical, I stop and ask myself: *Why am I being negative? How do I really feel
about what was said? Is my response appropriate?* Often the answers to
these questions lead me to say something more constructive. That way I
find myself building a conversation, not destroying one.

An old song tells us to focus on the positive and hold on to the
affirmative. I've discovered that life is a lot brighter — and a lot more
fun — when I do.

*Dear Lord, whenever my expressions are negative ones, remind
me to stop and think, then follow with ones that are constructive
and positive.* — Eleanor Sass

20
THURS
Be content with such things as ye have....
— Hebrews 13:5

I came home on one of those gray days that makes you think the winter
will never end, and for a moment I stopped outside the lighted windows
of our apartment and looked at the quiet scene inside.

Five-year-old Willy was at the kitchen table drawing with a crayon in
his coloring book, his tongue wagging between his teeth as he concentrated on his design. My wife Carol stood before the stove testing the
spaghetti sauce, furrowing her brow. *A little more basil? More oregano?* I
could only see the top of two-year-old Timothy's head, a feathery tuft of
blond ragweed.

Soon I would walk in the door and become a part of the scene, and
everything would change. There would be the boisterous greetings,
then someone would have to remind Willy to set the table and Timothy
to wash his hands before dinner. And before long the nightly ritual of
baths, books and bed would begin with its usual setbacks and outcries
("I don't want a bath tonight!"). Soon the evening would be over, con-
sumed in the hectic business of living.

Now, though, I stood outside gazing in, savoring what I saw.

The Bible urges us to be content with what we have. Sometimes all
that it takes is for us to stand back from ourselves for a moment so that
we can see our blessings and be content — as I am.

Thank You, Lord, for the loved ones who make my life full.
— Rick Hamlin

21 *...Christ in you, the hope of glory.* — Colossians 1:27
FRI

Several times a week I drive the stretch of Mississippi Highway 49 that passes the junior college I attended some twenty-six years ago. I remember as a freshman standing by the road just off campus watching cars pass me by. My dream was one day to own a car, head out on that highway and never look back on the poverty-stricken life of my hometown of Mendenhall.

What really happened I never could have imagined. A year later, I was offered a scholarship to a Christian college in California. While there, I went on an evangelism trip to the Far East and was invited to stay in the Orient to continue evangelism work. And all this poor, black teenager had hoped for was just to get me a car and drive old Highway 49!

But as gratifying as it was to be appreciated and to serve halfway across the world, somehow I couldn't get away from my roots. I knew God was calling me back to the poverty and hopelessness of Mississippi—and of Mendenhall. But when I surrendered to God's call, I found that God gave me a new dream: to bring hope and empowerment and change to my own people.

Today, I own a car and drive that familiar highway because I live and work in the community where I grew up, ministering to the people whom I had once longed to leave. I marvel at how many miles God took me before I ended up right back home.

If you are holding on to hopes of faraway things, check them again. Could it be that God is calling you to serve Him and others right where you are?

Lord Jesus, help me to hear Your call, and to serve You joyfully.
— Dolphus Weary

22 *Come near to me, I pray you....* — Genesis 45:4
SAT

"Dad, why don't you call some of your friends," I suggested. I'd been saying the same thing every Saturday morning since my eighty-two-year-old stepfather came to live with me almost two years ago.

"I will," he said, but rarely did. Finally, he admitted, "I don't have anything to say."

What could I say? I did the same thing with my friends. Unless something important was happening in my life, I didn't keep in touch. I thought I needed a reason to call or write.

Then, one afternoon, Dad got a call from a friend who had worked with him years before and retired at the same time. "Hi, Jimmy!" Dad said when I passed the phone to him, and his eyes lit up. From the next room I heard him asking questions about Jimmy's health, his wife and children, and reminiscing about the old days. He hadn't laughed that much in a long time. When he hung up and joined me in the living room, he was all smiles.

"What did you two talk about?" I asked.

"Nothing much," he answered, and then he looked at me in surprise. "Actually," he said, "we didn't have much to say. It was just so good to hear his voice!"

We grinned at each other as we reached the same conclusion: It doesn't matter what you have to say when you call a friend—it's just good to keep in touch.

Thank You, Father, for the many times I have felt blessed by the sound of a friend's voice.   —Phyllis Hobe

Getting in Touch with God
PRACTICING THE POWER OF PRAYER

Throughout this year, we would like to help you make prayer a constant and steady practice so that it can become the "fuel" of your existence, vitalizing all you do.

Each month, different writers will tell you about a practical technique that brought them a new understanding about prayer and helped put them in closer touch with God. Why not practice that kind of prayer all through the month, and briefly record your thoughts about your prayer practice and the results in the end-of-the-month Prayer Diary. Then watch God draw you closer to Him as you learn to practice the power of prayer.   —The Editors

23   Wake-Up Prayer
SUN   *My voice shalt thou hear in the morning, O Lord....*
                                        —Psalm 5:3

I've added a new spiritual practice this year that's had a profound effect on the quality of my life. I've tape recorded a wake-up prayer, an affirmation of life for the new day, and I start the tape as soon as I wake, while the doors to my deep soul are still wide open. It's such a simple thing, but since I've been doing this I feel more tuned to God's presence with me throughout the day, more clearly guided by the Holy Spirit. And each day seems to unfold like a rose, from that early-morning seed prayer.

Perhaps you'd like to try it, too. If it would waken others, you could use headphones. Or just read your prayer silently as soon as you wake. I'll share parts of my prayer with you, which you are welcome to use, but I urge you to write your own upbeat wake-up prayer, keeping it in the present tense, and tailoring it to suit your own life and style.

Thank You, Creator God, for this fresh day, unmarred by past pain or future worry. Today, I am spiritually centered, whole. Following Your guidance, I make strong strides toward accomplishing the purposes for which I am created. I now let go of past hurts, so that my mind is a clear channel for Your love. I live each moment fully awake, fully alive to the many wonders that await me. I now go to meet the miracles of this day with great thanksgiving to You, Creator of all my days. Amen.

— Marilyn Morgan Helleberg

24
MON
Charm is deceptive, and beauty is fleeting; but a woman who fears the Lord is to be praised. — Proverbs 31:30 (NIV)

My mother-in-law Joan had high cheekbones and deep-set eyes to die for, yet all her life she seemed oblivious of her good looks. She bought clothes for durability, not fashion, and never changed her hairstyle, explaining that the simple and everyday suited her best.

Convinced that a makeover would bring out her true beauty, I took her to my hairdresser, who washed, clipped and combed her delicate curls into a fashionable helmet of hair.

Joan seemed awed at her transformation — so awed, in fact, that she couldn't stop touching her sleek coiffure. At lunch, she carefully patted a lock at her neck. In the car, she tucked in a few loose strands near her ear. She ducked into the ladies' room at the department store to primp some more. By the end of our outing, the elegant bob had been plucked and tweaked back into the very same hairdo she had worn for twenty-five years!

"I've had such fun with you," Joan said, hugging me. "Do I still look all right?" Her eyes glistened with pleasure and her lips were parted in a delighted smile.

"Gorgeous," I replied with a grin, touched by her radiance. "Exactly right."

And truly, she was.

Father, so often false images of beauty blind me to the beauty that endures. Help me to choose character over conformity; strength over surface charm. And always help me to follow You.
— Linda Ching Sledge

25
TUES

I have showed you kindness, that ye will also show kindness.... — Joshua 2:12

While I don't like to admit this, it seems that most of my life I've had this need to be right. It was very important for me to be right — about almost anything. That is, until some years ago, when a minister and author whom I greatly admired quashed all my theories about being right. Jamie Buckingham's final statement preached in a magnificent sermon caused me to leave the church in a huff, wishing I hadn't come at all. He said softly, but powerfully, "It's more important to be *kind* than right."

Surely, there was nothing more important than being right! I later wondered if Jamie, who died in February 1992 after a staunch stand against cancer, had struggled hard to come to his decision about kindness. I know I did. Just recently, I met someone who doesn't believe as I do — at all. We had quite a frank discussion about our religious convictions. I remembered Jamie's strange statement and asked, "Can we be best friends anyway?" She looked startled, but gave me a tremendous hug.

Recently, when my grown sons forgot my birthday, I huffed and puffed and called them to say, "Hey, you forgot my birthday! I plan to forget yours, too. That's just *right!*" They didn't defend themselves, and when their birthdays rolled around, I happily selected gifts I knew they would like.

I'm finding that the amazing thing about choosing kindness is that it feels so good...to love, to give, to forgive. To be part of God's simple plan for happiness: *Be kind to one another.*

Father, help me to practice kindness today and experience first-hand its life-changing power. Amen.   — Marion Bond West

26 *For while bodily training is of some value, godliness is of*
<u>WED</u> *value in every way....*   —I Timothy 4:8 (RSV)

My son Phil, seventeen, enjoys bodybuilding. It is an intensely
demanding sport that takes great dedication. I've had to acquire an entire vocabulary just so Phil and I can talk the same language. When he
says, "That guy is ripped," I know he's referring to good muscle defini-
tion. I have learned his workouts consist of sets (specific exercises) and
reps (repetitions of each set), which are designed to increase muscle
mass. His training sessions work his pecs (chest) and lats (back), as
well as hams (back thighs), quads (front thighs) and calves (this one
I know!).

I exhaust myself just thinking about these workouts! But I believe
this capacity for muscular strength is Phil's gift from God and that He
will use it in some way that pleases Him. And so I encourage my
son...and do my best to keep pace with his voracious "size XXXL"
appetite (which is a workout in itself!).

Yet, what pleases me more than the muscle Phil is adding is the character I see him building. When his stolen motorcycle was recovered, he
remembered to give thanks to God for answered prayer. He took the
initiative in preventing a fight by reasoning with the two antagonistic
teen boys. At school, he's friendly toward everyone, whether they are
popular or not. His friend Abe says, "I was new to the class and kind of
shy. Phil taught me how to laugh."

Athletic fitness is great, but it wears out eventually. What lasts is the
Christ-like character I build. It blesses God and others and me, and it
carries on in the life to come (I Timothy 4:8). I will probably never be a
bodybuilder, but I am a builder in the body of Christ!

Lord Jesus, may my strength of character build up Your body of
believers here on earth.   —Carol Knapp

27
<u>THURS</u> *If any man have ears to hear, let him hear.* —Mark 4:23

I was waiting for the bank to open when I fell into conversation with a
man who was also waiting. He was retired. He talked about having
worked sixteen hours a day to educate his only child, a son, now a lawyer. The man's mother was a full-blooded Inca Indian who felt, "You
can't get the full benefit of the sun if you hide in the trees!" Then
quietly he said, "My wife died four years ago."

"Are you lonely?" I inquired.

"Terribly so," he said. "Yesterday was my seventy-fifth birthday and my son took me to lunch. But he was so busy peeking at his watch, twisting, turning and tapping on the table, because he had a client to meet." My friend gestured the emptiness of their luncheon.

As I entered the bank, I wondered about how many times I might have been too busy to listen to the things that were troubling people. I paused for a moment to reconsider: Was I working at too many community projects, too many volunteer ventures? Was I accepting endless invitations to social and civic affairs? Was it because of a need I felt to please *everyone*?

I couldn't help everyone, even if these activities were all worthwhile. I needed to be more selective. For example, I needed to spend time with Oscar, Jr. Recently, I discovered his distress with the constant demands and responsibilities of his profession. We needed to take walks where I could listen as he confided in me. I needed to listen better as my wife Ruby shared her thoughts. I could even get to know better my new friend at the bank. I would go further by asking his name and inviting him out to lunch!

Right then and there I prayed that my friend's son would learn the importance of listening—and that I would not forget it, either.

Father, help me to see who's most important in my life, and let me tell them—and show them. Amen.   — Oscar Greene

28 *Ye are the salt of the earth....the light of the world.*
FRI   — Matthew 5:13–14

For more than fifty years, my father was a much-loved family doctor in rural Wisconsin. He was one of those old-fashioned family doctors who often made house calls, lingered with his patients over a hot cup of home-brewed coffee, laughed and told stories with family members, and was generally known in the community as a dear and trusted father-figure.

I once asked Dad if he could sum up his guiding philosophy of life. I'm not sure what I expected to hear, but his answer surprised me because of its simplicity. He was a complex and highly intelligent man who thought deeply about life, yet this was all he told me: "When I go to bed each night, I look back over the day and ask myself if the world is better because I lived today. If it is, I'm content. If it isn't, I know what I have to do tomorrow."

That was it. And as everyone who knew him will attest, his simple philosophy worked. The world he left behind was, indeed, a much better place for his having been here.

Lord God, I want the world to be better because I'm here today. Show me the way. — Susan Williams

29 *He that is of a merry heart hath a continual feast.*
SAT   — Proverbs 15:15

I am a habitual pot-scraper and spoon-licker. When we entertain at dinner, I am usually so busy seeing that our guests are comfortable and well served that I hardly taste the meal at all. For me, one of the nicest parts of a dinner party is when everyone has gone home and I am in the kitchen alone with the leftovers and the pots and pans. All day long I look forward to filling the containers with bits and pieces of this and that, and sampling everything.

After one such dinner, I came to the moment when I sat down in a kitchen chair, cup of tea by my side. The chicken teriyaki pan was nestled on my lap, and I was ready for the bliss of a spoonful of the sticky goop of sauce in the bottom of the pan. As I picked up the serving spoon and popped it into my mouth, imagine my revolting shock to discover that my husband John had used it to spoon out the dog food. Instead of a delicious morsel, I had a mouthful of chopped liver and kidney bits!

The neighbors must have wondered what kind of a shriek came from our kitchen that night! When John heard what had happened, he howled with laughter — and so did I.

I am still a pot-scraper and spoon-licker, but no longer of the habitual sort. That never-to-be-forgotten disappointment has made me cautious in the kitchen. It also has taught me not to take routine things in my life for granted. Now, when things don't live up to my expectations and disappointments come my way, I grin and with good humor ask myself, "Having another *dog-food day?*"

Lord, when disappointments come our way, give us the whimsy of a sense of humor and the ability to pick ourselves up and carry on, knowing You have good things planned for us. — Fay Angus

30 *Those who oppose him he must gently instruct, in the*
 ‾‾   *hope that God will grant them repentance leading them*
 SUN   *to a knowledge of the truth.*   —II Timothy 2:25 (NIV)

Criticism. Sooner or later each of us will find ourselves on the giving or receiving end. I remember an evening church service many years ago when a grandfatherly stranger appeared and seated himself in the back. After the service, this sport-coated gentleman walked up and began taking our pastor to task. We stood agape as he loudly criticized the sermon, the Scripture used, the people and, finally, even a stained glass Scripture lamp in the vestibule. Pastor stood quietly and listened until the fellow wound down. The man then turned and paraded himself out of the church with a Bible tucked under his arm and the most smug, satisfied look I'd ever seen. We never saw the stranger again, but his bizarre criticisms left a wake of bewilderment and pain.

By contrast, I've known some very talented criticizers. When my former boss Mr. Horsman disagreed with a method, his first words were, "Perhaps you could tell me your reason for this decision." He'd listen carefully. Sometimes he'd even relent; sometimes he'd press on with his "druthers." But he never stripped away dignity.

Another supervisor, in the dietary department of a large hospital, took me aside about my leaving a butter wrapper on the cooler floor. When we were alone, he vociferated, "Someone could've slipped and fallen. Don't ever do that again." Do you know what I did when he was done? I thanked him. He was 100 percent right, plus he had disciplined me alone, away from curious co-workers' stares.

Without realizing it, these two supervisors were following Bible principles: "Gently instruct [the opposer]" (II Timothy 2:25, NIV); "Answer....with gentleness and respect" (I Peter 3:15, 16, NIV); "Go and show him his fault, just between the two of you" (Matthew 18:15, NIV).

I think the best critics are those who truly want a change—without alienation. Come to think of it, that's how Christ has always dealt with me, too.

Dear Lord, if I give or take criticism today, may Your "scriptural rules" be followed, yielding improvement and harmony.

                                              —Kathie Kania

HOUSE GUEST

<u>31</u>
MON

"For the ear tests words as the tongue tastes food. Let us discern...what is right...learn together what is good."
— Job 34:3–4 (NIV)

Using my high school Spanish and plenty of gestures, I often try to communicate with Maria, the Spanish-speaking wife of our Mexican ranch hand. She and I usually end up giggling because neither of us understands much of what the other is saying. But we have communicated something important in the process: We care enough to try.

I often wish I put as much thought into my English words as I do with my Spanish ones. Instead, words come too easily — I rarely think before I say them. And I'm often sorry for thoughtless words that slip out. With my family, especially, it's important to weigh my words more carefully.

So I'm starting a New Year's "control-the-tongue regime." I'm praying specifically for God's help with it each day. And I'm going to dust off praise words in my vocabulary and use them more creatively: praising the kids for a made-up bed (even if I've had to remind them to do it); thanking my husband for working hard to support us; dropping a note to a faraway friend to tell her what she's meant to me.

I want to speak the language of love.

Lord, please help me speak Your language in word and in deed today. Amen.   — Marjorie Parker

Prayer Diary

1. _____

2. _____

3. _____

4. _____

5. _____

6. _____

7. _____

8. _____

9. _____

JANUARY 1994

10._____

11._____

12._____

13._____

14._____

15._____

16._____

17._____

18._____

19._____

20._____

21._____

22._____

23._____

24._____

25._____

26._____

27._____

28._____

29._____

30._____

31._____

February

S	M	T	W	T	F	S
		1	2	3	4	5
6	7	8	9	10	11	12
13	14	15	16	17	18	19
20	21	22	23	24	25	26
27	28					

GIFTS OF THE SEASON

The Seed

In winter's dark womb,
planted prayer seeds germinate,
creating new growth.

*This month, Lord, I ask for faith to trust Your unseen
workings, as I quietly wait for answers to
my prayers.*

1
TUES
PRAYER CAN CHANGE YOUR LIFE
The Peaceable Kingdom Within

"The Kingdom of God is within you." — Luke 17:21 (GNB)

Five of my close friends have gathered with me in my living room. We are considering the teachings offered in *Prayer Can Change Your Life.* "There has to be something more substantial to life than getting up, going to work, coming home, going to bed," my friend Nancy is saying. "I've tried every self-help book on the shelf, and I've never been able to find peace of mind. I have so many doubts, so many frailties...I'm so discouraged."

"I'm with Nancy," I say, "in wanting a life that's more peace-filled. But I have all these mean-spirited habits like being overly critical and fearing what I don't understand, which keep getting in the way."

"It says here," Diane reads from the book, "that 'prayer can change your life anytime, anywhere, at any age. It can renew your mind and body, calm the storms of daily living,' which sounds so wonderfully peaceful to me. But how can we ever get there?"

"Do you think the book is telling us that even though we can't change the whole world and make it perfect," Gloria adds, "each of us can pray our way past all our conflicts and negativity and into a personal place of peace?"

"And by leaving all our flaws behind," Martha Kay says with the same longing we all feel, "we could really get in touch with God's love."

"To be free of all my mistakes, and believe that God loves me completely," Pam P. says, "in spite of those faults. I guess that *would* be heaven on earth!"

Meeting weekly, our little group learns to talk openly about bad habits, confusions, fears that block us from the kingdom of peace that Jesus says we can experience. *Father, I'm terrified of getting cancer,* Gloria admits in her prayers. *I tend to have negative feelings toward others and I want to stop,* Pam P. says. *My days are fragmented with activities — how do I get my life back?* Diane asks. *I say unkind things about people I'm jealous of,* I confess sadly.

As we try to dismantle our personal roadblocks through the honest approach offered in *Prayer Can Change Your Life,* we find ourselves moving toward this promised peace, which waits for all of us, past potholes and detour signs like envy, impatience, fear and rigidity. Inching forward, our group of six is astounded to discover the kingdom waiting not beyond some spectacular sunset, or up on a lofty mountaintop, but right here...right now...inside each of our hearts. As prayer changes our lives, we're learning to be honest about our feelings, to talk openly to God, to admit our missteps. We're beginning to believe that past all those self-made stumbling blocks, peace awaits.

God, I know You are here. I know You are listening. Help me to recognize and overcome all my shortcomings that separate me from my place of peace, the kingdom within. —Pam Kidd

---

2
WED *And ye shall seek me, and find me, when ye shall search for me with all your heart.* —Jeremiah 29:13

While looking at the new 1994 calendar on my desk this morning, I remembered something author Charles Swindoll wrote in a New Year's letter last year. When he looks over his new calendar, he begins to feel excited, wondering what God might do on any one particular day of the year. Then he takes a red pen, chooses a day at random and circles it. "For all I know," he wrote, "that day may prove to be one of the most significant days of the entire year."

I was intrigued with his idea and tried it myself last year, circling September 30 on my calendar. I added a small red cross inside the circle and prayed I would be especially aware of God's presence on that day. Every time I flipped through my calendar and saw the circle, I smiled with growing confidence that September 30 would be a special day.

Finally, September 30 rolled around...and I woke up feeling achy and feverish all over. "Oh, no!" I moaned. "Not today!" I crawled to my desk to check my calendar, and there was that circle. Suddenly, my circumstances took on a new meaning, and instead of resisting them, I began to embrace them. I made a few phone calls, grabbed a couple of books and went back to bed to spend a quiet day alone. On the surface, it seemed like anything but a good day, but deep down, it turned out to be a day when God led me beside still waters and restored my soul (Psalm 23). Yet, without my circle, I might have missed seeing God's fingerprint upon it.

Why don't you join me right now in boldly circling a couple of days on your calendar, or even in this book, and know with confidence that God will be real to you on those days.

Father, I look forward with anticipation to Your master plan for 1994. —Carol Kuykendall

3
THURS

PRACTICING THE POWER OF PRAYER
Prayer Capsules

*Thy words were found, and I did eat them; and thy word
was unto me the joy and rejoicing of mine heart....*
— Jeremiah 15:16

My husband George was a very unusual doctor. His patients were never
sure whether their prescriptions would be for medicine, vitamins or
what he called his "time-release prayer capsules." One thing's for sure,
George faithfully took the "capsules" himself.

"I just pick out a Psalm or a Scripture to read every morning, then let
it speak to my needs all day," George explained to me. "Take the Lord's
Prayer. As I drive to the office and see the sky overhead, the words 'Our
Father Who art in heaven' drift into my consciousness, and I know He's
there. As I greet the first patient, I become aware of 'Thy kingdom
come, Thy will be done.' And my mind responds, *This is Your kingdom,
Lord. With Your help, this person will get well.*

"As I break for lunch," George continued, "I'm reminded, 'Give us
this day our daily bread.' And, suddenly, it makes me feel good to realize that this is how I earn it, this is what I do for a living!

"As the day wears on, another line strikes me, which is almost funny
if I'm working on my books: 'Forgive us our debts as we forgive our
debtors.' Boy, if I collected on all the bills I've forgiven, I'd be a
millionaire!

"As for 'Lead us not into temptation,' no problem!" Beaming, he
squeezed my hand. "I already have everything I want.

"'But deliver us from evil.' Yes, we all need God's protection from the
evil in the world. But that prayer or any inspiring Scripture can drip
through our beings all day and deliver us, just as a time-release antibi-
otic can protect the body from infection."

Try George's prescription for prayer. Like all God's gifts, it's free.
And it could help you as it has helped me, now that George is gone.

*Dear Lord, the promises in Your book are true. Let me carry
them in my heart all day long, every day.*   — Marjorie Holmes

4
FRI *Love...in deed....*

HOUSE GUEST
— I John 3:18

It had been a disheartening week. In my room at the University of

Tennessee, I had seen the terrible devastation of a recent earthquake on the news. *If only I were rich,* I thought, *I could do something to help those poor people rebuild their homes.* A couple of days later, I read in a magazine a detailed report about widespread corruption in a government agency. *If only I had powerful political clout,* I thought, *I would straighten out that mess.* Then, in the local paper, I saw the face of an old lady who lived on the streets of Knoxville. *If only I had the resources to help,* I thought, *I would change that woman's life.*

My feeling of helplessness kept building so that by Friday I was feeling pretty low. Hitching a last-minute ride home with a buddy, I expected my mood to improve as we neared Nashville. Yet, there on the outskirts of town, a bedraggled man stood by the road holding a piece of cast-off cardboard. "Will work for food," his roughly lettered sign said.

Great, I thought to myself. *There's nothing I will ever be able to do to make a difference in all this misery.*

Being with my family would certainly cheer me up. And sure enough, my sister Keri came home bursting with news of her day, and as we all sat down to dinner she related a story that caused me to take a second look at my melancholy state.

"Mary's so excited about Valentine's Day," Keri began. I knew her friend Mary as a bright, talented girl who lived in a single-parent household with several siblings. I imagined that her mom had a pretty difficult time financially holding her family together. "Every February 14, as long as she can remember, a big pizza is mysteriously delivered to her house at supper time," Keri was saying. "Her mother has never been able to find out who sends it!"

For some reason, Keri's story struck home with me. Later, I wandered outside along the creek that borders our backyard. A single star was hanging in the sky. All week I had fretted over my lack of power to make big sweeping changes over the world's wrongs. The truth was that I could never completely change the world. But offering excuses of not enough money, not enough power, not enough resources was wrong, hopeless.

"I can't change the world," I said out loud, "but maybe I could send someone a pizza." And for one clear moment it seemed that might be the answer I was searching for.

Dear God, take my simple deeds — a small donation, an informed vote, an encouraging word — so that I can make a difference. Amen.   —Brock Kidd

FAITH: YOUR DAILY SURVIVAL KIT

None of us will ever forget the ordeal of the hostages seized in Beirut, Lebanon, during the 1980s. One of them, David P. Jacobsen, was an American who had gone there to be a hospital administrator. For eighteen months, David endured a harsh existence of chains and blindfolds, of cold dirt floors and terrible loneliness. Yet, the David Jacobsen who was released into the sunlight on November 2, 1986, was a man who came out strengthened by his imprisonment. "My patriotism, my faith and my belief in myself all grew during my ordeal. It had to," he said.

Now, for the next week, this former hostage will tell you about the tools he used to survive the despair and hardships of each day. They are spiritual tools available to all of us, no matter how bleak our lives may seem. And though Jacobsen puts them together as his "survival kit," his own experience shows that they are not intended for just getting through, but getting through triumphantly.   — The Editors

5 Day One — You Are Stronger Than You Think

SAT   *Create in me a clean heart, O God; and renew a right spirit within me.*   — Psalm 51:10

I was snatched off the streets of Beirut on a beautiful May morning in 1985. At the time, I was the head administrator of the largest hospital in Lebanon, and had assumed I was not a likely target for extremists due to the desperate need for medical care in the battle-torn city. I was wrong to think anyone was safe.

I didn't see the men. They threw me into a waiting van and shoved me into a special compartment under the floor of the back seat while quickly knotting around my head a coarse blindfold and a tight gag. My first reaction was utter terror. I waited for the bullet. But then, in the midst of this nightmare, an astonishing inner calmness took over: *If they're going to shoot you, they wouldn't be bothering with a blindfold.*

Calmness is a type of strength. In the following months, I discovered many different strengths — honor, patience, humility, compassion. Most I didn't know I had. If you'd described to me what my captors planned to put me through, I'd have told you that I couldn't have survived the first week. Yet gagged and blindfolded, stripped to my underwear and chained to a wall in a windowless, unheated room, allowed only one watery main meal and one supervised visit to the toilet daily, I *was* able to survive an ordeal that had been unimaginable to me. In fact, I grew stronger. I had to.

Of all the strengths I discovered in captivity, perhaps forgiveness was the most powerful. When you can forgive those who try to harm you, you lessen the harm they are able to do. You control your victimization. It seems like an impossible thing God asks of us, to forgive those whom we despise. Yet sometimes it is the only way we can rise above our adversity. When I was able to forgive the men who had beaten me, only then was I able to wash the bitter taste from my mouth. When I was able to forgive the men who had held me captive for eighteen months, I was finally able to get on with my life again back home in California. That is why Jesus commands us to forgive our enemies. So that we remain strong.

Lord, Your strength is the source of all of my strength; when I am weak You are strong for me.   — David Jacobsen

6 Day Two — The Saving Grace of Humor

SUN *When they were discouraged, I smiled and that encouraged them, and lightened their spirits.* — Job 29:24 (TLB)

Most of us remember the TV show *Hogan's Heroes*, where a madcap collection of Allied POW's made things hot for their Nazi captors while at the same time contributing to the war effort. No one is naive enough to think that captivity is anything like a sitcom. The grimmest moments of my life occurred in Lebanon — but so did some of the most humorous. Without humor, none of us could have maintained our sanity.

When one of my kidnappers held a gun to the back of my head and growled, "You dead," I suddenly found myself replying breezily, "This is Tuesday night and I still have a lot of work to do before you shoot me. Tomorrow I have a full schedule. How about Thursday?"

He swore at me and stalked off. The incident taught me that humor can overcome fear.

Whenever our guards asked us if there was anything we needed, a chorus would rise up: pheasant under glass, bottled springwater, a Bible concordance, an M-16 rifle.

Humor can be more than just jokes — it can be an escape from terror or depression or loneliness. It is a foundation of a well-balanced personality. Whenever one of us would lose his sense of humor, the rest of us knew it was time to gather round and give support.

Humor is a unique grace from God, the spiritual lifeblood of optimism. Without it I could not have survived. Not then, not now. Things can be bad, but there's always a time when you must stand back, look at your troubles and laugh.

Lord, let us use Your gift of humor to help lighten the burdens that seem unbearable. — David Jacobsen

7 Day Three — Body and Soul
MON

Every athlete in training submits to strict discipline....
— I Corinthians 9:25 (GNB)

A month and a half before my release, I was badly beaten and thrown into a tiny isolation cell. Of course, I had no way of knowing that freedom was imminent, so this was the darkest period of my ordeal. When the pain of the blows subsided, I began to feel angry, then enraged. *How dare they!* To be beaten like an animal and then shut off from my fellow prisoners. This seemed to me to be the ultimate deprivation of freedom, the final insult to my humanity. But what could I do in my dismal confines?

Push-ups. Believe it or not, the only effective physical escape from my rage came through vigorous exercise. It was something I'd learned from the other prisoners. On one of the first mornings I was held with the others, I remember being awakened by a rhythmic, clanging sound. I thought someone was signaling for help. Then I saw the source of the racket: Captive Terry Anderson, the American journalist, was doing sit-ups, his leg chain banging on the ground.

It was a strategy I soon adopted. In fact, I still practice it. If I'm upset, I go for a run or a swim. Even if I'm pressed for time, I can still jog in place.

Exercise is the body's own natural medicine for depression and anxiety — available without a prescription.

Lord, let me keep the body You have given me strong and healthy so that I may better serve You. — David Jacobsen

8
___
TUES

Day Four — You and Those You Love

The Lord is my strength and song....   — Exodus 15:2

Our captors weren't happy about us hostages communicating with one another, but by peeking up through our blindfolds and speaking in whispers, we could usually manage to put one over on the guards. One thing we were driven to talk about, talk about incessantly, was our families and loved ones. It was therapy, actually, and very close to prayer.

We'd take turns describing someone — wife, parent, child, old school chum — in loving, photographic detail. The longer we spent together, the further we traveled out along our family trees and network of acquaintances. But the discussions always got back to those we missed the most. I missed my sons and daughter more than I knew how to say.

Someone I grew close to in captivity was Tom Sutherland, a professor at the American University of Beirut. One day, we all noticed Tom was down. Finally, he admitted that it was his thirtieth wedding anniversary. That made us all feel pretty glum and forgotten by the world.

I don't really remember who started singing, but I think it might have been Rev. Weir or Father Jenko, also Americans. Whoever it was, he couldn't carry a tune very well. But that didn't matter. Soon we were all softly singing the "Wedding Song" (by Paul Stookey), and the young guard was peering in nervously, wondering, no doubt, what was going on.

> *He is now to be among you*
> *at the calling of your hearts....*

And once again we had found the strength to go on for our loved ones — whose hopes and prayers we truly knew were with us — when we didn't think we could go on any longer for ourselves.

God, help me to remember that Your love passes through others on its way to me.   — David Jacobsen

9
___
WED

Day Five — The Key That Unlocks

The eyes of the Lord are upon the righteous, and his ears are open unto their cry.   — Psalm 34:15

We christened it The Church of the Locked Door, and there was a rueful irony to that name. But there was also freedom in it.

The Church of the Locked Door had no permanent location, since we hostages were hustled from dungeon to dungeon around Beirut to confound any attempts at rescue. Yet wherever we were, in one big group or split into smaller factions, its door was always open to us through prayer. When we were unshackled, we would hold hands, and Rev. Weir or Father Jenko would lead us in Scripture and prayer. Services were twice daily, often constant. It was a busy church. It commanded respect even from our guards, who tried not to interrupt our services unduly. You have to remember that they, too, were religious men, and despite the conflict that irreconcilably separated us, they understood our deep need to pray.

When I was thrown into solitary confinement, I opened The Church of the Locked Door Annex Division. I couldn't have survived without it.

The point is, I prayed unceasingly. I prayed not only for deliverance from adversity, but for knowledge of the Deliverer. I prayed for loved ones back home who I knew were praying for me. Mostly, I prayed for the other hostages and asked them to pray for me. That's how we did it. We prayed for one another.

The power of prayer will never leave you, even in the darkest of times. It is, we discovered, the greatest weapon known to humankind, the freedom no one can take away.

Father, teach me to pray so that I may never lose touch with You.
— David Jacobsen

10 Day Six — God Is

THURS *He that believeth...shall be saved....* — Mark 16:16

I was released suddenly on November 2, 1986.

I was given no advance warning whatsoever of my imminent release, yet I knew with utter certainty when I went to bed on November 1 that it would be my final night as a hostage. I'd been kept in solitary since September 1. I tracked the days by positioning olive pits in one corner of my dark, tiny cell. There was just enough room to stretch out and do my push-ups. I devoted a lot of time to exercise and prayer. It was my sanity strategy. (It still is.)

Then, suddenly, during prayer time one day, I understood that I would be released on November 2. I didn't know why I was being released, just that I was. I trusted the knowledge completely because I felt it came from God.

On my final night, I swept up my room, gathered my few belongings and said a prayer of thanks. The next day I was taken to West Beirut and let go.

My life will never be the same. But for all its grim deprivations, captivity did bring me one blessing: a new closeness to God. It forced me into almost constant communication with Him, which was why I knew when my release would be. It is a communication I continue.

Belief in God is the most powerful survival technique available to anyone. You don't have to be a hostage. You can be held prisoner by many things—drugs, fear, greed, sex, envy. Yet God is. As long as we acknowledge His Lordship, His infinite power, there are no bonds strong enough to enslave us.

Dear Lord, let Your liberating love free me from all the chains in my life.　　　　　　　　— David Jacobsen

11 Day Seven—The Necessity of Hope

FRI　*We are saved by hope....*　　　　　　　　—Romans 8:24

One lovely summer's night, not long after I was released from captivity in Lebanon, I took in a California Angels baseball game at Anaheim Stadium. Gene Autry's Angels has always been my team. I got there early so I could relax and watch the crowd drift in. I wanted to soak up the delicious ambiance of a unique American tradition: the soft drink vendors barking in the stands, "Soda here! Ice cold soda!"; peanut shells cracking underfoot on the way to your seat; the whack of the bats and the slap of leather as the players warmed up. More than anything, I wanted to bite into a steaming hot dog smothered with mustard, onions and relish.

I'd done it a million times when I was chained to a wall in Beirut. We all did. Almost as a kind of prayer, we brought to life inside our minds the finest memories of freedom. There, in my dank confines, I could go anywhere: my daughter Diane's wedding, bouncing my grandson John on my knee at a Fourth of July picnic while he told a corny joke, or just a drive along the Pacific Coast Highway in my old Plymouth convertible.

I believed I would get to do all these things again because I had absolute faith that God would allow adversity to end favorably. More than anything, hope is the nourishment of survival. Like Job, you can lose everything — and still survive. Because with God there is hope. Always hope.

Dear God, in all adversity let me see the nourishment of Your hope.   — David Jacobsen

12   *"And the slave is free at last from his master."*
‾‾‾
SAT   — Job 3:19 (TLB)

On this day, I am thinking about two men, both of whom had a great effect on my life.

Abraham Lincoln signed the Emancipation Proclamation on September 22, 1862. This document freed, "thenceforth and forever," 3,063,392 of my ancestors on January 1, 1863.

On Christmas Eve, a week before the proclamation went into effect, a Union Army general named Samuel Chapman Armstrong wrote, "The first day of January is at hand — possibly the greatest day in American history — when the sons of Africa shall be free." I have always had my own reasons for thinking of General Armstrong in a special way. He was a graduate of Williams College in the town where I grew up, and after the Civil War, in 1868, he founded what is now Hampton University. It was created specifically to educate "the sons of Africa." I myself graduated from Hampton in 1941, just one of thousands who had done so before me.

I will never do the great things that President Lincoln and General Armstrong did, but I — and all of us — can try to follow their example. Today, on Lincoln's birthday, I want to give thanks to God for two men, one a president and liberator; the other an educator, another kind of liberator.

O Lord God, as I serve, let me not think of myself but of others in Your name.   — Oscar Greene

13   *Then I turned my face to the Lord God, seeking him...*
‾‾‾
SUN   *with fasting and sackcloth and ashes....saying "....we have sinned and done wrong and acted wickedly...."*
                                        — Daniel 9:3–5 (RSV)

All through Joan Kirchner's flute concert I wondered, *How does she get enough air in her lungs for those long passages?* Her phrases wound seamlessly on and on, with only an occasional pause for breath.

"Oh," said Joan when I had a chance to ask her later, "it isn't so much a matter of taking air in, as letting it out." It was the advice of her very first flute teacher, she said. "Work at blowing *out* all your breath — then relax and allow the air around you to enter naturally."

I'm thinking of those instructions as the season of Lent draws close. They help me understand the church's insistence on these weeks of fasting and doing without. The presence of God is all around us, too, like the air we breathe. We know this, but our lives fill up with busyness, and we lose the wonder of it. Lent is the season to clean house, to empty ourselves of ourselves, to sweep the place clean...to breathe out.

Then how naturally, how easily, how fully He will fill the expectant places of our hearts.

Teach me this Lent, Father, that I do not have to strain for Your truth...only make room for it.　　　　　　　— Elizabeth Sherrill

14
MON
Love one another....　　　　　　　　　　— John 13:34

I have made a discovery as a high school English teacher. Sydney Carton, in *A Tale of Two Cities*, wanted to be loved by Lucie Manette. In the end, he gave up his life for her happiness. Othello couldn't believe that his wife Desdemona was faithful to him. Rose-of-Sharon, in John Steinbeck's *The Grapes of Wrath*, longed for an embrace.

One of my students, during a conversation about Helen Keller and *The Miracle Worker*, said, "Helen's teacher Annie Sullivan was blind in a way, too, until she discovered that she loved Helen and Helen loved her." Another student said how she liked to read because she felt there are certain writers who seem to love her.

Most, if not all great literature, it seems to me, is about people who simply want to be loved. We all want to be embraced and cared for.

At the end of Leo Tolstoy's little novel *The Death of Ivan Ilyich*, the dying father fears death, realizes his life was full of vanity and ambition. Suddenly, his son appears at his bedside. The son takes his father's hand and the boy weeps. At that moment, the father finally sees what life is all about: *love*. Then the man dies without fear and with full knowledge about the world's true gift.

Robert Frost wrote that "earth's the right place for love." What I have seen as an English teacher is that the human heart is, indeed, the right place for love. We celebrate our nation's independence on July 4, the birth of Christ on December 25. Today, we celebrate the human need to love and be loved.

In the next ten minutes, embrace someone you love, or call someone on the phone and say, "I'm calling to say good morning, Happy Valentine's Day, and I love you."

God, Father of us all, I love You and thank You for this life. Amen.
— Christopher de Vinck

15   *To him that rideth upon the heavens…lo, he doth send out*
TUES   *his voice….*
— Psalm 68:33

It's five o'clock on a frosty Tennessee morning. *This timing is ridiculous,* I think as I tug at my gloves and readjust my hand-weights…but it's the only time I have. When I return from my run, my daughter Keri, fifteen, will be getting ready for school and my husband David will most likely be in the kitchen grinding beans for coffee. We'll talk as I pack Keri's lunch and later we'll snatch a few minutes together over breakfast before we go our separate ways for the long day ahead.

Out on the street, it's as dark as midnight. I don't see the moon, but everywhere there are stars. As I run my familiar course, I glance up into the heavens. "Look at that," I say out loud, "the Big Dipper's still there."

As I continue on, I chuckle at the sound of my unexpected words breaking through the silence of the cold morning, but they've set me thinking. Life seems to rush by so fast. There's always too much to do in too little time. But the Big Dipper's still there just as it was when I was four and fourteen and twenty-four. Something to depend on. Like God Who waits for us to look…to see…to feel His presence.

I round the block and head back home. Before I go inside, I stand and look at the sky. I don't feel so rushed now. In fact, I feel fit and energized, ready for anything. Sure, the day will stretch out long and busy, but I intend to remember my morning words and to remind myself often of the truth they have revealed: *The Big Dipper's still there…and so is God.*

In a world ever-changing, God, let me focus on Your never-changing presence.
— Pam Kidd

Quiet Time

A CHILD'S PRAYER

Ah, dearest Jesus, holy Child,
Make thee a bed, soft, undefiled,
Within my heart, that it may be
A quiet chamber kept for thee.
— *Martin Luther*

16
WED

The heart knows its own bitterness, and no stranger shares its joy.   — Proverbs 14:10 (RSV)

Spokane, Washington. May 18, 1980. It was a brilliant, blue-sky Sunday going into church, and a smudgy gray coming out. "Uh-oh," I cringed, "we're in for it." The sky grew steadily darker and more ominous. At home, Terry rummaged in the basement for our lanterns, certain we were going to lose our power. When the phone call came, we stared at each other, thunderstruck. This was no spring storm. Mount Saint Helens, nearly three hundred miles distant, had erupted six hours earlier, spewing a gigantic, volcanic ash cloud that was advancing straight toward us.

We watched the day turn black in the middle of the afternoon, as if the sun had been snuffed out. By the beam of the porch light, fine gritty flakes swirled from the sky in a polluting blizzard. When it was over, our spring greening lay obliterated beneath two inches of gray ash, creating an eerie barren landscape. Mount Saint Helens, meanwhile, had dislodged one thousand feet of its peak and considerable parts of its innards.

Since moving to Alaska, I have experienced two other volcanic eruptions, one on an Ash Wednesday. The feeling is the same each time: a deep sorrow for the earth's marred beauty, followed by rejoicing when eventually the cleansing rains wash away the ash.

Today, we usher in the somber Lenten season, when we purposefully take time to study our inner landscape and acknowledge the ash of sin. Beneath its gray blanket lie sorrows only God can know, only He can heal. Today, I am willing to look repentantly upon my darkened heart, and then accept, with rejoicing, His cleansing forgiveness that washes away all my sin.

There is nothing more beautiful in all the earth than a heart redeemed. Especially my heart. Especially yours.

Jesus, for me Your life's blood You did pour,
That beauty for ashes You might restore.
— Carol Knapp

17
THURS
But now in Christ Jesus you who once were far off have been brought near in the blood of Christ.
— Ephesians 2:13 (RSV)

I guess you could say I had a sheltered childhood. We were poor and black, and so was everyone around us. There were no whites in our schools, our churches or our neighborhood. They lived across town, and we avoided each other.

Imagine my shock when a friend and I arrived at a Christian college in California and discovered we were the only blacks on campus! For the first time, I was the minority. In the dorm, in classes and on the basketball team, I was always the minority. My teammates never made mention of it, yet I couldn't find the words for how alone I felt.

Until one night, in an unfamiliar city, I found myself "at home." Our basketball team was playing out of state and together we visited another school to watch its game. As we walked into the gym, I saw fifteen hundred fans who were my skin color. I felt comfortable and normal for the first time in months.

Now it was my teammates' turn to be surprised at being the minority. For the first time, they realized how I had felt — alone. On their faces and in their voices I saw and heard that familiar fear. "Dolphus, are they going to get us?" they asked.

I reassured them, "You'll be okay."

It was scary for them at first, fifteen hundred to ten. But they learned, as I had, that brought together one-on-one and one-by-one, we could get to know each other.

Where do we begin to overcome the barriers of race? By becoming friends with the stranger sitting next to us.

Lord, teach me to look beyond my fear to see You in others.
Amen.
— Dolphus Weary

HOUSE GUEST

18
FRI

A gentle answer turns away wrath....
— Proverbs 15:1 (NIV)

Determined not to be housebound my first winter as a new mom, I decided to take daily walks with Elizabeth bundled in the stroller. On our first outing, we turned the corner and heard a chorus of barking dogs. A boxer paced behind one fence, and a husky strained against his chain. Then an unrestrained, black "terrier mix" rushed onto the sidewalk, planted himself in front of us and growled. I spun the stroller onto the street, but he nipped at my heels the entire block.

The next morning, when we rounded that corner, he came at us again. Fighting fear, I called out, "Hi there! Come to give us a welcome?"

He stopped and glared. Suddenly, his fiery eyes seemed comical on such a scruffy face.

The following day, his bark sounded almost friendly. By the next week, I actually looked forward to seeing him.

Today, as I stood in line at the post office, I studied one stony-faced clerk. This man's surliness always bothers me, and I hoped I wouldn't be called to his window. Sure enough, when I reached the head of the line, he became the next available clerk.

Suddenly, I remembered my terrier friend. Instead of returning the clerk's gruffness with coolness, I smiled. After he finished stamping my packages, I said, "Hope you have a good afternoon."

To my astonishment, he quietly answered, "Thanks." Then his face softened and he added, "You, too."

Father, please help me look beyond a crusty exterior and respond with kindness.   — Mary Brown

19
SAT

Obey them that have the rule over you, and submit yourselves: for they watch for your souls....   — Hebrews 13:17

If you were fortunate enough to have been a child during the late 1930s or early 1940s, then you may recall Saturday afternoons at the movies. In my hometown, there was always a double feature with cartoons, newsreel, coming attractions and a serial where each week the hero faced a life-or-death situation. One had to hurry back the next week to find out what happened! My friends Mary and Johnny and I would be first in line when the theater's doors opened at noon. Hours later, after having viewed everything at least twice, we'd emerge squinting our eyes in the blinding daylight.

What I also remember about those Saturdays was the tall woman whose job it was to monitor the children's section. She wore a white dress and carried a flashlight that she'd shine on any misbehaving child. We called her "Matron" because we didn't know her name, but she certainly knew our names. "Eleanor, your mother wants to have supper at six o'clock. You'd better go home now." "Mary, keep your sweater on. It's chilly in here and you were sick last week." "Johnny, sit down in your seat and be quiet."

Years later, I learned from my mother that Matron's name was Mrs. Bauer, that she was childless, and had taken the movie job not because she needed the money but because she loved children. And even though as a disciplinarian she might have been feared sometimes, we children loved her, too.

Matron made us feel safe and cared for. She, like our heavenly Father, was there in the dark, always watching over us.

Dear Father, thank You for the caring people You put into my life.
           —Eleanor Sass

20
SUN
PRACTICING THE POWER OF PRAYER
Keep It Simple

When ye pray, say, Our Father which art in heaven....
           —Luke 11:2

What is the secret of effective prayer? That we are faithful enough? That we are persistent? That we are pure enough? That we are unselfish? That we pray regularly and often? I have come to believe that our best prayers are the simplest ones, the most spontaneous, the most full of love.

Richard Foster, in his inspiring book *Prayer: Finding the Heart's True Home,* retells a charming Leo Tolstoy story about three hermits who lived on an island.

Their prayer was as simple as they were:
> *We are three;*
> *you are three;*
> *have mercy on us. Amen.*

Miracles sometimes happened when they prayed that way. The bishop, however, hearing about the hermits, decided that they needed guidance in proper prayer, so he went to their small island. After instructing the hermits, the bishop set sail for the mainland, pleased to have enlightened the souls of such simple men. Suddenly, off the stern of the ship, he saw a huge ball of light skimming across the ocean. As it came closer, he could see that it was the three hermits running on top of the water. Once on board the ship, they said to the bishop, "We are so sorry, but we have forgotten some of your teaching. Would you please instruct us again?"

The bishop shook his head and replied meekly, "Forget everything I have taught you and continue to pray in your old way."

> *God, remind me my best prayer is the one*
> *That begins and ends, "Thy will be done."*

— Fred Bauer

21
MON
In thy book all my members were written....
—Psalm 139:16

As Presidents' Day approached, I found myself pausing with my almanac, which listed all the U.S. presidents and brief summaries of their lives. It seemed rather simplistic and cold, all those full, colorful lives reduced to a paragraph: "His policy aroused growing opposition..."; "...nicknamed 'Old Rough and Ready'..."; "...primarily concerned with the Cold War...." For the sake of space, of course, the almanac touched only upon high spots.

Ironically, as I was looking up something in the Old Testament later that week, I again saw brief summaries, included in Judges, I Kings, II Kings, this time of kings and rulers: "He walked in the way of his father, which was right..."; "He wrought evil in the eyes of the Lord...."

Then today I was thinking, *What if my name were to appear in brief summary beside a list of others? What would my "high spot" be?* "She was an artist." "She had a family." Or, maybe, "She tried to follow the Lord wholeheartedly."

According to Psalm 139:16, I am written about in God's book, so I'm going to try and keep this written record in mind as I begin each day.

Because if it should happen to be condensed into one sentence, I'm still hoping for "She tried to follow the Lord wholeheartedly."

Dear Lord, I pray for this nation's leaders today, that they might be guided and blessed by You in their choices and decisions regarding our people, country and world. —Kathie Kania

22
TUES

This is the day which the Lord hath made; we will rejoice and be glad in it. —Psalm 118:24

I tend to resist change. I don't want my favorite house slippers to wear out. Or my kids to get too independent. I shudder at the thought of moving or finding a new dentist. And I'm always a little reluctant to embrace new holidays.

I remember when Presidents' Day was first introduced on the calendar. I was furious! Never again would my hero George Washington be remembered on his "real" birthday. I mourned that the father of our country had been relegated to a convenient Monday in February.

But then I came across this fact: It seems that for the first nineteen years of his life, Washington celebrated his birthday on February 11. It was not until 1752, when the British Parliament replaced the Julian calendar with the Gregorian calendar, that Washington's birthday was moved to eleven days later. Washington was a man of tolerance and action, and I doubt if he wasted much time mourning the change. I'm sure the important thing to him was not the date, but the spirit of the celebration itself.

And that kind of thinking has helped me become more flexible in other areas of my life. Valentine's Day is any time I want to tell someone just how much they mean to me. If it rains on Mother's Day, we have our family picnic the next weekend. And when I couldn't get home for Christmas one year, my folks agreed to keep their tree up until my mid-January visit.

Holidays become hallowed days when we stop our bustle long enough to think about someone else. And sometimes the best holidays of all are the ones we create spontaneously with those we love.

God, help us not to relegate the memory of our founding father to a single day in February. Instead, enable us to emulate his honesty and strength of character on this his birthday and in the days to come. —Mary Lou Carney

23 *Freely ye have received, freely give.*   —Matthew 10:8
WED

I have to admit I was curious. So as the technician finished labeling my blood donation, I asked, "Is there any way to know where my blood is going?"

She smiled and shook her head. "Nope. The way it's separated into components, it could go to four different people in a month's time. You'll never know who you're helping, and they'll never know who helped them."

I thought back to my Bible study the previous month. In a way, Jesus was an anonymous donor. A centurion told Jesus that his servant was very ill, so Jesus offered to go to the man's house and heal him. The soldier protested: "Lord, I am not worthy to have you come under my roof; but only say the word, and my servant will be healed" (Matthew 8:8, RSV). Astonished at the man's great faith, Jesus healed the servant at that moment.

I wondered if the man ever knew Who made him well. I think the answer lies in the mysterious power of anonymous giving. Jesus asks us to give freely what we have received from God, so the satisfaction in giving quietly comes from merely passing on what God has given us. The ultimate Source, the true Giver, is God. I've received good health, so I like to give blood often. But you can be an anonymous donor in other ways, such as giving clothing or toys to a homeless family shelter, or by leaving a bag of groceries at the door of a family from church or in your neighborhood who's struggling to make ends meet.

I'll never know if I've given a premature baby an extra chance at life, or helped a burn patient grow stronger, but it doesn't matter. I'm giving only what God first gave me. As the centurion's servant must have known, the real Giver of all life-affirming gifts is God.

Use me, Lord, to pass on Your love and care to a needy world.
                                                      —Gina Bridgeman

HOUSE GUEST

24 *Therefore the prudent shall keep silence....* —Amos 5:13
THURS

When Dana Delany accepted her television Emmy for best actress in *China Beach*, she thanked her director for teaching her to trust the silences. A recent incident helped me understand what she meant.

Mavis, the activities director at my mother's convalescent home, is a vibrant, extraordinarily attractive young woman, who always seemed to have the world in her pocket. So when she shared with me the heartbreak of betrayal in her marriage and her subsequent struggle as a single parent, I was stunned. So stunned that I could manage only an occasional sympathetic murmur, unable to recall even one of my usual, ever-ready, "fix-it" bromides.

By the end of the conversation, I felt I'd failed Mavis completely, dumbstruck as I was. Imagine my amazement when she said, "This is the best talk we've ever had. I really needed to talk to someone today."

It was a humbling experience to learn that Mavis considered our best conversation one in which I'd said almost nothing! It made me take a hard look at how I conduct myself in conversation. I decided I must learn to "trust the silences" because often, like Mavis, people need me to listen more than they need my advice.

And I decided something else. Today when I talk to God, I'm going to spend more time listening and less time telling Him what to do for me. It may well be the best talk we've ever had.

Heavenly Father, remind me that sometimes silence really does speak louder than words.
— Bonnie Lukes

25
FRI   *I run in the path of your commands....*
HOUSE GUEST
—Psalm 119:32 (NIV)

One of my happiest childhood memories is of running pell-mell down the long driveway of our rural home. When I think about it, I can almost feel the *slap, slap* of the packed earth against the soles of my feet. Our graveled drive made an S-curve to our house. Tires had worn two smooth paths the length of it. Here and there, where a car had bogged down in winter mud, a cluster of imbedded fieldstones made bumpy paving.

By the time I was ten, my feet had memorized every angle and rock. I could run the length of it full speed at night without stumbling. Coming home from school on winter-dark evenings, the familiar driveway underfoot made me feel utterly secure. It led home, to the anchor of my young life: my mother, father, brothers and sisters.

Now that Dad and Mom are gone, the old house has been razed and the driveway has been amputated at a new property line. But my feet still remember the old way home.

That warm memory reminds me: I want to become just as familiar with the way to my heavenly home. I'd like the feet of my soul to know every step of my heavenly Father's driveway. Coming to Him quietly in prayer every day, recognizing His presence, is one way. And reading the Bible, the revelation of His love, is another way. Whatever my circumstances from day to day, from moment to moment, I want first to be at home with God.

Heavenly Father, thank You for Your Son, Who made the way for me to come home to You.   — Elsie Larson

26
SAT   *As ye abound in every thing...see that ye abound in...grace also.*   — II Corinthians 8:7

When I married Charles Shellenberger fifty-three years ago, my culinary know-how was limited to making fudge and popping corn. Gradually, over the years, I had to learn how to cook. Of necessity, I developed one dinner party menu and with it I gained the reputation of being an excellent cook. Friends raved about my stuffed Cornish game hen and bowknot rolls, and I guarded that entire menu like an old mother hen guards her chicks — especially my green bean casserole recipe.

One Saturday night, we invited a newly arrived doctor and his wife for dinner, and when Betty Jean told me her mother was visiting from New York, she was, of course, included. Betty Jean's mother begged me for that casserole recipe. "After all, Dorothy, I live in New York City. It will never get back to Waco." But it did. For the next six months, it seemed like every dinner party we attended we were served "Betty Jean's" green bean casserole.

Coming home one night, I complained to Charles, "That's the fifth time in the last three months that I have been served 'Betty Jean's' green bean casserole. I'm so mad I could chew nails. That's *my* green bean casserole."

To which Charles quietly replied, "Your green bean casserole? I thought Virginia Nash gave you that recipe!" After a few seconds of stunned silence on my part, we both broke into laughter, which lasted all the way home.

I learned a valuable lesson that night. Every good gift is meant to be shared. Whether it's a delicious recipe, a packet of marigold seeds from my bountiful garden blooms…or God's wonderful plan of salvation.

Dear Lord, where would I be without the love-gift of Yourself? Help me to realize that selfishness is deadly.

— Dorothy Shellenberger

From the Kitchen of: _Dorothy Shellenberger_

GREEN BEAN CASSEROLE

1 lb. sliced mushrooms
1 medium onion (chopped)
½ cup butter
¼ cup flour
1 cup light cream
¾ cup sharp cheddar cheese, grated
⅛ tsp. hot pepper sauce

2 tsp. soy sauce
½ tsp. pepper
1 tsp. salt
1 tsp. flavor enhancer (optional)
3 or 4 packages frozen French-cut green beans
5 oz. sliced water chestnuts
½ cup toasted almonds

Sauté mushrooms and onion in butter. Add flour, and cook until smooth. Add cream slowly, then cheese and seasonings. Simmer until cheese melts.

Cook green beans in salted water. Drain, and mix with sauce. Add water chestnuts, and top with slivered, blanched toasted almonds. Bake at 375 degrees for 20 minutes. (Can be made ahead; refrigerate, then bake for approximately 35–40 minutes.)

27
SUN

Love is very patient and kind….Love does not demand its own way. It is not irritable or touchy….If you love someone….you will always believe in him, always expect the best of him…. — I Corinthians 13:4–5, 7 (TLB)

The young couple had just returned from working with Wycliffe Bible Translators in the Caucasus region of the former Soviet Union. Excited and enthusiastic, they were sharing their experiences during the Sunday morning church service when, suddenly, what they were saying snapped me to attention.

"In translating the regional language," they explained, "we found they had no word for 'love.' The only comparable word we could come up with was *abaya*, meaning 'sees good in you.' To share how much God loves us, we have to tell them how much good God sees in us."

How beautiful, I thought. Yet in the same instant I realized how glibly I use the word *love* and how often I fail to *see good in* those I love. For instance, this week has been particularly irritating for me. Practically every day I was annoyed at something, and found myself tossing around the words *careless, irresponsible, untidy, inconsiderate*. Even that very morning I had snapped at my husband John, "What do you mean you have to tank up the car? We're running late! You should have done that yesterday!"

Sitting there in the pew, I suddenly was given a mirror image of my snapping, pouting self—a whole new perspective on love. "Help me, dear Lord," I prayed, "to *see good in* those I love even as You *see good in* me, despite all the times I fail to measure up and leave undone those things I ought to have done!"

There is little virtue in loving when it is easy to love—the "good times" kind of love. True virtue comes when we love when it is difficult to love, through the irritations, the hurts, the disappointments. It is continuing *to see good in*. It is then we are loving with the *abaya* love of our ever-loving God.

Let me see good, dear Lord, in everyone I meet,
Those I love and cherish, and the stranger on the street.
Help me love when loving's not the easiest thing to do,
Remembering that's the kind of love that comes to me from You!
                                                            —Fay Angus

28
MON   *HOUSE GUEST*

Finally, brethren, whatever things are true, whatever things are noble, whatever things are just, whatever things are pure, whatever things are lovely, whatever things are of good report, if there is any virtue and if there is anything praiseworthy—meditate on these things.   —Philippians 4:8 (NKJV)

There was a time when I was having real difficulty with anger toward a relative. He was treating some people in my family pretty shabbily, I thought. And the more I thought about it, the angrier I became.

The worst part was that I had no defense against it. One minute I could be totally content, and before long I'd be steaming. But I began to notice that it always seemed to happen while I washed the evening dishes.

Finally, I asked the Lord to help me past it, so my joy would be secure and doing dishes could be a simple pleasure again. Not a full week passed before I received an unexpected gift in the mail. It was a beautiful photo of the sun setting over the ocean, with Philippians 4:8 printed on it. I immediately knew where it belonged: on the window frame right above my kitchen sink.

The beautiful sunset gave me a place to focus my feelings. From that day on, I had better control over my angry thoughts toward my relative. It wasn't that I didn't have any, but now I knew to think "Philippians 4:8 thoughts" in place of the angry ones. In addition, I found myself wanting to pray for my relative. I asked God to help him through the unhappiness that made him treat others unkindly. One day, I was totally awed to discover as I prayed that a tender, genuine acceptance of him had begun to grow in my heart.

Some time later, a friend was telling me about trouble she was having with angry thoughts. I smiled. "I know just what you need," I told her, and went to the window frame. "This picture and the Scripture has helped me change my thought patterns, and even to pray for the person I've been angry with. I want you to have it—and hang it over *your* kitchen sink."

I wonder if she, now healed, has passed the picture on to another who's having difficulty with angry thoughts.

Father, thank You for keeping us in victory and joy through high and noble thoughts, and for replacing our anger with love.

—Ellyn Baumann

Prayer Diary

My Prayer Requests for February:

God's will + strong direction for mine + George's lives.

1. *Don't allow my peace to be stolen. Mom's health + move. Desire for Mom + Dads house in albuquerque to keep in family.*

Mom bought house in ___ 2-4-94

2. _____

3. _____

4. _____

5. _____

6. _____

7. _____

8. _____

9. _____

10. Be realesed from the bondage of suger and fat completely. Loose all desire for it.

11. To have stronger faith in my trials than I have when all is going right. Look to God first in all things

12. _____

13. _____

14. _____

15. Lord help me in the rush of daily living to stop & look up & remember you are always there never changing. Take time to stop and listen for what you might say or just to feel your presence.

FEBRUARY 1994

16. _____

17. _____
Protection for Lori Today. Let her feel God's presence
and know how much we love her. Help me
18. to see inside each person & not just the exterior

19. _____

20. _____

21. _____

22. _____

23. _____

24. _____

25. _____

26. _____

27. _____

28. _____

March

S	M	T	W	T	F	S
		1	2	3	4	5
6	7	8	9	10	11	12
13	14	15	16	17	18	19
20	21	22	23	24	25	26
27	28	29	30	31		

GIFTS OF THE SEASON

The Wind

Touch of Spirit's breath
offers lift to kites and prayers,
as March winds praise God.

*May this month's breezes remind me, Lord, of the Holy
Spirit's uplifting presence in all my comings and goings.*

1
─────
TUES

PRAYER CAN CHANGE YOUR LIFE
Pray the Cause, Not the Symptom

"Make me know my transgression...." — Job 13:23 (RSV)

"Look within and be honest about the cause of your problems," I read in the book *Prayer Can Change Your Life.*

Look "within"? I thought other people and other things were the cause of all my problems — never me! But the book keeps telling me to look for the *cause* of my distress in my *own* negative traits. ("Demons," it calls them.)

"Pray the *cause*," the book answered again. "Let the *symptoms* go." These symptoms, the book said, are only alerting me to the deeper problem within. *Okay, go for it,* I told myself. *Take the plunge, be honest.*

I was fretting over my distressed and lonely mother in Chattanooga, 130 miles away. *Distress* over my mother's plight was a *symptom.* My own feelings of *guilt* were the *cause.* I needed to use that misspent "guilt energy" to call her up, affirm her importance in my family's life and encourage her to visit us.

I searched further. "Why, God, do I take family members' rejection of my brother David's divorce so personally? If *resenting* them is the *symptom,* show me the cause."

I became aware that I was oversensitive to their criticism because I identified with David and therefore felt relatives were unhappy with *me.* The *cause* was *inferiority* — I didn't feel good enough about myself. With prayer, I needed to change that attitude.

The darkest of my demons lay in my feelings of *helplessness* (the *symptom*) over my daughter Keri's depression. I had taught Keri about God's goodness, and she saw her family disintegrating and cancer sucking away her younger cousin's life. Suddenly, I felt afraid. *How can I handle all of this alone?*

Afraid? Alone? There was my answer — the *cause* of my helplessness was *fear* because I had left out God. Now I could look within, acknowledge my own fear and turn my circumstances over to Him.

I mentally sealed in a box all my symptoms (distress, resentment, helplessness) and their causes (guilt, inferiority, fear), and in a prayer, handed them to God. For the first time in months, relief washed over me and a peace settled in.

God, my soul needs a spring cleaning, so I'm bringing You the causes and letting the symptoms go.   —Pam Kidd

2
WED

"Permit the children to come to Me; do not hinder them; for the kingdom of God belongs to such as these."
— Mark 10:14 (NAS)

Charles Francis Adams was a busy man. Born in 1807, the grandson of the second president of the United States, John Adams, Charles Adams spent his life as a successful lawyer, a member of the U.S. House of Representatives and the U.S. ambassador to Britain. Amidst his responsibilities, he had little time to spare.

Charles Adams kept a diary. One day he wrote, "Went fishing with my son today — a day wasted!" He closed his diary and thought nothing more of his hastily scribbled entry.

Some years later, it was discovered that Charles Adams' son Brooks Adams had followed his father's example and also had kept a diary from his youth. On the date that his father had written about his "wasted" day fishing, Brooks Adams had boldly printed in his diary, "Went fishing with my father today — the most wonderful day of my life!"

When I read this story, I felt as if I had been hit by a ton of bricks. How true it is that some of the most insignificant events that occur in the lives of adults have tremendous import in the lives of their children and grandchildren. It made me resolve to "waste" more time with my three children. Who knows? Maybe by giving myself the permission to do so, I may rediscover the joy and wonder of life myself!

Father, help me not to waste time by being forever busy. Amen.
— Scott Walker

3
THURS

"The Lord...has filled him with the Spirit of God, with skill, ability and knowledge in all kinds of crafts — to make artistic designs...."
— Exodus 35:30–31 (NIV)

There are two kinds of people in the world: those who enjoy throwing things away; and those who are always rescuing discards, hoping to use them. Take the huge tree stump somebody once tossed into our country woodpile. When my husband upended it and was about to chop it up, I halted him. "Wait! It's really beautiful. We could make something out of it."

"Yeah, a fire." Then he, too, noticed that it was table-high. Running his hand across the broad, flat surface, he noticed the grain. "Hey, I could fill in the cracks to keep it from rotting. Maybe we could use it in the yard."

So we rolled it down the hill and chose a scenic spot. There, he cemented its wounds and firmly grounded it. He inscribed the names of the children in the fresh cement and helped them carve their initials on the wood. Countless happy hours were spent around it — reading, writing, drinking coffee, entertaining. It supported typewriters and record players, and children who just liked to climb on it and jump off.

Years later, it inspired another couple who were forced to cut down a gigantic oak that had sheltered their family so long its roots were entwined with their own. "That's it!" they exclaimed. "That's what we can do with our family tree!" And although most of it went into firewood, its base made a magnificent table that they still gather around together today.

So you never can tell. An old tree stump rescued from a woodpile can affect many lives, and draw them closer in that most precious circle of all — the family.

Dear Father, help me to see the beauty and promise of all Your creations, however humble, and to share them with those we love.
                                                              — Marjorie Holmes

---

4   *New wine must be put into new bottles.*   — Mark 2:22
FRI

My friend Cheri and I had been walking at the mall three mornings a week for a couple of years, when she suggested trying something new. "How about swimming at the Y?"

Immediately, a whole list of excuses came sputtering out of me. "Oh, I haven't been swimming in years. Besides, I don't look good in a swimsuit anymore! And I'd get chlorine in my hair." And the final insurmountable obstacle: "It's *winter*, for goodness sake!"

"Well, never mind then. I just thought I'd ask." I think my answer was what Cheri had expected from me, someone who is eighteen years older than she. But as I was driving home, some words I'd heard from an energetic church friend in his eighties floated across my mind: "We grow old by consent." *Why should I consent?* I thought. *I used to love to swim. Why not enjoy it now? Indeed, why not? Every day I am a new person in Christ!* (II Corinthians 5:17).

Cheri and I have been swimming regularly for months now, and though I may *look* like an old wineskin, when I'm splashing around in the water I feel like a kid again. Besides firming my upper arms and tummy a bit, the swimming experience has taught me to question my "can't dos." No matter what your age, before turning down the opportunity for a new adventure, ask yourself, *Why not?* If there's no good answer, at least try it once. It may keep you young!

When I hesitate to try something new, Lord, remind me I'm a new creature in You. Then I'll ask, Why not?
— Marilyn Morgan Helleberg

5
SAT
When thou makest a feast, call the poor...And thou shalt be blessed; for they cannot recompense thee....
— Luke 14:13–14

Sally, a young friend of ours, recently suffered through a divorce. She has two small children and knew that she would be hard pressed to make ends meet. But with child support payments and income from her part-time work, she thought she could keep a roof over her head and food on the table. Then her ex-husband lost his job; his checks ceased and she was forced to turn elsewhere.

"I didn't want to ask my mother for help," she confided. "Pride, I suppose. But Mom didn't wait for me to ask. 'Come on home,' she said, 'you're always welcome.'" And though her mother is widowed and has limited income, she was willing to share whatever she had. "She's always been that kind of Christian," Sally added with admiration.

Robert Frost once wrote that "Home is the place where, when you have to go there, they have to take you in." Christ went that truism one better in His parable of the ninety and nine. In that story, the shepherd was not content that ninety-nine sheep were safely home; love compelled him to go in search of the single sheep missing from the fold.

If you are a parent like me, you have had lots of practice in welcoming children back into the family circle after some unwise wandering. The test for me is reaching out to a non-relative who could use my help. It is then I must remind myself that the family of God is all-inclusive...and to realize how deep is God's love, how much He values every one of His creations.

God, give us arms that reach earthly wide,
Sharing the love You've always supplied.
— Fred Bauer

6
SUN   *I will both lay me down in peace, and sleep: for thou, Lord, only makest me dwell in safety.*   — Psalm 4:8

Dear Father,

It's three in the morning, and I can't sleep, so I decided to get up and write You a letter.

To tell the truth, I'm having trouble with anxiety. I know, I know, You've told us repeatedly not to worry. But that's easy for You to say. You have everything You need. You can see the future. You never get tired or lonely or afraid. And You don't get bills from the IRS.

But down here I live in a complicated world that seems to be spinning out of control. I worry about my daughters and my granddaughter. What's going to happen to our country? What if I have a heart attack or a breakdown? What if I run out of money? *What if...what if... what if...?*

I try reading Your book, but it seems to be filled with warnings and commands. It only makes me feel more anxious. I'm having enough trouble just making a living. Where will I find time to do all the good deeds that need to be done?

I was almost ready to close the book and forget it when my finger caught at Hebrews 13:5–6 (NAS):

Let your character be free from the love of money, being content with what you have; for He Himself has said, "I will never desert you, nor will I ever forsake you," so that we confidently say, "The Lord is my helper, I will not be afraid. What shall man do to me?"

Is that really true, that You will always be with me? I don't expect You to protect me from all my troubles, but if You will be with me...*z z z z.*

Lord, thank You for the peace that Your loving presence brings me. Amen.   — Daniel Schantz

                                                    HOUSE GUEST
7
MON   *Behold, now is the accepted time....*   — II Corinthians 6:2

At a luncheon I attended, Susan Butcher told how, during the running of the Alaskan Iditarod, the grueling 1,158-mile sled dog race from Anchorage to Nome, she found herself in second place. When she saw she couldn't win, Susan vowed, "Next year, I'll win." She went home and trained more intensively. That next year, she gained the lead. Near the end of the race, however, another driver overtook her. Susan was too tired to hold the lead. "Well," she promised her dogs, *"next time we'll win."* Upon hearing herself, she was struck with the thought: No one wins *this time* who plans to do it *next time.* She called on everything within herself for one more burst of speed. Susan passed the leader and won her first Iditarod. After that she became a four-time winner of that exhausting race.

I went home determined to see how I could use Susan's do-it-now rule, and soon I was thinking of my old friend Bev. She and I had been best friends in high school, until I dated the young man she had dreams of marrying. Nevertheless, when I married Dick, she was my maid of honor. I moved away, and on my Christmas cards I always wrote, "Let's get together this year," but I put off doing it. Now it had been thirty years.

I called Bev right away. Our friendship blossomed. Only one year later, Bev died.

Susan was right—no one wins *this time* who plans to do it *next time.* Have you got something—or someone—that you've put on the back burner, vowing "next year"? *Now* is the time to get right on it.

Dear heavenly Friend, give me the courage to pursue that which I've put on hold. Now. Amen.   —Elsie Larson

8
TUES

The Lord thy God will make thee plenteous in every work of thine hand....   —Deuteronomy 30:9

I'd been stripping the walls of our dining room for weeks, taking off layers of old paint and flaking wallpaper, getting down to the original plaster. I'd filled up the cracks with spackle. That afternoon I was starting to apply the paint when my wife came home from a meeting at church.

"What was this one about?" I asked as I stirred the bucket of "biscuit" (a salmony sand color).

"Stewardship," Carol said. "This year we're going to do something different. Instead of just asking our members to pledge money, we want everyone to think about what stewardship means in all aspects of their lives."

I returned to my labors and began to think about what she had said. *Stewardship, was it?* By stripping and sanding the walls, I had undone a couple of lousy paint jobs. Urban renewal on a small scale. That could qualify as stewardship. And doing the job myself was a way of saving money. That certainly was good management of resources.

Two hours later the work was done. "Well," I told Carol, "all I can say is the next person who paints these walls will have an easier time of it."

"That's it!" she said. "That's what good stewardship is. Leaving a wall, a room, a church—a world—better off for the next one who comes along."

Together, we stood back and admired the room.

Lord, make me a faithful steward of Your bounty.

—Rick Hamlin

$\frac{9}{\text{WED}}$ *If we walk in the light...we have fellowship one with another....*   —I John 1:7

A Devotional Especially for Children (of all ages)

Boys and girls, I would like to tell you a true story about some ducks that live near me. There were two ducks. They were dark green and dark brown. One day a man came by our house and said, "I have a beautiful white duck who is all alone. Could he come and live in the pond with your ducks?" My husband and I agreed.

The man came and put the duck into the large lake. He quacked and swam just like the other ducks. They heard him and came swimming from way across the lake. The white duck swam out to meet them. A very sad thing happened. The two dark ducks decided not to like the newcomer. They pecked him and made mean quacks to him. The white duck, with an assortment of fancy feathers on the top of his head, swam behind the other ducks—longing to belong. When they ate, the white duck had to wait until they had finished, no matter how hungry he was. Every day he tried to become friends, but the two ducks would not let him become their friend.

Then one day the green duck hurt his orange, webbed foot. He had difficulty swimming and could not get out of the water to eat the food that we brought to the ducks daily. He tried and tried, but fell back into the water. Slowly, hopefully, the white duck swam right up to the green duck and let the wounded duck lean on him. Pretty soon the green duck caught on! The white duck was helping him out of the water so he could eat. The two ducks began eating hungrily, while the white duck waited in the water. Suddenly, the green duck turned to the white duck and gave a loud, "Quack, quack!" The white duck understood immediately. The green duck had said, "Thank you, friend. Please come and join us. You are loved." Now the three ducks swim and eat together and are best friends.

Do you have a best friend? Do you know anyone who is left out at playtime or at lunchtime? Have you ever been left out? Would you be willing to be a friend to someone who needs a friend tomorrow?

Dear God, please show me how to be a friend to someone who needs a special friend. Amen.   — Marion Bond West

---

10
THURS

Be ye therefore perfect, even as your Father which is in heaven is perfect.   — Matthew 5:48

The other day, a friend called me a *perfectionist* because I often compare myself to people I admire and feel bad when I don't measure up. "You're setting unrealistic expectations for yourself and aiming toward an ideal that is not *you*."

Bristling under this new label, I went home to see what Jesus had to say about *perfectionism*. "Be perfect," He commanded in the Sermon on the Mount, but as I dug deeper into the Greek and Hebrew translations of *perfect*, I found He meant three things:

1) Be complete, which means to be *who* God uniquely created me to be;

2) Be mature or *where* I am, within my own set of circumstances on my own level of maturity;

3) Be holy, which means surrendered in spirit to God, knowing that I am in the *process* of growing and changing, but will not reach perfection until I get to heaven.

My friend actually did me a favor, because now when I start falling into the comparison trap, measuring myself up against someone who prays more passionately or reads more books or maintains more friendships, I remember how Jesus calls me to realistic *perfection*: to be *who* I am and *where* I am and accept the fact that I'm in the *process*. Not flawless...but forgiven.

Father, may I seek to be perfect on Your terms.
                    — Carol Kuykendall

11
—
FRI
Live in harmony with one another; do not be haughty, but associate with the lowly....   — Romans 12:16 (NRSV)

Ashley — a pre-owned Yorkie from the Humane Society — came into my home with his head hung low. The neighbors were all waiting for me at home to meet the newest member of my family. That was when we learned that this little dog was terrified of men.

In their presence, Ashley would shake like a leaf. All my men friends are gentle, but their imposing sizes and booming voices seemed to terrorize him. I had to find a way for Ashley to be healed of his fear!

Whenever a male visitor came to the door, I would pick up Ashley and hold him in my arms. I would ask my friend to pet the dog gently and talk to him in a soothing voice. When the little guy relaxed, I would hand him over to my friend to hold and continue petting for a few more minutes.

After some weeks, Ashley seemed to remember each man he met in this way, and stopped cowering and shaking in their presence. In fact, after meeting my next door neighbor Bob, Ashley stole into his house, then reappeared a few minutes later to drop one of Bob's dirty socks at his feet. Bob, he seemed to be saying, was not only safe, he was accepted!

Since coming into my family, Ashley has been healed of his fear and to this day lives at peace with all men. It's the love he's been getting that's healed his fear — I'm sure of it. And not only is Ashley a beloved family member now, but he reminds me how to approach all the abused and fearful people I meet. The best way is to start with love.

Lord, give me a persistent love that makes healing possible for all the lowly and abused who come my way.   — Diane Komp

12
—
SAT
"I the Lord do not change...."   — Malachi 3:6 (RSV)

Last month, I spent one morning watching the snow fall and praying for my dad back East, who was taken to the hospital with a mild stroke. As I waited for word, I went back and forth between feelings of faith and fear. *Is my vacillation a disappointment to God?* I wondered. *What must He think of my apparent lack of trust?*

As I continued to watch the thick, swirling snow, I suddenly remembered the weatherman's prediction: "Clear skies." It wasn't supposed to snow! Yet fickle air currents had swept in a cloud cover so heavy it seemed as though the sun had never come up. Yet, I had never for a moment worried that the sun hadn't come up! I knew that the sun's path and the wandering clouds were two different systems.

For a few days, I found myself bursting into tears at the sight of the pot-holder rack Dad had made; the next moment I would find myself laughing to hear Mom tell of his complaints about hospital food or his joking with a nurse. I realized then that it wasn't back-and-forth *faith* I was experiencing, just back-and-forth *feelings; two different systems.* God was in control and would do His will. I knew it. But I knew, too, that because of deep love and memories, my feelings would swirl like fickle clouds, leaving a storm of tears here and there. And when Dad was sent home and began woodworking again, my sun shone brightly.

Fickle feelings that hinge on circumstances? Yes, I'm afraid that's often me. But He Who cried at Lazarus' tomb understands. So I don't have to pretend they're not there. I can depend on God's constant love that never fails.

Dear Lord, may the feelings my family and I experience today line up with our faith. But if they don't, please shine upon us anyway — especially Dad.   — Kathie Kania

13
SUN PRACTICING THE POWER OF PRAYER
Prayer-Letters

And you show that you are a letter from Christ delivered by us, written not with ink but with the Spirit of the living God....   — II Corinthians 3:3 (RSV)

I've started something new recently: I write prayer-letters. They are fun, they are nonthreatening, they can be read without embarrassment, and everyone loves to receive them. To give you an example of how I construct a prayer-letter, here's one I've written to surprise my friend Cathy Johnson in Missoula, Montana:

Dear God,

You sure gave me a solid-gold friend when You brought Cathy and me to-gether. You know, God, I really miss her now that I moved north to Alaska and she headed east to Montana. It is so wonderful that we both have You to keep us together.

I am praying right now that You will refresh her and brighten her day with the light of Your presence. Lord, thank You for all Cathy's work with her

church's teens, and for her generously giving spirit. Bring her thoughtful ways back to her in a swirl of blessings.

Guess I'm running out of space. But, Lord, You know I'll never run out of space for the love and smiles that thoughts of Cathy bring.

Love, Carol

Is there someone who needs a word of comfort or cheer? Perhaps you have a friend or family member whom you want to bring nearer to God? Write a prayer-letter to Him about them and your feelings for them. These letters can stay private between you and God, or you can send your prayer-letter friend a copy to lift their spirits and let them know they are cared for. Let your prayer-letter pray blessings into another's day.

God, teach me creative ways to pray for others that will draw them closer to You. Amen.   — Carol Knapp

14
MON   *[God] be not far from every one of us.*   — Acts 17:27

When my brother Bob and I were small boys growing up in Ohio, our father used to take us sometimes to an amusement park where one of the attractions was a maze, a labyrinth of artfully planned mirrors in which it was possible to get completely lost. Wherever you looked, whichever passage you chose, you ended by running into a reflection of yourself.

Being a minister, my father couldn't resist pointing out a moral. "This maze," he would say, "is just like life. No matter where you go, you can't escape from yourself. So you had better try to be a worthwhile person, because you'll never get away from that person no matter what you do!"

That was a valid lesson, and I remember it still. But what I remember best is the very first time we entered the maze and I somehow got separated from Bob and my father. Becoming more and more panicky, I finally cried for help. What a relief it was to hear my father's strong, reassuring tones: "This way, Norman. I'm right over here. Just follow my voice. I'm right over here!"

And so he was. What a blessing it was to find him. And what a blessing it is to know that whenever we're feeling lost or panicky as we move through life, a Person of infinite strength and love is calling out to us, "Just follow My voice and you'll find the Way. I'm right over here!"

Dear Savior, teach us to reach for Your hand, knowing that it will always be there.   — Norman Vincent Peale

Quiet Time

PRAYER FOR A NEW DAY

Help to keep my heart clean, and to live so honestly and fear-lessly that no outward failure can dishearten me or take away the joy of conscious integrity. Open wide the eyes of my soul that I may see good in all things. Grant me this day some new vision of Thy truth, inspire me with the spirit of joy and glad-ness and make me the cup of strength to suffering souls.

— *Phillips Brooks*

15
TUES *Therefore do not worry about tomorrow, for tomorrow will worry about itself. Each day has enough trouble of its own.* — Matthew 6:34 (NIV)

When our son Ross was about two years old, he loved to climb. One day at his baby gym class, he was climbing a ladder set at a gradual slope a few inches off the ground. The rungs were spaced too far apart for his young legs, yet he insisted on trying to take them two at a time.

"Watch your feet, honey," I said. "Don't go too fast. Take one at a time, one at a time!" He finally took my advice, and climbing the ladder became a breeze. But as I heard myself admonishing him, I wondered if maybe I should listen to my own advice.

For some time, I'd been trying to change some bad eating habits: too much junk food, skipping meals, sweets and snacking. "Starting to-morrow," I'd say, "I'm going to eat three meals a day, cut out all sweets and fat, no more fast food...oh, and I'm going to exercise a half hour every day, too." My intentions were great, but I set such an overwhelm-ing goal for myself I couldn't last one day. Discouraged, I'd go right back to my old ways. But once I broke down the job into tiny "rungs," climbing the ladder toward my goal was a lot easier. I started by cutting out snacking between meals only, and moved on to the next task when I felt ready. I'm still working on the overall goal, but I'm getting there.

Maybe this discovery can help you, too, if you're trying to tackle the whole world instead of just one small corner. Remember Jesus' advice: *Don't worry about tomorrow. You have enough to worry about today.* In other words, take it one rung at a time.

Loving Father, today with Your help I will focus on each small step of the climb instead of the mountain that stands before me.
— Gina Bridgeman

HOUSE GUEST

<u>16</u>
WED   *He who confesses...will obtain mercy.*
— Proverbs 28:13 (RSV)

"I don't believe it. It can't be true," I heard a chorus of unhappy voices saying as I stepped into the fraternity house after class. "Get in here, Brock!" my friend Ben called out from the TV room.

On the TV screen I glimpsed my childhood champion Magic Johnson. *What could be wrong,* I wondered. "I hope that others might learn by my mistakes," he was saying. Basketball great Magic Johnson was HIV-positive.

The shocked disbelief that one of my generation's major sports super-stars might be an AIDS victim filled us all with horror. And then came the critics. *Magic was being unjustly lionized. How could the news media make a hero out of a man whose mortal disease had come from moral reck-lessness?* But as the weeks passed, Magic never tried to make excuses. He just kept bringing himself back as an example of what *not* to do. He committed himself to the AIDS cause and encouraged others to do the same.

I was confused by the controversy — until I remembered David, the hero of legendary proportions in the Old Testament, who was also a man of equally legendary moral collapses. Despite all his sinful failures, God just kept loving him hugely. It's obvious that big sinners aren't the best role models for young people, but big character *is*. King David's greatness was guaranteed in part by the way he handled adver-sity: repenting his mistakes, then learning and going forward from them.

Maybe Magic was showing us a bit of the same. Taking the bad and trying to work it into good is a trait I could apply to my own life. Doing poorly on an exam should be a signal to study harder. Losing my temper might serve as a reminder to take time to cool down and center myself in prayer. Irritation when I don't get my way could be an invitation to look at the other person's side of the situation.

We all have regrets, times when we have fallen far short of our expec-tations. But we do have the "magic" to turn things around for the posi-tive. And we have a Father Who loves us hugely as we try.

God, I pray for wisdom to acknowledge my failures, and for courage to turn bad into good. Amen.   — Brock Kidd

17   *Love your enemies, bless them that curse you, do good to*
—————   *them that hate you....*   — Matthew 5:44
THURS

On St. Patrick's Day here in New York everyone wears green. African
Americans, Latinos, Anglos, Chinese — all of us are a little bit Irish
today.

That's as it should be. Ireland was Patrick's mission field, but his
message is universal. Born of well-to-do Christian parents in Roman
Britain around the year 385, young Patrick was no more interested in
religion than most boys. He was sixteen when a marauding band from
the savage island to the west made one of their periodic raids on their
neighbors. Patrick was captured and dragged off to Ireland to be sold as
a slave and put to work herding pigs.

And there, during six homesick years, he began to recall the
Christian teaching he'd absorbed without knowing it. Alone with the
animals through winter snow and summer heat, Patrick became a follower of Jesus.

He was twenty-two before he was able to escape to the seacoast and
hail a trading ship headed for France. From there he made his way home
to England and his rejoicing family. A happy ending to a bitter tale.

Except...what were these voices that woke Patrick night after night?
Irish voices...pleading with him to come back and teach them about
the God he'd come to know so well. Go *back*? Back to that place of suffering, to the very people who'd wronged him? But this, Patrick came
to believe, was exactly what God was asking him to do. It took him
twenty-five years to get his theological training and the endorsement of
the church, but eventually Patrick did return. He spent the rest of his
long life bringing the love of God to the place where he'd experienced
the cruelty of men.

There have been Patricks in every age. In our own, Corrie ten Boom
ministering to the Germans in whose prisons her father and sister died.
Elisabeth Elliot returning to serve the Ecuadoran Indians who mur-
dered her husband. Steve Mariotti, the New York businessman mugged
by a street gang, turning his business into a classroom where street kids
learn to be entrepreneurs.

Another Patrick is born each time you and I encounter hate and answer instead, "I love you."

*Father, I can never generate this kind of love on my own. Give
me, as You gave Patrick, the Spirit of Him Who died for us
"when we were enemies" (Romans 5:10).*   — Elizabeth Sherrill

18 *A friend loveth at all times....*   —Proverbs 17:17
FRI

Sometimes, when I'm cleaning my house, I wish I could replace every-thing in it. I notice every scratch on the tabletops, every scuff on the chair legs, every worn spot of carpet. "I've got to start replacing some things," I decided one day.

I was definitely in the mood for sprucing up when I took my father's watch to the jeweler's for a new battery that afternoon. And when the jeweler pointed out that the leather on Dad's watchband was worn, I said, "Let's put on a new one."

I thought Dad would be pleased with the new band. Instead, he looked sad. "What's the matter?" I asked.

"I'd rather have the old one," he said. "It was like an old friend." The watch had been given to him when he retired almost twenty years ago. Of course, it was like an old friend, a very special one.

I took the watch back to the jeweler and had the old band put on. When I came home, I began to walk through my house, seeing it in a different way. Some of the scratches and scuffs were made by playful puppies and kittens who had now grown up. The worn spots in the car-pet, especially the one by the front door, were made by the comings and goings of people I loved. My dishes, many of them chipped, had been settings for meals lovingly cooked and eagerly eaten.

No, I decided, I wasn't going to replace a thing. In fact, I really liked the way my house looked. It was filled with friends. And friends don't mind when friends get old and worn.

Even though I'm chipped and scuffed and certainly imperfect, I know You love me, Lord. Thank You, dear Friend.

                                              —Phyllis Hobe

19 *Whoso shall receive one such little child in my name*
SAT *receiveth me.*   —Matthew 18:5

The question was routine: "Why do some kids make it, others don't?" The unexpected answer made me feel glad I had taken time to attend this seminar on adolescent behavior.

"The difference," the session leader said, "has to do with what we call 'significant others.'" Her explanation was simple. If a child has the assurance that just one person believes in her, loves her no matter what she does, then that child will become a worthwhile adult. Studies suggest that a significant other can be a relative, a teacher, even a maid or a neighborhood handyman. Janitor or bank president, a significant other can be any person who believes in any child.

I thought back to my parents, my grandmother, Mrs. Setzer (my sixth-grade teacher), people who loved me as I was. They were my significant others.

Is there some future first-rate adult who will remember you as her "significant other"? A child is waiting out there, in the neighborhood, within the church family. A child who needs someone to look beyond her freckles, scuffed shoes, bad table manners. One person to call her special, encourage her, laugh at her "knock-knock" jokes. One person is all she needs to make the difference. Why not me? Why not you?

Lord, You have loved us unconditionally, looking past our faults and failures. Won't You help us pass it on?   —Pam Kidd

20
<u>SUN</u>

HOUSE GUEST

But when he saw the wind, he was afraid and, beginning to sink, cried out, "Lord, save me!"

—Matthew 14:30 (NIV)

When I read in the Bible about incidents of Peter's wavering faith in the Lord, it reminds me of my own weak faith during difficult times. Henry A. Ironside, a minister, wrote, "What Peter should have remembered was that he could no more walk on smooth water than on rough waves, except by the power of the Lord, and that power is as great in the storm as in the calm."

I have to continually remind myself of that truth. One of my waves of fear is financial. I know God provides, and He continues to prove it, as we try to be obedient in our giving. But when the porch roof is leaking, my car's odometer is at two hundred thousand miles, and my husband's surgery has added the strain of high medical bills, I start to sink. *Will I have to go to work full-time when I want to be an at-home mom? How can I budget more tightly when I'm already trying to be as frugal as I can? Will life ever be any fun again?*

When Peter cried out to Jesus, the Lord pulled him up. "Why did you doubt?" He asked him. When my storms blow in, I cry out the same thing. And somehow God lifts me up, whether it's with a new free-lance opportunity, or a friend's advice on a parenting problem, or the realization that a family outing such as a bike ride and a picnic can be as much fun as a movie and eating out.

His power is as great in the storm as in the calm. Why did I doubt?

Father, help me to remember Who's providing, and give me faith to trust in Your power to provide for me in good times and tough ones. Amen.   — Marjorie Parker

---

21
MON

Let thine heart keep my commandments: for length of days, and long life, and peace, shall they add to thee.
                                              — Proverbs 3:1–2

I read the blurb in the paper with dismay. Was next weekend when we had to set the clocks forward? Already? While I knew we didn't actually "lose" an hour, it sure felt like it to me. "I can't afford to lose any more time," I complained to my friend Dina. "I have so much to do already, what with my office job, classes and chores. And my boss just loaded another project on me. He doesn't realize how hard I work. I wish I were like Nan at the next desk, who gets away with murder...."

I went on in this vein, until Dina said bluntly, "You'll just have to do what I did a few years ago. I decided to cut W-A-S-T-E right out of my life. I constantly work on getting rid of *W*orrying, *A*nger, *S*elf-Pity, *T*attling and *E*nvy. You know, the time I save without these time-wasters more than makes up for the one hour we 'lose.'"

Soberly, I thought how I'd just *w*orried about the future, was *a*ngry at my boss, was deep in *s*elf-pity, *t*attled about Nan and *e*nvied her, too. Without W-A-S-T-E, I'd have plenty of extra time!

Dear God, thank You for the hours in my day. Let me not W-A-S-T-E one minute of the time You give me! — Linda Neukrug

22
TUES

HOUSE GUEST

May the God of hope fill you with all joy....
                                              — Romans 15:13 (RSV)

In the winter of 1988, I was trying to get back into the swing of teaching piano. I hadn't taught for ten years, and I was worried. *Will my students pass the state achievement tests?* I asked myself. *Will they be ready for a spring recital? Is my own training adequate?*

That year the Winter Olympics were held in Alberta, Canada, and I watched on television as a figure skater named Elizabeth Manley surprised everyone by winning the silver medal. Her exuberant performance and radiant smile captured the audience.

A few years earlier, she had suffered from depression and almost ended her career. When asked the secret of her comeback success, she said, "I worked on enjoying my performance and not putting so much pressure on myself. I just wanted to have fun."

Watching Elizabeth Manley sail across the ice, I decided, "From now on I'll teach for the pleasure of it." Instead of worrying about competitions or how I compared with other teachers, I relaxed. Loving my students, boosting their self-esteem, helping them have fun making music—these became my goals...and rewards.

Are you frozen with doubts about your abilities? Today, cut a winning smile and declare, "I'll perform my work for the love of it!" Newfound fun—and joy—could be awaiting you.

Father, please help me stick to what life is all about: loving and serving—joyfully.   —Mary Brown

---

23
WED

Then took Mary a pound of ointment of spikenard, very costly, and anointed the feet of Jesus, and wiped his feet with her hair: and the house was filled with the odor of the ointment.   —John 12:3

So many of my memories are culled from the past through the sense of smell. And often they are associated with a specific individual.

Take eucalyptus. "A terrible nuisance," complains my husband John as he fishes the leaves out of the swimming pool. But I love those trees. Frequently, I take a handful of leaves and crush them to capture the scent so evocative of my childhood—and feel again the gentle touch of my mother's hand as she rubbed oil of eucalyptus onto my chest for bronchitis.

In Shanghai, where I grew up, my Chinese *amah* (nanny) frequently tucked a jasmine blossom behind one ear. Even now the scent of jasmine here outside our bedroom window stirs my heart with loving thoughts of her.

I have often wondered what spikenard smells like. It was the expensive ointment with which Mary anointed the feet of Jesus, and its fragrance filled the whole house. Her deed, Jesus said, would always be remembered (Mark 14:9). Certainly, the disciples must have carried the memory of that perfume with them throughout their lives.

What kind of a fragrance do I leave behind?

In one of her prayers that I carry with me, Mother Teresa says that she wants to spread the fragrance of Jesus, the "sweet-smelling savor" of His sacrificial love (Ephesians 5:2). Today, as I go about my work, I'll ask for that fragrance to come from kind words spoken, a sympathetic ear, a forgiving spirit, a loving touch.

Dear Jesus, help me to spread Thy fragrance everywhere I go....Shine through me and be so in me that every soul I come in contact with may feel Thy presence. Let them look up and see no longer me, but only Christ.... (Mother Teresa)   — Fay Angus

---

24
THURS
Lord, grant us peace; for all we have and are has come from you.   — Isaiah 26:12 (TLB)

I am going bald. This is the first time I have admitted this to myself and to anyone else. My father is nearly bald, as is my brother. Now I have this wide, growing bald spot on the top of my head. This is difficult for me to admit — me, a child of the sixties who grew his moppy hair in the style of the Beatles.

When I go to the doctor's office and see the new, young doctor, when I drive on the highway and see the young state troopers, I realize again and again that I am no longer young myself, but middle-aged. I've thought about chemicals, special shampoos. I've also thought that vanity can be a dangerous thing. A man who is hungry, roaming the streets in ragged clothes looking for shelter each night, doesn't worry about how he looks.

Everyone tries to recapture their youth in one way or another. I have to accept the fact that I am growing older. "To thine own self be true," Shakespeare wrote. I should simply be happy and grateful for who I am now. But I could recapture some of the idealism and energy of my youth. I could turn my thoughts to that homeless man and strive to live up to the calling of the sixties, my growing-up years: a world of peace, love and harmony.

Youth has little to do with my appearance. It has everything to do with my behavior.

God, as I struggle with self-acceptance, help me to remember that Your love for me is greater than any earthly or material desire. I may grow to look like an old man someday, but in Your eyes I am always youthful. —Christopher de Vinck

25
FRI

HOUSE GUEST

You are not your own; you were bought with a price....
—I Corinthians 6:19–20 (RSV)

Just about every time I pass a hospital, especially at night when lights glow from curtained windows, I remember a promise I made to myself.

Awhile back, I had three major surgeries in less than a year. I spent a lot of time staring out hospital windows at cars and crowds passing below. I wondered where those busy people were going and if they ever thought about those of us who lay inside this big white building. I decided then to pray for patients when once again I became one of the passersby, enjoying my freedom and the outdoors.

But I'm afraid I soon forgot that resolve. At first, I was so busy enjoying my family and my restored health that I didn't think about it. And then I began to get caught up in the routines of everyday living and to take the gift of good health for granted. It took the jolt of a friend's hospitalization to remind me. Visiting, I was keenly aware of the monitored silence in the corridors and how it contrasted to the happy bustle of my life. Worried waiting room faces seemed to urge me to pray. Contrite, I prayed right then, asking God to help me remember to be both thankful and prayerful.

I need such jolts out of my life-as-usual complacency. And since my hospitalization, the coming of Good Friday gives me such a jolt. In the past, Good Friday had been just the beginning of the joyous Easter weekend, rather than a time to contemplate the suffering that paid for my freedom, when Jesus freely gave up His good health to suffer and die for all us "passersby." Next week, on Good Friday, I'm going to make it a day of remembering and deep, prayerful gratitude.

Father, help me to remember and appreciate the great price Christ paid for me. And help me to keep on praying for those who are ill and suffering. —Marjorie Parker

Keys to New Life
LISTENING TO JESUS' ANSWERS

Since he lives with three teenage sons and their many questions, it isn't surprising that Eric Fellman found his attention focused on all the questions posed to Jesus during Holy Week. "Throughout His short ministry on earth, Jesus was bombarded with questions, some less well-intentioned than others. Yet Jesus always had the right answer at the right time," Eric says, "making His questioners, even the disciples, stop and think.

"Since Jesus knew death and resurrection lay ahead, He chose the words of His last week very carefully," Eric continues. "Every question put to Him sparked answers profound with power and truth, and He built into His answers the tools for making ourselves new."

Come now, as Eric leads us through this Holy Week, looking at the questions Jesus answered. Perhaps within the conversations, the questions and the answers, we will find the keys to our own personal resurrection so that we can come closer to what God created us to be.   — The Editors

26
SAT

SATURDAY BEFORE PALM SUNDAY
QUESTION: *"Why this waste?"*...   — Matthew 26:8 (NIV)
ANSWER: *"Leave her alone....It was meant that she should save this perfume for the day of my burial."*
                                                        — John 12:7 (NIV)

Before His triumphal ride into Jerusalem on Palm Sunday, Jesus had been trying to tell His disciples He was going to die and rise again. They simply weren't hearing and believing. But a woman named Mary believed. She showed her belief by "wasting" a year's wages on perfume to honor Jesus. When others saw only the waste, Jesus saw the love.

After the Olympic Games in Paris in 1924, people around the world had heard of Eric Liddell. In honor of his Lord, Liddell had refused to compete on Sunday in his specialty, the one hundred-meter race. Then came his astounding win on a weekday in the four hundred-meter, an event he had never before entered in his life. With the fame he had gained, many doors of opportunity were open to him, but Liddell chose to go as a missionary to a small village in China. Many people said, "What a waste." Years later, his story, told in the movie *Chariots of Fire*, lifted countless millions to reconsider the value of faith in their lives. Can you hear the echo of Jesus' answer that long-ago Sunday? "Leave Eric alone. He has done a good thing for Me."

As we pause and prepare for the week ahead, let us take time to reflect on our own devotion to the Lord. Is there a way we can be "foolishly" extravagant because of our devotion to Him? Something only He can understand and honor? When we are willing to be remade through the lessons found in Jesus' long-ago conversations, the resurrecting power of Holy Week will be ours.

Lord Jesus, help me find the place in my life this week where I can be devotedly extravagant for You.   — Eric Fellman

$\dfrac{27}{\text{SUN}}$ PALM SUNDAY
QUESTION: *"Why are you untying the colt?"*
ANSWER: *"The Lord needs it."*   — Luke 19:33, 34 (NIV)

Imagine the sense of purpose that must have stirred in Jesus with the sunrise on Palm Sunday. On this first trip into Jerusalem He would be lauded and cheered—the most popular moment of His ministry. Calling two disciples, He said, "Go to the village...and...you will find a colt tied there....Untie it and bring it here. If anyone asks you, 'Why are you untying it?' tell him, 'The Lord needs it'" (Luke 19:30–31, NIV).

What is amazing is that the disciples experienced exactly what Jesus told them they would, even down to the words. Jesus gave them the question and the answer *before* the conversation took place because He wanted them to know that He had worked out all the details in advance. They could have faith in His plan for them.

Often, I find myself overly concerned with how something will get done, and I forget to trust God. Then, like the disciples, I am amazed and filled with gratitude when things turn out well. *Why didn't I believe in the beginning?*

Recently, when our company held meetings on planning for the future, I fretted for days, trying and failing to come up with creative ideas. Then, one morning, I received a small booklet from a correspondent. The first page read, "God loves you and has a wonderful plan for your life." *Of course.* I eased back in my chair and relaxed. Remembering the disciples in search of the waiting colt, I saw that I did not have to find the perfect answers — God already had them. I went to the next meeting confident that through all our discussion God would show us our next steps. And He did.

Like the disciples in Holy Week, we, too, have tough moments ahead of us. But we know that Jesus had a plan for them, and He has one for each of us. Perhaps this is the moment for a new turn of events, when you and I place our trust in Jesus' plan for our lives. After that, it is a simple matter of asking Him to reveal the details we need to get through today.

Lord Jesus, thank You for loving me enough to create a plan for me. Give me the faith to trust Your plan and give me the answers I need just for today. Amen.   — Eric Fellman

28
MON

QUESTION: *"How did the fig tree wither away so soon?"*
ANSWER: *"If you have faith and do not doubt, you will not only do what was done to the fig tree, but also if you say to this mountain, 'Be removed and be cast into the sea,' it will be done. And...whatever you ask in prayer, believing, you will receive."*   — Matthew 21:20, 21–22 (NKJV)

It was Monday morning. All the excitement of Palm Sunday was over. On His commute back to Jerusalem from Bethany, Jesus stopped to pick figs from one of the trees that grew along the road. Finding no figs on the first tree, He commanded that it never bear fruit again — and it immediately withered. Jesus did this to teach a lesson of believing and prayer to His disciples.

Jesus knew what was coming on Friday. He knew the disciples would soon be left alone to face a hostile world. He also knew that His Resurrection would redefine death for all time and would release great power into the lives of those who believed in Him. So on Monday He taught them that soon they would have power not just over trees, but also over mountains; in fact, "If you believe, you will receive whatever you ask for in prayer" (Matthew 21:22, NIV).

Just recently, I learned this lesson all over again. After seventeen years as a full-time homemaker, my wife Joy needed to return to work as we prepare to send three boys to college. After weeks of mailing résumés had produced almost no interviews, Joy said to me, "Honey, we really need to pray about this." Now, for me, praying for ourselves seemed selfish when so many in the world are starving and homeless. Somehow, I had the notion that God had given us so much that we were expected to fix our own problems and not bother Him. But that night we prayed specifically that Joy would find a job. That very week a friend called to set up an interview, which resulted in Joy's being hired on the spot. It was as though God was simply waiting for us to ask.

On that long-ago Monday, Jesus taught His disciples that a new power in prayer was coming to all who believed. The question we must answer today is whether we are willing to hear this lesson and accept the power He gives us when He says, "Everything you ask in prayer, believing, you shall receive."

Lord, as we listen to Your lesson for today, we can only echo the words of the grieving father You helped two thousand years ago: "Lord, I believe; help thou my unbelief" (Mark 9:24).

— Eric Fellman

29
TUES

QUESTION: *"Teacher, which is the great commandment in the law?"*
ANSWER: *"You shall love the Lord your God with all your heart, and with all your soul, and with all your mind.... And...You shall love your neighbor as yourself."*

— Matthew 22:36, 37, 39 (RSV)

When Jesus arrived in Jerusalem on Monday, the chief priests questioned His authority to teach the people. On Tuesday, various religious leaders asked Him questions designed to confuse and discredit Him. Finally, one of them asked, "What is the most important commandment in the law?"

I've wondered why he asked Jesus this question. Perhaps, because great crowds were now following the Master, this man thought Jesus might answer in a way that would reveal a selfish motive. Imagine the anticipation as Jesus prepared to answer. With His penetrating eyes, Jesus looked into the face of the man and found something different there — there was a hint of honesty in wanting the answer. And so He answered, not in the riddles or parables He had used all day long to confound the dishonest questioners, but simply and directly: "Love is the greatest."

The greatest lesson I ever learned about love began six weeks before Joy and I were to be married. I was critically injured while traveling on business and ended up in a hospital two thousand miles away from her.

The doctor told Joy not to make the trip because I would not survive the night. But her love for me never let her believe I would die, and she boarded a plane and twenty hours later arrived at my bedside.

My first memory is of awaking in the hospital bed, seeing Joy and wondering why she was there. The doctors said I would not live, so they let her stay. After twelve intense hours, the doctors decided I might live after all. For the next four days, Joy was there every time I opened my eyes, and her presence helped me hold on to life. Six weeks later, I hobbled down the aisle, arm in a sling and jaw wired shut, having learned a depth of love I never knew possible.

Jesus, knowing that His own death lay just four days ahead, put His message into its simplest form. Love God with all your heart, soul and mind, and love your neighbor as yourself. In John's Gospel, Jesus said, "For God so loved the world, that he gave his only begotten Son..." (John 3:16). It is His enormous example we remember with awe and deep gratitude during this Holy Week.

Father, let my life be filled with the love Jesus describes because I have accepted the love You gave me through Him. —Eric Fellman

30
WED

QUESTION: *"When did we see You...and [help] You...?"*
ANSWER: *"Inasmuch as you did it to one of the least of these My brethren, you did it to Me."*
—Matthew 25:37, 40 (NKJV)

On this day, Jesus' listeners wanted to know when the prophecies would be fulfilled and God would return to judge their enemies and reward their loyalty. Jesus makes the point that only those who get their eyes off the skies and on to the plight of people around them will be truly ready for God's kingdom. In short, Jesus was teaching His followers to focus not on *being* right, but on *doing* right.

Often we are protected from many of the painful everyday experiences much of the world faces. Sometimes a shock is necessary to wake us up. In 1983, I visited the People's Republic of China, shortly after Westerners were allowed into the country. The sight of armed soldiers patrolling everywhere was unnerving to me.

One morning, my student-friend asked if I was willing to take a "somewhat risky" trip into the countryside to better understand the growth of faith among the Chinese. A bit fearfully I agreed. There we saw people carrying water into a ravine, mixing it with earth and bringing buckets of mud up to a large building. "What are we watching?" I asked.

"You're watching a prison slave-labor brick factory."

"What are the crimes they've committed?"

"They were divinity students. This is a seminary that was taken over by the government in the 1962 Cultural Revolution."

"Do you mean these people have been here for more than twenty years for being divinity students?"

"Yes."

A few days later, when I was ready to leave China, someone brought me a packet of letters from the prisoners and asked that I smuggle them out to family members who had escaped. Although fear of those machine guns made me sweat, I carried those letters out under my shirt, next to my heart.

It was then I knew what Jesus meant when He asked us to do even the smallest thing to help those powerless to help themselves. Perhaps you are not confronted with such dramatic circumstances, but isn't there someone — homeless, hungry or hurting — whom you could help today? If you take time to do so, Jesus will be there to receive your Easter offering.

Lord Jesus, help me today to see someone who needs my help, and let me see Your face in their eyes.   — Eric Fellman

__31__
THURS

MAUNDY THURSDAY

QUESTION: *Lord, we know not whither thou goest; and how can we know the way?*

ANSWER: *I am the way, the truth, and the life....*

                                                — John 14:5, 6

Knowing His trial and death were approaching, Jesus tried to comfort the disciples. They didn't fully understand, and they were afraid. Jesus described a journey toward a wonderful future and told the disciples they would join Him there. But Thomas wanted a detailed road map. Jesus' answer didn't provide a map but something better. When He first called the disciples, Jesus often simply said, "Follow me." Once, when some people asked where He was going, He said, "Come along and see." Jesus didn't give directions; He showed the way.

Once, many years ago, I was canoeing in northern Minnesota with my father. There the lakes are often connected by short footpaths called portages. Traveling through the area can be confusing, especially for the uninitiated.

As we stopped for lunch on a beautiful pine-covered island, we watched two people in a canoe circling the lake, poking into every bay. Then, spotting us, they paddled in our direction. "Say, mister," said the young man to my dad, "can you show me the way into Lake Two? I need to get to the Lake One portage."

"You're sitting in Lake Two," replied Dad.

At this, the young woman burst into tears. "We haven't known where we've been going for three days," she sobbed. "We're on our honeymoon, and it's been awful. We just want to go home."

One glance at the husband's forlorn look melted Dad's heart. "It's tough to find. You'd better follow us." And so we showed them the way.

That is what Jesus was trying to do for Thomas. Jesus knew the next few days would be frightening and confusing. No set of rules, no words, not even Jesus' words, would hold Thomas and the others steady. But by focusing on Jesus Himself, His life and His actions, even Thomas could find his way through the days ahead. For despite his doubt, Thomas would still be with the group when Easter came.

Are you, perhaps like Thomas, uneasy about a difficult situation you find yourself in? Or, perhaps like the couple in the canoe, you have lost your way? Jesus' answer is the same today as it was for Thomas. "I am the way," He says. "Follow Me."

Lord Jesus, let me see You clearly today, so that I might follow You through all the moments of my life. — Eric Fellman

Prayer Diary

My Prayer Requests for March: George to be fine complete Healing
Safe trip for Mom
Good uplifting visit with mom

1. a terrific day for Mom. "Happy Birthday"

2. *Strength, wisdom, attitude, discernment*

3.

4.

5.

6.

7.

8. *Good Doctor report for Mother*

9. *Good Doctors reports for Valetta*

10. *Biopsy to be good for George*

11.

12.

13.

14.

15.

16. *Safe travel for Mom + Lashete*

17. _____

18. _____

19. _____

20. _____

21. _____

22. _____

23. *Safe travel for Mom* _____

24. _____

25. _____

26. _____

27. _____

28. _____

29. *Safe travel home for Mom* _____

30. _____

31. _____

April

	S	M	T	W	T	F	S
						1	2
	3	4	5	6	7	8	9
	10	11	12	13	14	15	16
	17	18	19	20	21	22	23
	24	25	26	27	28	29	30

GIFTS OF THE SEASON

The Rain

April world washed green,
fresh with apple blossom scent,
hails the risen Son.

Wash my heart, Lord. Make my spirit Easter-clean,
that I might live Your Resurrection
promise every day.

1
FRI

GOOD FRIDAY
QUESTION: *"Don't you realize I have power either to free you or to crucify you?"*
ANSWER: *"You would have no power over me if it were not given to you from above...."*   — John 19:10, 11 (NIV)

Good Friday certainly was not "good" for Jesus. He had been kept up all night, falsely accused, dragged from the priests to the governor to the king and, finally, back to the governor. Pontius Pilate had Him whipped with thongs containing iron nails and had allowed his Roman soldiers to jam a crown of thorns on His head. In the courtroom, Pilate demanded, "Who are You? Give an answer for Yourself!" Jesus remained silent. In exasperation, Pilate exclaimed, "Don't You know I can order You executed, or I can let You go?"

"I know you can't do anything unless God above allows it," Jesus replied. "And since God is in control, the greater guilt goes to him who has falsely accused Me, even though you may order My death." Pilate was so stunned by Jesus' answer that he considered releasing Him, but in the end he gave in to the demands of the angry mob and ordered the crucifixion.

Within Jesus' answer to Pontius Pilate is a magnificent truth for helping us through every rough spot in life: *Even when everything appears lost, God is in control.*

A very good friend of mine died this past year. Just months before, Susan had been alive and bravely fighting to fill every new minute with love and meaning. But on my last visit I ached to see how disease had robbed her of strength and mobility.

Susan said something to me I will carry the rest of my life. "I've had a great life," she said. "I saw everything I wanted to see, did everything I wanted to do...well, almost! So I'm ready for what's next. Besides, if you are right about God, I'm going to wake up one morning soon and be able to jump out of this bed and feel no more pain."

Susan reminded me of the only message Jesus thought was important at His trial. No matter what happens, God is in control and He will work out a wonderful conclusion.

On this Good Friday, Lord, help me to find renewal from my difficulties by remembering that nothing happens out of Your control.   — Eric Fellman

2
SAT

QUESTION: *My God, my God, why hast thou forsaken me?*   — Mark 15:34
ANSWER: Silence

On this Saturday, we cannot listen in on any conversation with Jesus. He is dead. Try to forget what you already know — that tomorrow is Easter — and try to feel Saturday. *Bleak. Quiet. Dark.*

The last question Jesus asked while He was alive came on Good Friday, in the early afternoon. Jesus was hanging on a cross, nails in His hands and feet. There should have been the full light of day, but the day became unnaturally dark. In those moments, Jesus fulfilled what He was born for: to die for the sins of the world (John 10:17–18).

We love to coo over the Babe in the manger and cheer at the door of the empty tomb. But all too often we hurry past the suffering Savior. For on the cross, Jesus did what only He could. On His shoulders came all the hate, guilt and shame of generations past and of those unborn. And in that moment His holy and righteous Father turned His face away.

"My God, My God, why have You left Me all alone?" It is a question we all ask sooner or later. Perhaps a loved one has died, maybe bankruptcy has crushed your dreams, or a child has gotten into drugs and alcohol. With Jesus, we cry out, "God, why have You left me?"

I've thought a lot about that unanswered question. In that vast silence, there is but one answer: "I cannot answer why, for I am still here." God was standing beside Jesus' mother Mary and His friend John who had her in his arms. God was with Peter who was seething with anger and self-loathing because he had denied Jesus. God was with Joseph of Arimathea who was hiding in the shadows, even then restoring his courage so he could ask for the body to be placed in his tomb. God was there beside all of them who were harboring frustration and wanting to scream their pain at Him. *God was weeping, too.*

So as you experience that place in your heart which seems hopeless, remember where God is today, right now. God has not left you alone. *He is weeping with you.*

Dear God, let me hear the answer You give in the silence, and let me take from it the strength You gave Jesus.   — Eric Fellman

3
SUN

EASTER SUNDAY
QUESTION: *"Sir...tell me where you have laid him...."*
ANSWER: *"Mary."*...　　　　　　　　— John 20:15, 16 (RSV)

Mary Magdalene went with two others to the garden near Jesus' tomb to anoint His body with burial perfumes. They entered the garden gate and were suddenly bathed in the glowing light of two angels. "Why do you seek the living among the dead?" asked one angel.

"He is not here, for He is risen, just as He said," explained the other.

Incredible as the angels' story seemed, two of the women ran to tell the disciples. The other, too worn from grieving, stayed behind. She didn't believe the angels and wanted to see the body of Jesus for herself. That's how Mary Magdalene became the first Easter doubter.

Before we shake our heads at her faithlessness, why not look into our own lives and find the moments when we have almost missed Easter. For me, it came when I worked with a young colleague who always seemed to be most focused on how she could do the least. Finally, I told her, "If your work does not improve, I'll have to let you go." To my relief, she transferred to another department.

A year went by, and it was decided a position of assistant supervisor was to be created. My errant colleague's name was proposed. I couldn't believe it! I argued with the manager in charge, but he stood his ground and pointed to her recent outstanding performance. Finally, the chairman of the meeting turned to me and said gently, "Eric, we publish stories of the power of God to change people. Why can't you believe it happens in our own offices?"

They were right. The woman proved to be a valuable manager and greatly influenced the project's success. I had almost missed the miracle.

So it was for Mary on Easter morning; she saw the Master, but didn't recognize Him. Jesus, full of compassion, put all the love He had for her in His voice and said, *"Mary."* Her name.

In our own need to be made new this Easter, may we be reborn in our lives throughout the year through participation in this celebration. Let us listen for Jesus calling our names to bring us resurrection power for today. It matters not what has gone before today — death, despair, hopelessness. You and I can be reborn as He calls our names. And not just at Easter. The miracle awaits us each day.

Dear Jesus, thank You for knowing my name and for loving me enough not only to die, but to live that I might have new life.
　　　　　　　　　　　　　　　　　　　　　— Eric Fellman

PRAYER CAN CHANGE YOUR LIFE
MON The Healing Power

A new commandment I give to you, that you love one another.... — John 13:34 (RSV)

"This is the great secret," says *Prayer Can Change Your Life*. "We can be born anew through love." As I was learning to pray honestly and faithfully, I was being healed by God's love. The healing involved leaving the old way of living in fear and mistrust, and with God's help, moving toward His kingdom of peace and joy.

Recently, I was very irritated with my co-worker on a volunteer project. *We'll never accomplish our goals*, I thought, *because she insists that everything be done by her unnecessarily rigid specifications.*

One morning in my prayer time, I was being honest with God about a different set of frustrations: my family's habit of "messing up" my perfect home. But as I talked to God, I saw the problem in a new way. Yes, I wanted to be a good home manager, but I felt greatly underappreciated when family members foiled my plans. Through my prayers, God seemed to tell me, "Loosen up! Muddy shoes and unmade beds don't have a thing to do with your family's appreciation for you. Don't you know that you're much more important than a clean house?"

As God's love filled me with warmth, my thoughts shifted to my co-worker. And I knew what I had to do: *Loosen up!* Appreciating my co-worker was more important than how the job got done. The next time our committee met, I gave her a quick hug and looked straight into her eyes. "You are so important to this project," I said, "and I want to thank you for trying to keep us on target. What we are trying to do is important, and we couldn't do it without you."

As the meeting moved forward smoothly, I felt a strange glow, a sense of peace instead of irritation. I had entered the kingdom. And no longer battling my irritation, my co-worker — and I — could relax in the atmosphere of love.

If you're still wondering if this new prayer life is worth your time and effort and energy, think of *love* as an action word. Then watch *healing, happiness* and *peace* follow.

Lord, Your love has healed my soul. I want to love others in response. Point the way. — Pam Kidd

5   *Remember me, O my God....*   — Nehemiah 13:14

TUES

Years ago, I happened to be in the neighborhood where my old friend
Fulton Oursler lived, and on the spur of the moment I dropped in on
him. Fulton was the father of the present editor-in-chief of *Guideposts*
magazine, Fulton Junior. (We called him "Tony" when he was a youngster. I still do.) Fulton Senior, who is gone now, was a writer, a great one,
whose books you've probably read.

Fulton's wonderful wife Grace met me at the door and welcomed me
in, but as for seeing her husband — "Sorry," Grace said, "you'll just
have to sit and talk with me. The candle's lit."

For a moment, I wasn't sure what Grace meant about the candle, and
then I remembered. When Fulton felt the urge to write, he'd head for
his study where, just before entering, he'd light a candle that always
stood on a table by the door. While the candle was lit, no one was to
interrupt him — no one, for any reason whatsoever.

Grace took me back to show me the flaming candle and the closed
door behind which the great man was writing. But there was something
there that I had not heard about. It was something that ever since has
been a part of my own prayer life. On the door was affixed a hand-
written sign: "Lord, I may get busy today and forget You, but please,
Lord, do not forget me."

Lord, please keep me from getting so wrapped up in my work
that I neglect others and You.   — Norman Vincent Peale

6   *So let us come boldly to the very throne of God and stay*

WED   *there....*   — Hebrews 4:16 (TLB)

My husband Gene and I know what to expect a few moments after we go
to bed and turn off the light. It has become a nightly routine. Minnie,
who isn't a very courageous cat, will pad softly into our room, hesitate
for a few moments, then spring gently onto our bed. She settles down in
between our feet. I suppose because it's dark and still, she thinks we
don't know she's there. But usually one of us says, "Hello, Minnie. We
know it's you. You're welcome to come and sleep with us. You don't have
to sneak in after the light is off."

Still, she comes only when it's dark and our voices have quieted. *Poor*

Minnie. She needs to become more…bold, I thought, just before I drifted off to sleep. Then my eyes popped open. Another thought came quietly, but defiantly. *I would like for you to come to Me, child, without such hesitancy, also. Sometimes you come almost apologetically, wondering if you'll be received. Come to Me, boldly.*

Right then and there, I approached my Father with a problem I had thought too small to bring to Him. In my mind, I sat in His lap like a small child and explained, "It's income tax time again, Father. I've procrastinated long enough. In the morning, will You help me to organize what my husband has asked me to do?"

And then I turned over and went to sleep. I liked the sound of Minnie purring at the foot of our bed.

I'm going to depend on You, Father, to help me remember my rights and privileges as a child of Yours. Amen.

— Marion Bond West

<u>7</u>
THURS   *And they remembered his words.*

HOUSE GUEST
— Luke 24:8

"Life is sweet," my friend Allen Carter was saying. We were sitting in my room at the Sigma Chi House at the University of Tennessee. A few hours earlier, Allen had scored the points necessary to lead our intramural basketball team to victory. Naturally, I thought he was talking about winning the game. But I was wrong.

"I wish you could have known my dad, Brock," Allen said. I remembered that Allen's father had died when he was fourteen, and at first I felt a little uncomfortable as he talked on.

His father had been a successful lawyer, enjoyed farming, loved life. One day, as he watched Allen playing tennis, he began to feel dizzy, but he got an "all's clear" response from the doctor. Yet, a few months before his forty-ninth birthday on June 26, 1987, he was taken to surgery and a tumor in the speech area of his brain was diagnosed. On December 22 of that same year, at 6:30 in the morning, Allen's mom woke him, saying, "You'd better come. You'd better say good-bye to your father."

"I went in and said, 'I love you, Dad. I'm going to be with you again, someday,'" Allen remembered. "He grabbed my hand before he died."

I looked at my friend sitting across from me. His eyes were clear and there wasn't a glimmer of self-pity. To bridge the silence, I asked him what he felt was the most important thing his father left.

"He taught me," said Allen, "that life is sweet. And so I try to live my life that way. Maybe he's not here, but I know he's watching. I want him to see that I remember him by living as he lived."

Thinking back on that conversation, I see a lot of truth in Allen's words, and I can't help but recall the message of Jesus. When we believe, when we truly believe the things He taught us, we know that everything really is all right and that we will be together again with those we love. Suddenly, everything's okay. Suddenly, yes, as Allen said, "life is sweet." Very sweet.

God, remembering that You are watching, let me live as You have taught. Life is sweet.　　　　　　　　　　　　　— Brock Kidd

8
FRI

Let the peace of Christ rule in your hearts....
　　　　　　　　　　　　　—Colossians 3:15 (NIV)

At a conference I attended recently, the keynote speaker was Mary Jo West, the station manager of a Phoenix cable TV channel. She began by sharing what she felt were the necessary ingredients for a successful life, each one beginning with the letters of one all-important word. When she started that word with the letter *S*, everyone in the room thought that the word was going to be *success*. But as she continued...well, I'll let you be as surprised as I was to discover how a most successful person spells *success* in the 1990s:

Service. Go outside yourself to derive the satisfaction of helping others.
Ethics. Be truthful in all your doings.
Reconciliation. Ask forgiveness and make peace with those you've harmed.
Enthusiasm. Open yourself to new things and take pleasure in your discoveries.
No. Did you know that "No" is a complete sentence? Don't feel guilty about using it to allow time for your needs.
Imagination. Have vision. Find a "passion project," and get to work on it.
Togetherness. Don't try to do everything yourself. Accept help, and lend a hand, too.
You. Take care of yourself. Remember, you are beautiful in God's eyes.

Now, let your year be filled with peace and *serenity.*

Loving God, let me not wear myself out chasing after success, now that I know a new way to spell it. Bless me instead with serenity in all my plans and pursuits.   — Gina Bridgeman

9 *May the God of love and peace be with you.*
SAT   — II Corinthians 13:11 (TLB)

How extraordinary it was, I thought, to find a retreat center in the middle of Anaheim, California. But the weekend at the spiritual center was full of surprises — arched arbors of fragrant rambler roses lined the parking strip, and the center courtyard was ablaze with hundreds of rosebushes in every shade.

"Roses are our hobby," said the director as she checked me in. "We grow them to the glory of God." And, indeed, I discovered roses everywhere, their scent filling the air.

Taking the stairs to my room, I came upon a small shelf hung from the stairwell banister. It was covered with sand and lit by a small candle that sent dancing lights across one deep red rose in a vase. Written in the sand were the words *God's Love*.

"Feel free to smooth the sand and write your own message," I was later told.

This stairwell shelf became for me a wayside chapel. That night, I paused for prayer and wrote the word *Rejoice*. By morning, someone had smoothed out my *Rejoice* and written *Hope*, and I paused to pray for them. On Sunday afternoon, before returning home, I made one more stop at my stairwell chapel. Two red petals lay curled in the sand with the word *Mercy*. I left it, but underneath I wrote, as I had found it, *God's Love*.

How good it is to set aside a still, small place of quiet. Now, on the terrace of my garden, I have made my own wayside chapel. A flagstone, set firmly on a large rock, holds a layer of sand. Instead of a candle, an abalone shell, mother-of-pearl side up, catches the light, and in its hollow floats one small rose.

In your mind's eye, come there with me now. Together let us smooth the sand and from your heart of hearts write the word of your present need, and I — for you — will write the words *His Peace!*

Dear Lord, how good it is to find deep within our hearts a small and quiet place of meditation and prayer. Enfold us with the assurance of Your ever-present love and cover us with Your peace.   — Fay Angus

10   *[The Lord] made darkness his covering around him, his*
SUN   *canopy thick clouds dark with water.* — Psalm 18:11 (RSV)

A five-by-seven-inch photograph hangs on our bedroom wall, a study of
sky and clouds. Not fleecy white clouds against a blue background—
these clouds are black and ominous; they block out the sun in a cheer-
less sky.

The picture was a gift, years ago, from a photographer friend in
England, Ray Cripps. He sent it at a time when the clouds in our lives
were ominous indeed: the imminent failure of our publishing company.
Not a cheering image to get in the mail from overseas, those gathering
storm clouds. In fact, the photograph did cheer us. For beneath the
photo, Ray had inscribed a verse by the eighteenth-century poet
William Cowper:

> Ye fearful saints, fresh courage take;
>   The clouds ye so much dread
> Are big with Mercy, and will break
>   In blessings on your head.

Rain-bearing clouds! Clouds bringing fertility and renewal...not the
portents of disaster our fears had made of them. And so it proved, as we
found a new format for publishing that freed us from day-to-day
management.

So clouds have proved time and again in the years since. The bedroom is where we do most of our praying for ourselves and others, so
that's where Ray's photo hangs. "Where is the mercy in this situation?"
we ask as we lift our concerns. "What blessing will flow from the sky
that looks so dark right now?"

Show me Yourself, Father, in the storm clouds of today.
                                                    — Elizabeth Sherrill

11   *And as they were eating, Jesus took bread and blessed*
MON   *it....*   — Matthew 26:26

I seem to dine alone more often these days. It's not all that bad. I go to
restaurants where I can be safe from my own cooking and be among
people. I like to play a little game with myself. I try to figure out who
the other diners are, where they come from, what they do for a living,
and I must confess that I don't mind catching snatches of their conversations. What I do mind are those couples who sit through a meal with-

out saying a word to each other. It makes me want to go over and say, "Look, you might just as well be eating alone like me. Stop wasting each other. Please!"

Then there's the matter of the food. Did you ever notice how, when you're with other people, you pay more attention to them than to what you are eating? Alone, however, you can concentrate on the dish in front of you. Which has led me to a new appreciation of food. Not only the food itself, but what it can mean to me in spiritual terms.

I remember the evening I was alone in a neighborhood restaurant hungrily waiting for the waiter to take the order. I reached for a roll, and as I took it in my hand, it became in some mystical way not just a roll, but something more. A symbol. It was as though I heard Moses saying to the Israelites, "This is the bread which the Lord has given you to eat." And I felt a gratitude so real and so deep that it has stayed with me ever since. Today, when I take a piece of bread in my hands and break it, I am saying a silent thank-You far more profound than any table grace I've ever heard spoken.

So you see, a lot can happen when you eat alone.

I am blessed, Lord, by Your daily bread.   — Van Varner

12 PRACTICING THE POWER OF PRAYER
TUES Victory Prayer

For we walk by faith, not by sight.   — II Corinthians 5:7

I seem to fight the same predictable battles every day: procrastination, a critical spirit, envy. But recently I learned a new way of praying that is helping me fight these old enemies. I call it the "Victory Prayer" and discovered it in Charles Stanley's book *The Wonderful Spirit-Filled Life.* Don't wait to pray until you are in the thick of a predictable battle, Stanley suggests. Instead, claim God's promise of victory in prayer *before* the battle. Then, when the battle comes, you know you've already defeated this enemy. The power behind this confident prayer is faith — believing God will do what He promises. That's how David won the battle against Goliath!

Goliath was the giant Philistine who terrorized the Israelite soldiers, but young David knew Goliath was God's enemy; that God would be with him in the battle; that God would be victorious over His enemy. So David claimed that victory before the battle began. Then he merely did what he knew how to do as a shepherd boy. He picked up his slingshot and five smooth stones and marched off to face the enemy. The result flowed from his confident faith.

I've been trying this spiritual battle plan. Each morning, I name my enemy (procrastination). I know this enemy is also God's enemy and claim God's promise that He will be with me in my battle. Then I thank God for His victory. After praying, I do what I know how to do. I sit down at my desk and begin the work that awaits me. The battle begins, and the result flows from my faith.

What familiar battles do you face today? Fill in the blank in Stanley's prayer:

Lord, I claim victory right now over the giant of _____.
I recognize that this giant is coming against the Christ in me.
Just as You defeated this giant when You walked on this earth,
You can defeat it through me now, for You are my life. I trust You
to produce peace and self-control through me. When the pressure comes, remind me that the battle is Yours. Amen.

— Carol Kuykendall

13
WED *But your sorrow shall be turned into joy.*   — John 16:20

The year our grandson Shawn was tri-captain of the basketball team, he dreamed of winning the New Hampshire championship. Instead, the team had four wins and fifteen losses. Shawn never complained. Maybe it was partly because of the advice from one high school teacher whom Shawn admired. Edward Metz taught his students English and much about life as well.

After the frustrating, heartbreaking basketball season ended, there was some unexpected good news. Shawn had written an essay entitled "A Teacher to Remember" about Mr. Metz. Unknown to Shawn, the theme had been submitted to a state essay contest, and Shawn had won the grades 9 to 12 category. Shawn was astonished, and Mr. Metz was elated.

Then, shortly before the prizes were to be awarded, Mr. Metz was in a car accident and broke his hip in five places. *If only Mr. Metz could be with us,* we thought on the evening of the awards ceremony. Then we looked up and saw Mr. Metz entering the hall. Although weak, he had traveled miles to come. As he hobbled to his seat, his face showed pain, yet his eyes sparkled with joy, pride and anticipation. He was there to see Shawn receive his award. Their greeting spoke volumes as they hugged warmly.

Both had overcome obstacles: The basketball season toppled Shawn's dreams for a scholarship; the mishap destroyed Mr. Metz's car and shattered his hip. But from this adversity had come good: Shawn awakened to his overlooked skill of writing; Mr. Metz saw one of his pupils fulfill the potential he had encouraged them to strive for.

Best of all, I learned, too. Shawn's flexibility and willingness to move on after a big disappointment, and Mr. Metz's courage in handling setbacks were inspiring. My teachers couldn't have been better ones.

Dear Jesus, You showed me how misfortune can become good fortune. May I not forget the lesson.   — Oscar Greene

14
THURS   *Love...hopes all things....*   — I Corinthians 13:7 (RSV)

Was that a knock at the door?
Or just the wind?
There it is again.
"Hello?"
It's just a little girl of seven,
With freckled cheeks and strawberry hair.
"Wanna buy some candy, sir?"
Her emerald eyes are wide with hope.
I mull it over in my mind.
It's overpriced. I don't need the sugar.
I have ten dollars to last till payday.
I don't even know this child.
"No, thanks, sweetheart."
She nods, politely, but her eyes lose luster,
And the hope is gone. She shuffles away.
"Wait! Just a minute! I'll take two boxes!"
Some things in life are more important than money.
Like hope.
There's just too little hope to go around.
This is the sweetest hope I've ever tasted,
For only seven dollars.
A real bargain at any price.

Lord, You gave me hope when I was hopeless. Now may I give it to others.
                    — Daniel Schantz

15 *The Lord is nigh unto all them that call upon him...in*
FRI *truth.*   —Psalm 145:18

My son Michael, eight, was playing with his bow and arrow set. Each
arrow has a small suction cup at the very tip. Michael was warned never
to shoot at anyone or any animal.

"Dad, I did as you said, so I shot the arrow way up in the air." The
arrow stuck in the oak tree, about twenty feet above our heads. Michael
tried knocking the arrow out with a tennis ball, with a stick, with his
shoe. After trying for half an hour, he decided to call me outside and ask
for help.

I tried knocking the arrow down with a tennis ball, a stick, my shoe.
No matter how many times we tried, the arrow stuck. That night, as I
tucked Michael into bed, he said, "Oh, well. No more arrow."

The next morning, while I was pouring milk into my cereal, I looked
out the kitchen window and saw Michael's arrow on the middle of the
lawn. I stepped outside, picked up the arrow, returned to the house and
put it at Michael's place. When he walked into the kitchen ten minutes
later, he was impressed that I was able to free the arrow.

"Well, Michael, I really didn't have anything to do with it. The wind
must have knocked the arrow free."

"That's okay, Daddy. Maybe we helped knock it out just enough for
the wind to finish the job."

If you are struggling with a problem today that doesn't seem to want
to budge, why don't you give it a nudge with a prayer? What you can't
solve alone (with a tennis ball, a stick or a shoe), you can depend on God
to help shake loose.

Lord, I give up all my struggling to solve this problem with no
results. I turn it over to You today and trust Your answer.
                                              —Christopher de Vinck

                                                        HOUSE GUEST
16
SAT *But the fruit of the Spirit is love, joy, peace, patience, kind-*
ness, goodness, faithfulness, gentleness and self-control....
                                              —Galatians 5:22–23 (NIV)

Yesterday, my husband Alex and I pruned the fruit trees in our backyard. Once again I can see through them to the field beyond. Like those
trees before pruning, lately my life is thick with excessive busyness. Yet

the guidelines we followed in reshaping the trees can help me reshape my life.

Limit a tree's height. Otherwise, it wastes energy and the quality of fruit declines.

As a rule, I have a hard time saying, "No." This year, besides teaching piano and music theory, I found myself agreeing to chair a competition. Next year, I'll limit my reach and only teach.

Prune cross branches rubbing against each other, or the branches scrape and the tree succumbs to disease.

Too many evening activities rub against our family life, leaving us little time to enjoy one another. Next time, instead of attending a town meeting, I'll write a letter, and strengthen our family time.

Cut away downward shoots blocking light. Shading reduces fruit and causes weak growth in the tree.

One more phone call to make, another bill to be paid, a new teaching assignment to plan—and soon I've frittered away my morning. I have a brighter sense of my day when I've first had my prayer and Bible-reading time.

As I watch the orchard today, light streams through the trees, and the branches sway with the breeze. I can tell that we will harvest a richer crop of apples this fall. And I hope, too, with proper care and attention, pruning will help produce the fruit of beauty and abundance in my own life.

Lord, help me make space for You, to choose carefully how I shape my life into one that will grow strong and full for You.
— Mary Brown

17
SUN

How good and how pleasant it is for brethren to dwell together in unity! — Psalm 133:1

"Why don't I go to church?" the middle-aged man heatedly answered his questioner. "Because down at the place I used to go, they're all a bunch of hypocrites. They're no better than I am."

"You're half right," the church worker replied quietly. "They're no better than you are, but they're trying to do something about it."

Someone once defined a saint as a sinner who keeps on trying. On that basis, all of us who recognize our faults and implore God's grace to help us change would qualify. Recently, the church has been roundly scandalized by people who took Christ's name in vain—posing as holy persons when they were in fact charlatans. As a kid, I thought "taking the Lord's name in vain" was using it to swear, and though that certainly doesn't honor God, it isn't in the same sinful league with pretending to be His follower in order to fool others and gain some material advantage.

But despite the widely reported failures of the church today, despite charges that it sounds a less certain moral trumpet, despite assertions that the church's role in shaping society has waned, it is still the place I want to be on Sunday morning. Why? Because in a community of believers who share my struggles with life's perplexities and defeats, I find hope. Together, in a little church where I have worshiped for the past thirty years, I am assured of Christ's presence. Together, we learn about our mutual needs and grow in our vision of what it means to serve others. Together, we bind up one another's wounds and go forth renewed and imbued with more faith than when we came. I know of no other place that offers so much.

> *Thank You, O God, for churches true,*
> *That guide us on our path to You.*

> — Fred Bauer

18 *Let every man be swift to hear....*   — James 1:19
MON

Visitors might think it odd to find a dandelion behind the glass doors of our dining room china cabinet. Surrounded by Great-grandmother's china and Aunt Kate's antique silver, it stands as it has for years in a clear crystal vase.

I pass through the dining room, look at the dandelion and remember a five-year-old Brock bursting with joy. His grandparents were on their way to visit us, and as I drove him home from kindergarten, he couldn't stop chattering. "Bebe's bringing me a real good surprise...and Pa's taking me out for hamburgers tomorrow...and...oh, Mama, did you see that giant dandelion over in that ditch?"

I hardly heard a word he said. My mind was on thawed chicken and ingredients for the lemon sauce.

Brock was still talking nonstop when his grandparents arrived. "And, Pa, my teacher gave me a 'good job' sticker today...and on the way home from school I saw the giantest dandelion in the world...I wish you could've seen it, too."

As you might expect, the chicken got cooked, the sauce got made, the dishes got washed and bedtime came.

Early the next morning, Pa had the coffee brewing when I woke up. I pulled on my robe and went into the kitchen. There on the counter, balanced in a mason jar, was the "giantest dandelion" you ever saw. I must have looked pretty surprised.

"It took a while," Pa chuckled, "but I drove up and down the road until I found it. I was back before Brock woke up."

And so the dandelion, carefully layered with hair spray to keep it intact, waits in the china cabinet. More than sterling pitchers and monogrammed plates, it reminds me of what's really important. It says, *Listen to those you love. Try to hear what they're saying.* After all, dandelion moments are few.

Lord, help me to listen to my family, my friends and You.
—Pam Kidd

Quiet Time

A BUSY MOTHER'S PRAYER

Dear God, this is the hour when in my day there comes a lull; breakfast is over, father has gone to his work, and I have helped the children into their rubbers and their coats and off to school. And now I have closed the door and find myself alone. O God, go with them all; beyond my sight and voice they live and move, but not beyond Thy care. Guide these precious ones of mine. Keep them from those things that make us weak and lesser souls. God be with my dear ones all this day. I pray in the name of Thine own Son, our Lord and Saviour, Jesus Christ. Amen.
—*Hazen G. Werner*

19
TUES   *[Jesus] answered, "Every plant that my heavenly Father has not planted will be uprooted."*
—Matthew 15:13 (NRSV)

For many years, one of my passions was growing orchids. In those days,

I was always on the lookout for new friends who shared the same obsession and had a collection worth visiting. It is called "going orchiding." Orchid lovers can *ooh!* and *ah!* over the plain green leaves of tiny seedlings that aren't even in bloom.

A true orchid maven knows each valued plant's genealogy without even referring to labels or records and can recite the generations that came before. Knowing those names in the pedigree helps me imagine what the flowers will look like when they finally come into bloom. The leaves spell out the name of the *genus* — the family that that plant came from — and the price of the plant is based on who its parents are. And if, when it blooms, the flower is not true to its heritage, the plant will be relegated to a back bench or be sold off at a bargain price.

These baby orchid plants remind me what it means to be my heavenly Father's offspring. Knowing Who my Father is spells out my potential. It makes me strive even harder to be a true child of God.

Father, help me to live up proudly to my Parentage.

— Diane Komp

20 *Commit thy way unto the Lord; trust also in him; and he*
WED *shall bring it to pass.* — Psalm 37:5

When our son Richard was in training at Williams Air Force Base outside Phoenix, he wrote an exuberant letter about flying T38 jets in formation. "Just think, Mother, we'll be flying those magnificent machines just a few feet apart!" I was anything but exuberant about his flying in formation. Why did the TV weather forecaster always report clear skies over Phoenix? Sunshine meant that Richard was up in the air, a fact that tied me in knots.

One day when I was confiding to a friend my almost paranoiac state, she said, "Dorothy, you need to be 'praying the promise.'"

"Whatever does that mean?" I asked.

"Well," she replied, "last month when I was asked to chair the women's division of the United Fund, I knew that I just could not do it until in my daily devotions I found Psalm 37:5. Now I am 'praying the promise' to 'commit my way unto the Lord and trust in Him.' And so far the whole drive has been a piece of cake."

From that day forward I followed up the daily weather report by "praying the promise." And you know what? I no longer worry about

Richard. He has been flying for eighteen years, the last twelve as a captain with a major commercial airline. I rest in God's promise that Richard is in much better hands than mine.

Thank You, dear Lord, that I can trust You to honor Your Word.
— Dorothy Shellenberger

<u>21</u>
THURS

"I am with you and will keep you wherever you go...."
— Genesis 28:15 (RSV)

On Monday, I had a biopsy as an outpatient at Good Samaritan Hospital here in Kearney, Nebraska. I prayed that Jesus would watch over me and I was quite calm about it all, until I got into the pre-op room and several nurses started working on me, placing an IV in my arm, monitor tabs on my chest and a hypo in my hip.

As I felt my heart beginning to race, a quiet, dark-haired woman with soft brown eyes took hold of my hand. "My name is Julie," she said, "and I'll be with you throughout your surgery and until you're ready to go home." Then Julie very carefully explained to me exactly what to expect when I was wheeled into the operating room, what would happen there, that I'd have an oxygen mask on when I woke up, and that she'd take it off as soon as I was able to tell her where I was and the day of the week.

My hand was in Julie's as I went under the anesthetic and also when I was coming out of it. I can't tell you what a comfort that was! And thanks be to God, the biopsy showed no evidence of cancer.

Jesus promised that He would be with me throughout this life, and I know He was there that day. When I'm frightened or insecure about anything, I can always turn within to hear that gentle voice saying, "My name is Jesus, and I'm with you in this all the way."

Thank You, Lord, for the blessed comfort of Your hand holding mine throughout this life.   — Marilyn Morgan Helleberg

<u>22</u>
FRI

God said unto them, Be fruitful, and multiply, and replenish the earth....   — Genesis 1:28

In her memorable book *Passages*, Gail Sheehy suggests that somewhere around the age of forty, it dawns on most of us that we are not going to live forever. Her observation came home to me not long ago as I was flying over a stretch of devastated Amazon rainforest in South America. For as far as the eye could see, the land had been stripped of its life-giving resources. What the people responsible for this ongoing destruction apparently don't realize is that the rainforests of the world — like our lives — are not infinite. Some day those jungles and their treasures will be gone, and future generations will suffer because of it.

But, of course, criticizing our neighbors to the south for having specks in their eyes and overlooking those in our own is the height of hypocrisy. Instead, we need to get on with the task of cleaning up our act: recycling, saving water, driving more efficient cars (or walking when feasible), conserving energy, being cautious with chemicals, planting trees, composting our garbage. Though our individual contributions may seem like a drop in the bucket, the cumulative effect could be enormous.

God may have given humankind dominion over the earth (Genesis 1:26), but we don't reverence His gift when we deface it and pollute it. Our job is to practice a piece of logic that I first heard from an Ohio farm friend whose family had worked the same acreage for four generations. "My hope," he told me, "is to leave this corner of God's garden a tad better than I found it." That's a good goal for all of us, and we'd better start today, because neither our land nor our lives is infinite.

> *When it comes to the beauty of Your earth...*
> *Lord, teach us how to love and enjoy it,*
> *How to use it wisely, not destroy it.*

— Fred Bauer

23
SAT *Be completely humble and gentle; be patient, bearing with one another in love.* — Ephesians 4:2 (NIV)

"And it really hurt my feelings when she cut off my sentence that way," I was winding down. I'd been telling my good friend DeLinda about a slight I'd received — intentional or not, I didn't know.

"I hear what you're saying, and I know how it feels. But, Kathie," she said in her warm, wise, country way, "that's nothin' but *junk mail*. Just toss it out unopened."

For the rest of the afternoon, I remained fascinated by this interest-

ing comparison. I remember once knowing someone who felt compelled to examine all junk mail that arrived. What a clutter! My
mail-reading friend didn't know what to keep or to toss after a while!

And I think that's where I was in my spiritual life right then: weighing and examining too closely, giving my own imagination free rein to
blow things out of proportion.

If a real impasse exists between people, the Bible instructs us to "go
and tell him his fault between thee and him alone" in a reconciliation
attempt (Matthew 18:15). And the questionable misunderstandings,
goofs and oversights? If it doesn't seem important enough actually to
"go and tell him his fault," then maybe it isn't important enough to be
sitting around in messy little piles in my mind.

The cutoff sentence I was agonizing over? Junk mail. Out it goes.

*Dear Lord, make me a holier "mail-sorter," able to dispatch the
clutter of questionable words quickly. And may others forgive
and toss any junk mail I've sent them.*   — Kathie Kania

24
SUN
There hath not failed one word of all his good promise....
                                        —I Kings 8:56

When my eighteen-year-old dachshund Heidi died, at first I mourned.
Then came a period when I tried to convince myself that freedom from
canine responsibilities had its advantages. After awhile, though, loneliness came back in a rush, and I found myself envying all the dog-
walkers in my neighborhood and asking God if He didn't have another
dachshund in mind for me.

His answer seemed to come in the form of a Maryland friend who
told me that she was going to breed her male dachshund. "Would you
like to have one of the anticipated puppies, Ellie?" she asked. Would I!

"Dear Lord, thank You for Your promise to turn mourning into joy" was
my prayer after hearing this good news. But the dachshund puppies
didn't materialize. Some biological complication in the female, I
learned. I was heartbroken.

Then one evening, I ran into a woman whom I knew casually. She
was a dog breeder, and she'd heard about Heidi's death through the veterinarian we both used. "I have a Dandie Dinmont for you," she said
with a smile.

"Oh!" was all I could reply. I knew the Dandie Dinmont terrier's size was perfect for a small apartment like mine, and that they were loyal, affectionate. But my heart was set on a dog like Heidi!

"An eight-week-old male," she added.

"Well...," I said doubtfully, "I don't know. I'll have to let you know."

In my apartment, I stood bewildered in the middle of my living room. "A Dandie Dinmont," I kept repeating. "But, God," I said aloud, "this can't be right for me. You promised me a dachshund."

"No," the answer seemed to come, "I didn't promise you a dachshund. I promised to turn your mourning into joy."

Today, as I write this, a Dandie Dinmont puppy sits at my feet. Wally is an eighteen-pound bundle of love. As with Heidi, we go for long walks together. And as with Heidi, Wally and I are bonding.

Now I can say with all certainty, God has kept His promise. He truly has. He always does.

Lord, I rejoice in the faithfulness of Your promises. — Eleanor Sass

25 *"Do not be afraid...for your prayer is heard...."*
MON   — Luke 1:13 (RSV)

Normally, when I go to New York City, I travel by bus or train, but on a recent trip I decided to drive. It was a poor decision. Since I moved out of the metropolitan area several years ago, I've lost the knack of driving in heavy traffic and avoiding pedestrians who leap out in front of cars to beat a changing light. Even worse, I stayed too long and found myself caught in rush-hour traffic on my way home.

I was inching my way along Ninth Avenue, heading for the Lincoln Tunnel, which would take me to the wide-open spaces of the New Jersey Turnpike, when the "Check Engine" light in my dashboard went on. Then the engine started making clanging noises. My car was breaking down — in the middle of New York City during the evening rush hour!

Gas stations are few and far between in a big city, and even though I was surrounded by cars, I felt utterly helpless and lost. Ordinarily, in that kind of a situation I would pray — and I did — but, frankly, I wondered whether God could hear anybody calling for help in the middle of this crowded, noisy city.

Suddenly, there it was. On my side of the street, too: a little old gas station with one pump. A man was locking up the office as I pulled in and the engine died. He turned out to be a good mechanic who not only replaced a broken fan belt but accepted this stranger's out-of-state check in payment.

Don't tell me God can't hear our prayers. He does — wherever we are!

Almighty Father, we thank You for hearing each and every one of us whenever we call You. — Phyllis Hobe

26
TUES PRACTICING THE POWER OF PRAYER
Generic Prayers

The...prayer of a righteous man [or woman or child] availeth much. — James 5:16

How often it is that I learn from those who are much younger than I!

I had been asked by seven young women, students at Baylor University and members of the church that I attend, if I would disciple them in Bible study. On this particular Tuesday afternoon we were talking about prayer, and I waxed forth (eloquently and informatively, I thought) on how we were to be specific in our prayers, spelling out to the Lord exactly what our needs were. I complained about those generic prayers like "Bless all the missionaries overseas" or "Watch over all the people who are traveling on the highways." "Even the Lord must find them innocuous," I said.

One of the girls interrupted me, "Oh, please, Mrs. Shellenberger, don't discourage anyone from praying those prayers. Usually, it is little children who are just beginning to pray who pray in generalities. My parents are missionaries in Uganda, and they are in constant danger. I believe when some child prays for 'all the missionaries overseas' that the Lord knows the specific ones in need of special care at that moment and dispatches one of His angels to protect them from danger, or encourages them when they are discouraged, or strengthens them when they are weak."

Another young woman spoke up, "And who knows but that prayer for 'all the people traveling on the highway' may avoid a traffic accident because the Lord assigned that prayer to someone in danger at that very moment."

I still believe that the Lord wants us to be specific when we can. But to insist that that is the only way to pray is, I see now, to limit God in my mind and put Him in a box. Never again will I do that.

Dear Lord, please remember Mona and David Entwistle as they teach young Africans at the Rift Academy. Guide, guard and protect them from hurt, harm and danger. And, Lord, for those other people serving in faraway places that I do not know, but You do, I pray that this request will include them, too. Thank You, Lord. Amen.
                                                        —Dorothy Shellenberger

Editor's Note: *Have you been practicing the power of prayer each month? You may want to return to the previous months and reread the devotionals on "Practicing the Power of Prayer." Then turn to the Prayer Diaries and review your written responses, adding new ones, too. If you like, you can write us about your prayer experiences or simply share one of your helpful prayer techniques with us. Write to* Daily Guideposts *Editor, Guideposts Books, 16 E. 34th St., New York, New York 10016.*

27
WED

A merry heart doeth good like a medicine....
                                                        —Proverbs 17:22

Most of us know exactly why doctors' reception areas are called "waiting rooms"—we usually have to wait such a long time in them! As I waited to see my doctor recently, I could almost feel my blood pressure rising as the minutes ticked by. *Why is it,* I fumed to myself, *that doctors seem to think patients have nothing better to do than wait?*

I angrily leafed through a tattered magazine, not really interested in the old news it contained. But one brief item caught my attention. It described a recent scientific study on the physiological effects of smiling. The researchers seemed convinced that the act of smiling ultimately triggers the release of certain chemical substances in the brain that act as natural mood-elevators and painkillers. Surprisingly enough, smiling seemed to produce a positive effect regardless of whether the smile was spontaneous or forced!

I was skeptical. Still, as I continued to read, I became aware of the tightness of my neck and shoulder muscles, the clenched jaw that was starting to give me a headache. Could a smile, even a forced one, really improve my mood? *It couldn't hurt to try,* I decided.

Glancing up from the magazine, I caught the eye of another patient and deliberately smiled as broadly as I could. She looked surprised, but smiled back. I held up the magazine and told her, "It says here that smiling makes us feel better — whether we have a reason to smile or not. What do you think?"

She paused, then laughed. "Now that you mention it, I think I do feel a little better right now."

I had to admit, so did I. Afterward, I realized that the best medicine was dispensed that day not in the doctor's office, but in the waiting room.

Father, when I don't feel like smiling today, please remind me that it's therapeutic to do it anyway!   — Susan Williams

---

28
THURS

And the Lord God formed man of the dust of the ground, and breathed into his nostrils the breath of life; and man became a living soul.   — Genesis 2:7

It was a busy morning, and I had worries on my mind. As the president of a Christian ministry to the rural poor, I was anxious about meeting our budget, training our staff and making deadlines.

I was about to leave town for some speaking engagements, and my mind was tied up in knots as I thought about the things I had to do in the few hours before my flight left. *I really don't have time for our weekly chapel service*, I thought as I walked to the church. I wasn't prepared for my trip. There were phone calls to make and letters to write. My mind raced through my agenda as I sat in the pew. A staff member got up to give the opening prayer.

"Thank You, Lord, for waking us up this morning," he said. "You didn't have to, but You did...."

The prayer continued, but the words stopped me short. How many days have I awakened with anxiety gnawing away at my heart and mind? How often have my own plans intruded, even in the quiet morning hours before I begin my devotions? How many mornings have I started stressed out, feeling as if everything would cave in without the immense effort of my own strength and will?

Let me begin again, Lord. "Thank You for waking me up." Yes, there are some difficulties before me, but thank You. Thank You for a new day, and a new opportunity to serve You.

Dearest Lord, thank You for the breath of life, and for breathing the Spirit of life into me. Amen.   — Dolphus Weary

HOUSE GUEST

$\underline{29}$
FRI   *The Lord reproves him whom he loves....*
                              —Proverbs 3:12 (RSV)

One night, while I did laundry, my nine-year-old son Zeb and I played rummy. I left to change loads during one of his turns, and when I returned, Zeb's manner told me something was up.

The possibility that he'd looked at my hand took me by surprise. *Zeb wouldn't do that,* I thought. But his big, blue eyes opened wide when I asked him, and with an embarrassed grin, he said, "I only peeked at your first card, Mom!"

After I gathered up the cards and called off the game, I talked to Zeb about honor and trust. He listened and agreed, then was ready—too ready—to start the next game. "No, son," I said, with a standoffish air.

"I'm sorry, Mom," Zeb replied and started upstairs to his room.

Now, usually corrections at our house end with hugs, not separation. *What's wrong here?* I wondered. I went over a mental checklist of how the Lord corrects me:

1. He loves me, so He corrects me (Proverbs 3:12).
2. When I apologize, He forgives and cleanses me (I John 1:9).
3. Then he forgets it (Isaiah 43:25).

Of course! I thought. *There's more to be said.* I called Zeb back downstairs. As we hugged, I said, "I forgive you, and the Lord forgives you. Now, let's put this behind us and play another game!"

"All right!" Zeb said. His joyful relief was evident as we shuffled and cut the cards. I was relieved, too. More than just learning right behavior, I wanted him to learn about love. Me, too.

Father, let my correction always be with love. Thank You for loving me—in firmness and tenderness.   —Ellyn Baumann

$\underline{30}$
SAT   *I will raise him up at the last day.*   —John 6:40

During my childhood, my mother and I would sometimes visit a little country cemetery in Bernardsville, New Jersey. We'd see the graves of some of my ancestors—Grandpa and Grandma Parry, Great-aunt Henrietta, Uncle Jack and Aunt Margaret Barnard, several cousins. Now my parents are there, too, and someday it will be my final resting place. It's a pretty spot, especially in the springtime when flowering trees shade the graves and honeysuckle grows wild along the stone wall.

Back when Mother and I visited it, we'd stroll around, stopping from time to time to place some flowers on certain familiar markers. Then Mother would tell me little stories. "Great-aunt Henrietta was engaged to a British Army officer who died in the First World War. She was devastated and never married, but she always said that her faith in God helped her. She was sure she would meet her fiancé again someday.

"Uncle Jack and Aunt Margaret once owned a very nice hotel in the village. They lost it after the 1929 stock market crash, but they never lost their sense of humor or their positive outlook on life."

Somehow those cemetery visits didn't depress me. In fact, I often envisioned how it would be at the Last Day when, as Jesus promised, He'd raise us up. It would be like a big, joyful family reunion, I decided. I'd meet relatives I never knew. I'd reminisce with those I'd loved. And, best of all, no need to bring flowers because there would be no graves to put them on.

Dear Lord, help me to rest in the blessed assurance of Your promises.   — Eleanor Sass

Prayer Diary

My Prayer Requests for April:

1. _____

2. _____

3. _____

4. _____

5. _____

6. _____

7. _____

8. _____

9._____

10._____

11._____

12._____

13._____

14._____

15._____

16._____

17._____

18._____

19._____

20.

21.

22.

23.

24.

25.

26.

27.

28.

29.

30.

May

S	M	T	W	T	F	S
1	2	3	4	5	6	7
8	9	10	11	12	13	14
15	16	17	18	19	20	21
22	23	24	25	26	27	28
29	30	31				

GIFTS OF THE SEASON

The Flower

Petal by petal,
the opening rose reveals
God's beauty within.

*This month, Lord, help me to watch for signs
of Your love unfolding around me.*

1
———
SUN
PRAYER CAN CHANGE YOUR LIFE
Make Prayer a Regular Activity

Seek his face continually.   —I Chronicles 16:11

Until this morning, it seemed I was moving forward in my new prayer life. But long before daybreak I found myself fretting over my troubles, my fear rising. Money—never enough. Would we have enough to pay for Brock's next semester in school? And Keri's future college dreams? What about the unexpected home repairs? Would we ever get ahead?

"God," I whispered, "I thought prayer was going to change my life." I closed my eyes tight, waiting for an answer.

Instead, a childhood scene drifted through my mind. Neighborhood children lined up to play that timeless game "Mother, May I?" where the players stand on the starting line and the leader directs them one by one: "Take two giant steps forward." "Mother, may I?" the player answers and moves two steps closer to the finish line. But if in her haste to get ahead the player forgets to say, "May I?" it's back to the starting line.

Like my prayer life, I thought. Follow the rules, you move ahead. Forget the rules and you're back at the starting point. I knew very well that the number one directive of *Prayer Can Change Your Life* is: *Make honest prayer a regular activity—from the moment you awaken till the time you sleep.* I had forgotten and had slipped out of my regular prayer routine. So it was back to the beginning for another try.

"God, I'm here, ready to begin a new day," I pray before I stir from the bed. "I didn't mean to leave You out of yesterday. Can we start over?"

I begin with new resolve. "Lord, we always seem to be teetering on the edge of financial disaster," I say. He reminds me of the unexpected check that came in the mail the year we thought there would be no vacation, the scholarship that put us ahead when Brock started college, the extra food in the garage freezer—more than enough to get us through the month. *Why do I keep doubting, Lord, instead of thanking You for always providing?*

Seek Him continually, I'm reminded. As the book suggests, I am learning to treat my God-time like a business appointment I wouldn't dare break. When I do that, the steps forward continue at a steady pace.

Lord, I need to talk to You every day. I know You are waiting for me to make the time.   —Pam Kidd

2 *The grass withers, the flower fades, But the word of our*
MON *God stands forever.*   —Isaiah 40:8 (NAS)

The best benefit of living a long life is you get to make a lot of wonderful friends. One of my dearest friends is Carl Erskine, former pitching great with the Brooklyn Dodgers. Carl was one of the magical "boys of summer" who dominated baseball a generation ago.

Last year, Carl, now a bank president, spoke at a luncheon I attended for corporate heads. The overall theme of the meeting was the importance of strong values in the drive to build and achieve. We expected Carl to give parallels between effort and achievement in baseball and success in business. We were wrong.

After a few enjoyable baseball anecdotes, Carl said, "I have a couple of things I'd like to show you. First is this World Series ring," he said, sliding it off his finger. "I have two of these, and I always thought there could be nothing better than the feeling of winning a World Series and wearing the ring. I was wrong.

"This," he said, pulling a small plastic box from his pocket, "gave me a greater feeling. You see, this box contains the medal my disabled son Jimmy won swimming in the Special Olympics. For me, winning the World Series was a matter of sharpening and using God-given talents to their fullest potential. For Jimmy, this medal meant overcoming a desperate fear of water. It meant fighting against great odds to make muscles do things they were never able to do before. It meant standing up in front of a large and confusing crowd and getting from one end of the pool to the other without being distracted.

"So as we proceed to our goal of adding excellence to ability in order to achieve, let's not forget the most important values of love, courage, struggle and perseverance against great odds."

Carl's words reminded me of how many of the things in life that we value, like a World Series ring, are really grass and flowers that will wither and fade. Remember with me today the Word of the Lord that calls us to courage, caring, truth and love as the pursuits that have lasting meaning.

Lord, let my life today be marked by selfless caring that adds value to the life of every person I touch. —Norman Vincent Peale

3 *Let the beauty of the Lord our God be upon us....*
TUES   — Psalm 90:17

I suppose if I were a photographer's model, putting on my makeup each morning would be a stimulating process. As it is, it falls in the category of any routine chore — necessary, but not wildly rewarding. But I've found a second use for the time spent in front of the bathroom mirror: a prayer time prompted by an inventory of the face. (A man could do the same with the equally humdrum act of shaving.)

Bible verses suggest the petitions. By now, I've memorized several dozen, such as "The very hairs of your head are all numbered" (Matthew 10:30). Brushing my hair, I ask that God's individual care for me continue through the day.

"Wash you, make you clean, put away the evil of your doings" (Isaiah 1:16) reminds me as I wash my face to confess the commissions and omissions of the previous day.

With the moisturizing lotion, I thank Him for forgiving me: "God...hath anointed thee with the oil of gladness" (Psalm 45:7). With the concealer: "Blessed are they whose iniquities are forgiven, and whose sins are covered" (Romans 4:7).

Applying eye makeup, I thank God for the gift of the senses: "The hearing ear, and the seeing eye, the Lord hath made even both of them" (Proverbs 20:12). Or ask Him to open my eyes to His truth: "Anoint thine eyes with eyesalve, that thou mayest see" (Revelation 3:18).

Putting on lipstick, I pray that today I may speak no hasty or unkind word: "I am purposed that my mouth shall not transgress" (Psalm 17:3).

And surveying the finished job in the mirror? I ask that those I meet today see not me but Him. "But we all, with open face beholding as in a glass the glory of the Lord, are changed into the same image from glory to glory" (II Corinthians 3:18).

It's a pretty wonderful promise, even for the photographer's models among us.

Father, show me how to make every activity of every day a doorway into Your presence.   — Elizabeth Sherrill

4 *There is no fear in love....*   — I John 4:18
WED

I am reading *Kon Tiki,* the book about the wonderful adventure Thor

Heyerdahl took in the late 1950s with five other men. They crossed four thousand miles of the Pacific Ocean, from Peru to the Polynesian Islands, on an Inca raft made of balsa wood.

At one point in the voyage, one of the men was washing his clothes, kneeling over the bucket near the edge of the raft. When he looked up, there, within just a few feet, was a huge, ugly creature staring at him.

When the man cried out in fright, all the members of the expedition rushed over to see what the trouble was. The trouble was the largest fish in the ocean: the whale shark. It looked ugly, horrible. A wide face, a huge body reaching under the raft until its tail surfaced many feet on the other side. For hours, this monster swam slowly back and forth under the raft.

Of course, what the men did not realize at the time is that the whale shark is perhaps the most gentle creature in the ocean. It eats tiny shrimp, swims peacefully, allows divers to hitch a ride on its back and likes to have its head scratched.

How often we judge situations and people by appearances. As a child, I was afraid of truck drivers. They seemed tough and formidable. Then during college, I worked at a truck stop pumping gas. I found most of the truckers were friendly and good-humored, and I enjoyed their road stories. I avoided classical music until my father gave me a record with small selections from many famous composers, and I learned to hear melodies and rhythms.

Is there something you've been afraid of that's preventing you from enjoying life? It can be something as small as meeting some new neighbors, or as large as getting on an airplane and flying to that dream vacation spot. Whatever it is, ask God to be with you, and take a chance. You know, you might like it.

Lord, may I look on new and unfamiliar things with the eyes of love.   —Christopher de Vinck

5
THURS   *Blessed is the people that know the joyful sound....*
                                        —Psalm 89:15

Years ago, on a guided tour in Europe, my parents visited an old monastery where there was a huge hammered metal bell. The monk who guided the group barely touched the bell with the cloth-covered striker and, according to my mother, the most glorious, reverberating sound resounded throughout the whole building, extending outward into the courtyard and beyond.

"How old is that bell?" asked my dad.

"Well," replied the old monk, "the metal part is not very old, maybe three or four hundred years." Then, lowering his voice to a reverent whisper, hand over his heart, he said, "But the space inside — *ah* — that is eternal."

It seems to me that prayer is like that old bell. The *words* we use when we pray are like the metal part: needed, but useless without the beautiful, ageless, eternal holy space within. Just as the old bell sounded by interaction between the perishable metal and the eternal space within, our prayers are also an interaction between our short-lived words and God's eternal Spirit.

This is the National Day of Prayer. Before and after our worded prayers today, perhaps you and I could take a few moments to tune in to that silent place within, where God's Spirit dwells eternally. Then, let the song begin!

May our prayers this day resound throughout creation, Lord, tuning our lives to Your eternal song. — Marilyn Morgan Helleberg

Quiet Time

Lord, might I be but as a saw,
A plane, a chisel in thy hand.
No, Lord, I take it back in awe;
Such prayer for me is far too grand,
I pray thee, rather let me lie
As on thy bench the favored wood;
Thy saw, thy plane, thy chisel ply
And work me into something good.
— *George MacDonald*

❧

6
FRI   *Each of you should look not only to your own interests, but also to the interests of others.*   — Philippians 2:4 (NIV)

It was Mother's Day, and I was in an airport preparing to fly home from a conference. I didn't want to be there. I wanted to be in church, surrounded by my husband and children, a corsage pinned to my shoulder. "We regret to inform you that your flight will be delayed another twenty minutes," the attendant said over the loudspeaker. I slumped even further into my chair.

That's when I noticed her, an attractive elderly lady in a pastel dress and straw hat. She sat with her head down, staring at her feet. She wore tennis shoes, bright white with pink accents. One shoelace lay untied on the floor. I was about to look away when I saw a man in a business suit come over and kneel down in front of her. Without a word, he proceeded to tie her shoe. She smiled back her silent gratitude.

Suddenly, it didn't matter so much that I was here among strangers. Sure, I wasn't with my family, but neither were these folks. *Could we be family for a bit?* I caught the eye of a mother with a small child sitting across from me. "Happy Mother's Day," I said, smiling. "You, too," she replied. "How old is your baby?" another lady asked. Soon we were all chatting, showing pictures of our faraway families—and having a rather pleasant Mother's Day after all.

Forgive me, Father, for failing to see the small opportunities You give me to pass on Your love. And remind me that we are all part of Your family.   —Mary Lou Carney

7
SAT
And be ye kind one to another, tenderhearted, forgiving....   —Ephesians 4:32

I grew up living next door to a tall, widowed woman with no children. She walked to work at the drugstore and walked home because she didn't own a car. She looked stern with her dark hair pulled back into a perfect ball. She always wore sensible, black shoes, long-sleeved dresses and an antique pin.

"Miss Margaret," as I was taught to address her, hated cats. I adored cats. My cat Josephine was forever having kittens in Miss Margaret's immaculate garage. Miss Margaret would see me out playing and call, "Yoo-hoo, Marion. Come here, please."

I'd run to her out of breath and often she said without a trace of a smile, "Your cat has had kittens in my garage—again." I would look up at her, nodding, chewing on my lip—and hoping. "They can stay there...this time." Miss Margaret and I went through this routine each spring and fall. I'd breathe a sigh of relief and take off for her garage to see the newborn kittens, calling out over my shoulder, "Thank you!"

Back then I didn't understand why Miss Margaret allowed Josephine such a luxury, but I didn't spend a lot of time pondering the matter. Lately, though, when the delicate pink and green spring days that smell of hyacinths and daffodils return, I think of Miss Margaret. I smile now at the clear evidence that Miss Margaret loved me more than she hated my cats. And I'm reminded that love isn't always "gushy." Sometimes it's hidden in a simple yet bountiful statement, "All right, this time."

Oh, Father! Help me see the less obvious ways love comes to me, and to embrace them with a full heart. Amen.

— Marion Bond West

8   *Her children rise up and call her blessed....*
SUN   — Proverbs 31:28 (RSV)

To My Mother on Her Day:

It's a bit late — you've been gone from us for years — but this is a note of appreciation nevertheless. I want to thank you for something I took for granted when I was growing up: your wonderful spirit of hospitality.

It is what made our old Kentucky home the why-leave-home sort of place it was for the three of us boys, not to mention all those dogs we collected. I still think of the people coming to the front door who were trampled in the canine rush to get inside, but front or back, the doors were always open to our friends. My own close friend was a skinny, red-haired kid from kindergarten who was around the house so much that he called you his "other mother." Ham and Jo-Jo had their school pals, too, kids that you would sit down and listen to and ask their opinion of things.

Generosity and caring. Those were the qualities you brought along with us when we left home. I went to a number of different schools and made a number of different friends after that, but wherever we went, you were always the same hospitable mom to us all. The extraordinary thing I've found, Mother, is that you still are.

To this day I hear from old (and aging) friends who tell me of the birthday cards that kept coming over the years or a wedding remembrance or something for the new baby. More than one friend has talked about the first homesick days in the service during World War II and how your letters arrived before anybody else's. (Apparently, you were clever enough to know that a serial number on an envelope would speed a letter through even to an inductee's station!)

After college, I was in New York City trying to make my living in publishing when the telephone rang. On the line was a friend from Kentucky days whom I hadn't seen or talked to in twenty years. He wanted to know if I'd be interested in a junior editor's job at a fledgling magazine called *Guideposts*.

"How'd you know where to find me?" I asked.

"Your mom," replied my once-skinny, red-haired friend from kindergarten named John Sherrill. "She keeps in touch."

I got the job. That was forty years ago, years for which I thank you. It just shows that some brands of hospitality reach far beyond just putting out a welcome mat.

God bless you, Mother, as God blessed me with you.

Thank You, God, for mothers whose arms are wide and warm.
— Van Varner

$\frac{9}{\text{MON}}$ *To be spiritually minded is life and peace.*   — Romans 8:6

Redundancy. It's a special word to me, one that my flight instructor taught me the first time I got into a plane. It has brought me much comfort.

Redundancy is the word that describes the construction of an airplane. For safety reasons, airplanes are built with backup systems. The engine has two ignitions, in case one of them fails in flight. The plane also has two compasses, two radios, two gas tanks and two steering yokes. This redundancy assures the pilot of alternatives in case of problems in the air.

I've found the principle of redundancy to be useful in many areas of living. When I prepare my college classes, I spend a few minutes thinking of a backup plan in case the lecture goes badly. A wise old friend gave me that suggestion. It may be something simple — a discussion idea, a worksheet — and I probably won't even need it, but just knowing I have Plan B puts my mind at rest and enables me to perform the lecture better.

I'm trying to notice other places in my life where this practice would grant me some peace of mind. For example, what will I do if that pay raise doesn't come through? I can drive my car another year and make my clothes last longer with some minor repairs at the tailor's. If our vacation to Texas doesn't work out, I can check out some of the tourist sites I've missed right here in Missouri. And if our daughters can't come home for the holidays, I can make a video and send it to them as a substitute.

Alternatives—they are always there. And when I take the time to think about them in advance, I feel better about the future.

Help me, Lord, not to be a one-track person, but to widen my vision to other possibilities.   —Daniel Schantz

---

10 *Taking the shield of faith...ye shall be able to quench all*
TUES *the fiery darts of the wicked.*   —Ephesians 6:16

Faith in God is a piece of cake for most of us when the sun is shining, when we've got a steady job, a good marriage, caring friends, healthy kids, a roof over our heads, money in the bank, food in the pantry and so on. It's when the good times quit rolling that we learn how firm (or how fragile) is our spiritual foundation. Last night, I was reading Dave and Jan Dravecky's book *When You Can't Come Back*. Baseball fans will recognize Dave as the former pitcher of the San Francisco Giants who lost his throwing arm to cancer. An active Christian before his career-ending loss, many wondered how it would affect Dave's faith afterward.

Though he and his wife don't minimize the mental anguish or the spiritual struggles that they've experienced, they credit God's grace for undergirding them. Dave writes: "I'm not getting through the loss of my arm because I am a great coper. I'm getting through it because I have a Father in heaven Who is a great giver. He is where I find the grace. At the time I need strength, He puts it in my heart or provides it through someone who is close to me, whether that's a family doctor or simply a friend. I don't earn it. I don't deserve it. I don't bring it about. It's a gift. And that is how I am able to cope...."

An acquaintance of mine who lost a top-paying job recently and was struggling to find another told me he had learned the truth of the hymn "I Need Thee Every Hour." Especially the second verse: "Stay Thou near by; Temptations lose their power when Thou art nigh." Which reminds me of something I heard as a kid at a revival meeting: *The secret of faith is to stick closer to God than bark to a tree in good times, and He will stick even closer to you in bad.*

You, Lord, are our trust today, our refuge for tomorrow,
A forever Friend from birth to end, in joy and in sorrow.
                                                      —Fred Bauer

11
WED

Relieve him...though he be a stranger....
                                    — Leviticus 25:35

My arms were full. I was carrying a book in one hand, a briefcase and umbrella in the other, and a Gap bag with presents for my nieces dangling from one finger. As I stepped off the subway to change trains, the Gap bag dropped, falling into the crack between the train and the platform. When the train pulled out, I couldn't reach for the bag, and jumping onto the tracks was too dangerous.

Aware of my quandary, a woman on the platform pointed to my small folded umbrella. No, I shook my head, it wouldn't reach. She gestured to a forbidding-looking man nearby who had a long, crook-handled umbrella. I tapped him on the shoulder and showed him my problem.

"Sure," he said, handing me his umbrella. "Try it."

I leaned down, fishing for the drawstring on the bag. With one scoop, I caught it and brought the bag up. The man smiled, I smiled, the woman smiled. In fact, there were a lot of people around me smiling. "Thanks," I said, as I returned the umbrella. "I couldn't have done it without you."

"No problem," the man replied.

I went on my way home with a warm feeling of faith renewed about people. Odd, isn't it, how people really want to help when you're in trouble. And most often you don't even have to ask.

Thank You, God, for a world of people needing people. We couldn't get by without one another.   — Rick Hamlin

12
THURS

Inasmuch as ye have done it unto one of the least of these my brethren, ye have done it unto me.   — Matthew 25:40

The conversation at the neighborhood coffee turned to complaints about the many appeals for donations that arrive in the mail each week. In frustration, one woman voiced the sentiments of many of us: "Well, there are so many needs in the world, so many starving children, so many diseases that need research funds, so many worthy causes. There's just no way to help them all!"

I was reminded of a little story I read somewhere about an old man who stood on the beach picking up stranded starfish that would otherwise die and throwing them back into the water. A passerby said, "Why are you wasting your time and effort, old man? Don't you know that there are miles and miles of shoreline like this, and that thousands and thousands of starfish are washed ashore and stranded each day? You can't help them all!"

"No," answered the old man. "But I can help *this* one."

I can do no great things, Lord. But I can do a few small things with great love.   — Marilyn Morgan Helleberg

---

13 *If anyone considers himself religious and yet does not keep*
FRI *a tight rein on his tongue, he deceives himself and his reli-*
gion is worthless.   — James 1:26 (NIV)

"Keep a tight rein on him if you don't want to gallop and keep up with the others," the riding instructor told me. I did — for a while. But when the horses up ahead slowed down, I relaxed my reins. *Mistake!* The tall, red horse "got his head" and thundered up the trail toward his pals, carrying one terrified rider.

That happened when I was a child. In the many riding lessons that followed, I learned the importance of a firm, controlling rein, especially in the two areas where a horse is most tempted to run away: heading back to the barn and trying to be with its pals. "Walk on," we were taught to instruct the horse with calm, firm control.

I thought of that runaway horse during a phone conversation with Mom last week. I happened to mention the name of a woman who had hurt my feelings badly. Suddenly, the details were pouring out — I couldn't seem to stop! Like the tall, red horse, my tongue "got its head" and I was only along for the ride. Sadly, I realized that when I did this, it wasn't aimless galloping; I was making a beeline for sympathy.

I'm wise to the ways of horses now, and know how to keep a firm, quiet control. I know how to look for the signs that a horse is going to bolt: a twisting tail, a hop-step with rigid front legs. So I take control before it starts!

The recent incident with my runaway tongue is teaching me to incorporate this same kind of watchfulness in my conversation. Better leave certain "hot-button" topics alone for now; better not bring up that person's name just now. *Heads up! Walk on.*

Dear Lord, help me to exercise firm control when I'm about to "bolt," by bringing my concerns to You first.   — Kathie Kania

14
___
SAT

Be humble, thinking of others as better than yourself....be interested in others...in what they are doing.
                                        — Philippians 2:3–4 (TLB)

My daughter has an attractive style that makes her fun to buy for. Dingle-dangle earrings, gossamer scarves sprinkled with glitter, tie-dyed T-shirts in purple, green and gold. Browsing through the stores, one is apt to gasp, "Oh, look, isn't that *exactly* Katrelya!"

She is a charming girl: sensitive, caring, with a heart extending out to others. And, yes, she is a nonconformist, sometimes of the most irritating sort. But then, I am a conformist of the most traditional sort, which to her is just as irritating! As I look through the kaleidoscope of her life and see brightly colored designs — without the dull and drab practicality that makes up much of day-to-day living — my heart tightens with the prayer, "Oh, dear Lord, help her make it through!"

Visiting her one day, her father and I noticed that the lawn in front of the small house where she lives was greatly overgrown. Foxtails, tall grass, dandelions tilting golden faces to the sun. "Why," we whispered to each other, "she doesn't have a lawn mower." So a couple of weeks later we showed up with the push-pull type purchased from a yard sale.

"What on earth would I do with that?" Katrelya asked curiously.

"Well," we said enthusiastically, "we thought you might need it to mow your lawn."

"Good heavens," she said, "I'm not growing a lawn. I'm growing a *meadow!*"

A meadow! It had never occurred to us that some people might prefer overgrown meadows to neatly manicured lawns! On our next visit we brought her several packs of wildflower seeds. Now she has sage tangled in with columbine, lupine and calendula mix with her own addition of red-hot peppers and miner's lettuce.

We no longer try to change each other, she and I. Though little things still irritate us, we are learning, instead, to celebrate our differences. To balance out our diverse yet together worlds, bridging them with love.

Thank You, Lord, for differences. Sprinkle our hearts with Your seeds of love and understanding for those who walk beside us to a very different beat. Help us to grow toward each other as we grow together toward You.   — Fay Angus

Editor's Note: *Just as* Daily Guideposts, 1994, *was going to press, Fay phoned us to express her delight that we'd chosen to place this devotional on this date. It's Katrelya's birthday! So, happy birthday, Katrelya!*

HOUSE GUEST

15
SUN
Comfort those in any trouble with the comfort we ourselves have received from God. — II Corinthians 1:4 (NIV)

After my mother died, my siblings and I comforted one another sharing family memories. To my great surprise, I discovered that Mom had not told them about our sister Lois' near-death experience. So that year, in my Christmas card to my niece Judy, Lois' daughter, I included a note to tell her about it.

While in the hospital with pneumonia, Lois' heart had stopped. Doctors successfully stimulated it. When Lois opened her eyes she said, "I have seen God and He's promised I will no longer have to suffer from my illness." Lois had myesthenia gravis, a disease that had weakened her for years. Although her lungs continued to fill with fluid, she felt no need for the oxygen at her bedside. Exhilarated, Lois lived one more day. She couldn't stop talking about her visit with God. And then she peacefully slipped away.

As it turned out, Judy, too, had not heard this story. She still tells me, several years later, "Aunt Elsie, I keep your note in my Bible and read it often. It comforts me."

I can understand that comfort because I, too, receive reassurance every day from Lois' near-death encounter with God. On good days and bad days, I think we all need to be reminded that we have a brighter life awaiting us with God. Just as He promised.

Heavenly Father, thank You for glimpses of You from the other side and that we will be with You some day in eternity. Amen.
— Elsie Larson

16
MON
"You shall be my witnesses...to the end of the earth."
— Acts 1:8 (RSV)

Marika was our favorite guide in Leningrad (now St. Petersburg), Russia. We were in The Hermitage, Catherine the Great's colossal winter palace, standing before Rembrandt's famous painting *Return of the Prodigal Son*, painted in 1669, the year the artist died. The young man is kneeling at his father's feet, the old man's hands on his shoulders, his eyes closed. Marika said, "What a pity that the old man was blind and could not see his son kneeling in front of him."

No one said anything, but en route to the next room I said quietly, "Marika, the old father was not blind. You can find the story of the prodigal son in the fifteenth chapter of the book of Luke in the Bible. It says the father saw him coming afar off. Would you like to read it?"

"No," she replied, "I don't have time to translate an English Bible into Russian."

"I mean in Russian," I said.

Her eyes widened. "You have a Russian Bible?" she asked incredulously.

"Yes, I do. And I would like to give it to you."

"Oh, I would love to have a Bible," she said, a smile on her face and a light in her eyes that had not been there before.

The next morning, I slipped the small Bible into her tote bag. "My husband has marked the fifteenth chapter of Luke. But there are other wonderful truths in the Bible about the love of the Lord for you. I hope you will read it."

"Oh, I will, I will," she whispered, smiling. "Thank you." And she hurried on to the head of the group.

I never saw Marika again. That was our last morning in Russia. But what joy would be mine if we should meet again in heaven and she should say, "Thank you for the Book, which showed me how to get here."

Dear Lord, help me always to be ready to give an account of the hope that is within me. And let me always be ready to share it with others. Amen.
                                                    — Dorothy Shellenberger

HOUSE GUEST

17
TUES
There is....A time to weep, and a time to laugh....
                                                    — Ecclesiastes 3:1, 4

One evening, my husband Glenn slipped a paperback book onto my lap. It was titled *Kicking Your Stress Habits* by Donald A. Tubesing, Ph.D. "Why don't you take a look at this?" he suggested. "I just finished it, and I think it could help you feel better, too."

These last few months hadn't been easy. We had just moved to a new state and said good-bye to dear family and friends, our daughter Lauren had moved south for a new career and, worst of all, Glenn had lost his job in a corporate takeover. We were in a crisis, and I hadn't even acknowledged it.

I thumbed through the book and stopped, puzzled, at the chapter on grief. That had nothing to do with how I was feeling. Stress, yes. But *grief?* Not me. I read that "Grief is the process of healing from the pain of loss. If you've ever had to say good-bye then you've experienced grief." Well, I certainly had said a lot of good-byes recently. "If you short-circuit the healing process by refusing to acknowledge your suffering," states Dr. Tubesing, "you will compound your distress." Otherwise, our buried feelings can show up as depression, insomnia, irritability, even sickness.

Now I better understood the enormous stress Glenn and I were under. We talked to each other about our feelings, cried, lent support when either of us had very tough days. Slowly, we were able to come out of our crisis. We thanked God the day Glenn found new work, and looked forward to visits from Lauren and our friends and relatives.

Have stress—and grief—been disrupting your life recently? Here are some suggestions for handling grief in a healthy way from Dr. Tubesing's book. Maybe they'll help you as much as they helped Glenn and me.

1. *Allow yourself time to grieve.* Expect this painful time; try not to fight it.
2. *Make new goals for yourself.* Give yourself something to look forward to.
3. *See the loss as an opportunity* to strengthen your faith.
4. *Reach out to others* for comfort—a support group might help ease your pain.

Grace us with Your strength, Lord, as we try and work through grief when it comes into our life. Amen.   —Ellen Secrest

---

18
WED *"If you are willing and obedient, you will eat the best from the land."*   —Isaiah 1:19 (NIV)

No matter how hard I try, my twelve-year-old son Geoffrey is a far better baker than I. Once, when he was wrist-deep in cookie dough, I pressed him for advice.

"I follow the recipe—exactly," he replied. "Do you?"

"Not quite," I hedged, recalling the many liberties I take with cookbooks. Watching him roll bits of dough painstakingly between his palms, I explained that I usually plopped the dough haphazardly on the cookie sheet with a spoon. "It's faster and easier that way."

"Faster and easier don't mean right," was his stern reply. "There are rules—" he began. Just then, a loud buzz from the timer interrupted his lecture. He opened the oven and stuck a toothpick into the top of a cookie. "Perfect," he announced. Carefully, he pried off two large, snowy spheres with a spatula and put them on a plate. My mouth watered as I watched him bite into a fragrant, perfectly baked snickerdoodle.

"*Ah,*" he sighed, "worth waiting for."

Remind me when I grow impatient, Lord, that the obedient earn a place at Your table. — Linda Ching Sledge

From the Kitchen of: _Geoffrey Sledge_ _____

SNICKERDOODLES

Put into a big bowl and mix:

1 stick of margarine	1 egg
¾ cup sugar	

Put into another bowl:

1¼ cup plus 2 Tb. flour	¼ tsp. salt
½ tsp. baking soda	1 tsp. cream of tartar

Add flour mixture to first bowl. Mix well. Dough should be soft and easy to handle. Add a tablespoon of flour if dough is too sticky.

Combine in a small dish and set aside:

1 Tb. sugar	1 tsp. cinnamon

Roll dough into balls the size of a walnut. Roll in sugar-cinnamon mixture. Place on ungreased cookie sheet, 3 cookies across, 5 down. Bake 8-10 minutes at 400°. Don't overbake! Cookies should be soft and puffy. Cool on rack. Makes 3 dozen.

Eat warm with a glass of milk.

---

19 *Lead a life worthy of the calling to which you have been*
THURS *called.* — Ephesians 4:1 (RSV)

I've learned a lot about myself from digging up my family roots. Growing up in New York City, I never knew any other family named Komp.

When I visited Germany on business several years ago, I took a side trip to the area from which my ancestors Heinrich and Elisabetha Komp came. It was strange to see my family name inscribed on so many headstones in the tiny farm villages of the Vogelsberg region.

My ancestors' farmland was some of the poorest sod in Germany. Sometimes without enough bread to eat, they would dream about the New World. They were so heavily taxed by the landed aristocracy that my ancestors bravely set out on a three-month sea voyage in the early nineteenth century. En route, they ran out of bread and had only sauerkraut to eat for the last week!

When I researched our name, however, I found that it was not German in origin. Way back, the name was shortened to Komp from Kompenhans. The Komps appear to have arrived in Germany from France in a time of religious persecution. And what did the name mean? The roots for Kompen are the same as for our word *companion: cum panis,* "The one who shares bread."

What a pleasant thought! Now when I prepare a meal for friends, I think of it as a "calling," a living up to my name.

You are my Companion, Jesus Christ, Who breaks bread with me and invites me to feast in my heart by faith. Help me to share Your hospitality with others. — Diane Komp

---

20
FRI
"Enter by the narrow gate; for the gate is wide and the way is easy, that leads to destruction...."
— Matthew 7:13 (RSV)

"I absolutely hate to clean house," I groaned to my husband Paul, as I got up from the floor after trying unsuccessfully to scrub a black smudge off the white tile. I hate it, especially here in Arizona, where dust is the state bird. So I usually end up neglecting it.

"If only housecleaning were something I could do once and then be done," I said. "Why can't it be like...." *Like what,* I wonder? What important task in my life is ever finished? Even the ones that do end, once completed, are immediately replaced by new challenges.

I soon realized that everything worthwhile in my life is ongoing and ever-changing, especially my relationships with family, friends and God. Then I wondered: *Do I take the easy way, expecting relationships to flourish by paying attention to them occasionally, like my housework, then forgetting about them? Do I give my friends the attention they need, or do I rely on a little emotional dusting now and then to take care of them?* I immediately thought of two phone calls from good friends that I haven't had time to return. I'll call them today. And what about the times I neglect my spiritual house? My new one-year Bible is still sitting on my nightstand unopened. I'll start it tonight instead of a new novel.

I see now that I must constantly work at everything worth having in my life. My house can't clean itself, and neither can I expect my relationships to take care of themselves without my continual care. So today I make myself a promise: I may not become a better housekeeper, but I will be a better "peoplekeeper."

Lord, may Your constant love remind me to care for and not neglect the important people in my life.   —Gina Bridgeman

21 *Whatever you do, work at it....*   —Colossians 3:23 (NIV)

SAT

Knocking on my childhood schoolmate's back door one day after a brisk walk, I heard Helen call out cheerily, "Come on in—I'm exercising!"

Making my way inside, I saw her sitting with an almanac in front of her and a glass of lemonade in her right hand.

"Some exercise!" I looked at her skeptically.

"It's *mental* exercise!" she said with a smile. "I try to do some every week. Don't you remember how we learned in school that our bodies have over six hundred muscles, and they require exercise to stay fit? Well, imagine how many millions of brain cells we have! So I try to do a *mental* exercise every week to strengthen my mind.

"Remember how, in school, we had to memorize poems, the times tables, the order of the planets—oh, all sorts of things. But as the years go by, I've gotten out of the habit. Then I got to thinking, God made our minds as well as our bodies, so doesn't it make sense to try to exercise our brains, too, by continuing to learn something useful every single week? This week, my assignment to myself is to try and memorize all the U.S. presidents. In order."

"Hand me that almanac, please," I said. "I'll start off this exercise session with the state capitals."

Thank You, God, for giving me all these brain cells. Let me never forget to exercise the mind You gave me!   —Linda Neukrug

22
SUN

Together shall they sing: for they shall see eye to eye....
—Isaiah 52:8

I love to sing. Some of my favorite hymns are the old heaven-bound songs ("Goin' Up Yonder") that we sang in the small church where I grew up. They aroused strong emotions in me then—and they still do. Songs of "Blessed Assurance" of knowing "Someday, I'll Fly Away." We all sang those songs of our heavenly destination. "When we all get to heaven, what a day of rejoicing that will be." Yes, indeed.

I grew up in the time when there were segregated schools, washrooms, and even separate drinking fountains for blacks and whites. Today, driving through rural Mississippi, you can still see some cemeteries with a fence running down the middle. That's the dividing line between blacks and whites.

Today, many of those divisions have been broken down. I can walk into most restaurants—not all—and get a seat anywhere I like. But as I sit there, looking around, I notice that most of us have segregated ourselves, choosing our seats as if they were color-coded. It's the same way in some churches.

It makes me wonder when Christians will show the world how to do it—how to love more and hate less. Because it seems to me that if we're going to spend eternity together, we might start by makin' harmony here on earth.

Lord, help us see past the differences that divide us to what we have in common in our love of You and through You. Amen.
—Dolphus Weary

23
MON

You are loving and kind to thousands....
—Jeremiah 32:18 (TLB)

Speaking in public used to make me nervous, and although I didn't do it often, I dreaded it. When I stood in front of a group, I felt as if I were facing a monster ready to devour me. I got over my fear with the help of my dog Suzy, who was a puppy at the time.

I was walking Suzy down our road on a day when I was to speak to a community group on behalf of our library. There are no sidewalks on our road, but very few cars, and almost every driver is a neighbor who waves hello. Suddenly, however, there was the noise of a large engine, and around the bend came a big, brand-new school bus with its headlights on. Suzy, who probably thought the bus was going to run us down, was terrified. She pulled at the end of the leash frantically, and it took all my strength to hold on to her.

Then the bus stopped, and the door opened. The driver, a pleasant-looking young woman, smiled and said, "I'm sorry your dog is so afraid of the bus. Is there anything I can do to help her get over it?"

"I think you've already helped," I told the driver. Suzy had stopped yanking on the leash and was wagging her tail. Just knowing that inside the bus was a kindly person made all the difference to her. She wasn't afraid anymore.

A little later, as I stood in front of my audience, I realized they weren't monsters ready to devour me. They were kindly people who knew I was nervous. I could see that they wished me well, and I wasn't afraid anymore. In fact, I began to realize that speaking in public can be — well, almost fun.

Lord Jesus, open my eyes to the kindness around me.
—Phyllis Hobe

24
TUES

PRACTICING THE POWER OF PRAYER
Positive Prayers

Have mercy upon us, O Lord…for we are exceedingly filled with contempt.   —Psalm 123:3

Through the years, I've struggled with a critical attitude. Almost without thinking, I find fault with the way the neighbors keep their yard or the politician expresses her views or the driver in front of me drives.

I confessed this to a close friend who admitted she faces the same struggle but has found a helpful solution. "I turn every criticism into a prayer of intercession for the other person. That not only helps me *stop* when I start being critical, it turns a *negative* thought into a *positive* action."

Her suggestion sounded simple enough, so I tried it for a few days, and it helped me, too. I started criticizing my teenage daughter's friend for her lack of thoughtfulness…*Lord, let someone today reflect Christ's thoughtfulness so clearly to her that she desires to be like that person.* Again, I criticized the politician…*Lord, Your truth is larger than my opinion. Give this leader discernment and a heart yearning to know Your truth.* I criticized the mailman for his tardy deliveries…*Lord, the mailman's task is a tough one. Dissolve his stumbling blocks today that he may sense Your presence.*

"Prayer enlarges the heart until it is capable of containing God's gift of Himself," I once heard Mother Teresa say. I'm learning that "God's gift of Himself" squeezes most of the contempt and criticism out of my heart.

Father, by Your mercy, may I continue to turn the habit of criticizing others into a habit of praying for them. —Carol Kuykendall

25
WED A man's life consisteth not in the abundance of the things which he possesseth.   —Luke 12:15

I have always been a book collector. Over the years, every spurt through Harvard Square in Cambridge, Massachusetts—past *twenty-seven* bookstores—brought temptation. Then those numerous thrift shops with shelves of books increased my appetite. The result: I was overrun with books. I purchased larger bookcases, but books still cluttered our home. How many books did I need? How many did I want? Something had to be done, but what? I was no longer a collector, I was a hoarder!

One day, I visited a supermarket where I spotted an overflowing bookcase. As I started forward, eager for new treasures, a woman said, "This is a different kind of library. It's sponsored by a hospital. Customers donate books and others purchase them, paying on the honor system. The money is used to buy instruments for the hospital. Would you like to donate?" I nodded without meaning to.

At home, I agonized. Which could I part with? I loved all my books. But I did select some and took them in. When I next visited the supermarket, all the books I'd given were gone—and I was glad!

From then on, I kept donating books weekly to the bookstall. And you know, a strange thing began to happen. I didn't miss the books from my shelves. I was getting a special feeling about things and how to use them: Cherish them for a while, then pass them on, so others can cherish them.

Merciful Lord, You shower me with an abundance. Continue to teach me the lesson of sharing, which increases abundance in a joyful way.   —Oscar Greene

26
THURS Love one another.   —I John 4:11

Our two cats Tuxedo and Tiger have been with us for a long time. Born in the same litter twelve years ago, they have moved with us through three states and have watched as three children have been born into our family. These cats are special members of our clan, though they have always lived outside. Fiercely independent, they roam their territory and fight their battles, but they are always home for supper.

Their appetites appear to have doubled, too. Now they stay around the back and meow for food every time the door is opened. Strangely, they often beg loudest when their bowls are brimming over with their favorite food. At first, such behavior perplexed me. For a while, I thought they might be having a problem with parasites, but our veterinarian assured me that was not the case. Then one day the explanation became perfectly clear to me.

The only time I had ever been able to pet these independent felines was when they were preoccupied eating. But once they left their food bowls, they were impossible to catch. All of their lives, these cats have associated petting with eating. So now, when they want more affection, they feel that they have to beg to be fed in order to be petted.

I guess people are the same way. As a pastor, I hear a lot of folks complain about many things. But behind most of the laments, there is a deep hunger to be loved and appreciated. Wise is the person who can see through the crazy ways people ask to be stroked and then simply give them a pat on the head or a warm embrace. After all, they are not really hungry. Their plates are full. They are simply in need of love.

Dear Father, above the complaints, criticisms and unrealistic expectations of people, may I hear what they are really saying. May I give to them the love and affection that they need. Amen.
— Scott Walker

HOUSE GUEST

27
FRI
My son, give attention to my words....For they are life to those who find them, And health to all their flesh.
— Proverbs 4:20, 22 (NKJV)

Days after his sixth birthday, my son Zeb got his foot caught in a bicycle wheel as a friend gave him a ride. X-rays showed no broken bones, but the pain was so intense that he couldn't walk. He gamely got around by crawling, and found it hard to sleep because the weight of the blankets put pressure on the foot. I could tell the situation was depressing him.

To cheer up Zeb, I copied out some Scripture verses and read them to him several times throughout the day: "When you walk, your steps will not be hindered, and when you run, you will not stumble" (Proverbs 4:12, NKJV); "For I will restore health to you and heal you of your wounds" (Jeremiah 30:17, NKJV); "The steadfast love of the Lord never ceases, his mercies never come to an end; they are new every morning" (Lamentations 3:22–23, RSV).

Later, I heard Zeb laughing heartily and deliberately. At what? I didn't know. At bedtime, I asked him about his laughter. "Oh," he said, "my Friend Jesus told me to laugh and my foot would get better." He smiled at me wearily and drifted off to sleep.

The Scriptures were working on Zeb in a way I couldn't have possibly imagined. The laughter came from God's prescription, "A merry heart does good, like medicine" (Proverbs 17:22, NKJV). He must have remembered that through lessons learned in Sunday school, in our family prayer and Bible story reading times. God's Word was beautifully lodging in my son's heart.

Three days later, wearing a big, triumphant smile, Zeb took his first awkward steps toward walking again. It was still a few weeks before he was back to full strength, but during that time he kept a merry heart and, with Jesus, taught his mama something about good medicine.

Dr. God, thank You for the encouragement You give us in Your written and whispered Word, which Your children — grown-up and small — are learning to receive joyfully.   — Ellyn Baumann

<u>28</u>
<u>SAT</u> *In whom we have boldness and access with confidence by the faith of him.*   — Ephesians 3:12

I almost didn't go.

It happened during my high school years, when I was trying my wings at oil painting. One evening at a party, another girl, who was as enthusiastic as I about seascapes, talked to me. And the more we talked, the more excited we became about the pleasures of dabbing colorful paints onto a clean white canvas.

At one point Marcia said, "Why don't we leave this boring party to go home and change? Then I'll drive us out to Jones Beach so we can be there to capture the sunrise."

At first, I hesitated. The invitation seemed wild! Go to the beach in the middle of the night?

"Oh, come on, Ellie," Marcia said. "It's a warm night and other people will be there."

Finally, I agreed, and off we went. So when the sun began streaking the eastern sky over Long Island, we were standing at our easels, brushes poised, ready to capture another of God's magnificent dawnings.

Today, I can still hear the roar of the surf, feel the wind whipping through my hair. I remember that as we worked, we sang, "When morning gilds the skies, my heart awaking cries, may Jesus Christ be praised."

That experience convinced me that sometimes God wants us to be bold, to trust Him and to try new things. Think of the magic memories I'd have missed if I hadn't agreed to go!

Lord, thank You for boldness and confidence that sometimes permits us to throw caution to the wind.   — Eleanor Sass

29
SUN
With God we will gain the victory.... — Psalm 108:13 (NIV)

HOUSE GUEST

Yesterday, after an especially rewarding prayer time, I set off in my car on an errand. Five minutes later — I'm embarrassed to report — I was yelling at another driver, "You jerk!" Then I was overwhelmed by guilt at this contradictory behavior. Unfortunately, it happens again and again. And always I begin to doubt how God can even stand me, let alone love me.

This morning in his sermon, the pastor quoted Ecclesiastes 1:2, 4, 9 (GNB): "Life is useless....The world stays just the same....What has been done before will be done again." *That's certainly true,* I thought grimly. But on the way out of church, I heard a young mother mutter, "He was probably referring to picking up after the kids."

I laughed, remembering how teaching my children to pick up after themselves had once appeared hopeless. They'd promise to do better, but soon they'd slip back into their old ways. "And isn't God just as good a Parent as you," prompted a voice within me. Of course He is! And just as I didn't give up on *my* children (and they did gradually get better), God doesn't give up on me.

In her book *Just As I Am,* Eugenia Price wrote, "God does not send more love when we behave. He loves us just as we are. Because of Him, not because of us." So if you're finding more guilt than joy in your walk with God, try memorizing these words today: *Because of Him, not because of us.* Then pray this prayer with me:

Lord, grant me the power to forgive myself when I fail You, just as You forgive me.   — Bonnie Lukes

---

30   *"Greater love has no one than this, that one lay down his*
MON   *life for his friends."*   — John 15:13 (NAS)

Like most of my generation, I was deeply touched by the Vietnam War. And so, on a recent family trip to Washington, D.C., I made time to visit the Vietnam Memorial Wall to stand in line and find a name.

Sergeant Olive wasn't a personal friend, but he was a hero who helped me come to terms with the war. And I wanted to honor his memory. You see, I was in college in Chicago during the last years of that war, safe from the draft and danger. I was angry that hundreds of young men and women were going over and dying for something no one could explain. And then I met Sergeant Olive...or rather I met his memory.

Wandering through a small park on the shores of Lake Michigan one day, I came through a grove of pine trees and found a statue of Sergeant Olive. On the base was inscribed the story of how he was on patrol one night and a grenade was thrown into the middle of his group. Instantly, without thought for himself, he jumped on the grenade. He absorbed the explosion, dying instantly, *but saving four friends.*

The story of his sacrifice soothed my anger about the stupidity of that war. All wars are stupid, *but the men and women who fight them are not.* They are selfless, placing themselves at risk and often giving the ultimate gift — their lives.

So I made my sons stand in line that Memorial Day and walk along the wall that cried tears of morning dew for all those who had gone for the rest of us and not come back. And I ask you to stop with me today, not to honor any particular battle or war, but to honor those who died for their country, their families, and unknown friends like you and me.

Father, even as we remember those who have died for our freedom, our hearts long to ask You to bring peace into conflict so that no one, from any country, will have to die in war.

                                                — Eric Fellman

31
TUES

"For the bread of God is that which comes down from heaven, and gives life to the world." — John 6:33 (RSV)

Who doesn't love a bakery? Just thinking of one stirs mouth-watering visions. When the children were small, we'd often visit a wholesale establishment nearby, carrying home a cardboard box crammed with wonderful frosted doughnuts fresh off the racks.

I've decided the true allure of a bakery is found in its attractive combination of delectable aromas, pleasing tastes, the sheen of golden crusts and something more...the simple satisfaction of a need for daily bread being met in a welcoming way.

I feel the same allure with *spiritual* bread. The hungers of my heart are many: how to tell truth from lies; how to find worthiness in a world that scorns imperfection; how to keep going when I've lost my motivation. And my appetite is satisfied when I turn to Jesus, the Bread of life, Who fulfills all those yearnings.

Over the years, I've collected some sumptuous Bible experiences. When our family wrestled with indecision over hosting a Japanese exchange student, Jesus' words in Matthew 25:35 (RSV), "I was a stranger and you welcomed me," encouraged us to open our home and our hearts to Ken Uehara—and we gained a lifelong friend. At times when I have faltered in my Christian walk, I have been immensely comforted and inspired to hear Jesus say to Peter in Luke 22:32 (RSV), "I have prayed for you that your faith may not fail."

Do you enter God's Word expecting your hunger to be met? I do...and when I do, I have His promise that "I am the bread of life; he who comes to me shall not hunger, and he who believes in me shall never thirst" (John 6:35, RSV).

Lord Jesus, today let me not starve or go hungry, when I can choose You, the life-giving Bread for all my longings and desires.
— Carol Knapp

Prayer Diary

My Prayer Requests for May:

1. _____

2. _____

3. _____

4. _____

5. _____

6. _____

7. _____

8. _____

9. _____

10._____

11._____

12._____

13._____

14._____

15._____

16._____

17._____

18._____

19._____

20._____

21._____

22._____

23._____

24._____

25._____

26._____

27._____

28._____

29._____

30._____

31._____

June

S	M	T	W	T	F	S
			1	2	3	4
5	6	7	8	9	10	11
12	13	14	15	16	17	18
19	20	21	22	23	24	25
26	27	28	29	30		

GIFTS OF THE SEASON

The Sunrise

June's splendid dawns of
pink and gold announce summer's
jubilant entry.

*May I begin each June morning expectantly, Lord, ready to
receive the warmth of Your everyday miracles.*

1 PRAYER CAN CHANGE YOUR LIFE
WED An Act of Surrender

Thy will be done....   —Matthew 6:10

One evening at a party, several friends were lamenting their teenagers' antics, and I related my daughter Keri's unsettling reaction to her cousin's terminal illness. Later, my friend Cindy, a practicing therapist, asked, "Pam, would you mind if I had a talk with Keri?"

"Of course not, Cindy," I answered. "But why?"

"I'm going to be honest with you," Cindy said. "As you talked about Keri, you described a very depressed teenager." My face must have turned ashen, for she hurried on to say, "Now, Pam, parents almost never recognize these signs of depression in their own child. They discount it as 'teenageitis.'"

After talking to Keri the next day, Cindy suggested we send her to a local counselor specializing in teenagers and grief.

Hand my daughter over to a stranger? I cried. I was her mother. I knew her. I knew how she loved to dance in the summer rain when she was two. I had spent an entire day helping her rescue tadpoles from a dried-up puddle when she was six.

I turned to *Prayer Can Change Your Life*, hoping for direction. "Surrender all to God," the book advised. "When you pray, 'Thy will be done,' that presupposes a God you can trust."

It was clear I couldn't help Keri by myself. "Thy will be done, Lord," I prayed over and over through the next months as I drove Keri back and forth to her appointments. Sometimes I sat in the parking lot and cried. But I kept praying as the book directed, surrendering myself and Keri to God. As I talked honestly with God, I began to let go of the image I had of myself as the perfect mom who could solve all my family's aches. Once again, honest prayer was helping me to trust God. "What a relief, Lord, to know that You are completely in control of life's unfolding. I want Your will to be done."

The golden day came out of the blue as I sat in the car reading and waiting for Keri. There was a tap on the window. I looked up and saw her counselor. "I don't think Keri needs to come back anymore," she said, smiling. "She's doing great."

Surrender everything to God now, the book says. Pray "Thy will be done," then hand every burden over to a God you can completely trust. I have found every word to be true.

To You, God, be the glory.   —Pam Kidd

2
THURS
God hath sent forth the Spirit of his Son into your hearts, crying, Abba, Father.   —Galatians 4:6

"Marion, I've just rediscovered some pictures of your father that you've never seen," my Aunt Sara said. "I'll mail them to you." I had seen very few pictures of him — there weren't many in existence. He died just before I turned two.

When the letter arrived marked "photos," I sat down at the kitchen table, just holding the envelope tenderly and listening to my heart thump. Finally, I opened it and five small, yellowed photos fell out. Slowly, I stood each photo up against the salt and pepper shakers.

My father Thomas Marion Bond, in his twenties, smiled back at me. I leaned very close, not to miss a detail. Tall, lean, hesitant to give the camera a smile, gentle hands, long fingers.... His red hair didn't show up in the black-and-white photo, but I had been told about his beautiful red hair. My four children have red hair — different shades from auburn to shimmering red. In one photo, he leaned against his prized new car. No one knew for sure what it was — perhaps a Buick. "Yellow," my aunt said.

"Hello, Daddy," I whispered. "I wish I could have known you. We would have had some fine times together...I love you, Daddy."

I had never expected to get to say those words, which I needed to express. The relationship I so longed for as a child, and all through my life, somehow seemed alive and real now. I looked into the deep eyes and handsome face of this stranger who was my father. Some deep void within me was filling up rapidly.

This marvelous emotion felt like something else I'd experienced somewhere. Something powerful. Life-changing.... *Of course!* It was years ago after I had become a Christian and made the discovery that God was truly my Father! My *Abba!* My Daddy! A relationship with God had filled that empty void.

I was thankful for this quiet reunion with Thomas Marion Bond. And I knew I would always experience the love I had missed growing up as I turned to my heavenly Father, God, each day in prayer.

Abba! Abba! *Thank You for being my heavenly Father-God. Thank You for making me whole. Amen.*   — Marion Bond West

HOUSE GUEST

3
FRI   *Let the light of your face shine upon us, O Lord.*

—Psalm 4:6 (NIV)

I'm a serious worrier with a fertile imagination. Nighttime, in particular, seems to send both my worry reflex and my imagination into overdrive. Because of that, I used to have a hard time falling asleep.

It's long been my practice to place the name of each of my loved ones before God prior to settling down for sleep. Unfortunately, instead of leaving them in His care, my imagination used to go to work conjuring up scary scenarios. *What if my grandchildren drop out of school? What if they get into drugs?* The fact that the oldest one was only seven didn't deter me. *What if something happens to my husband?* That John was perfectly healthy had no bearing at all. And more often than not I'd end up tossing and turning.

Then my friend Mary said, "Why don't you try imagining good things?" And thinking about her suggestion led me to a solution for my sleeplessness. Here's how I've learned to let my imagination work *for* me.

Going through my nightly list, I picture Jesus walking from house to house, room to room, bed to bed, passing His hand over each sleeping form, bathing them in His protective light. By the time we visit all the rooms, I'm asleep. If you are a nighttime worrier with an overactive imagination that's keeping you awake, I urge you to take a walk with Jesus.

Father, when dark, unreasonable fears overtake me, help me see the Holy Light that is Your Son.   —Bonnie Lukes

Quiet Time

Oh, God, I can't—
You never said I could.
Oh, God, You can—
You always said You would.
          —*Author Unknown*

$\dfrac{4}{\textit{SAT}}$ *When he went ashore, he saw a great crowd; and he had compassion for them....*   — Matthew 14:14 (NRSV)

It was a warm spring day with wildflowers underfoot in the Ozarks. A friend and I were staying at a monastery, renewing our friendship with the delightful guest master Father Ted. This special servant of God has a talent for finding vivid ways to teach a simple gospel message.

My friend and I had gone for a hike, crossing the swinging rope bridge, cutting across a sunlit meadow. Halfway up a steep path, I felt the pain in my lower back signaling a muscle spasm. By the time we got back, I could only walk without pain by bending. It was an odd sight as I came through the monastery door in the perpendicular.

At lunchtime, a shadow crossed in front of the still-bent me. It was Father Ted. He had bent down into the same position to join me, and we were now nose to nose. "Di," he said with a twinkle in his eye, "could you give me a clue as to what the correct pastoral response is to your painful situation?"

"Father," I replied, amused by his playful empathy, "compassion does not require that you be bent like me." But it certainly was an encouraging starting point. Soon I found another guest who was able to give me a muscle relaxant. I enjoyed a good nap and awoke able to stand up straight.

This was a valuable lesson for me to take home to my medical practice. I learned from Father Ted that sometimes more than medication is required to express compassion. Compassion is sharing someone else's point of view (even nose to nose). It is always the correct pastoral — and medical — response.

Lord, give me eyes of compassion that I can see another's needs from Your point of view.   — Diane Komp

$\dfrac{5}{\textit{SUN}}$ *Neglect not the gift that is in thee....*   — I Timothy 4:14

I was attending the funeral of a dear friend when the congregation rose to sing:

> *O Love that wilt not let me go,*
> *I rest my weary soul in Thee,*
> *I give Thee back the life I owe,*
> *That in Thine ocean depths its flow*
>   *May richer, fuller be.*

I knew those words because I had always admired the man who wrote them. His name was George Matheson, and he wrote that hymn one day in 1882, when discouragement darkened his world. Later, they were set to music by a famed organist, Albert Lister Peace.

George Matheson was unusual. In 1861, he graduated from Glasgow University with honors, then studied for the ministry and eventually went from a tiny church in Glasgow to be, at the age of twenty-four, pastor of the famed St. Bernard's in Edinburgh. Along with his sermons and parish duties, he squeezed out time to write lectures, articles and twelve books. Throughout his life he continued his college studies in French, German, history, philosophy and theology.

What is unusual about these accomplishments? George Matheson was blind.

When I sang Matheson's words at my friend's funeral, I couldn't help but think about what I was doing with the life God had given me. I wasn't talented like George Matheson, yet couldn't I contribute more?

In memory of my dear friend, I will continue to try.

Gentle Jesus, Your gifts are to be shared. Help me to use them more fully according to Your wishes. — Oscar Greene

---

6
MON

Thou hast commanded us to keep thy precepts diligently.
— Psalm 119:4

Last year, my husband Gary bought me a bike with gears...fourteen gears! "How do I use them?" I asked the salesman.

"It's easy," he assured me. "Just click into a gear that lets you pedal at a consistent pace. When you go uphill, gear down for easier pedaling. And when you go downhill, gear up."

Pedal downhill? How silly! One of the things I'd always loved best about biking was coasting downhill. But after a few days of riding, I decided to take his advice. When I topped a hill and started down, I shifted gears and kept pedaling. And the momentum kept me going well up my next hill!

I've applied that bike logic to my life now. When things are going well, I don't coast spiritually — reading only snatches of Scripture and skipping Sunday school. Instead, I "keep pedaling" and find that life, like the country roads I ride, seems much smoother.

I know, dear God, that You are always with me, no matter what the terrain. Help me in my resolve to pedal consistently close to You. — Mary Lou Carney

7
TUES

"Be merciful and kind to everyone."
— Zechariah 7:9 (TLB)

Do you like to go to the ophthalmologist? I do, and it's not just because Dr. Hoffman is an excellent eye surgeon who fixed my tear duct. His entire staff radiates a genuine kindness that makes us patients feel cared about.

After about a year of regular visits to his office, I finally asked him, "How do you maintain such a caring attitude here?"

To my surprise, he answered, "When I hire someone, my main concern is how she or he treats people. An impressive résumé means nothing to me — I can train them myself."

An impressive résumé means nothing? I pondered this all the way home, this system that seemed so incongruous in today's smartly competitive, career-climbing world. And yet musing through my Bible, I see this unlikely system again. Look at the strange conglomerate of disciples: fishermen, tax collector, bystanders. If an impressive résumé in religion were taken into account, wouldn't the disciple candidates have been filled with the snootiest Pharisees? But, no. Christ chose the former. Résumés meant nothing.

I'm curious now: What if the Lord said to me, "Kathie, I don't want to talk about your artistic achievements, or about the writing you've done, or the church activities you've helped with. What I'm wondering is, how are you treating 'the least of these my brethren' these days?"

No résumé. How would I stack up?

Dear Lord, I don't always stack up well, but by Your grace I'm forgiven. Remind me often of what You think of an impressive but loveless résumé.   — Kathie Kania

8
WED

Lay not up for yourselves treasures upon earth....
— Matthew 6:19

"She's got to go," says the tree surgeon. "She's diseased."

"But Grandaddy Banta planted her there by the cabin door before I was born!" I say, hoping to save the tall, majestic pine.

"I'm sorry," he says. "Take some time."

Silently, I say good-bye to my ponderosa pine:

How many summers have your protective limbs
welcomed us back, firm against the winds?

How many growing-boy sneaker prints have
left their marks on your roof-high branches?
How many front-porch sunrises have I seen
through puffs of pine while my family slept?
Yet where are these riches
if they're not in my heart?

"All right. I'm ready now," I say to the tree surgeon.
With love, thanks and tears, I offer her up.
Some say holding on makes you strong.
Jesus said letting go makes you strong.

Thank You, Lord, for Your strengthening presence at my letting-
go times.
                                    — Marilyn Morgan Helleberg

PRACTICING THE POWER OF PRAYER
Good Deed Prayers

Being...a doer of the work, this man shall be blessed....
                                    — James 1:25

Every other Thursday morning I meet for breakfast with a group of
like-minded, married men in their thirties. It's something between a
prayer breakfast and a support group. For want of a better term, we call
ourselves the Thursday Morning Breakfast Club.

One Thursday, one of our members told us about an impasse he faced
at work. He was distraught, at his wit's end. Fumbling for words, we
tried to give him advice, but by breakfast's end all we could do was offer
our prayers.

The following two weeks as I prayed, I kept thinking of things to
cheer him up, like sending a note or clipping an article from a magazine. I was not alone.

When we reconvened, our friend told us how the situation at work
had improved. Then, as he looked around our table, he said, "You
know what really amazed me? I asked for your prayers, but all of you
also did things for me. You called, you wrote, you dropped by, you took
me out for lunch, you brought books and tapes. You showed me that you
cared."

"That's called putting shoe leather on a prayer," I said jokingly.

"Perhaps," he said, "but I think all the things you did were in themselves actual prayers, too."

I stopped to ponder my friend's words. I hadn't thought of prayers as something you do. But, indeed, effective prayer can be not just words, but everyday caring acts.

Lord, make all my deeds prayers and my prayers deeds. Amen.
— Rick Hamlin

10
FRI

Let marriage be held in honor among all....
— Hebrews 13:4 (RSV)

Some friends gave us an unusual gift for our twenty-fifth wedding anniversary on this date: four country western dance lessons. "Learning the two-step is guaranteed to keep you together for the next twenty-five!" they promised enthusiastically.

We felt a bit skeptical. Lynn and I didn't dance much, and if our kids ever saw us twisting or bopping, they cringed with embarrassment. Yet, we showed up at the Grizzly Rose Dance Emporium that first night ready to give this gift a go. The first thing we learned was the strange, new dance position, "for better communication and just enough tension to create balance," the instructor informed us as we pressed our outstretched hands together. Then came the music and the instructor's commands: "Quick...quick...slow...slow...." Before long, I learned why the other ladies wore cowboy boots. Not to make a fashion statement, but to protect their toes!

"Men, your whole purpose is to make your lady look good," the instructor explained as he summarized the lesson.

"No wonder these dance lessons improve marriages!" I whispered loudly to Lynn.

"Ladies, your goal is to follow his lead," the instructor continued. I winced as Lynn nodded all too enthusiastically.

For the next four weeks, Lynn and I *worked* at learning to dance together, sweating some, disagreeing some and laughing some. Yet when it was all over, we actually twirled and two-stepped our way all around the crowded dance floor. Now I can't say that country western dancing guarantees marital bliss, but *working together* on a new challenge seems to strengthen and stimulate a marriage...especially when you can have some fun along the way.

Father, may we learn to work together in marriage.
— Carol Kuykendall

11 *"Rise up, my love, my fair one, and come away. For the*
‾‾‾ *winter is past....and the time of the singing of birds has*
SAT *come...."*   — Song of Solomon 2:10–12 (TLB)

They stood there together — my son Ian and his bride Melissa — in front
of the preacher. Young. Vulnerable. Hands clasped tightly together.
Vows exchanged, they were waiting for the homily, the final words of
spiritual direction and encouragement given to newlyweds.

"In all the frantic busyness of your day-to-day routines, *take time to
make time for each other!*" Pastor Bob said seriously, although a smile
played around the corners of his mouth. "There will be times, Ian," he
emphasized, "when you need to throw away your beeper, put your work
behind you. Remember, God created us as human *beings*, not human
doings!"

What important advice, I thought. My own life seemed to have been a
flurry of perpetual motion recently. Too much *doing* and not enough
being! Meetings and appointments stumbled over each other, I was up
doing laundry and dishes well past midnight, and even dinner was
caught on the run. It had been a long time since my husband John and I
had held hands for a quiet walk around the neighborhood or taken a
picnic to the park.

I leaned over to John. "Wanna just *be* with me this weekend, dearie?"
I whispered.

He squeezed my hand. "Honey, I wanna just *be* with you any time!"

Not only for newlyweds, but for all of us — how important it is to take
time to *be!*

Thank You, Lord, for making me a human being. *Help me in
the midst of all my* doings *to take time to* be — *with You and with
my family.*
                                                            — Fay Angus

12 *When I sit in darkness, the Lord shall be a light unto me.*
‾‾‾   — Micah 7:8
SUN

I was eleven the night I ran away. Angry with my family over some
minor disagreement, I traveled several blocks from home and hid myself in the tall grass of an abandoned field. There I sat in my self-
imposed isolation, gazing up at the few dim stars that hung in the summer sky.

How very alone I felt. The grass was dry and itchy. The ground was hard. I was terribly uncomfortable, but too embarrassed, too proud to go back. I was feeling pretty sorry for myself when, suddenly, I heard the unmistakable sound of footsteps. I looked toward the street and saw a large shadowy figure walking toward me. Before I could catch my breath, I felt a big hand touch my shoulder.

It was my father. He had found me in the dark.

Without a word, I took his hand and walked with him toward home. No explanations were necessary. He had come for me. I was glad.

I'm no longer a child, yet I often find myself doing childish things: running away from problems; allowing disagreements to separate me from the ones I love. And still, like that child of long ago, when I turn in my loneliness, I find my heavenly Father near.

The next time you feel alone, alienated, lost in the dark, think of a little girl sitting in a summer field. Don't be afraid. Just be still and wait for His presence. Wait for that big hand to rest on your shoulder. No matter how dark the night, He will find you. And you'll be glad.

Father, it is good to know that You are always near and ready to find us, even in the darkest night.   —Pam Kidd

---

$\frac{13}{\text{MON}}$ *I will forgive their iniquity, and I will remember their sin no more.*   —Jeremiah 31:34

I once wrote a children's novel called *Augusta and Trab* about a nine-year-old girl whose mother had just died. Wanting to fill up the empty feeling she had deep inside of her, Augusta goes off on a fantastic adventure with her slightly spoiled cat Trab.

Only after I wrote the book, and only after someone asked me where I got the idea for it, did I realize that much of the book came from my own empty feelings deep inside of me. My father was a busy man trying to hold down a demanding job, feed a family of six children and generally keep things together. I don't remember his having any time for any individual child in our family. I guess I wanted a father who would go off on fantastic voyages with me. And I guess you could say writing the book was my way of expressing long-buried feelings of disappointment.

Now my father is eighty-two years old, and he is very proud of me. His copy of *Augusta and Trab* sits on his desk next to the pictures of my brothers and sisters and me when we were children. This is his way of saying, "I love you. You're special, Chris."

There are many ways to tell each other our feelings. If there is some hurt you're holding, or if there are people who haven't lived up to your expectations, try to understand and forgive them today. Send them a letter or a card or a photograph and just say you love them anyway. Perhaps your small, quiet gesture, without a lot of fanfare, can set you both on a fantastic voyage of reconciliation to the land of "happily ever after."

God, I want to participate fully in the adventure You have for me. Help me to let go of old wrongs and start anew with those who are so important to me. Amen.   —Christopher de Vinck

---

14 *Lift ye up a banner upon the high mountain....*
TUES   —Isaiah 13:2

When I was a child, I lived near our town's Main Street, and every year on Flag Day I could be found waiting patiently at the curb for the parade to begin. I carried a flag over my right shoulder and waved it excitedly as the parade passed. My parents had told me that when you honor your flag, you're honoring your country, so I was careful how I handled it. I never let it touch the ground and I kept it in a drawer to protect it from fading.

Perhaps, because so many of us stopped waving flags after we grew up, we've forgotten that honoring our flag means taking good care of it. This Flag Day is a good time to remember:

Display the flag from sunrise to sunset.

Display it at night only if it is spotlighted.

Do not display the flag when the weather might damage it.

Do not use the flag as drapery or a decoration. Use bunting for those purposes.

Do not allow the flag to touch the ground.

Do not display the flag when it is faded or torn. Get a new one.

Dispose of a worn or tattered flag by burning it or storing it, never by throwing it in the trash.

A well-cared-for flag is a simple way for us to thank God for the blessing of freedom.

As we celebrate our national symbol of liberty, dear Lord, may we accept our responsibilities as citizens.   —Phyllis Hobe

15
WED

For who makes you different...? — I Corinthians 4:7 (NIV)

When Paul and I were newlyweds, I remember how our different habits caused a few clashes. He'd toss out the morning paper as soon as he thought we were done with it; later I'd search for it fruitlessly to reread something. He burns at the beach; I love to soak up the sun. He puts on loud music by Kate Bush to relax as soon as he gets home; I love quietly reading Agatha Christie mysteries.

When I was wailing about these "awful" differences to a friend, she surprised me by suddenly bursting into a few bars of song: "You say to-may-to, he says to-mah-to." I had to laugh, because that is quite literally true. Paul is English, so he *does* say "to-mah-to." He also says "chips" instead of French fries, "lorry" instead of truck, "lift" instead of elevator, and dozens of other phrases that I consider cute.

My friend persisted, "You wouldn't expect him to change his way of talking, would you?"

"I like those differences," I admitted. "I wouldn't want to be married to a cookie-cutter version of myself. Or 'biscuit cutter,' as Paul would say," I joked.

So the next morning, after a breakfast of "Sultana Bran" ("Raisin Bran" to us), I said to Paul, "Instead of the radio, why don't you pop that Kate Bush cassette into the car stereo today when we drive to work?"

He looked shocked. "Do you suddenly like her music?"

"No," I admitted, "but I like the fact that *you* do."

God, is there someone in my life whose personality I have been trying to change? Today, let me enjoy his or her uniqueness.
— Linda Neukrug

16
THURS

"For where you go I will go, and where you lodge I will lodge; your people shall be my people, and your God my God."
— Ruth 1:16 (RSV)

When I was growing up in the country, I learned how to play basketball by shooting a tin can into a bucket. It wasn't until I was in high school that I got my first basketball and a rim to go with it. As soon as I nailed the rim to the tree, kids from all around came over to play. When my son Reggie was nine, he asked, "Dad, can you put a basketball hoop in our backyard?"

"No," I said. "I don't want our yard to become the neighborhood playground." It would have been the only hoop in the community. I guess I liked my peace and quiet.

But God began working on me through my wife Rosie. "What's a little bit of grass and a quiet Saturday morning, when we can offer the children a chance to have fun?" she asked me. Finally, a year later, we put up a hoop. And guess what? Our yard was immediately full of kids.

Then, and at other times, I have wondered why we stay in a poor community. Almost every day there is a new crisis on our street or the next one over. I see children who go without, parents who work all night in a factory and people who struggle under the burden of poverty.

"We are here because God has called us to be *a part of,* not apart from, this community," Rosie says thoughtfully, wisely. "We are called to share the problems. When the creek spills over its banks, our house is flooded, too. We are called to look for the solutions together. And we are called to share ourselves and our resources."

Now when I pass the gym that our ministry helped build in our community — and play some ball myself — I'm glad I put up that first hoop. It confronted me with the needs of the young people and made me look for better solutions. The gym was one. And I look at the children around me and thank God for the privilege of lodging among them.

Our precious Savior, thank You for coming to earth to lodge among us. Help me to continue to follow Your example.

— Dolphus Weary

$\underline{\underset{FRI}{17}}$ *Our mouth filled with laughter, and our tongue with singing....*   HOUSE GUEST
ing....
— Psalm 126:2

It was a hot afternoon, and my eight-year-old son Zeb ran off to play with his friends Mike and Devin. What walked into the kitchen a couple hours later was a body Zeb's size covered with mud. In his ears, his nose, his hair, around his eyes, the stuff was all over him.

Although my mouth dropped open, words momentarily failed me. When I found my voice, I asked in amazement, "What did you *do?*"

"Oh, we were just playing in some mud," Zeb answered with classic understatement.

I wasn't sure if I should lecture him or laugh. So I drew him a bath instead, hoping the wisdom for an appropriate response would come to me soon.

As the tub was filling, Zeb said, "Mike was in big trouble when his mom saw him."

"What did she say?" I asked, feeling a kinship with Mike's mom.

"'You get in here *right now!*'"

I stifled a laugh as I found myself appreciating Mike's mom in a new way.

Devin was being cared for by his grandma that day, and I asked how she had responded to the awful sight. Zeb smiled with the memory as he told me, "She said, 'Wow! You're a *masterpiece!*'"

And suddenly it was my heart's prayer that, before he's fully grown, I'll be young enough to respond to my son's childhood as wisely and as lightly as Devin's grandma. At least, occasionally.

Father, please bless our parenting so that the children You've entrusted to us will grow from the love in our lectures and the lightness in our laughter.
— Ellyn Baumann

18
SAT
HOUSE GUEST
Let us hold unswervingly to the hope we profess, for he who promised is faithful.   — Hebrews 10:23 (NIV)

As I watched the waves crashing below me, I sympathized with the tiny creatures clinging to the rocks. Each breaker crashed against the shore with a force powerful enough to move boulders, blasting all in its path. I pondered how the shoreline inhabitants cope with the bashing, even making the waves work for them. Barnacles face the flow, sieving out food from the crushing water. Limpets cling, sea palms bend, shore crabs hide, and mussels cluster together with each approaching wave.

Lately, I've been feeling like a shore dweller. My husband Alex and I have been trying to conceive a second child for three years now. We have a beautiful daughter Elizabeth, four, but we long to give her siblings. No medical problem can be found for our infertility. "It can take longer to conceive when you are older," the doctor explained. But will we ever succeed? Each month, waves of disappointment and sorrow grow stronger. Yet watching the sea batter the rocks, I saw lessons in the survival of the creatures dwelling there.

Clinging to my Rock, I surrender my desire to Him: *Another baby is what I would choose, Lord. Nevertheless, may Your will be done.*

As I face waves of uncertainty, God feeds me with faith — not necessarily that I will have another child but confidence that I can be content regardless. I am assured that He knows our needs best, and He will provide. I may not know what's to be, but I welcome the tide of trust.

Dear God, I take refuge in Your steadfast love. Throughout my difficulties, help me find Your will and hold fast to Your Word.
— Mary Brown

P.S. Our family's tide of trust brought *good news:* I became pregnant shortly thereafter. A beautiful boy, Mark, is now one year old.

19
SUN   *HOUSE GUEST*
       How much more shall your Father which is in heaven give…?
— Matthew 7:11

I've always learned things the hard way. As a child, I always seemed determined to ignore any bit of advice my dad might offer, but still he was always there for me when I messed up.

"Brock, I'm burning some leaves down by the lake," I remember Dad saying when I was six. "Don't play near the fire." Thirty minutes later, he was gently applying ointment to my scorched foot.

One day, Dad took me fishing to Percy Priest Lake right outside of Nashville. Before cranking up the boat motor, he said, "Brock, for heaven's sake, try to be still in the boat. You might knock my rod and reel in the water and it's brand-new." Speeding over the water, I couldn't keep from squirming. *Plop!* "Uhhh…Dad…."

That dark moment wasn't mentioned again until… "You know, Brock, I really hated losing that rod and reel, but it turned out for the best." Dad went on to say he had been visiting a good friend, Dot Morris, who had recently lost her husband, and had laughingly told her the story of our ill-fated fishing trip. A few days later, Mrs. Morris showed up at our house with *two* dandy fishing outfits that had belonged to her husband!

I was ten the day Dad and I were in the backyard putting up my new basketball hoop. "Now, Brock, I want you to hold the ladder very carefully while I tighten the backboard," Dad said. If a certain frog hadn't hopped by, everything would have been all right. I released my grip on the ladder and went after it. Before I even caught the darn thing, there was a tremendous crash. I turned to see Dad sprawled out on the grass, breath knocked out, but luckily unhurt.

There's a kid in the Bible who reminds me a lot of myself — determined not to follow his dad's advice. His father is a lot like mine — arms wide open when the kid messes up. He's known as the prodigal son, and his father is like still another Father...our heavenly Father...always there for us, even when we stick our foot into the fire.

Dear God, on this Father's Day, thank You for my father, for all fathers. And help me to remember that You are the greatest Father of all.   — Brock Kidd

From the Wisdom of Ecclesiastes
FINDING THE JOY IN LIVING

"Until recently, I avoided a certain middle-aged man at church because he seemed so austere, so somber. He never seemed to smile," writes Daniel Schantz. "Then, at a social gathering, I discovered he had a wonderful dry wit that left me shaking with laughter. We've since become friends.

"The book of Ecclesiastes is a lot like that man," Dan goes on. "The author makes numerous dark pronouncements about life: 'All things are full of weariness,' and 'Vanity of vanities, all is vanity.' And yet there is also much in this book about how to enjoy life, in spite of the gloom."

Traditionally attributed to Solomon, Ecclesiastes does not name its author, who calls himself only Preacher (Teacher), a son of David (1:1). For convenience's sake, Dan refers to the author as Solomon, whom the Bible describes as the richest and wisest man of his day (II Chronicles 1:12, 9:22).

For the next six days, let's see what we can learn from this "truest of all books," as Herman Melville called Ecclesiastes. Together, let's allow Dan Schantz to help us discover the joy in living.   — The Editors

20
<u>MON</u>

Day One — Finding Joy in Our Daily Bread

Eat thy bread with joy....   — Ecclesiastes 9:7

Eighteen times in Ecclesiastes, the author uses the word *joy* or close synonyms such as *enjoy, rejoice* or *be merry.* He's urging me to adopt an attitude of appreciation for life. In the passage that urges me to eat with joy, I am reminded of the time my wife Sharon and I were invited to a banquet in Chicago, where the children's books I wrote were to be honored at the Children's Reading Roundtable. Sharon was thrilled at the sight of the Gold Room of our hotel, and she marveled at the lavish feast served by waiters in tuxedos.

"Oh, this is so exciting!" she said in a breathless voice.

I wanted to agree, but actually it was one of the worst meals of my life. Being a man of simple tastes, I refused to try the exotic-looking foods on my plate, and I looked suspiciously at the sauce on my tenderloin. I knew no one at the table and, shy by nature, I squirmed in my seat uncomfortably, while others ate heartily and chatted the evening away.

Finally, the last course — a more familiar dessert, ice cream flambé! And I ate so much of it I was ill the rest of the night.

I wonder if the wealthy Solomon, or any of the kings after him, really enjoyed the elaborate banquets served in his court? Did he, like me, balk at new dishes and pick at his food all evening? Did he draw back and miss out on the stimulating dinner conversations?

"Eat thy bread with joy." It sounds so simple. And yet I know I need to work at savoring the abundance God gives me, starting with my daily bread.

Lord, teach me to make each meal a celebration of Your goodness.
                                                             — Daniel Schantz

21
TUES

Day Two — Finding Joy in Work

He should make his soul enjoy good in his labor....
                                                             — Ecclesiastes 2:24

Throughout Ecclesiastes, Solomon moans about the futility of work, but he also admits to the great good in laboring. I have to admit that sometimes I, too, have mixed feelings about the work I do.

"I'm going to quit teaching," I announced one day to my wife Sharon as I dropped my briefcase to the kitchen floor. "I hate it. I detest it. It's miserable, and I'm not going back."

My wife listened patiently to my dirge of complaints about students, staff and procedures. Then in a sweet voice she said, "You do like *some* of your students, don't you?"

"Well, yes, some of them, but...."

"And you enjoy teaching the children's literature class."

"True, but...."

"You always seem to enjoy studying for your classes. I hear you whistling."

I nod. "But some of the people I have to work with!"

"But you like Richard, and Larry, and Patti, and Cheryl...."

I mumble my agreement.

"And you love eating in the cafeteria with students. You tell me all the funny things they do and say. And you have fun in the classroom, too. Remember that terrific discussion you had in Child Growth and Development?"

She pauses before driving the final nail of her argument. "And I know one thing you like a lot—your paycheck! Today is payday, remember?"

Lord, sometimes I'm awfully hard to please and it's hard to enjoy the good in my labor. Teach me to acknowledge the whole truth about my work—especially on those days when I'd rather be singing the blues.   —Daniel Schantz

22 Day Three—Finding Joy in Yourself
WED

Let thy garments be always white; and let thy head lack no ointment.   —Ecclesiastes 9:8

In the ancient East, I've been told, white was a symbol of festivity and joy. To wear white was to say, "I'm alive and well." I have an idea that nowadays secure and happy people have a way of presenting themselves as though they were wearing white. I'm thinking in particular of Candy, one of my students. She is a feisty brunette with a physical disability who zestfully pilots her motorized cart through the halls of the college where I teach. Let me tell you some of the things I have noticed about her.

1. *She takes care of her appearance.* Some of my nondisabled students seem to go out of their way to look shabby, but to Candy, "disabled" does not mean "dowdy." "How come the boys are always flirting?" she asks, amused. And I know the answer: Every day is a dress-up occasion for her. Her hair sparkles and is attractively arranged, her outfits are stylish and coordinated, and there's always a smile for everyone. People are naturally drawn to her because she likes herself and it shows.

2. *She is active.* No one would blame Candy if she just sat in her cart all day, daydreaming, but that's not Candy. She prefers to get out of her cart and navigate the halls with a pair of aluminum crutches, and you'd better be careful around her or she will reach out with a crutch and trip you just for fun.

3. *She makes the best of what she has.* Nothing is disabled about Candy's mind. In class, she is the first one to speak up, usually with a unique point of view. "Mr. Schantz, I'll have to disagree with you on that last point."

From Candy I have learned that a disabled *attitude* is the greatest disability of all. I'm trying to be more like her: grateful for my physical strength; careful to appreciate this temple of the Holy Spirit and treat it well; quick to use my body to accomplish goals of service and my mind to engage actively in important issues of debate and dialogue.

Thank You, Lord, for a healthy body, mind and spirit in which to glorify Your name.
— Daniel Schantz

23 Day Four — Finding Joy in What You Have
THURS

It is good...for....Every man also to whom God hath given riches and wealth...to rejoice....
—Ecclesiastes 5:18, 19

As a boy, I used to sit in church and piously sing, "I'd rather have Jesus than silver or gold...." Money was considered a grievous sin labeled "materialism." Today, I would probably sing, "I'd rather have Jesus *plus* silver and gold."

Why?

I've discovered that money and possessions are gifts from God to be used with care and thanksgiving.

Take our house, for example, an aged two-story beauty painted sky blue, with cloud-white shutters and candy-red doors. In this place, Sharon and I have put together a thirty-year marriage from a kit of youthful dreams. Here we have reared two beautiful and special daughters. One room of this house is my study, where I've written seventeen books and prepared thousands of classes. Sharon's kitchen has served hundreds of guests: students, missionaries, friends, neighbors. And from her bedroom writing table have gone thousands of cards and letters of encouragement to loved ones, friends and former students.

Possessions. Aren't they really just tools for service? How can I honor them? By using them to bless the lives of others around me. My car can become a friendship-builder as I pick up Larry, a fellow teacher, each morning on my way to work and we talk about things from sports to family life to financial worries. My television and VCR can be used to show a Christian video to the youth group that comes to our house after church. My computer bulletin board can be a tool to help locate a job for a recently unemployed friend. Our microwave can save cooking time so my wife can visit with students who have problems.

Like the kittens who live under our front porch and the birds who de-ice their wings over our chimney, I bless this old dwelling place. I pledge to continue using it and all my possessions to bless others.

Lord, help me to see the unselfish purposes of all the things I own, and to give praise and thanks for the true wealth You have bestowed upon me. — Daniel Schantz

$\underset{FRI}{\underline{24}}$ Day Five — Finding Joy in Laughter

Then I commended mirth, because a man hath no better thing...than...to be merry.... — Ecclesiastes 8:15

Question: How many psychiatrists does it take to change a light bulb?
Answer: Just one. But it's expensive, it takes a long time, and the light bulb has to want to be changed.

Okay, so it wasn't a side-splitter of a joke, but maybe you smiled a little.

Laughter. It's like an emotional sneeze that clears the heart of serious sludge. Or a kind of temporary insanity that keeps us from permanent insanity. I'm no comedian, but making people laugh has been one of my most rewarding hobbies. Every day I post fresh cartoons on the bulletin board in my classroom. I sneak silly questions into the exams to lighten test anxiety. I tell my students about my most embarrassing moments. I play jokes on my wife and friends. This week I put a rubber spider in Sharon's saucepan. She got even with a plastic snake under my pillow.

I wonder what laughter could do for you? It might break the tension of a deadlocked meeting, or slow down an argument with your mate, or dissolve a painful memory of a big mistake.

"Some day you'll laugh about this," they say. So why not laugh now? Look for the funny side of everyday problems. Check out a joke book from the library. Buy yourself a toy and keep it on your desk. And while you are at it, keep in mind this thought: "Angels can fly," G. K. Chesterton wrote, "because they take themselves lightly."

Join the angels. Take yourself lightly.

Lord, help me to understand that a laugh is just as holy as a prayer. — Daniel Schantz

P.S. Here's a favorite cartoon to help lighten your day.

"...and lead me not into temptation but deliver me from spinach."

25 Day Six — Finding Wisdom, Then Joy

SAT *For God giveth...wisdom, and knowledge, and joy....*
— Ecclesiastes 2:26

Our daughter Teresa called from the city where she was working at a temporary job in a publishing house. "Some of the people I've met here are so messed up," she said sadly. "Dad, even if they'd gone to Sunday school just one time I think they'd know better than to live the way they do."

Sunday school, I thought. *One of the most smiled-about institutions in the world. Something many people associate only with fruit drinks and finger plays and crafts.*

"You know," my wife Sharon reminded me later that evening, "I learned all the basics in Sunday school. The Ten Commandments, the beatitudes, the parables, The Golden Rule — all the things I need for a happy life I learned before I was in high school."

"I agree," I said. "It seems to me that our society is so unhappy because it has tried to go directly to 'joy' without first learning basic Bible truths about living."

Solomon was right, wasn't he, in putting wisdom, knowledge and joy in that order. When I work at learning God's will and doing it, then joy comes and lands quietly on my shoulder. I am "surprised by joy," as C. S. Lewis once described it.

How to have more wisdom and joy in life?

1. Teach a Sunday school class or home Bible study. "To teach is to learn twice," said the French moralist Joseph Joubert. No one learns as much about the lesson as the teacher.

2. Visit a bookstore and buy some inspirational books or tapes. Keep them in handy places where you can read them in snatches and bits.

3. Seek God "that giveth [wisdom] to all men liberally, and upbraideth not" (James 1:5).

Father, I want to be happier. Give me the wisdom I need to find the joy and contentment in living today and every day. Amen.
— Daniel Schantz

26
SUN
Jesus...saw a man called Matthew sitting at the tax office; and he said to him, "Follow me." And he rose and followed him. — Matthew 9:9 (RSV)

I've always marveled at this story. How was it possible for two words, *follow me*, to win such an immediate, unquestioning response? What was it about Jesus that engendered such trust?

I was given part of the answer in an unexpected place last summer, a detour in the Colorado Rockies. Driving down a steep mountain road, my husband John and I found ourselves at the end of a line of stopped traffic. Ahead we could see a flagman but not what the problem was. Five minutes passed, then ten, while other cars took their places behind us.

Coming up the hill from the other direction there was no traffic at all—until, at last, a line of vehicles appeared in the distance, following a lead car that passed the flagman, winding past us up the mountain.

And now we could read the sign on top of the lead car. Written in giant letters on a yellow placard were the words:

FOLLOW ME!

Follow we did, all of us, turning left on an unpaved road to parallel a streambed. "A bridge must be out," my husband said. It was a zigzag route on unmarked roads to the next stream crossing; as it became clear how complicated the route was, we were increasingly grateful for the pilot car with its simple command.

Was this the promise of Jesus' words, too? Did He see in Matthew a man whose life journey had reached a roadblock? Did the authority in His voice tell Matthew, I know what's stopping you. I know your destination. I know the way.

I'm so glad that in Jesus, Father, You sent us not a set of directions, but a Leader Who's traveled the route ahead.

—Elizabeth Sherrill

$\underset{\textit{MON}}{27}$ *I, John...was on the island of Patmos because of the word of God and the testimony of Jesus.* —Revelation 1:9 (NIV)

It was exciting for me to visit the Greek island of Patmos in the Aegean Sea where John wrote the book of Revelation. Walking down the mountain from the cave of John's mysterious vision, I took a side street to avoid the hot afternoon sun. A toothless elderly woman was sweeping the street.

She (who spoke no English) greeted me (who spoke no Greek), and I returned her greeting with a smile. She motioned for me to join her on her shaded balcony. I followed. She offered me coffee and expressed shock that I would drink the thick Greek brew without sweetener. As she chattered away in her Greek patois, gesturing expressively and fingering her wedding band, I grasped her continuing grief over her husband's death. Was I married? she asked by taking my left hand in hers. I gathered that her children did not visit often enough. What did I think of the holy *Apocalypse*? she asked, waving in the direction of the cave I had just visited. "A place to come face to face with *Christus*," I replied and gestured. She nodded her complete understanding.

For an hour we sipped and chatted, unimpeded by foreign words, sharing familiar thoughts and emotions. Where words failed, there was a glance of the eye, a motion of the hand. Then she showed me her beloved plants that shaded her balcony, telling me each of their stories. When we parted, she made a bouquet for me of fragrant, small white blossoms, fit for a bride. She kissed me on both cheeks.

What a wonderful gift, making this new friend, and just being two women together. Perhaps it was because he strolled down streets just like this one that John was able to receive that great vision of Jesus recorded in the book of Revelation. I thought, *Perhaps I, too, can take this gift I received here and let it bless others.*

Lord, teach me to look for all the side streets You have in store for me, and help me to appreciate the special people who wait to meet me there.   — Diane Komp

28
TUES   *"'Fool!...' So is he who lays up treasure for himself, and is not rich toward God."*   — Luke 12:20–21 (RSV)

My four-year-old runs into the house with a bucket of strawberries, a huge smile and his new shirt covered with red blotches. "Grandpa and I had a great time!" Ross hollers, but all I can see is his ruined shirt. As I take it off him, I don't say anything, but I mutter under my breath plenty as I stand over the sink scrubbing it. "If only I'd been here when they left the house. Who let him wear this good shirt? I'll never get these stains out."

Just then, an old story pops into my head, one I read years ago about baseball's great home-run hitter, Hall of Famer Harmon Killebrew. Once, when he was a boy, he and his two older brothers were wrestling on their newly seeded lawn. Their mother yelled for them to get off the grass and play somewhere else, but then their dad stepped in and said, "Let them have fun. We're raising kids here, not grass."

I've always remembered that story, and now I understand its philosophy. What's more important, my child's joy or a closet full of perfect clothes? Sometimes I get so caught up in wanting things to be "just so," I forget God's purpose for my life. As preschool paintings cover our refrigerator and creep toward the kitchen walls, and a small army of toys fills our family room, I wish my house could look more beautiful and less lived-in. But then I have to smile. Our house will never be in an interior decorating magazine, but all who see it know a lot of joyful living goes on inside.

So I wring out the shirt and hang it to dry, not perfect, but good enough. It's just not as important as the little boy who made a wonderful summer memory today, picking strawberries with Grandpa and gobbling every other one, letting the warm, sweet juice run down his chin and onto his shirt.

Remind me, Lord, to treasure people, not things.

—Gina Bridgeman

29
WED   *His mercy endureth for ever.*

HOUSE GUEST
—Psalm 118:1

"What's your secret for having such a long and happy marriage?" I asked the woman seated next to me at a luncheon recently.

"Oh, that's easy, dear," she replied. "I have lots of staying power. From the beginning, I thought it over carefully, so I knew for sure that I wanted to stay in this marriage through all its ups and downs."

Staying power, she called it. I had to admit that stick-to-itiveness has never been my strong suit. Impulsively, I tackle a new interest, then get bored or overwhelmed, and quit.

A few days after that conversation, I was asked to do volunteer work at the local nursing home. "I'd love to!" I said with my usual beginning enthusiasm.

But the director surprised me with her response. "Why don't you ease your way into the work?" she suggested. "Come as often as you'd like, get to know the patients and then, if you decide this is for you, you can make a commitment."

Her approach made good sense. Remembering the words of my luncheon partner, I saw that a basic ingredient of staying power was thinking a project over carefully before jumping in. A few weeks later, I was sure I wanted to be a volunteer. And I'm still one, almost a year later.

If you're like me, always charging headlong into new endeavors, why not start developing some staying power by easing into that next activity? Think it over carefully and ask yourself: *How much of my time will be involved? What are my responsibilities? Will I like doing it?* Talk to others who have held the same position. In other words, get the facts, think them over and, if you decide the job's for you, make a commitment. Then watch your staying power grow.

Staying power, Lord—will I ever have enough of it? I will, if I "stick with" You!
                                                                        — Ellen Secrest

---

30   *A merry heart maketh a cheerful countenance....*
<u>THURS</u>   — Proverbs 15:13

The Wimbledon tennis match was growing tense.

I was watching the games on TV, and even on a small screen I could see the lines of stress on the faces of players and fans alike. I could hear shouts of protests at close line calls and volleys of angry words.

Suddenly, a cloud opened overhead, and silver rains covered everything. I could almost hear God saying, "Let's cool this game down a bit."

The TV cameras abandoned the court and began a kaleidoscope of shots: fans fleeing for cover, young lovers sharing an umbrella, camera operators flinging tarps over their equipment. Line judges were drenched of their dignity, and young people danced around in the torrents, laughing and squealing.

Later the games resumed, this time with a friendlier spirit.

The incident set me to thinking about times when I myself get too intense for my own good. Like the time when I let a marital disagreement go on too long until it turned into a full-blown battle. And the day I worked long past my limits and got so irritable I hurt my students' feelings. Then there was the faculty meeting where I tried a little too hard to be "right" and ended up being very wrong.

Next time you find yourself getting too serious for your own good, why not *stop. Cool down.* Take a walk around the block or flip on the TV to a harmless sitcom. Better yet, dip into a Psalm. Then, *lighten up!*

Lord of Laughter, help me to see the sometime silliness of seriousness.
                                                                        — Daniel Schantz

Prayer Diary

Healing for John

Strength + Faith for John + Tammy

1. Prayer requests from church

Salvation for:

Larheta	Matt (Rosemary) Mar...
	Uncle Doc
Jaunna	Terri Lynn Kim
Danny	Cal
Liz + John	Ronnie
Bob + Carol	Cherrone
Mike + LaDon	Mary Anne
Linda + Mark	Dalles
Janice + Ken	Charlie
Charlie Jr.	Nancy
Ron	Carson
	Tom

Salvation + Closer walk for:

Self + George

Valetta + Ed + Sharrena

Bell + Lucy + Billy, Roger, Frank, Timothy

Sharnna + Harry, Nicole, Jonathan, Jered

Lori + Buck, George, Kenneth, Sharetta

Cathy + Tom, Julie, Bobby, Joshua

This country + its leaders

world revival

Guidance + direction for our lives

Open doors from God

Free of debt

Be a real servant

Increase our giving

Thousand Trails / NACO more God centered

9. _Jews For Jesus Campaigners_
Lionel, David & Patti, Aleene
What do you want me to do?

10. _Possess Me Lord_
Laura Gilbert
David & Barbra

11. _Merri & Ken_
Bonnie & Bert, Ed & Harriett,
Doug, Debbie, Jessi & Baby

12. _Richard & Louise_
Betty & Ron Baker
July 3rd Concert

13. _____

14. _____

15. _____

16. _____

17. _____

18. _____

19. _____

20.

21.

22.

23.

24.

25.

26.

27.

28.

29.

30.

July

S	M	T	W	T	F	S
					1	2
3	4	5	6	7	8	9
10	11	12	13	14	15	16
17	18	19	20	21	22	23
24	25	26	27	28	29	30
31						

GIFTS OF THE SEASON

The Light

Fireflies, shooting stars,
bursting rockets of light dance
on warm July nights.

*Blessed Christ, may the celebratory flares of July call
me to reach for Your light to illuminate my world.*

1
FRI   PRAYER CAN CHANGE YOUR LIFE
Make Prayer Positive

> *Whatsoever things are...good...think on these things.*
> —Philippians 4:8

Prayer Can Change Your Life reminds me: *How you believe is how you'll be—and how you'll find the world around you.* If you're negative, sure enough you'll see it reflected around you. How can I change? Authors Parker and St. Johns suggest praying positively. By holding in my mind a picture of the *positive changes* I'm aiming for, I'll see them realized.

A morning appointment in downtown Nashville offers me a perfect opportunity to change. I hate driving in rush-hour traffic. Until now, I have pictured myself as a scared rabbit, dodging traffic, pursued by armed hunters in blue and silver cars. I am a personal wreck by the time I reach my destination.

But for this trip, I decide to pray positively as I drive and interject good into every situation. According to the book, I can change the face of the freeway through positive prayer! As I drive onto the entrance ramp, I imagine myself as a sort of emissary of good. "Look at all these people in their remarkable cars," I say out loud. *Lord,* I pray, *it's wonderful that all these men and women have jobs to go to. Stay with each of them through the day and grant them the satisfaction of work well done.*

A man cuts sharply into my lane. I want to blast my horn. But, no...*How awful to be in such a hurry, Lord. Give this man safe passage. But let him slow down enough to see beauty along the way.*

A lady to my right is honking madly. I notice that her face looks tense. *She needs Your peace, Lord. She needs to feel Your love.*

A few minutes later, I calmly arrive at my destination. *I really enjoyed the drive, Lord. Thank You.*

Do you want to change? In each situation, visualize the person you want to be. Hold on to that image in every prayer you pray, in every deed you do. Paint a picture of the life you want to live and pray positively, as if it were already so. By taking each moment as a new opportunity, you will move a little closer to the person you want to become. Because slowly, but surely, you're letting prayer change you.

Father God, I want to take the positive path, because it is the straightest way to You.
—Pam Kidd

2
SAT *And thou shalt write [these my words] upon the door posts of thine house, and upon thy gates.*   —Deuteronomy 11:20

They're painted or carved over the doorways of older houses in Switzerland—mottoes in antique German script.

Some express a homely philosophy: "Who has wood in the stove and meat on the spit need not envy princes."

Or welcome the guest: "Enter, friend, and take a chair, if you're content with simple fare."

Or comment on life's inequities: "A rich man has many admirers, a poor one, many critics."

Suppose, I thought, we put slogans on housefronts in America. What would mine say? What message would I want to give the world?

A greeting? "Welcome, stranger! I have much to learn and you to teach."

Or a KEEP OUT notice? "PRIVATE PROPERTY, stay away; I have no time for you today."

Hypothetical mottoes...weren't they? Or is a message carved for all to read in everything I do, everything I am?

Father, let others read Your handwriting across my life today.
                                          —Elizabeth Sherrill

3
SUN *"Let them come to me for refuge; let them make peace with me, yes, let them make peace with me."*
                                          —Isaiah 27:5 (NIV)

Jason wrecked the car. Isn't it funny how four little words like that can ruin a good day? I heard them recently after Jason, sixteen, was driving with his aunt and brothers and went too fast, sliding off the road into a stone fence.

I rushed upstairs to his room to find him cowering on his bed. Before I could say a word, he blurted out, "Dad, you're not going to kill me, are you?"

Ignoring that absurd plea for a moment, I asked, "Was anyone hurt?"

"No."

"Did you hit anyone else?"

"No, I just went off the road and hit the stupid fence."

"Uh, Jason, I don't think the fence is the stupid one here."

I waited for the frown to begin forming from that comment, then sat down and hugged him, chuckling with relief.

"Dad, I really thought you were going to kill me."

"Jason," I said, "never forget that I'd much rather yell at you and have to fix the car than visit you in the hospital or worse."

Sitting there with him, I thought for a few moments how he had been afraid to see me and tried to hide. It reminded me of how I sometimes try to hide from God when I've done something wrong or stupid. When I get angry at a co-worker and don't resolve the matter, it is hard to sit down in my quiet time the next morning. I'm afraid for God to find me out. Or when I've been selfish with my wife Joy and not considered her needs. That always seems to happen before dinner when I am supposed to quiet down the family and lead in prayer. Somehow the words won't come. I think God doesn't want to hear me.

At those times, I need to remember that He is waiting to sit next to me and hug me and tell me He loves me. I only need call for Him.

Dear Lord, thanks for watching over everyone in that car. Help me to remember You love me no matter what and that You are always waiting to receive me.   —Eric Fellman

---

$\underset{\text{MON}}{\underline{4}}$ *By the rivers of Babylon, There we sat down and wept, When we remembered Zion.*   —Psalm 137:1 (NAS)

My family left the United States when my parents decided to be missionaries in the Philippine Islands. As a six-year-old boy, I don't remember being homesick while we adjusted to a new country. But I sure missed my dog Butch—I cried my eyes out over leaving that old stub-tailed bulldog.

A long four years later, it was time to return to the United States on furlough. I will never forget sailing into New York harbor on the SS *United States* and standing on the deck with my father. Leaning on a life-rail, we gazed at a radiant sky and saw the Statue of Liberty loom larger and larger as we glided past Bedloe's Island (now called Liberty Island). I was mesmerized by her immensity and stateliness. But as I looked at my father, there were tears brimming in his eyes.

"Son," he quietly spoke, "that tall lady over there is one of the most beautiful sights you'll ever see. Many a soldier or sailor coming home from war stood right where you are today and wept when he saw her. She's a wonderful lady. She welcomes us home."

I was just a boy then, sharing a reflective moment with a dad who, in serving God abroad, had seen so much hopeless suffering and poverty. But I never forgot his words or the depth of his emotion that day as we came home to America. Now every Independence Day, when I hear "The Star Spangled Banner" and see Old Glory unfurled with her "broad stripes and bright stars," I understand why my daddy cried.

Perhaps the most precious feeling in the world comes when you realize that you have a home—a place to belong, the cradle of your birth. It's worth celebrating, not just today, but every day.

Dear God, I thank You for family and friends, country and heritage, a place I can call "my home." Amen.   —Scott Walker

---

5   *I stay close to you; your right hand upholds me.*
<u>TUES</u>   —Psalm 63:8 (NIV)

The last time I saw my friend Eileen was when I drove her and her husband George to the airport to catch a plane bound for the Caribbean. It was their first vacation in years, and I was happy to see them go.

The next thing I knew, Eileen was dead, the victim of a boating accident. It was so sudden, I couldn't accept it. I couldn't even ask God for help because I was numb and empty inside.

"How can you bear the pain?" I finally asked George.

His eyes were tired and red from lack of sleep, and he sighed deeply. "I have my faith," he said quietly.

"*My* faith," he had said. I had faith, too, but I didn't call it *my* faith. Somehow, calling it *mine* made it something to cling to. It was like stretching out my hand and finding God's hand right there, ready to comfort and strengthen me.

That night I was able to talk to God about my grief. I began to cry as I asked Him to take away my anger, resentment and loneliness. And as He walked with me through the days and months ahead, healing my pain and replacing it with happy memories of my friend, I learned what it means to have not only faith, but *my* faith.

Lord Jesus, let me lean on You.   —Phyllis Hobe

6   *Be ye steadfast, unmovable, always abounding in the*
‾‾‾   *work of the Lord....*   —I Corinthians 15:58
WED

While on the beach in Florida recently, I trained my binoculars on a couple of double-crested cormorants (they have twin cowlicks and a yellow face) that were fishing for lunch in the surf. Bobbing along like corks, they swam until, detecting a fish below, they disappeared like magic into the deep. After they had had their fill, they took flight, leaving behind them a rainbow mist in the sun.

How different from the cormorants I'd seen in the Galapagos Islands a couple of summers before. Those cormorants were earthbound. Like their Florida relatives, they, too, had once been able to soar, but probably because of the ideal climate and an abundance of food, they had quit migrating and lost their ability to fly. Now they swim and fish with the same skill as other cormorants, but when it comes time to go home, flightless cormorants can only slither awkwardly up on the rocks and dry off at water's edge. Their bony wings are powerless and graceless.

We, too, can become graceless...especially in the spiritual sense. When we forget our manners, forget to be kind, forget the One Who is the source of all grace. When you and I forget to be thankful for our blessings and forget to ask forgiveness for our bobbles, we become calloused and insensitive. And if unarrested, such arrogance can lead to a hardened heart incapable of feeling or belief. Faith is much like the flightless cormorants' wings: That which we don't use, we lose.

> *Wake me, Lord, shake me, Lord, when I would stray,*
> *Remind me: You are the Truth, the Life, the Way.*
>   —Fred Bauer

7   *Knowing that tribulation brings about perseverance;*
‾‾‾‾‾   *and perseverance...character; and...character, hope.*
THURS   —Romans 5:3–4 (NAS)

The most annoying thing happened at our apartment in New York City last summer. The neighbors upstairs began to remodel their whole place, moving walls, changing electrical and plumbing systems. All this activity caused quite a lot of banging around and caused a shower of dust to sift down into our apartment. Water leaked and ran down our walls, creating a real mess. Nothing could be done to stop the dust and mess—we were stuck until the workmen finished.

For the first few weeks, I scurried about cleaning up everything every day. I washed, mopped and dusted until I was exhausted. And the next evening another powdery layer covered everything like new-fallen snow. Dirty snow, that is.

At last, I realized my efforts were ridiculous. I needed to wait for the activity to end and then I could clean once and for all.

Sometimes difficulties in life come in repeated waves, too, like the flu that sweeps through one member of the family after another. Now I see that the important thing is not to struggle too hard against something I cannot change, but to hold on until the trouble passes. I know that it is in the trials of life that God can do His most important work in our souls.

Lord, grant us the wisdom to know when to stop fighting and let You take over.
                                                    — Ruth Stafford Peale

8
FRI   *HOUSE GUEST*
"But I tell you who hear me: Love your enemies, do good to those who hate you, bless those who curse you, pray for those who mistreat you."
                                                    — Luke 6:27–28 (NIV)

I've skimmed over the above passage before, thinking, *I don't have any enemies.* But yesterday the word *mistreat* stood out when I remembered an incident from six years ago. I had taken my wedding dress and veil to a local dry cleaner to be cleaned and preserved. Five months later, I offered to lend a friend my gown. Opening the yard-long white box, we found the dress carefully wrapped in tissue paper — but no veil.

The dry cleaner refused to replace it. "You should have checked the box when you picked it up."

"But I was told if I opened it, the contents would no longer be preserved."

"That's ridiculous, we wouldn't tell you that. You can't prove we lost the veil."

I raged inwardly, *He's calling me a liar,* but only said firmly, "You did lose it. It's your responsibility to replace it."

He shouted, "No way! Never! Go ahead, take me to court. You won't win!" Then he hung up on me.

I slammed down my phone, shaking with fury. Six years later, when

I passed his store, I still heard his caustic voice and my anger burned again.

Pray for those who mistreat you. "Pray for Mr. B? That disgusting man who...." Somehow I couldn't start my usual tirade. I whispered, "Lord, have mercy on him. Bless him. Please forgive me for holding on to anger."

An icy chunk of snow stored inside me all these years melted. Six years ago, I had called Mr. B, then written a letter. I had contacted the Better Business Bureau, and I had even tried to forgive. Nothing worked, and the bad feelings persisted. But finally, now, praying *for him* washed away my bitterness.

Today, I drove by his store, and you know what? I said, "Thank You, Lord, for blessing Mr. B. Please draw him close to You."

Dear God, thank You for the healing I find when I obey Your Word.   — Mary Brown

9
SAT
Worship the Lord in the beauty of holiness.
— I Chronicles 16:29

"Pick your roses early," an old gardener once told me. "If you get them still heavy with dew they'll last twice as long." Good advice, easy to forget. Yet when heeded, those words do double duty. Put beauty first and it will make the whole day brighter.

One day I had to get up extra early. Company was coming, the house needed cleaning, there were classes to teach, errands to run — "And you'll want flowers on the table," a small voice reminded. "Pick your roses early."

I groaned, one eye on the clock. But leaving the coffee to perk, I slogged through wet grass to the garden, shears in hand. Birds were singing like church bells, a squirrel and a bluejay were playing hide-and-seek among the trees. In the first sunlight the roses were sparkling, drenched with the sweet wine of morning. My arms were soon full of an offering less vital than groceries; but breathing deep of their fragrance, my own spirit sang. All day, each time I saw them, their bright blossoms cheered me on.

And I thought, *Wouldn't it be wonderful if everybody could start the day like this?* By reaching out to claim some gift of beauty God has provided for us? It wouldn't have to be roses — or even flowers (although flowers are best because other people can enjoy them, too). It could be a glorious golden sunrise, or a winter dawn when the sky is still roofed with glittering stars and the snowy earth paved with diamonds.

Even these intangible treasures can enrich and brighten your spirit all day, because there's something about gathering beauty in the morning that gives you energy and vitality. It puts a bounce in your step, a lilt in your heart. It makes you want to smile more, hug more, pay compliments, call out to friends and neighbors, and scatter little nosegays of love wherever you are, all day.

Dear Lord, don't let me sleep too late. Give me the willpower to hop out of bed in time to see the sunrise and hear the birds' first chorus, as I set out to gather whatever gift of beauty You have for me today.
— Marjorie Holmes

---

10 *Wherefore seeing we also are compassed about with so*
SUN *great a cloud of witnesses....*   — Hebrews 12:1

Our church has been standing at the corner of 99th Street and Amsterdam on New York's Upper West Side for one hundred years. To celebrate the building's birthday, a professor of art history, a member of our congregation, led a group of us on an informal tour.

He praised the Tiffany stained-glass windows for their iridescent colors. He drew our attention to the detailed mosaics behind the altar representing the four Gospels. He pointed out the baptismal font hand-carved of warm Indiana marble. He noted the pews done in a solid native walnut.

As we walked through the century-old edifice with new eyes of appreciation, I found myself pausing to look at the brass plaques beneath the windows. "In memory of a beloved friend," read the inscription on one. "Donated by the altar guild," read another. "Given by St. Cecilia's Choir," said another. All of them showed names of people who had worshiped, preached and prayed here over the years.

"Of course," our guide said, "a church is more than a beautiful building like this one."

Yes, I thought as I looked at our own group of Sunday school teachers, women from the altar guild, soup kitchen volunteers and my fellow choir members. *Yes, the church is a living thing. The church is us.*

Lord, may I be one of that cloud of witnesses that has built Your church to last forever.
— Rick Hamlin

11 *In old age [the righteous] still produce fruit; they are*
————— *always green and full of sap.*   —Psalm 92:14 (NRSV)
MON

You already know that I love orchids. And that the love of orchids leads
to orchiding. That is because orchids are not only beautiful flowers to
look at, they can introduce you to beautiful people. Avid orchid growers
are always on the lookout for new friends with the same passion.

When I visited my sister Marge in upstate New York some years ago,
we called on a retired doctor in her area with a famous orchid collection.
As we entered the greenhouse, the fragrance of a vanilla bean plant
wafted up to greet us. On every side we were surrounded by the most
exotic flowers I had ever seen. Big *Cattleyas* and tiny *Oncidia* thrived
side by side in the doctor's garden of love.

Although my sister knew nothing about the plants he was showing
us, she was as captivated as I was by this elderly but quick-witted physician. After an hour of discussing Latin-named hybrids, we reached a
plant that gave him special pride. As he lovingly took it in his arms and
gently fingered the breathtaking spray of yellow blooms, he started to
recite its genealogy. But the Latin names would just not come. He
thought for another moment and then shook his head. "Whoops!" he
grinned. "I just burned out another synapse." Then he laughed, and we
shared his laughter with him.

These days, I not only recall my elderly friend's beautiful orchids in
all their majestic colors, but I remember with fondness the gracious orchid grower who taught me a new kind of gentleness, a gentleness with
the self. Now, when my own aging brain slows down, instead of berat-
ing myself, I take it in stride and just say, "Whoops!" It cuts down
greatly on the self-condemnation, and allows me to flower into a more
gracious human being.

Father, help me to become more fruitful with age, gentle on my-
self and all those I meet.   —Diane Komp

12 *Let your light so shine before men, that they may see your*
————— *good works, and glorify your Father which is in heaven.*
TUES   —Matthew 5:16

"Would you be so kind as to take my picture?" the stranger asked, extending his camera. We were standing in front of the statue of the great
missionary-explorer David Livingstone at Zimbabwe's Victoria Falls,

that wonder of nature that Livingstone had been the first European to see. I'd spent the afternoon wandering tropical paths and climbing spume-wet rocks in search of a good view of the spectacle so vast that no single vantage point could provide a full vista.

I snapped my fellow tourist's picture. He came back and the two of us lingered before the tall statue of a man who was himself larger than life. Perhaps we were thinking the same thoughts about Dr. Livingstone's explorations — his courage, his sense of brotherhood, his obstinate efforts to salve the "running sore of Africa," the slave trade.

"I've heard of a quality the Arabs call *baraka*," my friend mused out loud.

"Baraka?"

"No word for it in English. It's a power some people have for making life better by their presence. I think Livingstone had baraka."

We talked a little more, shook hands, and that seemed to end that. Except that this idea of baraka kept swimming in my head. Was it something that only great men and women had? Did you have to be born with it? Who among the people I knew had that quality for enhancing life?

Long after returning home, I was still pondering these things — until the day it came to me that whether people had or did not have baraka was not the key question. What mattered was that they should strive to have it. Then came the sobering thought: The striving should begin with *me!*

Lord, with You, through You, my light can shine.   — Van Varner

13
WED

Love covers a multitude of sins.   — I Peter 4:8 (NAS)

My husband Gene and I and my twenty-four-year-old son Jeremy were having lunch at a popular restaurant when, suddenly, without warning, the conversation between Jeremy and me took a sharp, unexpected, angry turn. I hate to admit it, but I've often lost my temper with this son of mine and this time I did it again. I snapped back at him loudly. People stared. Our friendly waitress' smile froze. My husband glanced down beneath our table as though he might crawl under it. Jeremy looked at me in disbelief. Soon I was dissolved into tears. "Why can't we get along, Jeremy? Do you know how much I love you?" I asked, a familiar helplessness overtaking me. Finally, we left the restaurant.

Outside, we stood awkwardly, silently. Suddenly, Jeremy broke the silence. "Hey, Mom, you want to ride in my new Corvette?" he said, smiling openly, confidently, waiting for my answer.

Still blowing my nose, I answered curtly, "No. No, thank you." Jeremy jumped into his car and roared off.

As Gene and I drove home, he said, "Marion, Jeremy can't express love the same way you do. He was telling you that he loved you when he asked you to ride in his new car. It was his way of reaching out."

Almost physically sick, I ran to the phone when we got home and dialed Jeremy. *Please let him be home, Lord.* "Jeremy! I'm sorry for the whole bad scene and for ruining our lunch. Please forgive me. Will you ask me to ride in your car again?" (*I love you! I love you!*)

"Sure thing, Mom. No problem. See ya, okay?" At midnight, I was still wide awake, looking at the ceiling in the bright moonlight, remembering Jeremy as a baby, a little boy, a teenager...a devastated fifteen-year-old when his father died. *Oh, Jeremy, I love you.*

The phone's shrillness interrupted my thoughts. I answered it quickly. "Mom? You okay? Were you able to forget about today? I did. Go to sleep. Okay, Mom?"

"Okay, Jeremy."

Dear Father, You know how deeply my children and I love one another. Show me how to communicate that love. And when I fail, help me to forgive myself. Thank You. Amen.

— Marion Bond West

14 **THURS** *This one thing I do....* — Philippians 3:13

There are so many things I've wanted to do in my life that I haven't done...become an actress, a Peace Corps volunteer, a pianist or any number of other unrealized dreams. People often tell me they've always wanted to be a writer but have never found the time. I wonder if it's really a matter of time. This afternoon, while I was waiting for inspiration to fall from the skies and sprinkle itself onto my word processing screen, an old maxim came to me: *Inspiration follows aspiration.* Could it be that inspiration doesn't come until we truly aspire — *reach for —* a goal?

As long as I just have a fuzzy desire to do or be something and sit waiting for inspiration, it'll probably never happen. On the other hand, if I'm really serious about it, I'll pray about it, and then reach for it by making a commitment. Only then can I expect God to provide the inspiration. I know it's true. *Inspiration* always *follows aspiration.*

Spirit of God, I offer You my aspiration to: _____.
My first step is _____. *If it's mine to do, please confirm it with Your inspiration.*   — Marilyn Morgan Helleberg

15 *You care for the land and water it; you enrich it abun-*
FRI *dantly...for so you have ordained it.*   — Psalm 65:9 (NIV)

> *July 15. Our two-week drive along the Atlantic coast leaves my husband Gary, twelve-year-old son Geoffrey and me exhausted. We have gone through our itinerary at top speed, yet the perfect vacation spot continues to elude us.*
>
> *Faster and faster we speed on our futile quest until somewhere in the backwoods of northern Maine we are hopelessly lost. We wander along narrow gravel roads, growing more and more frustrated as the precious hours tick by. We have a schedule to keep, an itinerary to follow. How else can we get to where we should be?*
>
> *Suddenly, we go around a curve. There, before us, stretches a breathtaking expanse of water with a small green island floating on its silvery surface. Has it always been here beyond the superhighways and fast-food restaurants? We pull our car onto a strip of sand to find our location on the map. Two hours later, we have forgotten that we ever needed maps or itineraries or schedules. There was a beach to explore, water for wading, rocks for climbing and small round stones to skip along the shore....*

I have two pictures of that blessed and unnamed place. Yet I do not have to look at it to recall the lake, the trees, the faces of three contented travelers who had finally found the best place to be that memorable July day.

Searching madly for your heart's desire? Rushing around won't get you there any faster. Instead, take the long, slow, scenic route toward your true destination — the one the Lord planned for you all along.

Slow me down, Lord, so that I may see, really see, eternity all about me, and Your hand leading me down each lane.
                                          — Linda Ching Sledge

16 *If God is for us, who is against us?*   — Romans 8:31 (RSV)

SAT

Halibut fishing out of Homer, Alaska, is one of life's finer performances. On the summer day our friends Ked and Diane Schoming invited us aboard their boat *Morning Glory*, the beautiful mountains rimming Katchemak Bay were obscured behind a screen of rain. After several hours of fishing, I had caught one small halibut. I remained undeterred—my big fish was down there somewhere.

When the big one struck, my rod bent clear to the water and I panicked. As I instinctively fought the halibut, Ked hollered, "No! Let him take the hook!" He then instructed me in a cardinal rule of fishing: *Let the pole do the work.* For twenty minutes I kept a rhythm going, drawing the tip of the rod slowly upward, keeping the line taut, and then cranking in the slack as the pole dipped back to the water. Twice the fish dove with the line. I let it go, thrilling to the singing of the reel spinning wildly. When I finally pulled my fish alongside the boat, I'd caught a fifty-five pounder! Not a record as halibut go, but definitely a keeper.

What a difference it made to "let the pole do the work," instead of exhausting my own strength against the superior might of the fish. As with the sea, so in the flow of life I hook into things that are too powerful for me to combat with my limited human resources. But by trusting the Holy Spirit dwelling within me, I know there is a way to win.

Whatever your personal leviathan, try doing less resisting and allow God to do more assisting. In rhythm with Him, "let the Spirit do the work." Together, you will land a victory!

Father, by Your Spirit, any success I gain—however large or small—is a "keeper," and I thank You for it.   — Carol Knapp

17 *"I have many people in this city."*   — Acts 18:10 (RSV)

SUN

Two summers ago, while I was visiting Los Angeles, there was a major earthquake. Amazingly, this was the *second* major earthquake I had experienced since moving to California several years ago. Later, when I told a friend that I had been in San Francisco during the Loma Prieta quake, too, she said, "Oh, yes, I prayed for San Francisco after that, and I prayed for Los Angeles as well."

"You prayed for an entire *city?*"

She smiled and shrugged. "Why not? Cities are made up of people. When I read of some horrific tragedy—a flood, a tornado, an earthquake—I ask God to heal the city and the people in it. So even though you didn't know it, I prayed for you during the aftermath of both of those quakes."

Although I must admit the idea sounded a little grand to me, I did feel comforted by the idea she'd been praying for those cities. So I began praying for entire cities, too. If I read about a city in trouble—whether through natural disasters or man-made violence—I often look it up in an atlas and read a little bit about its background and history, its geography, what the climate is like, what it produces. My knowledge makes me feel closer to it, and this closeness leads me to pray for its healing.

Is there a city that you would like to ask God to watch over? Perhaps your own?

God, please bless the city I live in today.   —Linda Neukrug

18 *Make sweet melody, sing many songs....*   —Isaiah 23:16
MON

I played cards with my grandmother for hours and hours when I was a teenager. She sat on one side of the dining room table and I sat on the other. We often shared a bowl of potato chips. Often, when it was her turn, I'd begin whistling and soon enough she would begin singing the tune I'd be whistling.

I remember one summer afternoon I began whistling "Stars and Stripes Forever." I turned over a card, made my move, waited for my grandmother to move, then I began to whistle. She began to sing. I began to add some drumrolls on the tabletop; she began to clink a spoon against the potato chip bowl. Between the banging on the table, I added a few claps; she stood up and began singing at the top of her voice. I made trumpet sounds with my mouth; she made crashing cymbal sounds. You would have thought an entire Marine Corps band was marching around the dining room table.

After we finished our performance, my grandmother sat down, took a drink of water, smiled and said, "Your move." She was eighty-nine years old at the time.

If you think you are too old, or too tired, or too depressed, or too lonely to whistle, sing or crash cymbals, I think you're wrong. You have in your heart the ability to create a symphony today. Try it. A single song, a whistle while you prepare yourself for today's challenge.

"Your move."

Lord, give me a spirit that unabashedly celebrates You and the joy of living.   — Christopher de Vinck

19
TUES *Mercy triumphs over judgment.*   HOUSE GUEST
                                          — James 2:13 (RSV)

I knew I was the right man for the job the minute I heard about the opening at Electric Motor Rewind. It was the summer before my freshman year at the University of Tennessee, and since I was twelve my summer jobs had been labor intensive. Working with construction crews, I had always been the step-and-fetch-it guy who was handed the dirtiest chores. Now Neal Horner, a member of our church, offered me a cushy job driving an air-conditioned truck making pickups and deliveries around the Nashville area. What an opportunity! I could learn about the motor rewinding business, and I could even listen to the radio while I worked!

Like all Mr. Horner's workers, I found myself eager to do my job well. Soon I was a real pro. But one morning while backing up to a loading dock, I heard an unfamiliar crunch. *Couldn't be me,* I thought over the sounds of the radio. I turned the volume down and backed a bit farther. *Crunch.* Oh, great! I had run the truck into the bay door. Jumping out, I found a two-foot crevice in the side of Mr. Horner's newest delivery truck. I felt faint, then terrified.

"Hi, Brock," Mr. Horner smiled as I entered his office. "How's the road treating you today?"

"Well, Mr. Horner," I said, thinking he might fire me on the spot, "I really messed up. You'd better come outside." Trembling, I rubbed my hand across the depression in the side of the truck. It seemed to be getting larger by the second.

"Brock," I could hardly believe the words Mr. Horner was speaking, "you're all right, that's my first concern. And I'm sure you've learned something today. That's all that's really important. Trucks can always be fixed."

That was it. And Mr. Horner was right. I did learn something. Not only about driving, as he was probably thinking, but about the kind of man I want to be. A man like Mr. Horner, slow to blame and mighty quick to forgive.

Dear God, I want to live by Your rules so that I might influence others the way Mr. Horner influenced me. Help me never to forget that. Amen.   — Brock Kidd

20
WED

HOUSE GUEST
PRACTICING THE POWER OF PRAYER
Wish Prayers

And this also we wish, even your perfection.
— II Corinthians 13:9

At noon each Wednesday, I used to walk from the dental office where I worked to my friend Bonnie's house nearby. There, we met for prayer. Through the months, I saw many of our prayers answered, but I also discovered the power of a wish.

A dear friend, who had been rejected for a position in her church, began to resent the one who had been chosen for it. I watched sadly as envy ate at my friend. I silently wished she would stop finding fault and take an honest look at herself. Within a week, she called and said, "I've decided to get rid of my bitter attitude. Please remind me, if I start to say anything negative about that person."

I thought, *that's like an answer to prayer...only I didn't pray!*

Later, my new daughter-in-law JoAnn said she would never be baptized. I couldn't say anything without sounding like a meddling mother-in-law, but I often wished she would change her mind. I'm sure I would have prayed about it after awhile, but before I could, she announced that she wanted to be baptized.

My fulfilled wishes reminded me of God's message to Isaiah, "Before they call, I will answer" (Isaiah 65:24). God knows our wishes — what we hope for — before we even realize we should pray for them. Since I discovered what can happen when I wish something good for someone, wishing has become fun for me. Every greeting card I send is really a wish and a prayer. Throughout my day, as I see a need, I offer wishes for others like good thoughts blown their way. The rest I leave to God. He understands and answers.

Heavenly Father, guide me to wish what You wish and remind me at every opportunity to sow those wishes as prayers.
— Elsie Larson

21

THURS   *You have a very special place in my heart....*

— Philippians 1:7 (TLB)

A child from our town died last week. Kelsey was a healthy and energetic nine-year-old, glad that summer was finally here, when she was
gravely injured in a freak bike accident.

At Kelsey's funeral, the pastor urged us to appreciate the gift of
life. He said that if we have people to love, we should continually show
them and tell them how we feel. As I listened, I began thinking about
Thornton Wilder's play *Our Town*. The main character, a young woman
named Emily, dies during childbirth, and from her grave realizes how
beautiful life is. Longing to experience just one day again, she ignores
other deceased souls around her who warn that it will be too painful for
her to return. The day she chooses to relive is her twelfth birthday. Her
mother is busy preparing breakfast as Emily pleads with the unhearing
woman, "Look at me, Mama." But the day's activities hurry on, without the mother stopping to look and really *see* her daughter.

It all hit home this morning. While making a birthday cake for an
elderly neighbor with my ten-year-old Zeb, I'm all business, trying to
keep things neat, orderly and efficient. Zeb's having a good time helping in his enthusiastic way. Sensing my order is about to overtake his
fun, the message I've absorbed from these recent days comes to me in
an instant. I put down the mixing spoon, look at my freckle-faced red-
head, hug him and tell him how glad I am he's in my life. He says,
"Thanks, Mom," and hugs me back. And we get on with the baking,
both of us now lighthearted.

Our neighbor is surprised and pleased with our gift. And I'm thankful that in the busyness of preparing it, I didn't miss an opportunity to
look upon my son and really see him.

*Father, thank You for the loved ones with whom we get to cele-
brate this precious life. Keep us from taking them for granted
and letting our busyness overtake life's sweetest joys.*

— Ellyn Baumann

22

FRI   *What manner of persons ought you to be in holy conduct
and godliness?*

— II Peter 3:11 (NKJV)

HOUSE GUEST

This past summer we visited the Shaker community in Canterbury,

New Hampshire. The Shakers, a religious sect best known for their celibate and communal life-style, were founded by devout men and women whose primary objective was to bring honor to God. During our tour, the guide mentioned that when a Shaker is guilty of "wooden swearing," he or she must confess to the appropriate elder or eldress. "Wooden swearing" refers to such actions as slamming a door or stamping one's foot.

Now I've always prided myself on not using crude language, but I'd never thought about wooden swearing. I began watching for it. Time after time, I caught myself in the act. Everything from jamming the phone on the hook following an irritating call to slamming my notebook on the table at a heated parish voters' meeting.

Wooden swearing may not be a heinous sin, but it leaves an impression of my faith just as surely as if I mutter an oath. It's a hard habit to break, but yesterday when I started to slam a pan down on the stove, I remembered the gentle Shakers and stayed my hand. Just as their loving, obedient faith has reached across the years as an example to me, can't I be a faithful example for someone today? With His help, I'm certainly going to try.

Dear Father, help me to curb my wooden swearing so that everyone I meet will have no doubt that I truly desire to honor You.
— Bonnie Lukes

23
SAT
Simon answered, "Master, we've worked hard all night and haven't caught anything. But because you say so, I will let down the nets." — Luke 5:5 (NIV)

On Saturday mornings, my friend Jimmie and I — we were about seven then — would get up early and walk a mile through the woods to a small river, toting our bamboo poles and a tin pail with the worms we'd dug up the night before. As we walked barefoot (shoes were saved for church), we looked for the best place to fish, then ran the snakes out, baited our hooks and waited.

If we didn't catch anything, we'd come back at night and set out several fishing poles to try to catch a fish for Sunday breakfast. I remember one morning finding a five-pound catfish dangling on our line. What a catch! When Mama fried that up, I mean finger-lickin' good!

But I also remember all the hot Mississippi days sitting on the riverbank, the air hanging on us thick and heavy, the mosquitoes biting, but not a nibble from a fish.

I think of those days when I read about Peter. I know how discouraging it is to fish and catch nothing. Yet Peter had faith to let down his net again because he trusted the Lord's Word.

Although I don't fish anymore, there are many times I need to remember to "let down my net" in faith and the Lord's promise. Many times I don't know where the resources or the strength will come from to sustain our ministry, to sit through a child's illness, to see a friend suffer. But I have learned from Peter to say to the Lord, "Because You say so, I will do."

Lord, help us trust Your say-so in all we do for You. Amen.
— Dolphus Weary

24
SUN

And of some have compassion, making a difference.
— Jude 22

Recently, I read a story about the friendship between two Olympic distance runners, Australia's Ron Clarke and Emil Zatopek from the former republic of Czechoslovakia. Clarke was a world-record holder, the top runner of the 1960s, but his dream of winning a gold medal died in 1968 in Mexico City. He had trained hard and was in top physical shape, but Mexico City's high altitude was too much for him, and he finished sixth. He returned home brokenhearted, unable to pull himself together until he made a trip to see Zatopek, a triple gold-medal winner at the 1952 Olympics.

The two men spent a week together. Zatopek was understanding and comforting. As Clarke boarded his plane for home, Zatopek quietly slipped a small package into his hand. During the flight, Clarke opened the box, and there lay a gold medal. It was one of Zatopek's. Clarke was stunned. He lifted the medal out of the box and read the new inscription: "Not because you won it, but because you deserved it."

Zatopek's selfless gift raised Clarke's spirits as few things could have done. It makes me think about how acts of unexpected kindness, even the simplest ones, have often lifted my own spirits. I think of the friend who sent me a sympathy card when my little dog Coco died. And the stranger who saw me struggling with my tired, crying three-year-old and said with a smile, "You've got a tough job today. Hang in there." It's people like that, and like Emil Zatopek, who make God's light shine when days grow dark.

Lord, help me not pass silently by those who need to be encouraged, but let me lift them up as You have lifted me. Amen.
                                                            — Gina Bridgeman

25
<u>MON</u> *Be ye angry, and sin not: let not the sun go down upon your wrath.*   — Ephesians 4:26

"Put it back where it goes." That's a saying I used to hear a lot the year I worked on a horse farm in Ohio with two other girls.

"Girls," our boss Mr. Duffner admonished us often as he guided us through our stall-building project, "always put a tool back where it goes. If you just set it down anywhere, you'll find yourself searching for it again and again, wasting time."

That was a long time ago, yet even today I try to remember Mr. D's words and put them to work in my life. Take my problem with anger, for instance. I'm a great one for not facing it honestly. Instead of putting it where it goes—acknowledging that I'm really angry about something—I'm liable to set it down here or there where clutters of activity may cover it up for a while. But I always find it later and have to deal with it. When I felt pressured into being a group leader and it proved to be too much for me, my resentment popped up in all sorts of places—a flash of anger at my kids or husband, moods of dark self-pity. I finally saw that I had to put my anger where it belonged by being honest with myself and others about its cause. And then I resigned from the leadership role.

Perhaps the Scripture "let not the sun go down upon your wrath" is like the saying "Put it back where it goes." For me, that's facing my anger, bringing it to God and then taking an appropriate action, if need be. As Mr. D would say, putting anger just *anywhere* is wasting time.

Dear Lord, are there any tools of anger—or envy, or grief, or pride—around in me today that I should put in their proper place? Teach me to "put it back where it goes." Amen.
                                                            — Kathie Kania

                                                            HOUSE GUEST

26
<u>TUES</u> *The memory of the righteous is a blessing....*
                                                            — Proverbs 10:7 (RSV)

Migraine headaches. Shortly after my grandmother died, I started getting one or two a week. Our family doctor wrote me this prescription: "Buy a notebook and fill it with memories of your grandmother. Write in it every day for the next two weeks and call me at the end of the month."

Gram was just like my best friend and since she lived for 101 vigorous years, she was also my oldest friend. I missed her terribly. I dreaded writing down my memories; it would be too painful. I thought after things settled down and my family and I got back in the usual routine, well, maybe then I'd have the time to face my sadness.

The headaches didn't let up. And one afternoon I was so miserable that I grabbed a pencil and found an old spiral notebook. "I'll just write a few words," I said to myself. Two hours and a box of tissues later, I looked up and was amazed — my head wasn't throbbing. And half of the pages in the notebook were filled. I felt so much better that I followed the doctor's orders exactly and wrote about Gram every day. By the end of two weeks, my headaches were gone and I had a book full of wonderful "Gram Memories": staying overnight at her apartment and eating hot fudge sundaes; learning how to thread a needle and baste a hem. I included her recipe for Irish soda bread ("always use buttermilk") and her favorite Irish limericks. I wrote about our trip to Maine when I was twelve, the luncheon she gave before I was married, the walks we took with my children when they were babies. I pasted in some snapshots and copied down some of the prayers Gram said every day. That old spiral notebook crackled with sparks of Gram's laughter and wit and her strong faith. And the act of writing about someone I missed so much helped ease the pain in my heart and got rid of the pain in my head.

Like a good patient, I called the doctor at the end of the month to report my progress. Holding "Gram Memories" in my hand, I thanked him for some of the best medicine I ever received.

Help us to face our pain and to savor the sweet memories of those who have left us to be with You, Lord.   — Ellen Secrest

P.S. Here is one of Gram's and my favorite Irish limericks to brighten your day:

> *There was a wise man from Bray*
> *And this he had to say:*
> *If you're kind and you're nice*
> *God will bless thee thrice,*
> *But don't forget to pray.*

From the Kitchen of: *Ellen Secrest*

GRAM'S IRISH SODA BREAD

1½ cups raisins
4 cups flour, sifted
½ tsp. baking soda
1 tsp. baking powder
1 tsp. salt

3 Tb. sugar
3 tsp. caraway seeds (optional)
½ cup butter at room temperature
1½ cups buttermilk
2 eggs, beaten

Heat oven to 450°. Mix raisins with sifted flour, baking soda, baking powder, salt, sugar and caraway seeds. Cut in butter with a pastry blender or two knives used scissor-fashion until the consistency of coarse cornmeal. Gradually add buttermilk and eggs, and mix gently until just moistened. Knead lightly until smooth on a floured board and shape into a round loaf. Put the dough in a greased, round baking pan. With a sharp knife, cut a cross in the top of the dough. Bake 10 minutes at 450°; reduce heat to 350° and bake for 45 minutes. Cool on wire rack. Slice and dunk in a cup of hot tea!

HOUSE GUEST

27
WED
If anything is excellent or praiseworthy—think about such things.
—Philippians 4:8 (NIV)

"Flip a coin, Mommy," the children cried. They'd decided heads meant Joanna would get the last purple Popsicle, tails meant Sarah would. The loser would get the orange one.

If only all choices were so easy, I thought as I spun the silver dime up in the air. *Heads.* The kids raced to the freezer, accepting the coin's impartial verdict.

I turned the dime over in my hand. Lately, I'd "gotten my head down," as my husband Joe calls it, feeling frustrated with our muddy well water. Our soil here is a fine red sand that, if it gets in the well, turns the water red, makes it undrinkable and gets ingrained in our clothes when I wash. It was so frustrating that I seriously wanted to move away, believing somehow that would solve it. But I knew it wouldn't.

I looked at my attitude. It was one thing that *could* move. I tried the "coin-flip method" I'd used with the children. *Heads:* Appreciate my mother-in-law a few miles away and take up her offer to share her washing machine. *Tails:* Keep on complaining about the soil.

I decided to choose heads. My new attitude cleared the mud out of my disposition. And shortly thereafter, we managed to buy a system that filters the red sand out of our water.

There are never easy solutions to anything. But a "flip" of the right attitude, I'm finding, is a big start.

Heavenly Father, today I want to choose an attitude of praise, no matter what my circumstances. Please help me to trust You. Amen.
                                                    — Marjorie Parker

Quiet Time

Thou that hast given so much to me,
Give one thing more, a grateful heart.
...

Not thankful, when it pleases me;
As if thy blessings had spare days:
But such a heart, whose pulse may be
    Thy praise.

                                        — *George Herbert*

28 *Behold, I have set before thee an open door....*
THURS
                                        — Revelation 3:8

I am not technologically adept. In fact, I'm downright scared of most of the stuff. But my job demands I work with some high-tech machines like computers and fax machines and laser printers. One of the things that intrigues me most is the modem, that tiny apparatus which, when linked with my computer and phone line, can magically transfer print from one of my faraway colleagues right onto my screen.

One day, when I was having difficulty with a transmission, I punched a key I'd never punched before. Instantly, the screen lit up with bright purple letters and a border of opened doorways. It seems I had come upon the "Doorway to Unlimited Doors" — and a whole host of options I didn't even know I had!

Often I find myself doing habitual and methodical things. I eat at the same restaurant, frequently ordering the same foods. I read the same authors. I even wear my "favorite" outfits, leaving much of my wardrobe hanging in the closet. But the next time I'm tempted to settle for the commonplace and familiar, I'm going to remember that new doors can open up lots of unexpected pleasures. A book review group at the library could bring me a new friend. Walking a different route may waken my senses to new scenery. And that computer class could teach me to exercise — and maybe even enjoy — my options when it comes to technological *stuff.*

Life is full of doorways leading to new possibilities. I'm going to push open a few new ones today.

Nudge me, Father, when I plod along instead of plow ahead. Help me experience the world of unlimited doors You have placed within my reach.   — Mary Lou Carney

29
FRI
      Be still, and know that I am God....   — Psalm 46:10

Every summer our family trundles up to the High Sierra of California and spends two weeks tucked into a log cabin beside a rushing stream. We call it our "wilderness experience."

Here we can run in fields splattered with Indian paintbrush and buttercups, gather cones from the towering ponderosa pines and listen to the call of the whippoorwill in the twilight. Here our children learned to fish. Here, also, we stopped frozen in our tracks the morning we saw the huge wet paw prints of a bear dripped across the patio to our front door!

Away from alarm clocks, telephones, TV and all the pressure points of the calendar, we have no schedule. We get up when we wake up. We eat when we are hungry. We go to bed when we are tired. We talk less and listen more — to the sounds of the woods, twigs snapping underfoot, squirrels chattering in the trees, the clatter of rain on a sloping tin roof. The Chinese call it "the pause that lets the soul catch up with the body."

Spiritually, our wilderness experience has taught us the importance of bringing that "catch-up pause" down from the mountain so that our body and soul keep sync one with the other. Daily, now, we pause in the frantic busyness of our lives and take a few moments to cultivate an inward stillness. The poet Longfellow called it an inward healing — a time to listen to the voice of God speaking through the quiet.

Take that quiet now, and in your inward stillness may you come into the peace of inward healing.

We take a silence, Lord, where our lips and heart are still and we no longer entertain our own imperfect thoughts. We wait quietly to hear Your voice and know Your will in the silence of our spirits, that we may do Your will and do that only. (Adapted from Henry Wadsworth Longfellow.) — Fay Angus

30
SAT
He causeth his wind to blow, and the waters flow.
— Psalm 147:18

Early one summer morning at Alamitos Bay in California, when seagulls were bobbing up and down on the buoys, my father took me out in our small wooden dinghy for a sailing lesson. I sat next to the tiller and he sat across from me. I already knew how to tack and maneuver the sail. This morning he was teaching me about the wind.

"Look at the flags on the shore, son. See which way they are flying." I looked. "Look at the wake in the water. Which direction are the waves going?" I saw. "Feel the wind on the back of your neck and how it ruffles your hair." I could feel it coming across our port (left) side. "A good sailor can tell which way the wind is blowing in even the lightest breeze."

He handed me the tiller and the mainsheet. I let out the sail and watched the wind fill it like a kite in air. Our wake hissed in the water, and I felt the goodness of being at one with nature. Not fighting the wind, but going with it, harnessing it.

I looked over at Dad and he smiled. And then he said something that I've never forgotten, "The wind is everywhere, son, but you have to find it. It's just like faith in God. When you have it, it can take you anywhere."

Lord, fill me with Your ever-constant breath of life.
— Rick Hamlin

31
SUN

All this is from God, who reconciled us to himself through
Christ and gave us the ministry of reconciliation...
— II Corinthians 5:18 (NIV)

During a visit abroad, I was deeply moved and inspired by a symbol of reconciliation between two former World War II enemies. In Lübeck, Germany, I visited a war memorial that tells a story of a cracked bell and a charred cross. I felt as though I was standing on holy ground.

The Marienkirche (St. Mary's Church) in Lübeck was a target for bombing in World War II in retaliation for the destruction of the cathedral in Coventry, England. The Allies scored a direct hit. As the flames reached the belfry of the church, the bell began to toll wildly, alerting the people. They came from around the countryside to form a bucket brigade to save the rest of the church. In its death throes, the bell fell to the floor below. It remains there today, cracked and silent, its own memorial.

After the war, teams of Christians came to Germany from Allied nations to help rebuild the churches. With them came charred timbers from Coventry Cathedral. In Lübeck, next to the cracked bell, two pieces of wood from Coventry form a simple cross, not unlike the charred cross that stands today in the ruins of the English cathedral, in front of the words "Father forgive."

I tarried there for a long time on that holy ground, thinking about these symbols of faith whose scars tell a story of reconciliation. I thought about all the broken relationships in my life, all of my so-called enemies. If Coventry and Lübeck could do it, if the cracked bell and charred cross can live side by side, then surely I can try.

Lord, wherever You are is holy ground. Wherever You are there
is the possibility for reconciliation. Thank You.   — Diane Komp

Prayer Diary

My Prayer Requests for July:

Healing: John Freitas
           Mr. Tweedle

1.   Gabes daughter, son-in-law & Destiny
          Ron & Betty Baker
Strength for Tammy & family

Salvation: Gabe & Cal   Bill & Lucy
2.   Liz & John   Lori & Buck
                           Sharnna & Harry
       Carol & Bob   Larketa
       Jounna & Danny   Mike & LaDon
3.   Janice & Ken   Dalles
       Mark & Linda   Uncle Doc
       Ronnie   Mary Anne
       Cherrone   Pat
4.   Bruce   Nancy & Ronnie
       Carson   Tom
       Terry Lynn & Allie   Charlie
       Chailie Jr.   Kim
5.   Maria   Art
       Dave   Jay & family

Closer more obedient walk:
6.   Self & George
       Kids & Grandkids
      This country
7.   Our leaders
World revival
New car
8. Free of debt
Work with Lionel
See Lori & family, Cathy & family
9. Guidance & direction for our lives
Be a real servant
JJ & NACO to become God centered

JULY 1994

NACIE Leaders
10. Jews For Jesus Campaigners
Lionel + Aleene

Travel Safety:
11. _____
        Bonnie + Bert
        Richard + Louise
        Harriett + Ed
12. , Family Reunion in Sept. _____
Lift up:
    David + Barbra
13. Merri + Ken _____
    Laurie Gilbert
    Mom
    Durees + Orlando .
14. Marci + Steve + Kids _____
    Tammy + Kent + Kidd
    aunt Gwen
15. Sandy + Allen _____
    Pam + Shelly
    Renee + Carl
16. Moffitt + Oleta _____

17. _____

18. _____

19. _____

20. _____

21._____

22._____

23._____

24._____

25._____

26._____

27._____

28._____

29._____

30._____

31._____

August

S	M	T	W	T	F	S
		1	2	3	4	5	6
7	8	9	10	11	12	13
14	15	16	17	18	19	20
21	22	23	24	25	26	27
28	29	30	31			

GIFTS OF THE SEASON

The Water

Sun-sparkled ripples,
coolness of splashing waves, bring
August's refreshment.

*As vacation time restores my body and mind, Lord,
may Your living waters also renew my spirit.*

1
MON

PRAYER CAN CHANGE YOUR LIFE
Make Prayer Receptive

"Whatever you ask in prayer, believe that you have received it, and it will be yours." — Mark 11:24 (RSV)

"My dad called this morning from Florida," Gloria announces joyfully to our *Prayer Can Change Your Life* study group. "Mother's cancer has disappeared! The doctor can't understand it. Dad was so happy he was crying!"

"Maybe the doctor had the wrong diagnosis," Pam P. comments.

"Perhaps he read the first X-rays wrong," Nancy says.

"Well, I guess the chemotherapy worked. And your mother's positive attitude," I tell Gloria.

There's a moment's quiet thought. Then Gloria asks, "Why do we avoid believing that our prayers are answered?"

All of us have prayed many prayers for her mother's recovery. Now her question calls each of us to account. It's true, we admit, that we didn't really expect our polite prayers for Gloria's mother to be answered this way. We don't really expect *any* of our prayers to be totally and miraculously answered.

As we turn to our well-worn copies of *Prayer Can Change Your Life*, Martha Kay stumbles across an appropriate statement: "We did not know how to receive, and in many cases did not even expect to receive."

"The Bible says," Nancy adds, "that when you pray, you should believe at that moment that you have received."

"I marked this statement in my book," Pam P. says. "'Let your prayer go, let it grow, and give thanks to God.'"

"How strange it is," I say, "that I can look back and see God's hand in my life, see one thing leading to another as God works His will out. And yet every time I look toward tomorrow, I forget to trust. I limit God's effectiveness by denying the possibility that He can and will handle any situation that arises."

We all decide to keep struggling toward a more perfect trust by believing as we pray that God *will* answer each petition that we make. We vow to keep alert for the answers, to recognize them when they come and to give thanks.

Let us give thanks that already as we pray, even before we say *amen*, God is working His way — unfolding tomorrow — on our behalf.

God, everywhere I look I see Your answers to my prayers. Thank You.
— Pam Kidd

$\frac{2}{\text{TUES}}$ *I was young and now I am old, yet I have never seen the righteous forsaken or their children begging bread.*
— Psalm 37:25 (NIV)

As my wife Rosie and I toured the small private college that our daughter Danita might attend, my heart was full. As we walked through its gorgeous stone buildings and beautiful tree-lined grounds, my mind went back to the time my daughter was in ninth grade, trying out for the high school drill team. She came home in tears because none of the black girls was chosen. The next year she tried out again, and again she was turned down. My heart ached to tell her to give up, but she kept trying, and the following year she was accepted.

She brought this same quiet determination to her painful recovery from a degenerative hip disease. And she brought it to her schoolwork, earning the spot as high school valedictorian, the third black in our community to win the honor.

And now we were walking on the campus of a college that in so many ways for so many years was beyond our reach, and this time they were asking Danita to try *them* out.

How thankful I am that my daughter can know of my Father's righteousness, and the opportunities He offers His faithful.

Lord, You are truly righteous and worthy of honor and praise.
— Dolphus Weary

$\frac{3}{\text{WED}}$ *Then God said, "Let there be light"; and there was light.*
— Genesis 1:3 (NAS)

My seven-year-old son Luke has that Tom Sawyer look. Strawberry blond, he is all boy, full of good-natured mischief. But under that skinned-nose toughness is an incredibly sweet disposition.

Last week, Luke and his younger sister Jodi, four, went to the toy store. Luke had earned a few dollars at his corner lemonade stand, and it was burning a hole in his pocket. It didn't take long for him to spend his money, yet he spent every penny of it buying a doll for his sister.

As we walked out of the toy store, I thought, *What a sweet-natured little boy. His kindness will be the key to his future success. I hope the world doesn't snatch it away.* Keeping my thoughts to myself, I patted him on the head and walked silently to the car.

That night, as I tucked Luke into bed, I again reflected quietly on his wonderful gift of sweetness. Suddenly, I knew that I needed to say something. "Luke, it really made Daddy feel good when you spent your hard-earned money on Jodi. You are one of the most thoughtful little boys I have ever known. That is a gift God has given you. And I hope you will be kind and generous all of your life."

Luke smiled bashfully, but he was obviously delighted with my words. I leaned over and kissed him good night, trying to hide the tears in my eyes.

The *spoken word* has power. God created the world through the *spoken word*. "Let there be light!" He said, and there was light. So do we create and shape the nature of one another through our spoken words. When a child is affirmed for his goodness, he grows to be good. When an adult is commended for her kind actions, she becomes kinder yet. Spoken affirmation and encouragement are the gentle hands that create goodness in our world.

Dear God, change my silent thoughts of appreciation into spoken words of inspiration. Amen.
                                                                — Scott Walker

---

$\frac{4}{THURS}$ *Be ye also ready....*   — Matthew 24:44

A couple of years ago, my son Christopher joined a group of young people brought together by the organization Outward Bound for the purpose of climbing Africa's tallest peak, Mt. Kilimanjaro. To get ready for the ascent (over nineteen thousand feet), he went through a lengthy physical conditioning regimen of running, lifting, bicycling and swimming to build himself up. Bodybuilders have an expression, *hardgaining*, to describe the process of strengthening their muscles, and that is just what Chris went through to get ready for his climb. But it all paid off. Hard work provided him with the stamina needed, and he reached the summit successfully.

Once I heard an experienced marathon runner explain why he had dropped out barely halfway through the twenty-six-mile race. "I didn't have time to get myself in top shape," he explained. "I wasn't adequately prepared." Having won previous marathons, he knew he would have to work harder next time. Rather than berate himself, his ability or talent, however, he analyzed the problem and pinpointed the fault.

Too often when we fail to scale metaphorical mountains or finish a race, we tell ourselves it was because of personal inadequacies — our looks, our brains, our physiques, our background, our social status — when lack of preparation may be the major rub. Before a baby walks, it crawls; before a flower blooms, it buds; and before a Christian develops an indomitable faith, he or she usually experiences "hard-gaining" times of uncertainty and doubt. Faith in ourselves has a prerequisite: faith in the One by Whom we were "fearfully and wonderfully made" (Psalm 139:14).

> *Strengthen our souls, God, so when tested,*
> *We'll know a power that can't be bested.*
>
> — Fred Bauer

5
FRI *This book of the law shall not depart out of thy mouth...for then thou shalt make thy way prosperous....* — Joshua 1:8

For almost seventy years, I have tried to convince people that if they live by the principles of the Bible, their lives will be successful ones. The stories I hear of this working out continue to amaze me.

A man came up to me at a conference last year and told me that he had followed my advice with some surprising results. It seems he had lost his job and the only work he could find was driving a milk delivery truck. Soon he ran into a problem because in June, in Georgia, sales of milk and dairy products drop off. Just about that time, the company added a line of fruit punch to try to boost sales. But there was lots of competition in the soft drink market.

"I was reading my Bible," the man said, "and I came across the verse that says, 'All things work together for good to them that love God' [Romans 8:28]. I knew I loved God, so I was sure that something good was going to happen. Then one morning the thought came to me, *Where could I sell this fruit punch that no one has thought of selling it before?*

"Well, in the first town I drove into I saw a big hardware store. I went right in and told the manager that I'd like to sell fruit punch at the front of his store. In fact, I told him I wanted to bring a barrel of ice and fill it with fruit punch.

"He thought I was crazy, but let me go ahead. By the next morning, orders were going out for more punch! It seems people got so hot doing repair work that they were thirsty when they came into the hardware store for supplies. Again and again they'd buy not just a container of punch, but sometimes a whole case to take home.

"So what you said about having successful lives by believing in Scripture really works, Dr. Peale!"

Well, you know, after hearing his story I wasn't so amazed after all. In all my years as a minister, I've never heard that God's promises have failed the honest seeker. And my guess is that I'll keep on hearing posi-

tive, astounding stories of people who came upon success through faith
and hard work. And so will you.

*Lord, thank You for the power of Your Word to change lives. Give
us a strong faith and belief to trust Your guidance every day.
Amen.*   —Norman Vincent Peale

$\frac{6}{SAT}$ And God saw that it was good.   ﹨ —Genesis 1:18

It was the simplest of structures: one room, with glassless screened windows and hinged boards to let down in case of rain, bunk beds and a
picnic table. Outside was a fire pit with a metal grill, outdoor restrooms
and a pump. The Marriott it was not! Yet my friends and I found it wonderfully refreshing and renewing.

We stood outside as night came on and watched the stars being born.
How much more clear and bright they seemed, undimmed by glow
from city lights. And what fun we had talking into the wee hours,
zipped into our sleeping bags, falling asleep to the sounds of crickets
and the flowing waters of the nearby creek, then waking up to sunrise
and birdsong.

Most of the time, I'm insulated from God's natural world by air conditioning, central heating, and airtight windows and doors. Now, after
experiencing the sights and sounds of a gentle summer night and dawn-
ing day, I feel linked again to that wonderful creation story of God flinging the stars across the night sky and speaking the world into being.
It's a link I intend to preserve, by opening my windows on summer
nights, by moving my bed close to the window so I can watch the night
sky, by stepping out into the yard to greet the morning, and by doing
everything I can to protect and preserve this precious, fragile earth we
all share.

*Loving Creator, let my actions this day express reverence for this
gentle home You have created, so that when evening comes, I
may join in Your resounding pronouncement: "It is good."*
                                          —Marilyn Morgan Helleberg

$\frac{7}{SUN}$ And be it indeed that I have erred, mine error remaineth
with myself.   —Job 19:4

I was driving with my family through New York State on my way home
from a visit with relatives who live in Canada.

It was a Sunday afternoon. The interstate highway was nearly empty. I was peacefully driving when I saw in my rearview mirror flashing red lights. The first thing the police officer asked when he stepped up to my window was, "Do you know why I am stopping you?"

I not only clearly knew, but I apologized and admitted my guilt. Yes, I was driving over the speed limit. The policeman, who was very nice, said with a bit of sadness, "I'll have to give you a ticket."

"Of course. I'm sorry, officer."

Everyone makes mistakes — but trying to avoid them or cover them up distorts our lives with a heavy burden of guilt. Somehow, at that moment I realized that instead of arguing or making excuses I had to admit my error, take responsibility and make amends. As I continued down the highway, I drove not only at a safe and legal speed, but with a much lighter heart.

I wondered, *What helped me to do the right thing?* I think it may have been those three children in the backseat listening — and looking to me as an example.

Lord, I was wrong. I'm sorry. Help me to make the necessary amends. Amen.   — Christopher de Vinck

 When a Child Grows Up
A SEASON OF CHANGE

In every family, that delicate relationship between a parent and child undergoes dramatic changes over the years. In this six-day series, a most sensitive moment — when a young person leaves home — is captured by Linda Ching Sledge and her college-bound son Timothy. Let's listen to mother and son's firsthand discoveries about themselves and each other during a season of change.   — The Editors

8
MON

Day One — Remembering the Moments

"The Lord watch between you and me, when we are absent one from the other."   — Genesis 31:49 (RSV)

Tomorrow, my eighteen-year-old son Tim leaves home for college. What does a mother of a grown-up son remember while he packs his gear and cleans out the old station wagon in preparation for the trip to come?

I remember a day in spring long ago. Two-year-old Tim is running across the lawn straight to me, his chubby legs churning, his brown curls dancing. He wears a white vest embroidered with a red heart that his grandmother has given him, and his hazel eyes are bright with mischief, for he is playing a game of his own devising. In the next second, he will veer away from my open arms. Now he is racing away from me to a nearby maple tree, laughing with delight, then to the tree beyond, challenging himself to run as far from me as he dares. Back and forth he runs as I call to him, in and out of my embrace, always choosing his own moment of departure and return.

Then it is time to go home, and I catch him up, wriggling and squealing, into my arms. I smell the sweet, apple scent of his cheeks, wishing I could cherish and protect him forever. I promise myself that I will remember this moment as long as I can.

Sixteen years later, I do remember — flesh of my flesh, bone of my bone — now that Tim is tall and strong and about to venture beyond the farthest maple tree to a place where he cannot hear me call. My heart races in panic — *who will care for him? Who will help him in time of need? Who will be there for him at the first sign of trouble or distress?* And I remember, too, that the God Who knows the number of hairs on my head and every sparrow that falls to the ground (Matthew 10:29–31), also knows each heartbeat of concern I have for my loved ones. He will not fail us.

Lord, whenever I fear losing those whom I love most, remind me that You are before, behind and beside them, keeping them in Your care. Amen.   — Linda Ching Sledge

---

$\dfrac{9}{TUES}$ *HOUSE GUEST*
Day Two — Savoring the Friendships

There are friends who pretend to be friends, but there is a friend who sticks closer than a brother.
— Proverbs 18:24 (RSV)

On an October Sunday, I joined hundreds of nervous college freshmen at the doors of the fraternities for the annual rush season. I had only gotten close to a couple of guys at my dorm. Surely, I believed, finding friends would be faster and easier at a frat. I was immediately attracted to one fraternity in a stately brick building with ivy crawling on its walls and a lazy beagle on the doorstep.

By "bid night" in November, I was among the few still in the running. I had tried my best to dress like the "brothers," to laugh at their jokes and echo their opinions, so I was sure things would be going my way. But midnight came and went without any word from them.

At 3:30 A.M., two guys with frat pins knocked softly at my bedroom door. "You didn't make it," they told me politely. "But, hey, you're still cool."

I awoke the next morning to rage and confusion. *What was wrong with me? Did I say or wear the wrong things? Wasn't I cool enough?* I spent the day feeling like a total reject and avoiding my dorm buddies.

Sometime that evening, I heard feet kicking at my door. I knew it was the guys from the floor below, because they never knocked, only kicked. The door burst open, and my two friends tumbled in, laughing, pushing, insulting each other good-naturedly.

"You weren't at dinner," they accused. "C'mon, let's grab a pizza."

Why hadn't I realized how famished I was? There was just time enough to grab my favorite jacket, the blue one with the torn pocket, and stuff my hair under a baseball cap. Together the three of us strolled into the cool autumn night, arguing loudly about what kind of pizza to order and savoring the richness of our growing friendship.

Lord, You don't always give us the friends we want; instead You give us the friends we need.   — Timothy Sledge

10 Day Three — Becoming an Encourager

WED *"No, I will not abandon you or leave you as orphans in the storm — I will come to you."*   — John 14:18 (TLB)

In the first two lonely months of college, Tim called home often for advice. I urged him to find a congenial group to make his adjustment to campus life easier. Finally, in early November, he phoned with good news.

"I'm rushing a fraternity. We're down to the last fifty guys, and the 'brothers' say I have a great chance of getting in. I'll know for sure Sunday night after the voting."

"Terrific," I replied, feeling my own spirits soar at his excitement. "Call me when the votes are in."

Yet Sunday night came, and Tim did not call. Monday and Tuesday passed the same way. It wasn't until Wednesday that the phone rang.

"I didn't get in," he said, sounding tired and strained.

Although the news was no surprise, I still felt his disappointment as keenly as if someone had slammed a fist into my stomach. My mother instinct warned me to tread carefully, but unwisely I blurted out, "You didn't call!"

"No," he replied carefully. "I needed to work things out by myself."

He didn't need me? Me? His mother! Who had picked him up when he fell? Who had wiped away his childhood tears and listened to his boyhood laments? Reproachful words rose to my lips, but before I could utter them, he said, "I just signed up to audition for a men's barbershop chorus. Two hundred other guys are trying, too...." More wistfully he added, "You think I've got a chance?"

I heard the need in his voice. This time I heeded my mother instinct, which told me exactly what to say. "Go for it! And call me when the votes are in."

Lord, we cannot soften life's blows for those we love. Assure us, nevertheless, that we are always needed to encourage. To affirm. To lift them when they fall.   — Linda Ching Sledge

11
THURS

Day Four — Honoring the Privacy

"Go into your room, close the door and pray to your Father, who is unseen...."   — Matthew 6:6 (NIV)

Tim, who is home for college break, is in his room with the door shut playing his guitar; he is upset at — who knows what? — a girl, perhaps, or college, or maybe even me. As he sings, his voice cracks with youthful emotion, and I hear again my own long-ago frustration at a world I was sure did not understand me.

I want so much to walk through the door in order to soften whatever pain has driven him to such sad music. I touch the doorknob. His fingers strike a chord...and my hand drops away.

What right do I have to interrupt his solitary song? I myself have sat behind a similarly closed door, overwhelmed temporarily by some burden. With my loved ones waiting on the other side, I would read, rest, pray until strength and understanding returned and I could open the door to them again.

My heart aching, I turn to go downstairs, and grant him what he needs and desires: time-out with God.

Lord, when our loved ones seek solace alone with You, give us the wisdom not to intrude, trusting that they will open their hearts to us again. — Linda Ching Sledge

<u>12</u>
FRI

HOUSE GUEST
Day Five — Releasing the Love

He who loves his brother abides in the light, and in it there is no cause for stumbling. — I John 2:10 (RSV)

My little brother Geoffrey was only ten years old when I went off to college. Overnight, it seemed, our relationship had shrunk to a few moments on the phone every week. Gone were the video game contests, the ice cream feasts, the pillow fights during commercials for Saturday cartoons.

On the phone, he was shy and unsure, as if he were talking to a stranger. One night, he signed off saying, "Good-bye, and thank you for your time."

Why would my little brother have to thank me for my time?

Worried that I was losing his love, I asked my parents to make a special trip so Geoffrey could spend the night in my dorm room. When he arrived, he seemed taller, older, more serious. He refused any help carrying his suitcase, preferring to drag it up three flights himself. As he was unpacking, I saw that Mom had put his favorite stuffed animal, a big fuzzy fish named Mr. Whale, into his bag. Geoffrey indignantly insisted he had never seen it before.

He sat on my bed, trying so hard to be grown-up, yet not knowing what to say.

I couldn't stand it! So I did the wildest thing I could think of. I picked up a pillow and whacked him over the head. And suddenly, Geoffrey was laughing and shouting and beating the daylights out of me with Mr. Whale.

For one glorious weekend, never were the pillow fights fiercer, nor the ice cream sweeter, nor two brothers closer.

Dear Lord, sometimes we forget the simplest thing about love. To get it, give it — wildly, joyfully, abundantly! — Timothy Sledge

13 Day Six — Cherishing the Uniqueness
___
SAT *Sons are a heritage from the Lord, children a reward from him.*   — Psalm 127:3 (NIV)

I guess because I've always been one myself, I love "nerds" — those shy, quiet types more at home with books than people. While he was growing up, Tim was a lot like me, I'd tell people. Or so I thought, until the sweet, gangly bookworm I had raised to teenagehood suddenly turned into a social butterfly!

Overnight, my home changed from a quiet sanctuary into a bustling summer hangout for the home-from-college crowd. Now I wake up some mornings to hear the phone ringing off the hook with customers for his summer house-painting business. At lunchtime, he and his pals will be noisily cooking spaghetti in my kitchen with the radio blasting cacophonous sounds. At night, they are hauling amplifiers and electric guitars into the TV room and playing rock music until midnight.

When I saw my neighbor in the supermarket recently, I was overwhelmed with anxious thoughts. What would she make of the noisy parade of youngsters? Of the raucous music? Of the paint cans littering the yard? But before I ducked past, she nabbed me in the pasta-and-sauces aisle.

"Congratulations!" she exclaimed.

"What for?" I blurted out suspiciously.

"Your terrific son!" she declared. "His painting business has kept seven kids employed this summer! And the recreation center's hired his band to play next week. Shy little Timmy's grown up to be a leader!"

I gave her a sheepish grin, and began to pull items off the shelves: six packages of spaghetti, three jars of sauce, two pizza shells. Enough to hold my son, the nerd-turned-leader, and his enterprising crew for at least half a day. After all, I told myself, a young man who works as hard as he does needs food to keep leading.

Lord, help me to cherish my children for who they are, not for what I expect them to be. And let me support their dreams, too, through all their seasons of change.   — Linda Ching Sledge

14 *Let us give thanks, by which we offer to God an acceptable*
___
SUN *worship with reverence and awe.* — Hebrews 12:28 (NRSV)

If you lived near me, you could learn a lot about tending God's creation.

To get to my country home, I have to drive along a winding road lined with exotic plantings and inhabited by strange animals.

One of my neighbors spent the whole summer cultivating his garden and planting a new border of witches'-broom shrubs for all of us to enjoy. The first weekend, one of his new shrubs disappeared. A little farther down the road lives a new "neighbor" — a wild turkey who has moved into our woods. On a pleasant day, she thinks nothing of sitting down in the center of the road to enjoy a midday sunbath. The first time I saw her, I was driving a bit faster than usual and nearly ran her down. Within one block, two endangered species!

But I don't see the situation as hopeless. The gardener replaced the shrub and planted a large, clearly worded sign: SHAME ON YOU. Six weeks have passed and his garden — our garden — remains inviolate. And our turkey-lady is still out there strutting and sunning. She has not changed her ways at all, but I have changed mine. I'm careful to obey the posted speed limit on our country road.

I think about the missing witches'-broom and the predictably unpredictable turkey, and I realize that there is hope for all endangered species if each of us will do our part. I can start on my own country road. Reverence and respect for nature is a lesson that is best taught one plant and one wild turkey at a time.

Creator God, I thank You that You have treated me with respect and reverence. Teach me to do the same to all of Your creation.
— Diane Komp

15
MON
This has been my practice....   — Psalm 119:56 (NIV)

When a friend asked, "How's your American Sign Language study going?" my face fell.

"I'm afraid I'm not keeping up with it," I said. "I really miss it, but I have no time. What with school, and my two part-time jobs and all."

He smiled. "Do you have five minutes a day?" he asked.

I laughed. "Who doesn't have just five minutes a day? But that's hardly enough to keep practicing a subject."

My friend shook his head. "I used to be an 'all-or-nothing' person. But now I've become a 'some-is-better-than-nothing' person! When I felt I didn't have time for my Bible study, I did a little math. That told me that just five minutes a day is thirty-five minutes a week, which equals eighteen hundred and twenty minutes a year. That's over thirty hours! I reread quite a few books of the Bible in thirty hours. Surely, that's enough time for you to learn a few more signs?"

Thirty hours! I smiled, then shaped my hand into a fist and then moved it as if I were knocking at a door.

"What does that mean?" my friend asked.

"That means 'yes, yes, yes!'"

God, is there a task I think I don't have time for? Please help me become a "some-is-better-than-nothing" person, and work on that task for five minutes, starting today! — Linda Neukrug

---

16 *And the Lord shall guide thee continually....*
TUES   — Isaiah 58:11

I'm a basketball fan. When Larry Bird, one of my heroes, retired in August 1992, after thirteen years with the Boston Celtics, he had played in 1,100 games, helped to establish 541 home-court sellouts and led the team to three national championships. At thirty-five, he was leaving an occupation that he loved. He was retiring because a painful back prevented his continuing.

At the noon press conference Larry said, "I'm joking to keep from crying. I didn't want to go out like this."

I felt Larry's anguish. Twelve years ago, I agonized over retirement. Like Larry, my skills as a technical writer were valued and needed. I loved my work, and I worked hard, but I knew that fatigue had lessened my performance, threatened my health and disrupted my home. I had to let go. My career was over. Yet, in my heart, I felt I was quitting, and that hurt!

Surprisingly, retirement became a joy. Frank Seluk, a friend of mine in the retirement group I joined, gave me some "retirement guidelines":

> *One needs direction and purpose.*
> *One must accept change.*
> *One must remain curious.*
> *One must communicate.*
> *One must remain confident.*
> *One must be committed.*

This list has helped me. Interests that were put on the side during my career now get to be fully realized — watching my grandkids participate in sports, long walks with my wife Ruby and stacking up the books I never had time to read.

Letting go is difficult, no doubt. But when you see change — whether it's retirement, a move, a broken relationship — as a movement into something new and not an end in and of itself, then it makes the transition that much easier, that much more exciting.

Larry, this is for you. Thanks for all of those dazzling performances. And this is also for you, my dear reader-friend, as the changes in life sweep you along toward God's awaiting blessings.

Heavenly Father, You opened my eyes to see letting go is making room for Your gifts to enter.   — Oscar Greene

Quiet Time

O God of peace, who has taught us that in returning and rest we shall be saved, in quietness and in confidence shall be our strength: By the might of thy Spirit lift us, we pray thee, to thy presence, where we may be still and know that thou art God; through Jesus Christ our Lord. Amen.

— from *The Book of Common Prayer*

17 *The wise heart will know the proper time and procedure.*
WED   — Ecclesiastes 8:5 (NIV)

It was a gorgeous August day, but I hardly noticed. As I hurried down the driveway to the mailbox, I checked my watch. So much to do today! Pick up the dry cleaning, stop by the travel agency, buy stamps, balance my checkbook, call my church committee members....

Suddenly, a burst of butterflies erupted in front of me, their wings fanning the air in a kaleidoscope of color. Startled, I paused — and then smiled, remembering the day my daughter Amy Jo, then only three, came rushing inside, breathless with excitement. "Flutter-byes, Mommy. There's flutter-byes all over the yard!" As I reached into the mailbox, I watched the butterflies disappear into an adjacent field. So beautiful. Gone so quickly. I almost missed seeing them at all.

What other things am I missing in my hurry? I wondered. How long had it been since I'd taken time to share a bowl of popcorn — and some real conversation — with my son Brett? What was it my elderly neighbor Katie had said in response to my glib, "How are you?" How many "quick menus" had my husband Gary endured good-naturedly in the last few weeks?

So I'm working harder these days on *unhurrying* my schedule. I'll take time to touch Katie's hand when she talks to me about her problems and ask concerned questions. Brett and I have a Ping-Pong game scheduled for later this week. It's been so long — I wonder if I can still beat him? And won't Gary be surprised to come home to a dinner celebration of freshly baked ham and real mashed potatoes?

It's not easy to slow down, but I don't want important moments to "flutter-bye" while I'm hurrying along.

Thank You, Father, for the gift of time. With Your help, I'll balance daily duties with the beauty and joy of every moment.
— Mary Lou Carney

18
THURS

And he said…put off thy shoes from off thy feet, for the place whereon thou standest is holy ground.
— Exodus 3:5

I can see it as though it were yesterday. Blue paint is flaking off the front porch, stuffing is coming out of the chaise longue, the white chenille bedspread is so worn the pattern has disappeared. Sand clogs the bathroom drain, the hall light flickers on and off (pound the middle of the wall to keep it on), the bedroom bureau is missing a handle on the bottom drawer.

It's a beach house we rented for two weeks every summer in my youth, and again and again I return to it in my mind. There beneath the stairs is where we stored the dinghy in which I learned how to sail. Sitting on that lumpy chaise longue, I painted my first seascape. Precious shells and starfish I kept in the bedroom bureau drawer — until their odor gave them away. Lying on that chenille bedspread, I finished reading my first favorite book, *The Yearling* by Marjorie Kinnan Rawlings. And at night as the hall light flickered on and off, I listened to the ocean waves pounding on the jetty and felt the presence of a God more powerful than the sea.

I like to think of this place in my memory as a sacred place. You must have one, too, reminding you of the simple things you once loved. Go there when you feel lost. It's holy ground.

Dear Lord, let me treasure Your peace found in the memories I've stored.   — Rick Hamlin

___

19
FRI

It is not for you to know the times or the seasons, which the Father hath put in his own power.   — Acts 1:7

Once we were hiking on the Appalachian Trail — my wife Shirley, four kids and I — and it was getting dark. Though we had a tent, the rocky trail was not an inviting mattress, so we pressed on toward a wooden shelter that our guidebook said was not far. But as the shadows fell longer, it seemed farther and farther away, our knapsacks heavier and heavier. Then it started to rain. Still we pressed on...up a steep grade, down a jagged blade, over a fallen tree, through a boot-sogging creek.

Finally, in the fading light and distant mist, the silhouette of the three-sided lean-to came into view, and the kids gave a resounding cheer. After we had eaten hot stew, gotten into some dry clothes and climbed into warm sleeping bags on the smooth wooden floor, we laughed at our ordeal. "It's a good thing I didn't know how far away this place was," my daughter Laraine ventured, "or I'd have given up before the creek."

I've thought about her comment in the years since. How many times would I have given up on some undertaking, some goal, some assignment, if I'd have known the full price, the whole distance, the total time and effort? Isak Dinesen, the author of the best-selling book *Out of Africa*, once wrote that God made bends in roads because He didn't want us to see too far ahead. I think she may have had it right.

Teach us, God, that growth requires
Perseverence in all life's fires.   — Fred Bauer

___

20
SAT

Even though the fig trees have no fruit and no grapes grow on the vines...I will still be joyful and glad....
                                        — Habakkuk 3:17–18 (GNB)

It was a total disaster.

I love working my little garden plot out behind the college where I teach, and this particular year my garden was a showpiece. Mounds of fat, fragrant cantaloupe. Tall rows of creamy sweet corn. Plump beefsteak tomatoes next to teepees of baby lima beans. The entire plot surrounded with giant Russian sunflowers. It would soon be ready to harvest, so I took a few snapshots of the garden for my records.

I had to leave town for a few days, and when I returned, I found the garden in ruins. Coons had ravaged the corn. Some animal ate large cavities out of the cantaloupe. Worms and bugs banqueted on the tomatoes and beans, and some pranksters smashed the pumpkins. Only the sunflowers survived.

"It's a total disaster," I said to my daughter Teresa, who was surveying the damage with me.

"Not so," she argued. "You had loads of fun growing it."

"Well, *yes, but....*"

"And it was beautiful — you have pictures to prove it."

"*Yes, but....*"

"And the birds will go wild over the sunflower seeds. You see, it wasn't a *total* loss."

I think each of us could use someone like Teresa to remind us that seldom is any failure a total and complete failure.

That business deal fell through, but it left you with some new contacts. You dented your car, but you're a more careful driver now. Your thoughtlessness cost you a friend, but it also caused you to grow up....

Lord, keep me from watering my woes and fertilizing my failures. Help me to focus on what's left, not what's gone.

— Daniel Schantz

21
SUN

PRACTICING THE POWER OF PRAYER
Faith-Picture Prayers

But when ye pray, use not vain repetitions....

— Matthew 6:7

I have a list of people I pray for stuck in the back of my Bible on an index card. They're all categorized — the sick in one section, the searching or unbelieving, the ones with certain material needs. Yet for all my organization, I used to find myself droning, "Lord, be with Tom. Be with Joan...." *If it even bored me what must God think?*

Then, among some old letters and clippings my mom sent me last year, I found a yellowed article that she had cut out of a Texas newspaper long before she and Dad were even married, many years before anyone knew there would be a Kathie who would grow up to be an artist. In part, it read:

"Sometime during the day make a special prayer for those you want to help. If they are ill, picture them with Christ by their side, taking their hand, putting new strength into them. If they are miserable, imagine them with joy gradually filling their hearts. They may not know why, but things will soon look less black, and they will realize that Jesus Christ is by their side. If they are getting cynical or going downhill or being fiercely tempted, a different picture can be made. Make your own pictures — become an artist in praying."

With damp eyes, I read this bit of studio-wisdom. Here I was an artist, using no creativity at all in my prayers.

But now I am trying to hone my artistic skills as a pray-er. "Lord," I offer, "I ask and see Jenny in less pain this day. I see her enjoying her food. I see Jack with a new awareness of Your presence. I ask that he be drawn into the circle of Your irresistible love. I see Jack letting go of those old barriers."

I think my keener "eye" has me spending a little more time with each request, and has increased my interest. After all, art should never be boring.

Dear Lord, please transform my faith-pictures into loving prayer-answers for those who need Your touch today.
                                                        — Kathie Kania

---

22
MON
You saw me before I was born and scheduled each day of my life before I began to breathe.... — Psalm 139:16 (TLB)

Holding our new little grandson, delighting in the wonder of tiny hands, button-nose and eyes blinking in the unaccustomed light of a bright new world, my heart skipped a beat as I thought, *If only my mother could have seen him.*

Just two years before, I had held Mother's frail body in my arms and whispered the gentle reassurance, "Don't be afraid, Mummy darling. You are going right from my arms into the arms of Jesus. He is waiting for you, and when you see Him, tell Him how much I love Him."

With a quiet little, "Oh!" as though surprised by some angelic light, she went limp in my arms and into the presence of her Lord.

Life taken. Now I was holding *life given*.

I was reminded of the story I'd heard of another new baby. "Come," said the young father, taking his four-year-old daughter by the hand and leading her to the nursery, where they had just tucked in her brand-new baby brother. "Come and say hello!"

The little girl pulled back. "I want to see him all by myself."

Both parents looked at each other, eyebrows raised. "You mean no one else in the room with you?" they asked with some concern.

She nodded, curls bouncing in agreement.

With some hesitation, they let her into the nursery alone, watching and listening carefully from around the corner of the doorway. Standing on tiptoe, leaning over the bassinet, she patted the baby. "Tell me...tell me quick," she whispered, "what does God look like? I've forgotten!"

Father, it is in the sacred moments of birth and death that we feel Your presence most deeply. Thank You that You are with me in my ordinary moments, too.
— Fay Angus

23

TUES

HOUSE GUEST

In the way of righteousness there is life; along that path is immortality.
— Proverbs 12:28 (NIV)

As the boat bumped against the dock the captain announced, "We sail back promptly at three."

Our family had just arrived at South Manitou Island off the northeast shore of Lake Michigan. My two-year-old daughter Elizabeth and I strolled to a nearby beach while my husband Alex set out on a six-mile hike leading to a sand dune overlooking a famous shipwreck and ending in the Valley of the Giants, a rare grove of virgin white cedar trees.

The afternoon passed quickly. Soon Elizabeth and I shuffled behind a line of boarding passengers. Just in time Alex came jogging down the dock. Between breaths he said, "I barely made it. It took longer than I expected."

"How much of the shipwreck could you see?"

"None. I skipped it. I didn't have time to see both sights so I kept going to the Valley of the Giants." Walking among the towering cedars, which existed before the arrival of Columbus, he knew he had chosen best. He added, "I saw life instead of death."

When we returned home, his words came back to me as I made daily choices. On days with few quiet moments, I, too, have a choice: I can read the newspaper or my Bible. After supper, we can watch a TV sit-com or enjoy a family walk. I can dwell on an unpleasant interaction with someone or forgive. In short, I can stare at a sunken ship or stroll among the living cedars.

Lord, please help me choose today what will point me toward You. — Mary Brown

24
WED
For God hath not given us the spirit of fear; but of power, and of love, and of a sound mind. — II Timothy 1:7

For years, I suffered from a terrible fear of snakes. Mine began as a child when an older playmate teased me with a garter snake. I couldn't bear even the word in a book; a picture was a horror. When we sum-mered at our cabin on Lake Jackson in Virginia, I lived in misery lest my anathema appear. I even made the children wear boots lest they step on one outdoors.

Meanwhile the children's enthusiasm for all living things, whether they flew, swam, hopped or crawled, drew me into their world. When our four-year-old Melanie ran up excitedly carrying a twining length of living ribbon, I managed not to scream, stopped by the sheer delight on her face. *I must not curse her with my phobia,* I thought.

After that, little by little, the V-shaped silver patterns that an occa-sional water snake drew in its gentle course became a source of pleasure instead of horror. I could even study a snake book with the family, so we'd know the poisonous ones if they ever came around. We learned that blacksnakes are actually friends — they keep down rats and other rodents. More importantly, harmful snakes are seldom found in a black-snake's territory. So when a fine stout blacksnake adopted our point of land one summer, it actually gave me a sense of security.

I learned to appreciate what I had once feared. Such fears are false. If you have such a fear, you can overcome it, too. It's a slow process; it takes both the will and the desire to learn. But when you do, it's like discovering this beautiful world anew.

Dear God, I know You have a reason for every form of life You create. Help me to respect and honor that life, whatever form it takes — even when I don't understand why it's here.
— Marjorie Holmes

25 *Whosoever drinketh of the water that I shall give him*
——— *shall never thirst....*   —John 4:14
THURS

When I want to get away from the world and close to God, my favorite hideout is a retreat center near my Arizona home called Canaan in the Desert. I can easily spend an hour walking through the small prayer garden, a beautiful, quiet trail lined with blooming desert plants.

At the end of the trail is a fountain unlike any I've seen. Water tumbles off a huge pedestal into a seven-sided pool, and on each side are words inlaid in tile: *Father of Comfort, Goodness, Faithfulness, Patience, Grace, Love* and *Mercy.* Above each phrase is a spigot, and a paper cup dispenser sits nearby.

On one of my first visits, I was standing by the fountain feeling the cool mist spray my face, when a small boy and his mother approached. The little boy grabbed a cup and began walking around the fountain, carefully pouring a little water from each spigot and drinking. His mother chuckled and said to me, "He wants to drink from every one."

So do I, I thought. Suddenly, prayer became so simple. When I come to God, I can ask for what I need, then drink from the cup He offers and let Him fill me with His refreshing mercies. It helps me to visualize that image now when I pray. "Cool me off with patience, Lord," I might pray silently, when I'm about to lose my temper. "Quench my fears with Your comfort," when Ross, my little boy, is ill. "Fill me up with Your grace," when I've acted thoughtlessly toward my husband Paul and I'm feeling quite unlovable. Sometimes I even take a drink of cool water to remind myself that when I ask God for a taste of His goodness, He offers it in abundance to refresh and strengthen my soul.

Lord, when I don't know how to pray, remind me that it's as easy as asking You for a cool drink on a hot summer day.
                                                     —Gina Bridgeman

26 *And rejoice with the wife of thy youth.*   —Proverbs 5:18
———
FRI

As our twenty-fifth wedding anniversary approached last year, my husband Lynn and I found ourselves buried in all sorts of work deadlines and projects. "Maybe we'll just go out to dinner or do something quiet," I wearily told an older friend.

"Oh, you have to *make a celebration*," she urged, "to mark the importance of this milestone for your children *and* yourselves."

Her words kept coming back to me over the next couple of weeks, but I still felt reluctant. Planning a celebration seemed like lots of work and worry. Yet, with the encouragement and help of Derek, twenty, Lindsay, nineteen, and Kendall, fifteen, Lynn and I began planning a backyard reception and sent invitations to the friends who have been important to us in the last twenty-five years.

As the date approached, I still worried about the possibility of rain and whether we'd forgotten to invite anyone and whether we'd have enough food. But when the day finally arrived, we had a great party, complete with a spectacular sunset, music for dancing, plenty of cake, and a toast from Derek who bravely stood up in front of all the guests to *thank* us for getting married and giving them a living example of the word *commitment*.

Looking back, I'm thankful for the advice to *make a celebration*, in spite of the work and worries, because we made a permanently pleasant memory of the importance of our silver anniversary. Do you have a birthday, baptism, graduation or any other milestone coming up? *Make a celebration* — it's a good way to mark its importance and publicly thank God for the good things He gives us.

Father, may we always celebrate Your goodness and the special people and milestones that make up our lives. —Carol Kuykendall

27
SAT
HOUSE GUEST
"He will turn...the hearts of children to their fathers...."
— Malachi 4:6 (RSV)

"Brock," my dad begins as he casts his line out onto the mirrored surface of Lake Weiss. It's late afternoon and we are out in the little red fishing boat that Mom bought a few years ago, thinking to surprise us. "About the car," Dad continues as he reels his line back.

I knew that my parents had hoped to help me buy a car by my junior year in college. Hitching rides back and forth to school was getting more difficult, and working part-time off-campus with no transportation was a pain. But summer was almost over, and I knew the car wasn't to be. It had been a summer of unexpected expenses. Medical and dental bills, car repairs (our family's newest car had more than a hundred thousand miles on it), a broken water heater one month, a broken air conditioner the next. August was here, and the savings account held just enough to get me back in school. No more.

So here we were, Mom, Dad, Keri and I, spending a few vacation days at a cabin in Leesburg, Alabama. None of us had mentioned the car till now.

Long ago, my father made the choice to give his life to God. Being a minister has brought a lot of rewards, but a huge salary is not one of them. Sometimes it's hard to see Dad rejoicing when others describe their fancy vacations, country homes and their two cars. It's hard because I know how much he would love to give us those things...how much it hurts because he can't.

"Dad," I answer, looking out on the horizon where the sun is just beginning to set, "remember when Mom bought us this boat, she was so proud that she got it for a hundred dollars." We laughed, remembering our first horrified glimpse of the strange, too-small, too-slow boat, which Dad teasingly named Thunder. "A big fancy bass boat couldn't ever replace the good times we've had in old Thunder. You know, Dad, there are lots of things more important than a car. Some of them you can't buy. Why, I wouldn't trade this time with you for any car in the world," I say.

I hope he understands. Because I have spoken the truth.

God, help us to never lose sight of the things in our lives that really matter *the most.* Amen.   —Brock Kidd

28 *For you did not receive a spirit that makes you a slave*
SUN *again to fear, but you received the Spirit of sonship....*
—Romans 8:15 (NIV)

Can you remember your childhood fears, like being afraid of the dark? Today, my own children are still afraid of the dark, the furnace in the basement, the sounds of the wind pressing between the cracks in the windows.

I remember being afraid of bats when I was a youngster. My grandmother would sit outside reading on the evening summer lawn. The bats would flap their wings and zigzag above us chasing mosquitoes.

My older brother Bruno had the idea of throwing stones into the air. One bat, thinking the stones were insects, dove down, swooped among us and zoomed within inches of Grandmother. She screamed, the newspaper flew in the air, and I ran into the house calling my father. "They're after us!"

Of course, most bats are harmless. I know now that they are far more interested in eating gnats and hanging upside down in caves than in carrying grandmothers or little boys off to the dark woods.

I've learned — through bats and other things — that often what I fear is what I do not understand. One way to disarm a fear is to face it head-on and examine it closely. For instance, you might find that fear of a big city is really about being in different surroundings. And you might discover that the cosmopolitan atmosphere of a city can open you to new people and experiences. Or that your fear of a career change is really about not succeeding. Maybe taking a college course or talking to professionals in that field can help boost your confidence.

In other words, whatever your fear, the more you know about it and can do something about it, the sooner you can enjoy what you used to fear.

Lord, help me to understand and face my fear, and see what's positive that awaits me on the other side. —Christopher de Vinck

29
MON
He got into the boat with them....   — Mark 6:51 (RSV)

A friend and I recently canoed down Nebraska's Niobrara River. It's a beautiful, day-long trip on mostly gentle waters that pass by sparkling waterfalls along the river's rocky banks. Golden eagles fly overhead while deer and buffalo graze on hillsides. My friend Curt manned the rear of the canoe, while I paddled from the front.

The course starts out at an easy pace, but a couple of hours into the trip, the speed of the water picks up, swirling into rapids that cause the currents to keep shifting. Suddenly, it's necessary to be totally alert in order to avoid the boulders that can't be seen until you're almost upon them.

I found myself paddling like crazy, first on one side of the canoe and then on the other, trying to keep us going straight so we wouldn't capsize. Then Curt called from the back of the craft, "You just watch the water ahead, and if you see a problem coming, point it out to me. Let my paddling steer us." An amazing thing happened when I took his advice. We became a team! As my paddling became less frantic, quiet spaces opened up, and the movement of the canoe became stable and sure.

I have a busy week ahead, with work deadlines to meet, a talk to give on Wednesday and an eight-hundred-mile round-trip drive to South Dakota for a family gathering on the weekend. I could "paddle frantically" through the week and end up exhausted. Instead, I'm going to try to put into effect the lesson of the canoe. If I can just relax and trust God to steer me, I know that some quiet spaces will open up, and my week's course will be navigable and steady.

Thank You, Holy Spirit, for being a trusted Teammate. Steer me through any rough waters ahead. — Marilyn Morgan Helleberg

30
TUES
I will carry, and will deliver you.

HOUSE GUEST
—Isaiah 46:4

"Try and cheer up," my husband Glenn said to me as I huddled glumly in the cockpit of our sailboat. "This weather can't last forever." Rain dripped from everything—the sails, our jackets and shoes, our hair. The weather matched my mood—soggy. I'd looked forward to this boat trip, but after three days of fog and drizzle, I couldn't wait to get home to some dry clothes and a hot shower. So we decided to keep on going even though we were heading straight into another storm.

Soon we were surrounded by an angry-looking horizon. From out of nowhere, a flash of black and orange flickered past us and a beautiful monarch butterfly landed on my bright pink baseball cap. The butterfly was perfectly content to sit on my head as the wind picked up and the boat crashed through the choppy water. Suddenly, thunder, lightning and blinding rain hit us with fury; gale-force winds tossed our boat around like it was made of paper. We had on life jackets and safety lines, but each time the enormous waves smashed across the bow, I was sure we'd be flung overboard. Finally, it was over and we were very lucky. We'd made it safely to shore.

Amazingly, the butterfly rode out the entire storm in the safety of our boat and when the wind died down, it unfolded its wings and flew toward shore. As I watched it dart up into the sky, I marveled at its incredible instincts—it had come on board, made itself at home and accepted our protection.

I learned something about strength from that fragile creature. It showed me that being strong often means knowing when to reach out and look for help.

Father, anytime I need Your help, Your arms are wide open and waiting. All I have to do is ask. — Ellen Secrest

31 *We give thanks to God always for you...Remembering*
───   *without ceasing....*   — I Thessalonians 1:2–3
WED

Two years ago today, I had a phone call from the island of Nantucket, Massachusetts. It was my friend Barbara Nelson calling to tell me it was her ninetieth birthday.

"Barbara, I wish I'd known!" I apologized. "I ought to be the one calling you!"

"Oh, no!" Barbara sounded startled at the thought. "To me, a birthday's the time to say thank you to everyone who's made the year special."

She was having a wonderful day, she went on, recalling all she had to be grateful for. "I enjoyed your visit to the island in June, for instance. Today gives me a chance to tell you so."

Now, of course, I have Barbara's date in my birthday book to remind me to call her today. But, I suspect, it won't be the remembrances she receives that will make her day special. It will be her remembrance of others, seasoned with gratitude and expressed with love, that will make this ninety-second birthday, as she said of her ninetieth, "the best one yet."

Give me the gift of a grateful heart, Father, and the grace to put my thanks into words.   — Elizabeth Sherrill

Prayer Diary

My Prayer Requests for August:

1. _____

2. _____

3. _____

4. _____

5. _____

6. _____

7. _____

8. _____

9. _____

10. _____

11. _____

12. _____

13. _____

14. _____

15. _____

16. _____

17. _____

18. _____

19. _____

20. _____

21._____

22._____

23._____

24._____

25._____

26._____

27._____

28._____

29._____

30._____

31._____

September

S	M	T	W	T	F	S
				1	2	3
4	5	6	7	8	9	10
11	12	13	14	15	16	17
18	19	20	21	22	23	24
25	26	27	28	29	30	

GIFTS OF THE SEASON

The Moon

Harvest moon, full, round,
shining on God's abundance,
radiates His grace.

With joyful heart I pause to remember, Lord,
Your many blessings in my life.

1
PRAYER CAN CHANGE YOUR LIFE
Give the Moment to God

The Lord is good, a stronghold in the day of trouble....
— Nahum 1:7

Nine months into the disciplines offered by *Prayer Can Change Your Life*, and I still find myself losing my way, stumbling back to the beginning, feeling that there is so much I don't understand about prayer. Fortunately, the book acknowledges that I will sometimes be confronted with seemingly unsolvable problems, and it offers a clear solution for those times: *Give the moment to God*.

Remember the family division created by my brother's divorce I mentioned back in January? Here's how this simple directive healed my personal hurt. I recently attended a big family gathering in another city, hoping the time with my relatives would let us regain the closeness we used to have. But my place card directed me to a table of strangers instead of to a seat with my relatives. While they shared old times across the room, I felt left out — embarrassed and humiliated.

Then I remembered the words from *Prayer Can Change Your Life*. "Give this moment to God and you can emerge with a clean heart." So I sat at my table and silently prayed, "God, I'd give anything to be back home with David, Brock and Keri, but I am here. So if You would see fit, take this situation and use it for good."

About halfway through the evening, one of the younger men at the table mentioned being a high school football coach. I began telling the story of Brock's coach, how I had watched him change the course of many lives, how boys that might have dropped out of school were now in college because of him. Thus the evening ended.

I was walking back alone to my car, when the coach's wife tapped me on the shoulder. "I just wanted to thank you," she said. "All summer we've been trying to decide if the coaching job is worth it. Tonight, your story told us everything we needed to know."

Standing there, I was overwhelmed with God's grace. I had given a situation I couldn't change to Him, and He had used me to bring a bit of His kingdom to earth.

What are you struggling with right now? An enemy? An impossible predicament? An embarrassing moment? If you can't do anything about it — *give it to God*.

You have used me, God, and Your love has made me free. Thank You.
— Pam Kidd

2	*If ye have faith as a grain of mustard seed...nothing shall*
FRI	*be impossible unto you.* — Matthew 17:20

A few blocks from where I live in Princeton, New Jersey, stands Nassau Hall, the historical centerpiece of Princeton University, which was founded in 1746 by Presbyterians. Nassau Hall was occupied by colonial and British militia during the Revolution; it served as the nation's capitol for five months in 1783 when the Congress of the Confederation met there; and its prayer room was used to honor George Washington for his leadership. Today, Nassau Hall is the symbolic goal of thousands of college-bound seniors, but only a few hundred of the country's best students will gain admission. That's why a story I read recently caused my heart to cheer.

It was about a young lady from a nearby city, notorious for its troubled school system. Plagued by racial disharmony, poverty and violence, its high school drop-out rate is inordinately high and its test scores abysmally low. Hardly the place one would expect to find an aspirant for Princeton. But there was one. When told she couldn't get into a prestigious university like Princeton, she refused to listen. And even if she made the grade, detractors said, it was one of the most expensive schools in the country, far beyond her family's means. But she had a dream. She wanted to become a doctor, and she worked and studied and prayed — night and day, weekdays and weekends, year in, year out. In addition, she took an after-school job and did volunteer work at a nearby hospital. Finally, she graduated at the top of her class and won her way into Princeton on a full scholarship. When saluted for her accomplishment, she credited the high school others had disparaged, and "the wonderful help I got from my dedicated teachers."

Strange, isn't it, when we have a goal and commitment and faith, how the most formidable obstacles crumble. Even mountains, according to Christ — if we have the faith of a mustard seed. I need to remember that next time I'm tempted to give up on some dream of mine.

> *Teach me, God, to pray*
> *as if all my hopes depended on You,*
> *And to work each day*
> *as if all depended on what I do.*
>
> — Fred Bauer

3 *And my God will meet all your needs....*

SAT						— Philippians 4:19 (NIV)

We were coming to the end of our family vacation in the Colorado mountains when our six-year-old son Reggie started having problems breathing.

By the time we got home to Mississippi, his neck had started to swell. When antibiotics didn't work, our doctor sent us to specialists. Pediatricians, hematologists and oncologists ran test after test while our son grew worse. Finally, they ordered a biopsy. The diagnosis: cancer of the lymph nodes.

Not cancer! I felt nauseous and weak. I couldn't believe it. My wife Rosie and I helplessly watched our little boy suffer ten weeks of painful chemotherapy and radiation treatments — without a guarantee that he would recover. Many times we found ourselves questioning God. *How could this happen? Why us? Why all this suffering?* It was a terrible time.

One day, when I was shouting all my anger to God, it was as though God reached out to touch me. Somehow I felt His love surround me — and I knew that God did love us, that He loved Reggie and that He would never leave us no matter what happened. And then I saw that I had a choice. I could go on demanding that God heal Reggie and save us all from this suffering. Or I could surrender Reggie into God's loving hands, trusting that God would do the best for all of us. With His help, I quit fighting and gave Reggie and his future to God.

Reggie wasn't healed immediately. He had to finish the radiation therapy and was a pretty sick boy for several weeks more. But six months later, the doctors could find no trace of cancer in him.

During those terrible weeks, we learned that while our circumstances change, God doesn't. He is still present, loving us, caring for us and carrying us along, even when we can't feel His presence.

What a comfort it is to know that our God, Who leads us to many mountaintops, is the God of the valleys as well.

Jesus, thank You for the mountains, and thank You for walking with us through the valleys, too. Amen.				— Dolphus Weary

4 *Let your gentleness be known to everyone. The Lord is*

SUN *near.*					— Philippians 4:5 (NRSV)

Gentleness and peacefulness don't come easily to me, but they come easier in some places than others. I've always had a sense of peaceful-ness here in this country house where I live, for instance. My bedroom is almost in the trees. It seems fitting that the place I do my dreaming is at the top of the house. This is truly a place where I can let God speak to me.

Sometimes I write down my dreams in a journal, even if I don't understand what the dream means at the time. One day, I noticed that my house is a prominent image in my dreams! As I browsed through my written dream stories, I realized that in my dreams, my house repre-sents me.

One time I dreamed that I was out in the garden, looking at the border of my property. It was hedged in with a neat, tight row of attrac-tive, tough pachysandra. Then I looked again and the pachys were gone, replaced by tender plants of perennial periwinkle. The peri-winkle seemed more vulnerable than the pachy, but there was a strength and solidity in the soft carpet of blue and white flowers.

I realized that this is exactly what God is doing in my life. God has been taking away an impenetrable border I have constructed around the house — myself — and is replacing it with something gentler. I am learning medicine alone is not enough for my young cancer patients; I can help them better in their fight when I also let them know that I understand their fears and care for them. And it has become easier to let my friends know me better, too.

The pachy and the periwinkle told the story of the healing — the growing gentleness — in my soul.

Father, let me not worry about being fragile, so that I might touch and be touched by others. — Diane Komp

---

5
MON

Blessed are the peacemakers: for they shall be called the children of God. — Matthew 5:9

"Blessed are the piecemakers." So reads a small framed needlepoint hanging on my mother-in-law's kitchen wall.

"Did you know this is spelled wrong?" I ask.

"I never really noticed, I guess," she says, laughing a little.

I laugh, too. Then I wonder if it really is a mistake. It's certainly true. I think of all the people who do their small part to make our world spin around, including myself. Sometimes my small part feels too small. I want to be bigger, more important, taking care of the whole pie. But I'm not. I'm taking care of my small piece, raising my child, singing in the church choir, teaching adult classes. Often the task seems so small and insignificant: to color with my son, to sing on Sunday morning. Neither will change the world.

Then I think of my brother-in-law Danny. He's mentally handicapped, employed at a sheltered workshop with hundreds of other people like him at all levels of ability. They're working on a huge order for one of the big carmakers. Dan's job is to separate foam pieces. Then a more skilled person stacks the pieces. The next person, more skilled yet, staples them to a plastic form. The next attaches those forms to other forms by machine. And on it goes, each worker doing what he or she is capable of: the seemingly smallest piece but at that moment the most important. Then all of it goes back to the manufacturer, and by the time they're done, they've built a car. Each worker is a part of the whole, making a piece of the pie.

Blessed are the piecemakers, you wonder? Where would we be without them?

On this Labor Day, Lord, help me be content to do my small part, knowing I'm a "piecemaker" in the work of Your larger creation. — Gina Bridgeman

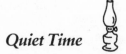

Quiet Time

Lord, may I not put a question mark
where You put a period. Amen.
— *Author Unknown*

6
TUES

But now abide faith, hope, love, these three....
— I Corinthians 13:13 (NAS)

Jan is one of the most radiantly beautiful young women I know. She is the daughter of a dear, dear friend, and I have known her since the day she was born. Jan has been married for eight years, is the mother of three small children under four and is finishing up her doctorate in religion at Baylor University. How can she be so calm, wear so many different hats, and have such well-behaved and happy little ones? Last week I discovered one of the clues.

Tucked in a book I had borrowed from her was a dog-eared copy of a poem written by her mother and sent to her when she left home to attend the University of North Carolina at age seventeen. The clue was wings — the gift of freedom bequeathed to a daugher in these love lines:

> *Discover, fledgling, who and what you were meant to be...*
> *Yet hear forever in the winds of flight —*
>   *"We love you!*
>   *W-e l-o-v-e y-o-u!*
>   *We-----love-----you!"*
>
> *Mother*

This week our oldest grandson leaves for college. I called Jan's mother Suzie and asked permission to use her poem and send it to Gib. Charles Gibson Shellenberger has his grandfather's name. He is only a tiny student speck in a gigantic circle of fifty thousand more student specks at the University of Texas, but I want him to know that God knows his name and loves him as if he were the only one there. So do his parents and so do his "Dodaddy" and "Dodolly" (his names for us).

He is Yours, Lord. Help him to become all that You have intended for him to be.
                                        — Dorothy Shellenberger

---

7
WED
The steps of a good man are ordered by the Lord: and he delighteth in his way.   — Psalm 37:23

"What makes a successful life anyway?" I asked myself forlornly as my friend Joe and I arrived to pack up the belongings of a friend who had died. He'd been an artist, a good one, but his paintings hadn't provided much of a livelihood. Now, in the cramped quarters of his tiny apartment, I saw that it would not take Joe and me long to do our work. There was room here for only the bare necessities of living.

It had to be done, this chore, yet handling these personal possessions only added to the melancholy. We worked in silence. The afternoon wore on. Then, unexpectedly, the sadness I was feeling turned to a kind of gladness. It had to do with these bare necessities.

On the windowsill, I picked up a slender, silver bud vase, a pink rose still in it, now faded and dry. Then I remembered: Every time I visited there'd been a fresh flower of one kind or another in that vase.

In a low-lying bookcase, I sorted out the small collection of carefully chosen books. Some of them, lovingly inscribed, were written by friends. *So many good friends he had*, I thought, *but what a good friend he had been to them*. And on the bedside table lay the Bible. Yes, that was *always* there.

From a high shelf, Joe took down a small wooden object and shrugged in puzzlement. "It's a bird cage," I said. "Don't you remember all those wounded sparrows he'd pick up off the streets and try to nurse?"

The job done, Joe and I sat and talked for a while about our friend and what the essential qualities of his life had been. You could put them all in one cardboard box, just as you could the bare necessities of any good life: love of beauty; fidelity to friends and to God; a caring for all living creatures. And the more we talked, the more the success of our friend's life filled the room.

Thank You, Lord, for good friends who inspire us to love life and live it fully.
— Van Varner

8
THURS
Each one should test his own actions. Then he can take pride in himself, without comparing himself to somebody else, for each one should carry his own load.
— Galatians 6:4–5 (NIV)

A few years ago, I took an "Effective Parenting" course at our grade school. I absorbed the discussions of misbehavior, communication, child self-esteem, all agreeably until we got to one point: "Don't do for your children what they can do for themselves."

"I can't go along with that," I blurted to Mr. Wicksnin. "I often tie shoes for my girls or button coats. I sometimes feed their pets. It only tells them I love them."

"Of course you do," the kind counselor soothed. But, he explained, "Doing things for children can cause them to feel even more helplessly little, robbing them of the joy and satisfaction of 'doing it myself.' In essence, your doing it implies, 'No, you can't.' It can prove to be a growth inhibitor."

My head whirled all day with the realization that Mr. Wicksnin was right! In fact, when I got home I decided I would try to practice this new "effective parenting" method. I began cutting back on indulgently taking over my girls' chores. Instead, I would comment on specific successes: "You did a great job of feeding the cats — not a bit of food spilled!" or "It really helped me with the housecleaning when you put away your paints and papers. Thanks!" And for myself I prayed:

Dear Lord, help me not always to expect the "quick fix" or immediate comfort in my pursuits. Walk by my side and guide me as I make my choices, take action and grow, so that You might be my proud Parent.   — Kathie Kania

9
_{FRI} *My needs were supplied by the brethren....*
          HOUSE GUEST
          — II Corinthians 11:9 (RSV)

I'll never forget the day that my parents, my sister Keri and I made that long, three-hour drive from our home in Nashville to the campus of the University of Tennessee in Knoxville, where I was enrolled as a freshman. Too soon the car was unloaded and it was time to part ways. We said our teary good-byes, and I stood in the parking lot watching my dad's old station wagon drive out of sight.

Alone. Of course, every university is ready for the freshman class. Events were offered one after the other, all sorts of orientations, mixers, get-togethers. All that planned activity and yet I felt unplugged.

When friends encouraged me to go through fraternity rush, I decided to give it a try. It turned out not at all like the *Animal House* chaos people sometimes associate with college fraternities. It became for me a family away from family. I found myself among boys of all backgrounds who had come together to form a kind of brotherhood. When news came the day before spring break that "Pop-Pop," my grandfather, had died, my room in the fraternity house became the center of attention. My brothers came to offer their condolences, to share experiences of their own losses. I was amazed when an older member that I hardly knew volunteered to drive me home to Nashville.

Back home after the funeral, I got a call from the guys spending spring break in Florida. "It's not the same without you," they said. "We're sending a frequent-flyer ticket. You're to catch the next plane down." *Brothers!*

Today, if you visit my home on campus at Sigma Chi House, don't expect perfect order or Mom's cooking. What you will find is a group of fifty very different individuals making a home together in the midst of a large college campus, a group of guys who adhere to a common prayer memorized during their pledgeship: "Teach us to be true to each other, ourselves and to Thee." I have found the fraternity to be a supportive community like the ones we need all through life, where we commit ourselves to principles, demand the best from one another and push one another toward common goals. A community like a family, a church, a civic or fraternal organization.

God, help us all to seek and find community. Amen.
— Brock Kidd

10 *Moreover the light of the moon shall be as the light of the*
SAT *sun....*   — Isaiah 30:26

Late one crisp Saturday afternoon in September, our friends Wayne and Joyce called. "It's almost a full moon tonight. How about a hike?" This wasn't an unusual suggestion. The four of us often enjoyed moonlight hikes together.

"Great!" I said after checking with my husband Lynn. Hastily we planned a potluck picnic, packed our backpacks and headed for the Mesa Trail, a familiar path along the flatirons and front range of the Rocky Mountains near Boulder, Colorado. The top sliver of a harvest moon peeked over the eastern horizon as we huffed and puffed up the first steep part of the trail. By the time we reached the top of the mesa, the mountains around us glowed in the silver moonlight, and we cast clear shadows as we followed the trail through the tall pine trees. Periodically, we paused to look up at the starry sky or listen to the great stillness or appreciate the softness of the surroundings, so different in the moonlight than in the harsh sunlight. After about an hour, we found a level spot in a clearing, spread out our blanket, and with a fresh sense of worship, we thanked our Creator for the beauty of His awesome creation. We then shared pita bread sandwiches, apples and cheese, carrot sticks and brownies. By the time we started back down the mountain, we felt awed by God.

You don't need to hike a mountain trail to feel close to God. The same bright moonlight fills up a garden or illuminates a path through a familiar park or neighborhood and gives you an opportunity to see anew the wonder of God's creation in your own backyard.

Creator God, thank You for the everyday wonder of Your light.
— Carol Kuykendall

11
SUN *For you are our glory and joy.*

HOUSE GUEST

—I Thessalonians 2:20 (NKJV)

While we were growing up, my two sisters Mary and Katy and I journeyed every summer from Denver to North Platte, Nebraska, for a special week-long visit with our grandparents.

A visit to Grandma and Grandpa's meant at least two or three *breakfasts* of chocolate cake with white icing, as well as noon meals of pot roast with all the trimmings, or chicken and dumplings.

Then there was the apple tree in the backyard—just right for climbing and eating its sour green fruit. "Not too many," Grandma would caution, "or you'll get stomach aches."

We went on downtown errands with Grandpa where he'd introduce us to his friends. "These are my lovely granddaughters from Denver—Ed and Mary Ellen's girls." His gentle pride always showed in his smiling eyes and soft, friendly voice.

Early evenings, we'd amble with Grandma through the wide, tree-lined streets. Once she led us to a new park in town and told us, "I won twenty-five dollars for naming it 'Park Allura.'" That was the prettiest name I'd ever heard for a park.

For that week, we reveled in the treats, the attention, the knowledge that we were loved just for being who we were. My grandparents died some years ago, but their loving example inspired me to pass on those same traits to my child, and one day, hopefully, his children. It's a legacy of love that never runs out. So, "Thank you, Grandma and Grandpa, for being you!"

Father, thank You for loving grandparents, and for Your love that accepts me as I am. Help me to look on the people in my life with pride and joy.   —Ellyn Baumann

12
MON *Be ye therefore merciful, as your Father also is merciful.*
—Luke 6:36

Many years ago, I was visiting my son's friend, a Vietnam veteran and an amputee in the Naval hospital. An old man appeared, lugging a bulky sack, and with a kind of shy eagerness he approached Harry's bed.

"I do tricks," he said. "Don't let me butt in or nothin', but I come here to see you boys and try to cheer you up. If you want me to, I'll show you some."

"Sure. Great!" Harry said. "What kind of tricks?"

"Oh, nothing much. Just things I make up." Fumbling in his sack, the man produced a box with colored plastic sides and a little fan on top. Inside was a tiny motor, which hummed when his trembling fingers touched a switch. The fan whirled merrily. "Wait. I got a star to put on it." And now the little glass star was spinning, too, spilling rainbows on the sheets.

"You hurt bad, son?" the old man asked.

"Not too bad," Harry said. "I'll make it."

"Sure you will. I got banged up in a couple of wars myself. So I try to do what I can to help. I'm an old sea dog, and I tie all kinds of knots." He brought forth another box containing a garland of sailor knots. "That there's a true lover's knot," he pointed out. "That's the Pope's knot—nobody else can use it...." With pleased authority, he gave the history of others.

"Get well, son," he said finally, packing up. "Hope you liked my little tricks."

"Wait! Don't go yet." Harry exclaimed. "Hey, guys! Come here!" he called out to the other patients.

They came rolling up in their wheelchairs, unsteadily on their artificial limbs, making a circle to examine and praise the man's little gadgets. They asked questions and listened to his stories. And when it was time to leave, they encouraged him, "Good-bye, Pop. Come again."

Turning, the man's face was shining as bright as his little star. "Get well, boys," he said. "I'll pray for you."

Jesus, my heart is warm as I remember Your tremendous compassion. Let us all be kinder to one another.   —Marjorie Holmes

---

13
TUES

HOUSE GUEST
PRACTICING THE POWER OF PRAYER
Upside-Down Reminders

Blessed are those whose strength is in you....
—Psalm 84:5 (NIV)

Our shy, twelve-year-old Joanna was understandably nervous. We'd recently moved, and not only would Joanna be attending a new school that had more kids in it than the total population of our former town, but this was her first day in junior high.

I stood in line with Joanna in the gym as she waited to get her class schedule card. When she got it, her blue eyes filled with tears. She hadn't gotten the basketball elective she'd chosen; no friends were in her homeroom; her classes were spread out over the large and unfamiliar grounds. She couldn't make changes that day, so with an encouraging smile (hiding my own heavy heart), I patted Joanna's shoulder and left when the bell rang.

Like the typical concerned parent, I drove away feeling anxious. When I got home, I went straight to my "prayer chair," a rocker in the bedroom where I spend my quiet times. There I offered a support-prayer for Joanna, asking God to guide and reassure her on this first, uneasy day. *And* to help me leave my own anxious feelings about Joanna with Him.

As I read through one of my devotional books, I found it: a suggestion that I wear my watch *upside down* so that each time I looked at it I'd be reminded that God is with Joanna (and me) every moment. I did it—I turned my watch upside down. That day, any glance at my watch brought me a gentle reminder of Who is in control. When the school day ended, Joanna bounced in the door with an excited look on her face. "I think I'm going to like it here," she said.

Next time you or someone close to you is feeling anxious or uneasy, try wearing your watch upside down. Or pick some familiar object in your home or office that you look at often and set it askew or off-balance as a constant reminder of Who is in control. Watch it work wonders!

Father of all things, comfort us in all our times of need.
— Marjorie Parker

$\underline{14}$ *My times are in thy hand....*   —Psalm 31:15
WED

I used to be easily annoyed by interruptions on a busy day, the unexpected telephone call or the co-worker who dropped by my office to talk. That was before I interviewed Richard Bolles for an article I was writing. An ordained minister and author of the popular job-hunting manual *What Color Is Your Parachute?*, Bolles talked with me about the importance of organization and careful planning.

"But how do you handle interruptions?" I asked, pointing out instances of how they could upset some of the best-laid plans.

"They shouldn't really upset you," he said. "Maybe the interruptions are there to remind you of other priorities. After all, the Holy Spirit is the Lord of our time."

It was a chance remark that had a deeper meaning than I recognized at the time. I thought about the friend who called to talk about his mother's heart operation just when I was working against a deadline. And my five-year-old son Willy who wanted me to admire his coloring book at the moment I sat down to watch the evening news. "Other priorities," Bolles had said. I began to think differently about interruptions when I saw them in that light.

The Holy Spirit is the Lord of our time. Think about it.

Lord, especially when interruptions upset my plans, help me see Your purpose in everything that happens today. —Rick Hamlin

---

15
THURS
So teach us to number our days, that we may apply our hearts unto wisdom. —Psalm 90:12

It was growing late, twilight turning into dusk as I trudged home from work. Fumbling with my house keys, I paused on the sidewalk before our door and glanced down the street. All was quiet except for a boy pedaling his bicycle at a distance.

For a moment, I stood still...the first reflective moment in an active day. Something about the boy on the bike had caught my attention. Framed against the darkening sky, I could dimly see that he wore a red University of Georgia sweatshirt—a rare commodity in South Carolina! My old Georgia bulldog blood surged, and I responded with a faint smile. *Glad there's another fan around*, I thought, as the boy drew closer.

Staring through the dimness, I glimpsed a shock of blond hair, wide shoulders. A young teenager, I guessed. Thinking of my own little boys inside the house, I turned and inserted the key in the lock. "It won't be long before Drew's that age," I mumbled. "Ten years have flown. Absolutely flown!"

As I turned to close the door, I looked down the street again and, suddenly, the young fellow on the bike was right before me. "Hi, Dad!" he said, as he braked and coasted up onto the sidewalk.

Blinking, I stared at my own son with disbelief. Sure, it was dark.

But not that dark. Drew had grown older before my unsuspecting eyes, more mature than I was ready for him to be. Shaking my head and placing my hand on his firm shoulder, as if to prove he was real, I walked with him into the light of our house and closed the door.

I was jolted. But it was a jolt I needed. Quite simply, my three kids will not be here forever. The hymn text is true:

> *Time, like an ever-rolling stream,*
> *Bears all its sons away.*

We cannot stop the world and get off. The present time is all that we have. I have resolved this day not to wait for another day to enjoy my children and rejoice in the goodness of their youth. They are a precious and fleeting gift. They need me now, not later. Not even tomorrow.

O God, help me not to postpone for tomorrow what should be done today. May I love this day as if there were no tomorrow. Amen.   — Scott Walker

16
FRI

HOUSE GUEST
He healeth the broken in heart, and bindeth up their wounds.   —Psalm 147:3

I grew up in a depressed area of southern Illinois, where medical care was considered a luxury, and was also hard to come by. The nearest doctor was fifty miles away. But happily there was Old Doc Brown.

Doc Brown was our town pharmacist. He never pretended to be a doctor, but since he was the closest we came to having a doctor, the townspeople affectionately called him "Doc." (In the tradition of small towns, he became Old Doc Brown when his son Young Doc Brown joined him in running the drugstore.) He provided much more than the ointments, cough medicines and stomach powders that he dispensed (whether or not people had the money to pay). He gave his time. Whether it was a physical complaint or a personal heartache, he always took time to listen.

Even after the town got its own doctor, my dad preferred to see Old Doc Brown. "I've got a little problem," he'd tell him, "and I know you can fix it." But Doc Brown knew his limitations, and would insist my dad see the doctor. Still, after Dad saw the doctor, he'd stop by Doc Brown's. The doctor was knowledgeable, but he didn't make time to ask Dad about his new hunting dog.

Sometimes when I walk into my local, neon-lit, well-stocked modern pharmacy, I feel a twinge of nostalgia for someone like Doc Brown. But then I remember that I have Someone better. Someone I often go to, saying, "I've got a little problem, but I know You can fix it." And like Old Doc Brown, He always has time to listen. The difference is that, unlike Doc Brown, *He has no limitations.* He is the ultimate Healer.

Thank You, Father, for daily healing my physical and spiritual bruises.   — Bonnie Lukes

---

17 *In the morning sow thy seed, and in the evening withhold*
SAT *not thine hand: for thou knowest not whether shall pros-*
      per, either this or that....   — Ecclesiastes 11:6

Some years ago, I ran across a back-page news item describing a bill pending in our state legislature. The ambiguous bill inadvertently could have allowed custodial parents to seek "child support" after the children had reached adulthood or even senior age. I was immediately struck by the long-term negative impact of this bill and the unreasonable financial burden it would place on the ex-spouses and their new families paying out child support. And I was astonished that it was about to become law without public discussion.

I called a number of friends about the bill. Most simply shrugged and said, "You're probably right, but what can one or two people do?" When I asked the Lord the same question, the answer He seemed to give me was this passage in Ecclesiastes.

So I immediately called my state representative's office and discovered that the vote was only forty-eight hours away. I decided I would hand-deliver a letter to its members, adding my voice to the democratic process. At least then I could say I'd "sown my seed."

"You're against the bill?" an aide asked incredulously the next morning when I handed him my letter. "Why? Everybody is for it!" I briefly outlined my objections. "You know, you have some valid points," the aide said. "I'll mention them to the senator."

Two days later, when I called the chairperson's office to find out how the vote had gone, I had a surprise coming. "The bill was set aside," the secretary told me. "The members decided it needed further study." It never did make it through committee.

While there's no way to gauge exactly how much impact I had on the process, I've wondered what might have happened if I hadn't "sown my seeds" when I did. One thing is sure: The experience taught me never to hesitate to sow what I could — regardless of how small or how few my "seeds" might seem to me.

Father, on this Citizenship Day, show me how I can sow good seeds — in my world, my nation, my city, my neighborhood, my family — trusting You for the harvest.   — Susan Williams

18
<u>SUN</u>   *As the hart panteth after the water brooks, so panteth my soul after thee, O God.*   — Psalm 42:1

My new Dandie Dinmont terrier puppy Wally doesn't hesitate to let me know when he needs something. By a persistent bark or a cold-nose nudge, he tells me when he wants to eat, go outside or play.

Recently, I was sitting in my bedroom chair reading. Wally raised himself on his hind legs, his forepaws touching my lap. It wasn't his mealtime. He'd just come in from being outside. "Do you want to play?" I asked, reaching down for his yellow rubber ball. But when I threw it, Wally didn't run. Instead, he gave me another nudge with his nose.

"Do you want to come up here?" The answer seemed to be yes, because he attempted to jump. But he didn't make it. His legs were too short. So I lifted him up into my lap. After some turning and shifting, he settled down. When I heard him give a big sigh, a warm feeling of contentment enfolded me.

This is how God must feel, I thought, *when one of His children comes to Him, not with a need but simply wanting to be with Him, to have a quiet time in His lap.*

Dear Lord, let me think of more reasons to come to You, simply because I love You.   — Eleanor Sass

19
<u>MON</u>   PRACTICING THE POWER OF PRAYER
Prayer Portions

For the word of God is quick, and powerful, and sharper than any two-edged sword....   — Hebrews 4:12

My friend Sylvia has constructed a booklet entitled "Alphabet of Who

You Are in Christ." Part of the introduction says, "Until now, your sense of personal worth may have been determined by what your family, your friends...or others think of you. Nothing is more liberating than agreeing with God about how He sees you and how He feels about you."

At last count, Sylvia listed 255 Scriptures explaining our relationship with God. She has given them all subject titles and then organized them alphabetically. When she runs into a problem, or doesn't know exactly how to pray, or gets depressed and doesn't *feel* like praying, or just has to wait at a red light, she goes through her list of Scriptures, beginning with *A*, and turns them into "prayer portions." Her prayer might go something like this:

Able to do all things (Philippians 4:13). *Sometimes I feel so helpless, Lord, but thank You that with Your help I am capable of doing any task You give me.*

Beautiful (Isaiah 61:10). *Lord, thank You that I am beautiful in Your sight, for You have given me wonderful garments and jewels of salvation and righteousness.*

Cared for with compassion (I Peter 5:7). *Thank You for Your love and care that surround me.*

Disciple (Hebrews 12:5–11). *Lord Jesus, You've called me to a strenuous race that requires lots of discipline, but I gladly accept it because I'm following You Who ran the course joyfully.*

Empowered to obey (Philippians 2:13). *You're asking me to forgive, and it seems impossible. But I do want You to keep on working in me and to create in me the desire to obey.*

When we "agree with God" about how He sees us, we are letting Him change us and produce in us the **M**ind of Christ (I Corinthians 2:16).

Father God, help me to take Your Word more seriously for today's living. Amen.   — Marion Bond West

---

20
TUES

But Jesus called the children to him and said, "Let the little children come to me, and do not hinder them, for the kingdom of God belongs to such as these."
— Luke 18:16 (NIV)

In the first few days of kindergarten at our ministry's school, my youngest son Ryan came home almost every day with notes from his teacher for some disturbance he had caused in class. He brought home more notes that first week of school than his older sister and brother had ever brought home in a year. In fact, from birth he has proven to be a very determined child. While his sister and brother would respond to a look, my youngest looks right back.

As I talked to Ryan about the teacher's note regarding his talking in class, he looked up to me with absolute trust and innocence and said, "Dad, she told us not to talk to other children in class. I wasn't talking to other children. I was talking to myself!"

I had to stifle a grin as I explained what the teacher said versus what she meant, and that he needs to talk less—both to himself and to others—in class.

But later, as I thought about his five-year-old innocence, I wondered, *When was the last time I took people at their word?* Wasn't I always reading a meaning into a mere glance, and whole attitudes into a turn of the head?

Maybe my youngest son has something to teach me about taking people at their word. His problem understanding what the teacher really meant has prompted me to speak more clearly, to try always to say what I mean, to make sure my words match my intention.

Thank You, Lord, for the blessing of children, and what they can teach us, when we stop to listen—and learn. Amen.

—Dolphus Weary

21 *The promise of the Lord proves true....*
WED
—II Samuel 22:31 (RSV)

This true story is about a promise made that was not kept:

There was a young teenage girl who dearly loved her cat Jewel. One autumn, a large, fluffy, white dog appeared in the woods near her house. He liked to chase after her cat, which worried the girl a great deal. But her mother assured her the cat was much faster than the dog and could always get away. And, as parents will do, she kept promising that "one of these days" she would have the stray dog picked up.

Winter came and with it, deep snow. One night, after setting Jewel outside, the mother was awakened by a loud commotion. She raced for the door to scare off the stray dog. When she called for Jewel, the cat did not come.

The next morning, her daughter came shrieking up the stairs. She had just discovered her beloved pet, still and lifeless, lying in the snow-bank. "You promised she could get away!" she sobbed. The promise had proved worthless. The mother sat down next to her daughter. Together they cried.

I am the mother of that brokenhearted girl. I have learned a thing or two from my sorry performance. First, don't fling promises around as if they were loose change. Second, strike the expression "one of these days," since it usually means "*none* of these days." Third, step off my pedestal and admit I am capable of failure. Fourth, keep a leash on regret, so I am freed to forgive myself. And fifth, accept comfort from the God of all comfort. He never breaks His Word, but He has plenty of experience in consoling those of us who do.

Jesus, even Your disciple Peter wept bitterly over his broken promise (Matthew 26:75). Dry our tears, precious Lord.
— Carol Knapp

---

22 **Open thou mine eyes, that I may behold wondrous things....**
THURS — Psalm 119:18

I suspect I'm the only male in North America who doesn't like sports.

Normally, I don't even read the sports section of my morning newspaper. I give it to my students in the cafeteria, and they devour it with breakfast. But today, for some reason, I decided to read the sports section. At first, I was lost. Lots of strange names and statistics that I neither recognized nor wanted to recognize. (Yawn.) I kept reading, however, and soon became mesmerized by the clever writing style of the sports journalists. I jotted down some of their creative expressions.

"A tie game is like kissing your sister."

"Their team is like an ugly baby. It ain't much to look at, but you gotta love it."

"He plays hockey like a Rolls-Royce in a street race."

On page four, I found a sports sweepstakes that offered a new car prize, and I clipped a dollar-off coupon for a new razor. I was happily surprised to find that the sports section carries the automotive ads, and I do love cars. I even found an article on caring for feet, which I read with interest because I have a foot problem. When I finally took the sports section to the cafeteria, it had a well-worn appearance — ragged edges and extra folds.

I wonder how many interesting things I've missed in life because I prejudge them and wave them off with a "not interested." Do you do that, too? I'll make a deal with you. Today, I will start reading one of my wife's mystery novels (I hate fiction!). Now it's your move. Maybe you could try a different radio station while driving, or choose a different food item from the menu of your favorite restaurant. I dare you. Be prepared to be pleasantly surprised.

Lord, show me what You have hidden behind the door marked "not interested."
                                                    — Daniel Schantz

---

23   *O God, listen to me! Hear my prayer! For wherever I am,*
 FRI   *though far away at the ends of the earth, I will cry to you*
         for help....   —Psalm 61:1-2 (TLB)

Friends of ours have a cabin in Idyllwild, a rustic, artistic community in the hills of Southern California, and we jump at the chance to join them there. "Get on the road early," they cautioned us one autumn weekend. "By mid-afternoon, the fog is apt to start rolling in, and the hairpin turns can be treacherous."

We thought we had allowed ourselves plenty of time, but halfway up the mountain the clouds were so pea-soup thick we could hardly see the taillights of the car in front of us, and they were moving farther and farther away. Suddenly, we were alone in the terrifying fog—scared to go on but even more scared to turn back.

"Hug the centerline," I said to my husband John, my voice tense.

John stopped the car and turned an ashen face to me. "I can't even *see* the centerline!" Taking the flashlight out of the glove compartment, he said, "You drive. I'll walk ahead, shining the flashlight on the centerline."

Thank God for the guidance of that centerline, I thought, as I hunched over the steering wheel. Then, remembering that prayer is the centerline of our faith, I turned to God. "Dear Lord, You are Lord of the fog. Give John the strength he needs to keep on walking. Quiet my frightened heart and give me a steady hand on the wheel."

At last, we made it to the cabin in the woods. Keeping our eyes on the centerline had guided us through.

Today, there are times when the fog of confusion and self-doubt can disorient me and blur the way ahead. Then I tell myself, "Remember

Idyllwild." I pray and wait...and then, the right opportunity comes, the fog lifts, and I am able to see the way to go, thanking God once again for that *centerline*.

We cannot always see the way ahead, dear Lord. Lead us through the fog of our confusion into the bright, clear light of the path You have prepared for us.   —Fay Angus

$\underline{24}$ *Dwell in a peaceable habitation...and in quiet resting*
SAT   *places.*   —Isaiah 32:18

Each day there's a general routine I follow. On my way to work, I stop and buy the newspaper. My school day then becomes so hectic, I can't get to my paper until evening when I'm home — *after* spending time with my wife Roe; playing Sorry with my daughter Karen, ten; helping my son Michael, eight, with a math problem; and talking with my older son David, thirteen, about his science project. After the children are in bed, after the cat is fed and sleeping, I get to sit down and read the newspaper filled with almost-old news.

But on Saturday morning — well, Saturday's different. I wake up, shower, dress, drive to the local store and buy the newspaper. Then I step into the sweetshop next door and buy a medium chocolate ice-cream cone. There aren't any children next to me needing a napkin, biting the cone from the bottom, arguing with a sister that her cone is bigger.

By the time I have finished eating my cone, I am pulling into the driveway. I step into the house, walk to the couch and read the fresh, morning paper from cover to cover. Then my daughter begins to ask, "Want to play Sorry?" or the boys begin chasing each other around the house. The cat is crying to be let out.

During your demanding day, try and stop a moment and treat yourself to a special quiet moment, alone — a drive down a picturesque country lane, a walk through a new gallery exhibit, a stroll outside at beautiful sunset, or even a double scoop of chocolate ice cream at your local parlor. It is a wonderful thing to give and give and give, but it is also okay to receive.

Father, little things I do for others are acts of love for Your glory. Help me to take time to be good to myself — also for Your glory. Amen.   —Christopher de Vinck

25
SUN

What you have heard from me through many witnesses entrust to faithful people who will be able to teach others as well. — II Timothy 2:2 (NRSV)

When I was in college, I taught Sunday school at Craig Colony, a residential colony for epileptics in New York State. Although many of the clients had normal intelligence, my students were severely retarded and had the most seizures. My first Sunday, one of my students fell on the floor in a "fit." I was seventeen years old and in shock. "That's okay, dear," one of my other students said to me. "We'll take care of this. You just keep on teaching." And I did. For four long years.

As you can imagine, my youth and inexperience made this difficult teaching situation even harder. Every Sunday I went home with a headache, but I never told anyone. I often questioned just what I was accomplishing. Did my students understand anything I said? But I went on faithfully for the entire time I was in college.

After I left school, I rarely thought about Craig Colony. It was eventually closed in favor of bringing the people closer to their own families. But some thirty years later on a Sunday afternoon, I visited a regional center for the developmentally disabled in the same area.

The chaplain invited me to their worship service. There I met a short, rotund, retarded man who kept smiling at me. *Strange! He acts as if he knows me.* Finally, I asked him, "Do you think you know me?"

He nodded energetically. How could he possibly know me? I had never been there before. "Craig Colony," was his reply. "I was at Craig Colony."

Mother Teresa said that God does not call us to be successful, but simply faithful. But it is kind of Him to give us a clue, every thirty years or so, that our headaches and our faithfulness are not in vain. It was not so much my words as much as my faithfulness that had told that little man about Jesus.

Help me to be faithful in my commitments, Lord, and to trust the results to Your knowing hands. — Diane Komp

26
MON

"He [God] will...fill your mouth with laughter...." — Job 8:21 (NIV)

When I first began teaching high school, I was terrified I'd do a poor job. I feared that the kids would hate me and my principal would be disappointed in me. "Don't smile until Thanksgiving," one education professor had said. So I didn't. Or, at least, I tried not to. I pretended to be severe and all-knowing—and all of my worst fears began coming true. The kids did hate me. I was doing a crummy job.

One day in class, as I reached for a stack of tests, I thought I saw something moving in the papers. Carefully, I lifted the top sheets to reveal a hermit crab wriggling its way across the page. Instantly, instinctively, I laughed. And everyone else did, too. It was the beginning of much shared laughter—and knowledge—in my classroom.

Since then, I have found laughter a valuable tool in lots of other areas of life. It can break the tension when my daughter Amy Jo and I don't agree on weekend plans. Or when my son Brett accidentally squirts ketchup on my good tablecloth. A playful wink has been known to diffuse a volatile situation between my husband Gary and me. And laughing at myself often helps me keep other people's foibles in perspective. And that's a lesson *everyone* needs to learn!

God of joy, help me sow laughter wherever I go—and reap a crop of holy humor on my heavenly journey.   —Mary Lou Carney

27
TUES
                                        HOUSE GUEST
Praise be to the God and Father of our Lord Jesus Christ, who has blessed us in the heavenly realms with every spiritual blessing in Christ.   —Ephesians 1:3 (NIV)

The doorbell rang and there stood a delivery man with a package for me. "My goodness! What's this? I haven't ordered anything. And it's not Christmas or my birthday!" I told him. I tore away the brown paper, revealing a shiny red box. Inside was a white leather pouch containing a bottle of a new perfume and underneath the pouch a card. Opening it, I recognized the flowing handwriting:

> Mary,
> *I started counting my blessings one day and concluded that I'm the richest person in the world. And you are one of the priceless gems in my life. I just want to thank you and let you know I love you very much. Have a wonderful day.*
>
> Love, Mom

"Oh, Mom," I whispered. Here I had been worried about Mom the past month. Over the telephone her voice sounded weary. Although her seven children are adults now, she still shoulders each one's struggles. When my dad died ten years ago, Mom took over his wholesale business, and things weren't going well. Although almost seventy, Mom will run the company several more years until my younger brother Karl can take over.

I read her note again. In the midst of work and pressures, Mom had found time for joy — by giving. *What an example for me*, I thought. Today, I'm going to sit down and list my blessings. And as for those priceless gems in my life, I plan to let them know I love and need them.

Father, help me look beyond my troubles and see my treasures: the riches You have given me.   — Mary Brown

28
WED

A word spoken in due season, how good is it!

HOUSE GUEST

                    —Proverbs 15:23

Last fall, I drove down the southern Oregon coast to visit a friend. On the last stretch of the 150-mile drive, a highway sign, which appeared again and again, confused me. It seemed to indicate there would be concrete traffic islands on the road, but as I drove on, in rain and growing darkness, I couldn't see any. I resented this sign, and not knowing its meaning on an unfamiliar highway really worried me. When I finally arrived at my friend's house, I vented my frustration. "Why would anyone place a warning sign with an unclear message on a busy highway?"

She explained that the signs alerted drivers to upcoming turning lanes marked by *painted lines* on the road, not the usual concrete structures that were familiar to me. "The winding and narrow roads here are safer for driving because of the painted lines," she told me.

Later, as I recalled those confusing signs, I remembered my husband Dick's recurring complaint about me: "You don't communicate clearly, Elsie." It was true. As a child, I'd learned to keep quiet about my feelings in order to stay out of trouble. After I married, however, silence *caused* trouble. I'd substitute actions for the words "I'm sorry" or "Please forgive me" or "I love you" — only to discover that the message behind my actions wasn't understood. Because of my unhappy experience with those highway signs, I began to understand Dick's frustration with me, and I resolved to speak up whenever I had strong feelings about something, instead of thinking my actions would speak for me.

I'm finding it takes great effort to express myself clearly, but it's all worth it. Just ask my husband.

Heavenly Father, fill me with the love of Christ and help me to say what He would say.

— Elsie Larson

29

I thank my God upon every remembrance of you.

— Philippians 1:3

About suppertime one fall evening, my thirty-two-year-old daughter Julie phoned. "Hi, Mom. How do you make gravy to go with pork chops?" I could hear the pork chops sizzling over the phone. I gave detailed instructions and she followed them, asking questions. Toward the end of my explanation, Julie said, with emotion that had very little to do with cooking, "Mom, it seems like *you* should be making the gravy, frying the pork chops...."

Yes! My thoughts plugged into her memory. "Baked sweet potatoes, stewed tomatoes, turnip greens, cornbread and gingerbread with raisin sauce...."

"Yes, yes!" Julie remembered. We both held that exact same memory for a few nostalgic moments. Julie continued, "I'd be in the living room doing my homework with Jen — I can remember the dresses we wore. We'd be watching Jon and Jeremy for you, and we'd all be listening for the sound of Daddy's car in the driveway."

"And I'd start telling you children to put your books away and wash your hands for supper...only I said it in a nagging, tired voice. I was always barking out orders like an army sergeant."

She ignored the comments about my being tired and nagging. (Maybe she didn't remember that.) "I can smell the food, remember being a child. I smell gingerbread coming out of the oven! Now I see Daddy coming in the back door smiling at all of us."

"I remember too, Julie. I can smell it, feel it." A moment of almost reverent silence over the phone as together we remembered an "ordinary fall evening and supper."

"You always made pork chops and gravy when fall came, didn't you, Mom? Well, thanks for the recipe. My gravy looks lumpy, but thanks, anyway. *Thanks*, Mom. Bye."

The gravy wasn't really the issue, of course. Memories had crowded in on my daughter on this crisp, fall evening as she cooked for her husband and three children — and she needed to share them with someone who remembered, someone she loved.

How marvelous, Father, that You created us able to remember and cherish the past, that we might remember to cherish one another in the present. Amen.   — Marion Bond West

30 *And he shall give you another Comforter....* — John 14:16
FRI

It's been a long, tiring week as I've pushed myself to meet several deadlines, sometimes getting up before the sun and often working until I fell into bed at night. Yes, I'm a procrastinator, but lately I've become aware of something: *I like it this way!* Deadlines are good for me. Yet after a long push, there's often a harsh letdown. That's when I get out my "soul-mothering" list. I like to think that the Holy Spirit works with me in this process of soothing and renewing my spirit.

Maybe today, you'd like to start a soul-mothering list, a log of things that nurture you, that make you feel whole, that warm your heart and heal your spirit. Then when you're tired or blue or letdown, you can turn to your list and find something that will lift your spirits. Your list will be uniquely yours. But to help you get started, here are a few of the things on mine.

Have a quiet talk with a close friend over a cup of tea.

Sit in the recliner in the dark, listening to Bach.

Walk alone along the river, letting flowing water and birdsong renew me.

MY SOUL-MOTHERING LIST

1. _____

2. _____

3. _____

Spirit of the living God, fall afresh on me.
                                   — Marilyn Morgan Helleberg

Prayer Diary

My Prayer Requests for September:

1. _____

2. _____

3. _____

4. _____

5. _____

6. _____

7. _____

8. _____

9. _____

10. _____

11. _____

12. _____

13. _____

14. _____

15. _____

16. _____

17. _____

18. _____

19. _____

20. _____

21. _____

22. _____

23. _____

24. _____

25. _____

26. _____

27. _____

28. _____

29. _____

30. _____

October

S	M	T	W	T	F	S
						1
2	3	4	5	6	7	8
9	10	11	12	13	14	15
16	17	18	19	20	21	22
23	24	25	26	27	28	29
30	31					

GIFTS OF THE SEASON

The Leaf

Leaf by leaf by leaf,
the old cottonwood lets go,
shedding its cover.

*Let falling leaves remind me, Lord, to let go of old
hurts, one by one by one, to make room for
new possibilities.*

1 — PRAYER CAN CHANGE YOUR LIFE
SAT — What Do You Truly Desire?

I press on toward the goal....   — Philippians 3:14 (RSV)

It's 7:00 P.M. on a fall Friday. Two hours ago I waved my husband David off for a weekend church retreat. My daughter Keri just left for a football game. And my son Brock is away at the University of Tennessee in Knoxville. Alone at last! I can settle in my favorite chair and read the new spiritual growth book I got for my birthday, or I can pop myself a big bowl of corn, melt some cheese on top and watch TV. Oh, the luxury of being home alone doing whatever I want!...

"Hello! Anybody home? Hellooo? Mom?"

Startled, I peep around the corner into the foyer and see Brock standing there with an overflowing laundry bag over one shoulder and a book bag hiked up over the other. "Brock! Honey! I didn't know you were coming home." I try to put a lilt in my voice and not sound disappointed as I watch my home-alone night sprout wings and fly away.

Then, just as quickly, an incident from this morning flashes through my mind. I was driving to work, thinking about one of the lessons in *Prayer Can Change Your Life* about attaining a richer, fuller life. "Ask yourself daily," the book said, "what you truly desire." The book has told me that whatever condition I am in, it is what I have chosen for myself. So if I want to be known as one who loves, not as one who worries and frets and fusses in her own self-centeredness, I must choose to be that way.

"Lord," I remember praying as I drove along, "help me keep my focus on what I truly desire in my life: to be less selfish and more giving, to be known as a positive friend, wife, mother, one who serves, one who makes life better for others...."

Back in the foyer, I throw my arms around my college-weary boy. He has come home for a good meal, some clean clothes, some encouraging words. Though I had not welcomed this unique opportunity moments earlier, I know with some certainty that God is offering an answer to my morning prayer.

"Oh, Brock," I say, "I'm so glad you're here." And I am.

Father God, keep me flexible. Help me to see past momentary, self-centered plans that block my vision of what I truly desire to be.
                                          — Pam Kidd

2
─────
SUN

WORLD COMMUNION SUNDAY

This is my body which is given for you: this do in remembrance of me.... This cup is the new testament in my blood, which is shed for you.   —Luke 22:19–20

A few months after Pearl Harbor, my mother and I, along with six hundred other foreigners from Shanghai, China, were shipped up the Yangtze River by the invading Japanese to a POW camp in Yangchow.

There, in the shabbiest of circumstances, in the midst of starvation and suffering, when day-to-day survival tested the bedrock of our faith, the sacrament of Communion became for me (and continues to be) a lifeline of courage, unity and hope.

We internees came from many ethnic, cultural and social backgrounds, yet each Sunday we held a united service of worship in the dining hall, putting aside our spiritual differences. We saved our bread, one slice rationed daily, to break and pass at Communion. We had no grape juice to commemorate the shed blood of Christ, but just as sweet was the tea diluted almost colorless. At Communion, we were transformed by the glory of God's grace as we remembered the crown of thorns, the scourge, the cross and spear-pierced side. Remembrance of the empty tomb and the victorious power of the Resurrection gave us strength to carry on.

For several of our services, a Japanese guard stood outside the open doorway of the hall, as though yearning to come in. It was not unusual to see him close his eyes as if in prayer. Then, one day, a camp chum and I saw him marching along the top of the wide city wall adjacent to our prison camp. He was singing, full volume, in Japanese, "Onward Christian Soldiers"! "Why," we gasped in amazement, "that guard is a Christian!" He used a song to show that he was a brother in the faith. While the war had placed us in the bleakest of circumstances that no outsider could possibly comprehend, we took this as a sign that God was with us.

So it was in that prison camp that I began to understand the universal power of who we are, knit together as *one* in the family of Jesus Christ. From that day forward, our worship and Communion services embraced, in spirit, that unknown brother.

Today, Lord, as we break bread together on World Communion Sunday, we celebrate the unity of Your family and pray for our brothers and sisters everywhere. Amen.   —Fay Angus

3
MON

But the Lord thy God turned the curse into a blessing unto thee....   — Deuteronomy 23:5

A few years ago, my husband and I visited the Milan, Ohio, birthplace of the great American inventor Thomas Edison. The volunteers at the quaint little house are filled with stories of Edison's early exploits and his later years as the world's most successful inventor, with more than one thousand patents. I learned, for example, that Edison originated the now-famous proverb "Genius is one percent inspiration and ninety-nine percent perspiration."

But my favorite anecdote concerns Edison's work on a new storage battery. A friend remarked to him about the huge number of failures he'd encountered in his search, some fifty thousand experiments before he achieved results. "Results?" said Edison. "Why, I've gotten a lot of results. I know fifty thousand things that *won't* work."

How I know the feeling! Yet too often when I make a mistake, I see only failure and get discouraged, instead of focusing on what I've learned. For instance, I've found that yelling at my little boy Ross doesn't work; I'm learning to say I'm sorry. I now know that trying to be a "superwoman" means doing a lot of things not very well; I'm learning to concentrate on the most important ones and say "no" to the rest. I've discovered that in my quest to be efficient, I sometimes clumsily trample over people, saying, "Here, I'll do it!" I'm learning to slow down and give others time as well as consideration.

So, I guess I've gotten a lot of results, too. Often not the ones I expected, but always gentle lessons that leave me, like Thomas Edison, anxious to try again.

Open my eyes and ears, Lord, so I may always be ready to learn and grow.   — Gina Bridgeman

4
TUES

He tends his flock like a shepherd: He gathers the lambs in his arms....   — Isaiah 40:11 (NIV)

I didn't know the family by name, only by sight, but when their home was destroyed by fire I grieved for them. They had just moved into the house on the corner a month earlier. Miraculously, no one had been injured, but I could imagine how terrible it must be to flee your home in the middle of the night and see it reduced to ashes.

What could I do to help? There wasn't enough room in my house for two adults and three children. I could offer them food and clothing, but that wasn't enough. I was only one person, and the need was so great.

In my frustration, I called a neighbor whose children were away at school and asked her if she could take in some of the family. "Yes!" she said. "I'm glad you called. I wanted to help, but didn't know how." That gave me an idea. Maybe my other neighbors felt the same way: powerless in the face of such a catastrophe.

I started calling around and within an hour I had more offers of food, clothing and warm, friendly places to stay than the stricken family could possibly use — plus help in filling out insurance claims and contacting faraway relatives.

That evening, as the family and neighbors crowded into my dining room to feast on covered dishes of steaming hot food that appeared almost magically, I was moved to tears. Only a few hours ago each of us had felt helpless, but together we became channels for God's love and compassion. I think we all felt grateful for the experience.

Beloved Father, increase my usefulness as I gather together with others in Your name.   — Phyllis Hobe

---

5
WED   *Love is patient and kind....*   — I Corinthians 13:4 (RSV)

The day I discovered the wonder of love was not on my wedding day when, wide-eyed and hopeful, I took the hand of my young bridegroom and stepped out of the chapel.

It was the day many years later when I pulled on an old and favorite pair of pants and found, to my dismay, that the ten pounds I thought I had lost had simply shifted south and stuck.

When my husband Gary came home that night, he found me weeping before the mirror over my too-tight pants — and the new sags and wrinkles that I had discovered on my face. To his credit, my husband didn't laugh. He took me into his arms and assured me that, yes, he would love me even if the pouches under my eyes sagged down to my chin and the bulges at my hips migrated to my knees.

"You look the same as you always did — beautiful," he said. And to prove it, he drove me to the ice cream store and bought me a frozen yogurt — low-calorie, of course. With fresh strawberries. Just the way I like it.

Here I am, Lord, precious and beautiful in Your sight.
                                                    — Linda Ching Sledge

Quiet Time

Dear Lord, who sought at dawn of day,
In solitary woods to pray,
In quietness we come to ask
Thy presence for our daily task.
> — *Harry Webb Farrington*

❧

6
THURS

The uneven ground shall become level, and the rough places a plain. — Isaiah 40:4 (RSV)

One evening in a conversation with my teacher-friend Mary, I happened to ask what she would be presenting to her third graders the next day. "The concept of symmetry," she sighed, adding wryly, "and I think I'll tell them life is rarely symmetrical."

Her offhand remark prodded me to look up *symmetry* in the dictionary: "Beauty as a result of balance." I have always associated symmetry with art. But then I wondered, *What about my life? Does it have symmetry — beauty as a result of balance?*

Captivated by this curious thought, I dipped into my past and present to see what I could find. I made an amazing discovery. My life is full of symmetry, but I didn't put it there. *God did!* By my own leanings, I am hopelessly off-balance. I am afraid to try new things, I worry too much, I'm easily angered, I think of myself first and others later, and my friend Mary will tell you I *never* share my chocolate.

But the picture changes dramatically when I see God's firm and loving hand on my life. My worries dwindle as I give them to Him in prayer and accept His sovereign right to order the events in my life. So when my mother became critically ill while visiting me, I trusted Him completely for her future, which enabled me to cope with her illness more calmly. The fruit of God's Spirit, planted in me, has encouraged gentleness and self-control, helping me to respond more patiently to my four teenagers and to refrain from always insisting on my own way.

Symmetry. Yes, the Master Artist is at work bringing graceful balance to my life.

Loving God, in Your hand, my lopsided life is being transformed into vibrant symmetry.
> — Carol Knapp

HOUSE GUEST

$\frac{7}{FRI}$ *...That they may see your good works, and glorify your Father which is in heaven.*   — Matthew 5:16

When Bebe, my grandmother, first announced her remarriage, I had mixed feelings. Sure, I wanted her to be happy, and my grandfather had been dead for almost nine years. But their marriage had been special. Together, they had been my example of real Christianity, always doing for others. So I wondered, *Could Herb Hester, the man Bebe planned to marry, really be right for her?*

The answer came along with their wedding announcement, which read in part:

In lieu of gifts, Arlene and Herb would like to ask that you: Take a lonely friend to lunch, buy a needy kid a pair of tennis shoes, make a donation to your local youth group, or find your own way to make this world better for someone else.

I knew then that there was something very right about this marriage.

Visiting the newlyweds later, Bebe shared a note with me that was written by a good family friend, Frances Faulkner. "What a beautiful way you had," her note said, "asking your friends to share in the celebration of your marriage by giving happiness to someone else. My effort to carry out your wish was giving a day to an Alzheimer patient on her birthday. I took her a box of her favorite candy, then out for lunch and a drive in the beautiful autumn weather. I think your generosity in wanting to share your happiness with others was fulfilled."

When I got home, I took the announcement and slid it under the glass on my desktop. It's a timeless reminder of the small and ordinary ways that I can glorify God every day.

Welcome to the family, Herb. And thanks.

God, let all my deeds glorify You.   — Brock Kidd

$\frac{8}{SAT}$ *He and all his family...prayed to God regularly.*
                                        — Acts 10:2 (NIV)

You may recall that I wrote two years ago about the monarch butterflies that come to our daughter Sally's ranch outside Fredericksburg, Texas, each October (see *Daily Guideposts, 1992,* October 8). Well, as of this writing, they have not appeared again. But we have seen a few in flight over the vacant lot across the street from our home in Waco, so we know that they are on their way.

Last year, we had a number of telephone calls from people who had read my devotional describing how these magnificent monarchs settle in the woods behind my daughter's home, painting it a brilliant black and white and orange. One lady who called from Michigan told me that she enjoyed reading *Daily Guideposts* each day. "My husband and I feel like we know you," she said excitedly. "We're about your age and also love grandparenting and traveling and being retired." She said that occasionally they, too, realized that time was flying by and that they had begun the habit of praying for us each time they read one of my devotionals in the book.

Her call touched me so much that when I told my husband Charles about it, he suggested that we do likewise. So now each morning at the close of our devotional reading, we are going to remember the writer of that day's devotional and the *Daily Guideposts* readers all across the country, along with members of our own family. After all, when you share your deepest feelings with others over the years, they do become like family — as brilliant in our hearts as the beautiful monarchs who rest in the woods in Fredericksburg.

Dear Lord, thank You for the wondrous creatures in nature that reflect Your glory, and for the lessons learned, truths shared and blessings received from "our family" of Daily Guideposts *writers and readers. Amen.*   — Dorothy Shellenberger

9 *Old things are passed away; behold, all things are become*
SUN *new.*   — II Corinthians 5:17

Last year, I ran into trouble with my church pledge. No matter how hard I tried to keep it up to date, I kept getting behind. When the amount owed became too great, I feared I'd never catch up. *God must be very disappointed with me,* I thought.

Around this time I accompanied my friend Nancy and her dog Casey to the Westminster Dog Show at New York's Madison Square Garden, where Casey was competing in the long-haired dachshund group. For security reasons, the rules stated that all dogs entered in the show could not leave the Garden until after 8:00 P.M.

The competition in the dachshund ring was intense. There were many entries, and though the judge paused several times to study Casey, she didn't award him a blue ribbon. Now all we could do was return to the dogs' benching area for a long wait.

Finally, it was 8:00 P.M. Casey, Nancy and I joined the great exodus of hundreds of dogs, owners and handlers. As we headed for the exit ramp, we could hear the roar of the crowd in the Garden. They were cheering for the dogs out in the ring, those that had survived the day's judging and were going on to try for bigger "bones."

"Never mind, Casey," Nancy said as she bent down to give him a pat. "I'm not disappointed in you. You did your best. We'll try again at the next show. I love you."

Suddenly, I thought about my church pledge. Like Casey, I'd done my best. I hadn't quite succeeded, but I'll try again next year. Most important, God wasn't disappointed in me. He loves me still.

Lord, be with me as I try, and try again.   — Eleanor Sass

10
MON
And there arose a fierce gale of wind, and the waves were breaking over the boat so much that the boat was already filling up. And He Himself was in the stern, asleep on the cushion....   — Mark 4:37–38 (NAS)

My dad would have called it a "sod-busting day." Others would call it "being up to your neck in alligators." No matter the metaphor, it had been one of those days — hard, tense, grueling. When I finally made my way home, I knew I had to get out and run to chase away the stress.

As I began to jog, I noticed that the pleasant breeze was quickly turning into a storm. I thought of turning around and going home. But, no! I had come to run, to battle the elements. And, by George, I was going to do it!

Facing into the gusts, I attacked the storm. Leaning forward like a sprinter, I felt like I was standing still, buffeted backward by the wind's fury. Gritting my teeth, I continued to do battle, pushing and pummeling my invisible adversary until, panting and aching, I grew exhausted.

As my own fury began to ebb and flow away, I quit fighting the wind. It no longer mattered if I ran a mile in record time. Soon I became aware of the pleasant sensation of rain on my face and wind in my hair — as though I were dancing with nature. Gradually, a runner's toiling snarl turned into a lover's foolish grin. I was enjoying the stormy elements, feeling the mystery of the presence of God and the strong caress of Mother Nature. Released from the rigors of the day, my muscles relaxed, and I grew calm.

Too often, when life crashes in on me, I choose to fight and rage against its fury. But fighting only exhausts me. If I battle less, relax more and trust God, I can find a way through the storm to a place of peace.

O God, help me to relax and grow strong in the midst of the storm by seeking Your presence even in the most difficult of days. Amen.   — Scott Walker

11
TUES   *I am their music.*   — Lamentations 3:63

Subway musicians with their hats out for donations are a common sight in New York City, so their presence is often taken for granted by regular riders. Though I'm no longer a regular commuter, I was giving my best imitation of one the other day. Hurrying down the platform, looking up the tunnel for the next train, checking my watch every couple of minutes, I was fretting that I would be late for my appointment.

Then I looked about me and was amused as I realized others were doing the same dance of impatience. It was at that moment I noticed a blind electric keyboard player. He was rendering a lively version of "Five Foot Two" when I tuned in. A couple of passersby dropped coins in his plastic container, but for the most part it was a free concert.

Then the man turned to another part of his repertoire and began playing "Amazing Grace." You should have seen the transformation that took place around me. A hot and bothered executive with a fancy leather attaché case quit fidgeting and began keeping time with his feet; the face of a dour-looking woman brightened as she mouthed the words; a couple of teenagers kept time with their hands and swayed to the beat; even I had relaxed. Business increased dramatically for the musician, whose collection plate was filling. He had apparently hit upon his most successful selection because he was still playing it when my train finally came and I was whisked away.

Although I was late for my appointment, my appointee was later. I passed the time humming:

> *When we've been there ten thousand years,*
> *Bright shining as the sun*
> *We've no less days to sing God's praise*
> *Than when we've first begun.*

Thank You, God, for music glorious
That promises hope and life victorious. — Fred Bauer

12
WED

A word fitly spoken is like apples of gold in pictures of silver.
— Proverbs 25:11

When Mr. Welch, our eighth-grade English teacher, spoke, my heart dropped. "Next week each of you will give a three-minute speech. Pick your subject. You'll be timed, and I will grade you."

I worried. *Speak before the class?* All those honor students, and I, barely passing? I didn't want to be laughed at. I had never given a speech, and in my heart I knew I would fail. I grew more anxious until the moment I spoke. I don't recall my subject, but I did finish within the time limit.

Mr. Welch critiqued us the next day. I held my breath as he approached and said, "I'm giving Oscar an A!" A hush fell over the room. I couldn't believe him. "I'm giving him an A because he held your attention."

This was my first compliment concerning schoolwork. My work up until then had been so poor that I had almost stopped trying. But Mr. Welch's words were a boost. I began to study — really study — not only in English, but in all of my courses. Teachers took notice and were eager to help. Soon I felt I could do the work. I believed in myself. When doubt crept in, hard work chased it away. I went from failing grades to the honor roll.

Mr. Welch alerted me to the magic of encouraging words. I had hungered for reassurance, and he assured me. Even now, though those school years are far behind me, I can do the same. I can praise a neighbor's garden, a mechanic's skills, our postal carrier's durability and a child's accomplishments.

That eighth-grade compliment has lasted my lifetime. Who knows? Maybe your thoughtful comments will do the same.

Our Father in heaven, may I never leave words unspoken that may make others feel happy and encouraged. — Oscar Greene

13
THURS

HOUSE GUEST
"The eye is the lamp of the body...."
— Matthew 6:22 (NIV)

Just before my dinner party, after cleaning all day, I walked through the house one more time, looking at everything through "company eyes." I employ these to see all the things my "everyday eyes" don't see: a stack of magazines that's grown a little too high; the shabby hand towel; those little cobwebs on the ceiling. Even when I think I've finished everything, it's amazing what I see that still needs doing when looking through "company eyes."

As I dusted down a corner cobweb, I mused about all that I miss seeing or hearing because of the "everydayness" of life. Often I only half-listen when my chatty children talk about events at school that may have important undertones. I'm remiss in stopping my busy evening routine to massage my husband's stress-tensed shoulders, or just to sit by him and be still. Many hectic mornings I rush through my daily Bible reading, missing the blessing.

I've determined to use "company eyes" in dealing with my family and my Lord—after all, I do have Company every day. Looking at my life through His eyes helps me see what needs to be "cleaned up."

Father, help me to see my life through Your eyes and become all You want me to be. Amen.
— Marjorie Parker

14
FRI

HOUSE GUEST

A wise man is strong; yea, a man of knowledge increaseth strength.
— Proverbs 24:5

I carried my then-two-year-old daughter Elizabeth up three flights of stairs to our Paris apartment. Both of us were crying. She, because she couldn't have the spaghetti she had seen in the university cafeteria. I, because I hadn't been able to communicate in French sufficiently to obtain the necessary meal ticket.

I persuaded her to eat a croissant and settled her down for a nap. Exhausted, I sank into a chair. When I first learned my scientist-husband Alex had been invited to work in Paris, I was eager to accompany him. Now I cried, "Lord, why did I come? I'll never survive a whole month here."

Blinking away tears, I opened my phrase book. I had thought French might come easily because I already knew Spanish. But the pronunciation was so different. "Impossible!" I slammed it shut. "I can't learn another language at my age." Then I remembered Grandpa.

At age eighty-seven, Grandpa's heart began to fail. This man who had been chopping wood, walking several miles a day and playing kickball with his grandchildren had to sit all day. But he refused to stop exercising his mind. Borrowing my Spanish textbooks, he pored over them. I remember the twinkle in his eye one day when he greeted me, "¡Hola! ¿Cómo está?" He beamed as we carried on a conversation.

"Oh, Grandpa," I whispered twenty years later in France. Then I picked up that phrase book and started practicing. Soon I was ordering meals in cafés and restaurants, and making friends along the way.

"Did you speak French in Paris?" people asked when I returned.

"Sure," I said. "Enough to survive anyway."

Is there a skill you're struggling to master? Does a new job or machine or computer program seem impossible? Maybe Grandpa, adjusting to changes at eighty-seven with the enthusiasm of a teen, can encourage you, too.

Thank You, Lord, for challenges. With Your help, I'll tackle them.   — Mary Brown

15
SAT
HOUSE GUEST
PRACTICING THE POWER OF PRAYER
Mood-Breaker Prayers

Pour out your heart before him: God is a refuge for us....
— Psalm 62:8

Delightedly, I listened to an interview with Oscar the Grouch of *Sesame Street* fame on a local radio station. It was October 15, National Grouch Day, and Oscar talked about how much he loves to moan and complain. Then he belted out, "Have a rotten morning!" and was off to spend the rest of the day in his beloved garbage pail.

Occasionally, there are days when I'd make a great stand-in for Oscar. When that happens, I usually run out and buy an enormous chocolate candy bar. It's terrible for my cholesterol, but it works like a charm at improving my mood! Some of my friends go on cleaning binges when they wake up in a bad mood. One straightens her kitchen junk drawers, another heads for the closets. A neighbor takes her dog for a long walk on the beach. My husband Glenn tries to avoid people until he feels better (the whole family appreciates that!).

But what to do when none of these quick fixes works? At a prayer meeting recently, someone suggested praying for others when we're caught in an ugly mood. I decided to give it a try. A family friend had been sick with Lyme disease for more than a year, so the next time I felt like snapping at everyone around me, I concentrated on Kevin, visualizing God's healing love all around him. Whenever the ugly mood would start to overtake me, I'd say another prayer. After awhile, I started feeling better and, I hope, Kevin did, too.

I've done this many times since then and now use it as my "bad-mood breaker." Why don't you try it the next time you wake up on the wrong side of the bed? You'll be helping someone who needs your prayers, it's great for family harmony, and it will take you a long way *away* from that nasty mood that's hard to shake.

Father, praying for others is a wonderful way to center ourselves and do good for others. Help me choose it as a calming path back to You.
                                                              — Ellen Secrest

16 Be ye all of one mind, having compassion one of another....
SUN   — I Peter 3:8

My nine-year-old daughter Karen woke up one Saturday night with great pain in her right foot. The next morning we took her to the doctor for X-rays. After seeing two more doctors, it was determined that Karen might have cancer.

After six weeks of tests, my wife Roe and I were sitting in a waiting room while a surgeon in a New York City hospital performed a bone biopsy on Karen. The doctor said he could determine if Karen had a tumor and if the tumor was cancer.

That was the longest two-hour wait Roe and I have endured in our married years together. We didn't tell Karen of the potential threat. All she knew was that we were trying to find out what was wrong with her foot.

Karen was allowed to bring her stuffed toy dog with her into the operating room. After the surgery, the doctor came to us with the good news that Karen did not have a tumor and she would be fine — a stress fracture they discovered would eventually heal itself. Roe and I stepped into the recovery room to find Karen still asleep. Sitting at her side was her stuffed dog wearing a green surgical mask and cap.

Perhaps the doctors will never know what that small act of kindness and humor meant to me and to my family. The playfully dressed dog told us others were watching over our daughter and caring for her, too, and it comforted our spirits.

Father, where I can sow kindness, let me offer gestures — no matter how small — that can bring hope and strength in large doses to the receiver and those closest to them. — Christopher de Vinck

The Hardest Part of Prayer
WAITING

The theme of this year's Daily Guideposts *is the power of prayer. Throughout this year, we've been learning how to practice this great power in our lives. This week, Elizabeth Sherrill helps us to understand the hardest part of prayer: waiting.*

It's that in-between time after we've brought our requests to God and are waiting for His answers. This period can be excruciatingly long for many of us, especially during those times when we feel that our prayers require immediate attention. How, then, do we wait with faith and trust during those uncertain and anxious times of prayer? Join Elizabeth as we learn about the other side of prayer: waiting. — The Editors

17
MON

Day One — Learning Patience

O Lord, how long shall I cry, and thou wilt not hear!...
— Habakkuk 1:2

The question of the prophet Habakkuk is our question, any time we pray earnestly, repeatedly, in accord with what we believe is God's will...and nothing happens.

O Lord, how long?

Waiting...it's the hardest part of prayer. If it's any comfort, it was hard for great figures of the Bible, too. Sometimes the Scriptures provide an explanation of the wait, such as the one an angel gave to Daniel, who for three weeks had prayed and fasted seemingly in vain: "Fear not, Daniel: for from the first day...thy words were heard...But [Satan's warrior]...withstood me one and twenty days" (Daniel 10:12–13). In other words, more may be involved in our prayer battles than we know; our prayers may be only a skirmish in a cosmic struggle whose size — and importance — we can scarcely imagine.

Or what seems prolonged to us may reveal only how different heavenly time is from our own: "But do not ignore this one fact, beloved, that with the Lord one day is as a thousand years, and a thousand years as one day" (II Peter 3:8, RSV).

Usually, though, the Bible is silent about why we must wait, insisting only that we not lose heart as we do so. "Wait on the Lord: be of good courage" (Psalm 27:14). Promising: "Wait on the Lord...and he shall exalt thee" (Psalm 37:34). "The Lord is good unto them that wait for him" (Lamentations 3:25).

Waiting, in fact, is so often linked with promises that we can expect something very wonderful to occur in the wait itself, before the answer to our prayer appears. In our day of "quick" this and "instant" that, waiting is not a skill much valued. But with the psalmist, you and I can say to God, "Teach me: for thou art the God of my salvation; on thee do I wait all the day" (Psalm 25:5).

Father, teach us to wait.

— Elizabeth Sherrill

18 Day Two — Listening for the "Now"

TUES

Behold, as the eyes of servants look unto the hand of their masters...so our eyes wait upon the Lord our God, until that he have mercy upon us. —Psalm 123:2

It's a vivid image: the servitor's eyes fixed on the hand from which will come a signal. *Now! Act! Fill the role assigned you.*

Easy enough to detect a human master's hand-sign, but what about God's signals? Can we learn to wait for His silent *"Now"* in our hearts?

I know a man who did. I met Gregory Vojae at his home in St. Petersburg, Florida. But the test of his ability to wait had occurred in Atlanta, Georgia, during a catastrophic hotel fire. That night in 1946, Gregory awoke in his tenth-floor room at the Winecoff Hotel to the screams of fellow guests. The door to his room was hot to the touch. From his window all he could see was smoke — and an occasional plummeting form as people leapt from the floor above.

The only thing that kept Gregory from joining the 121 who died, he told me, was his long habit of listening for God's guidance — not only for His *what,* but for His *when.*

"Make a rope of bedsheets," he believed he heard God say, "and tie it to the center post of the window frame." Though he knew the makeshift rope would extend no more than two floors, Gregory obeyed. Through the smoke he heard the wail of sirens; he'd lower himself to the end of the sheets on the chance of being spotted by a fire fighter.

Wait.

Wait? Wait while the paint blistered on his room door? But each time he hoisted himself to the windowsill, the order came again.

Wait. Not yet.

The floor beneath his feet was smoking when through the inferno of noise all around him came a quiet word.

Now.

Gregory lowered himself into the blackness outside. He reached the end of his sheet-rope, eight dizzy stories above the street. And just as he did, through the thick smoke directly below, rose the tip of a ladder, then the helmet of a fire fighter climbing up.

Lord God, You have prepared the perfect time for each event of my life. Give me grace to ask before I act: Father, is it now?

— Elizabeth Sherrill

19 Day Three — When the Time Is Right

WED *Be still before the Lord, and wait patiently for him....*

— Psalm 37:7 (RSV)

You'd think by now I'd have developed better waiting skills. Here in my own house I live with an expert. For forty-six years, I've watched my husband John weigh the moment…hold off on an action…wait till the time seemed right to speak a word. Like the message John "heard" for our friend Jim.

It made such a strong impression that John repeated the message to me: *Do not condemn yourself. Rest in the love of your heavenly Father.*

We stared at each other, bewildered. Reassuring words, to be sure, but what could they possibly mean to Jim? Though he no longer lived nearby, as far as we knew he was still happily married, still doing well at work. Nevertheless, John wrote the words down beside Jim's name in our prayer log. And there they remained, month after month, with no entry in the follow-up column. "Call him. Tell him," I'd urge. "If it doesn't make sense, no harm done."

But John, of course, was waiting. It was three full years before he announced one evening, "I wrote Jim today. Passed on that message." In the letter, he'd told Jim how he'd waited and that he still had no idea what the message meant — or why now seemed the time to send it when he'd sat on it so long.

Jim, however, did know. He phoned three days later to tell us he'd been in a near-suicidal depression following the death of his father from whom he'd become estranged. And what meant the most to Jim in John's letter? It was the fact that "God knew three years ago what I'd be going through today." That "so long ago He was setting His help in motion."

Father, help me to trust in the love that knows no past, no future, only an eternal now.   — Elizabeth Sherrill

20 Day Four — Unexpected Rewards

THURS *They that wait upon the Lord shall renew their strength....*   — Isaiah 40:31

My friend Barbara Gordon is recovering from reconstructive spine surgery. It's taking a long time, and her friends are getting impatient.

"Are you sure you're doing the exercises right?" we ask. Or, "Shouldn't you see another doctor?"

The only one who seems satisfied with the slow pace of her recovery is Barbara. Despite pain and setbacks and the awkwardness of life on crutches, Barbara tells me something valuable is taking place in the process itself. "In the waiting, I'm learning to listen...to my body, to my emotions, to God."

If she'd plunged back into her busy daily schedule, Barbara says, she'd have missed the important lessons God has to teach in the crucibles of life.

Her words reminded me of a literal crucible, the 1,500-degree furnace where Steuben glass is shaped at the factory in Corning, New York. The glass is never returned directly to the outside air, but placed in a superheated oven where cooling takes place in a gradual process that frees it from "interior stress."

In the waiting, we learn to listen...to bring the stresses of our lives before the One Whose hands are shaping us...to let His healing have its perfect way.

Teach me to value the wait, Father, as well as the answer.
                    — Elizabeth Sherrill

21 Day Five — Hidden Reasons
FRI

The Lord is not slow about his promise as some count slowness, but is forbearing toward you, not wishing that any should perish.... — II Peter 3:9 (RSV)

"The houses here are so bleak in wintertime without their window boxes," my friend Susan Reiner wrote last June. Sue's husband had taken a job in Mosbach, Germany, where Sue had made a discovery about waiting.

Sue had heard about Mosbach's famous flower boxes, and as the dark days of February crawled by, she'd grown impatient for spring to come. By March, she'd started seed sets in a living room corner; by April, she'd put their empty window boxes outside. Still, up and down the street, no other boxes appeared. *Why were the town's renowned gardeners so slow in starting?*

Throughout March the weather warmed. All April long birds sang, the sun shone. May arrived on a heat wave. At last, Sue could take those empty receptacles no longer: "I transplanted all my flower sets to the window boxes."

That afternoon her next-door neighbor knocked on her door. *"Eisheiligen!"* the woman said with a vigorous shake of her head. *"Eisheiligen!"*

"The word means 'ice spirits,'" her husband said that evening, as baffled as Sue.

A week later the mystery was solved. On the tenth of May a hard freeze struck Mosbach, killing the brave new plants in Sue's boxes. The freeze lasted three days, and on the following day the local newspaper carried a headline:

Die Eisheiligen Sind Vorbei ("The Ice Spirits Have Passed")

Next day flowers bloomed on building fronts all over town.

"That's what they were all waiting for," Sue wrote. "This cold spell comes every May. They know enough to keep their flowers indoors until the threat is past."

Help me to accept this waiting time, Father, as the protection of Your farseeing love. — Elizabeth Sherrill

22
SAT

Day Six—Believing in the Promise

For since the beginning of the world men have not heard...neither hath the eye seen, O God...what he hath prepared for him that waiteth for him. —Isaiah 64:4

He arrived in New York in November, our friend from Uganda, to begin a six-month internship in journalism. Concerned with how Kiloto would handle the cold, we'd bought and borrowed a winter wardrobe.

But cold, it turned out, was not the problem. The problem was Kiloto's reaction to gray skies, leafless trees and lifeless fields. Uganda is a land of vibrant color—lush green foliage, brilliant flowers, jewel-like birds.

"I cannot remain here," he would say. "I cannot live in such a place."

"Wait!" we kept telling him. Spring will come. Trees will grow leaves. Birds will come back. Flowers will bloom.

But to wait, for Kiloto, was too hard. Mental pictures of the beauty-to-be, so clear to us, were absent for him. Kiloto had never seen a crocus poke through the snow or an apple tree in blossom. He went home in January.

And I understood better why waiting is so hard for us all. We don't see the end of the vigil. We can't visualize the promise fulfilled in the glowing colors of reality. All we can see, as we wait, is the wintry landscape before our eyes, not the new life burgeoning just beneath the surface.

Father, fill this season of waiting with the faith that sees what eyes do not. —Elizabeth Sherrill

23
SUN

Day Seven—His Higher Purpose

Let both grow together until the harvest....

—Matthew 13:30

As a gardener proud of her weed-free flower bed, I used to puzzle over Jesus' parable of the wheat and the tares. Unwanted plants had sprung up in a wheat field. Why didn't the farmer root out the miserable things?

Then my husband and I rented a house for a year in Oxford, England.

No, I said grandly to the realtor's offer to find us a gardener, we'd manage the small yard ourselves.

Small, but oh, dear... I'd reckoned without the fecund English climate and the many plants I didn't know. Every day a score of nameless shoots thrust up. I'd stand uncertainly on the garden walk, weeding fork in hand. Weeds or flowers?

That must have been the dilemma facing the farmer in Jesus' parable. Botanists believe the "tare" of the parable was the bearded darnel, a weed indistinguishable through much of the growing season from a wheat stalk. Only as harvest approaches do the differences appear.

Coping with that English garden helped me understand why answers to prayer are sometimes long in coming. "Lord," we protest, "why do You let evil go on and on? Why don't You uproot the wicked and prosper the good?"

"Do you know which is which?" I'd hear Him ask as I hesitated before some unpromising-looking plant. "Can you tell which of the plants in My garden are weeds? The changes coming to your neighborhood...the employee promoted over you...those disruptive voices at your church...can you detect My long-range plans in these situations?"

"Let both grow together until the harvest," He answers when our prayers seem unavailing. "I am doing greater things than you can dream."

Father, give me a farmer's faith, which sees the harvest in the seed time. Teach me, dear Lord, to wait. — Elizabeth Sherrill

24
MON

And they shall beat their swords into plowshares, and their spears into pruninghooks: nation shall not lift up sword against nation, neither shall they learn war any more. — Isaiah 2:4

"Today is United Nations Day," the radio announcer informed me. In honor of the occasion, I made a detour while on an errand past Woodrow Wilson's old house, which is just a few blocks away from my home in Princeton, New Jersey.

The former president of Princeton University, governor of New Jersey and president of the United States was the driving force behind the League of Nations, forerunner to the present peacekeeping body. He proposed such an organization in his famous "Fourteen Points" speech in 1918 to be used as a guide for making and keeping peace after World War I.

But the League of Nations failed to match Wilson's vision. In fact, he couldn't even persuade Congress to let the United States join other countries in this pact. Yet this son of a Presbyterian minister, who believed he was ordained by God to lead this country and work for peace, was not deterred. In his very last speech, weary of the fight and near death, he predicted his dream would someday become a reality. "I am not one of those who have the least anxiety about the triumph of the principles I have stood for," he stated. "That we shall prevail is as sure as that God reigns."

The United Nations, with one hundred fifty members (including the U.S.), testifies to his faith. Like the League of Nations, the U.N. is not everything Wilson's successors had hoped, but it has been a significant force for good and a symbol of the aspirations of peace-loving people everywhere.

"Blessed are the peacemakers," Christ said in the greatest sermon ever preached (Matthew 5:9). And blessed are visionary people like Woodrow Wilson who put their faith to work.

> *God, make us united in a common creed*
> *That deplores hatred, eschews greed.*

— Fred Bauer

---

25 *Bear with each other and forgive whatever grievances*
TUES *you may have against one another. Forgive as the Lord*
forgave you. —Colossians 3:13 (NIV)

The onion I picked up had a soft, dark spot. Oh, well, I could salvage most of it for the beef stew in progress. I marveled at the unusual, layered construction of this tasty vegetable as I pulled off the bad layers. Finally, I reached the perfect, pearly white onion to chop for the stew.

While peeling back that onion, I thought of what Pastor Martin had said recently about forgiving old, deep hurts: "Sometimes you have to forgive in layers." *How true,* I thought. Some people seem to be able to forgive and be done with it, but for me, it's usually the "Onion Method."

An old friendship came to mind. When we met, I felt sure Marie (not her real name) and I had much in common, that we'd soon be very close.

Her little digs and hurtful comments, though, would surface now and then, and after many months I had to admit that she disapproved of much about me — including some of the very things I considered my God-given assets. When I backed away from the relationship, she seemed agreeable. But it actually took me months of peeling away spotty layers of hurt, anger and resentment. Finally, I was down to disappointment. I found it helped to admit in prayer the layers I was feeling: "Lord, I'm still angry." But as long as I progressed inward, peeling and giving those layers to Him, I could see I really *was* progressing.

Sometimes it takes awhile, but I eventually do get to that pearly white forgiveness layer, where the offense, even upon remembrance, no longer hurts or matters.

Dear Lord, just as I wouldn't allow spotty vegetables in my stews, help me to be just as diligent at peeling away any stubborn unforgivenesses that might be clinging.   — Kathie Kania

26 ...*Making the most of the time....* — Ephesians 5:16 (RSV)
WED

Football — perhaps more than anything else, it has taught me the value of a second and a minute.

I don't generally join my husband in watching all of a televised game, but I will frequently come in for an exciting final quarter. And it is nothing short of extraordinary what a team can do in just a few brief moments. They can throw a touchdown pass, recover a fumble, make an interception or kick a field goal to win by a slim, three-point margin. Sadly, they also can lose a game with just seconds left to play.

Football has taught me how to strategize my moments, effectively using the clock — or "quarterback calling" my time. Now, instead of getting bogged down with too much to do and not enough time to do it in, I think in terms of minutes.

Ten minutes does a lot. It can scrub down the bathroom, empty or stack the dishwasher, fold the laundry, pay the month's utility bills, put on makeup, comb hair out of curlers...the list goes on. *Five* minutes dusts half the living room furniture, bookshelves and such, with the other half done in segments — *three* minutes here, or *two* minutes there — while waiting for the kettle to boil. *One* minute. *Ah,* that vital sixty seconds! Why, *one* minute jogs in place and burns off calories, or brushes teeth.

In terms of minutes, there is a time for everything. And it is also good to remember that it only takes *one* small minute to recover a fumble and say, "I'm sorry!" *One* small minute to intercept a harsh word and convert it into a smile instead. *One* small minute to go for the touchdown, with hugs and kisses for those we love.

Let's play to win!

> *Let us take one small minute today, Lord,*
> *to call and tell someone we care.*
> *To write a short note, send a blessing,*
> *so they know if they need us, we're there.*

— Fay Angus

27
THURS   *To every thing there is a season, and a time to every purpose under the heaven.*   — Ecclesiastes 3:1

On November 1, I'll become, officially, a senior citizen. When I told a friend I planned to write about being sixty-two, she said, "Don't tell me you're going to publicly *admit* that...before God and everybody!" I laughed, because it reminded me of a speaker I'd heard at a retreat last spring, a man in his eighties who said, "My wife is always telling me I should act my age, but I tell her, 'Why in the world would I want to do *that?*'"

Yet aging does have its rewards. At last, I have an *excuse* for my lifelong absentmindedness! I can now get by with being a bit silly, I've dropped many of the unnecessary "shoulds," and I can say what I think, letting the raised-eyebrow people whisper, "*Tsk, tsk*, senior citizen, you know!" I've also been playing more than I have since age twelve. Second childhood? Well, yes! I think I'll claim that! The first one was much too short.

Each age brings its own gifts, so I'd like to propose, right here before God and everybody, that we *celebrate* our aging, whether we're thirty, fifty, sixty-two or older, by making a thank-you list of the special blessings that come with the stage of life we're in. Then write A + at the top of the page and offer your list, with thanks, to God. (Bonus for seniors: When your list is done, reward yourself by hugging a grandchild!)

Thank You, Creator God, for the special gifts of this wonderful time of life: _____ .

— Marilyn Morgan Helleberg

HOUSE GUEST

$\dfrac{28}{\text{FRI}}$ *Am I my brother's keeper?*   — Genesis 4:9

I jumped out of the car and ran up the front steps of the old apartment house. It was my turn to deliver a hot meal to the elderly woman in Apartment 23-C. She was very sweet, very lonely and loved to chat, but I never gave her a chance to say anything.

You see, this woman was fond of cats and shared her tiny apartment with six adored felines. The problem was litter boxes. There just weren't enough of them to handle this household. So each time I stepped inside her door, I smiled, put the lunch tray down on the nearest table and made a rapid retreat — holding my breath until I got back into the hall.

Then one day, I heard a story about an old rabbi who asked his students how they knew when nighttime had ended and the new day had begun. One pupil thought it happened when one saw an animal in the distance and was able to tell whether it was a sheep or a dog. Another guessed that it happened when one looked at a tree in the distance and could tell whether it was a fig tree or a peach tree. The wise rabbi shook his head at both of these answers.

"Then how can you tell when night has ended?" the students asked.

"You can tell when you look at the face of any human being and see that he is your brother or sister. If you cannot do this, then it is still night."

The next time I visited the old woman's apartment I lingered for a little while. Her smile and the light that came into her eyes made the place bearable. Shortly after, a group of us contacted a local social services agency, explained the situation and made arrangements for weekly housecleaning to be done. Now she is living with the cats she loves in a healthy environment — and I'm taking the time to get to know her better.

Father, often it's difficult to see You in the faces of others — my brothers and my sisters. Let it always be daytime in my heart.
           — Ellen Secrest

HOUSE GUEST

29
SAT

The one will lift up his fellow.... — Ecclesiastes 4:10

Driving home in rush-hour traffic one day, our car began to cough and sputter. As my husband John edged it over to the slow lane, impatient commuters careened past, blasting their horns and mouthing angry words. We eventually made it home safely, but I felt disheartened by the irate attitudes we'd encountered.

The next day, still upset, I visited my mother at the convalescent home. Taking her in her wheelchair for an outing to a nearby ice cream parlor, I approached — with dread — the wide, busy street we had to cross. When the "walk" sign flashed, I yelled to Mom, "Hold on!" and broke into a trot. But the rough pavement forced me to slow down, and in despair I saw the light changing. Then I noticed that the waiting drivers were all waving to my mother. And Mom, who rarely responds to people anymore, was happily waving back.

That's the difference, I thought, feeling the disillusionment of the previous day melt away. *There are wavers and there are honkers.* But which one am I? Am I one of those who restores hope, or am I too often the impatient and irate one? Standing with my mother safely upon the sidewalk, I silently asked God to help me recognize when my fellow travelers need encouragement and affirmation. Because I know which kind of person I want to try to be.

Lord, let my words and actions seek to uplift another whose load may need lightening or brightening today. Amen.

— Bonnie Lukes

30
SUN

But the Lord said...man looketh on the outward appearance, but the Lord looketh on the heart. — I Samuel 16:7

Years ago, when I was a widow, I attended meetings of an organization called Tough Love. The purpose was to learn to love your teenagers with tough love, no matter how difficult it might prove. I felt I needed help rearing my sons without their father. Just as the meeting started, a man in his twenties entered the room. Quite obviously, he didn't fit in our group of concerned parents. He wore a loud shirt and tight jeans with holes in them. He had shoulder-length, curly blond hair. He also wore an earring, and he chain-smoked. *Lord, please don't let me get in a sharing group with him. Why doesn't someone ask him to leave?*

To my horror, he plopped down in a chair right by me. I was determined to ignore this young man. We all shared a bit about ourselves. "I'm fresh out of jail," he said softly. "Was there seven years. You name it, I've done it. I came to see if I might help some of you parents. I got some answers."

No one else had questions for the stranger but, suddenly, I was asking him everything I always wanted to know about teenage rebellion. "Why don't my sons ever talk to me? Why do they always seem angry with me? Why do they make fun of me? Am I really too tough, as they say I am?" Questions and answers were flying back and forth when suddenly I blurted out, "Why are you wearing that earring?"

He smiled. "To see if anyone here would accept me with it, my long hair and my torn jeans." We laughed some and then talked seriously for nearly two hours. I learned a lot from Paul. "Your sons don't think it's cool to talk to you. Give 'em time. The anger only *seems* directed toward you. Laugh a little bit with 'em. But too tough? Man, I wish I'd had a tough mom like you."

At home, the moment I walked into the den, both my sons mocked, "Hey, how was your 'love tough' meeting?" They rolled on the floor laughing. I sat down on the floor with them and laughed, too. I didn't criticize the TV show they were watching. I didn't comment about the homework left undone. Nor did I nag that they were eating on the new carpet again. These were minor offenses. When the serious ones occurred, I would remember Paul's words: "Man, I wish I'd had a tough mom like you."

Oh, Father, how many Pauls have I brushed by? Will You help me to make friends with people who are different from me? And to continue to "love tough" my children through all their problems — and mine. — Marion Bond West

---

31
MON
But many that are first shall be last; and the last shall be first. — Matthew 19:30

When we were in the third grade, my best friend Marguerite and I memorized the little childish ditty "The Purple Cow." So we thought it would be fun to dress up as a purple cow for the town's annual Halloween costume parade that year. Trouble was, we couldn't seem to agree on who should be the front end of the cow. Marguerite felt she should because her mother was making the costume. I said that I should because I was older than she was. Finally, after we'd argued endlessly about the matter, I stomped off in a huff. So Marguerite asked our friend Connie, and I made plans to go as a gypsy.

Halloween night came and the town's children gathered in the local school yard to parade. I tried to smile as I swished my colorful skirts and shook my tambourine, but I couldn't keep my eyes off the purple cow up ahead. Obviously, Connie was delighted to be the rear end! She kicked up her heels and pranced in time with the music. Everyone was laughing at the purple cow's antics, including the judges, who eventually awarded Marguerite and Connie first prize.

Somehow, I've never forgotten that Halloween event and the lesson it taught me: the importance of subduing one's ego now and then and cheerfully accepting what seems to be a secondary job. It's good for the soul. And with a little luck it can also be fun.

Dear Father, thank You for Your words, meant for Your disciples but just as relevant for me today.　　　　　　　— Eleanor Sass

Prayer Diary

My Prayer Requests for October:

1. _____

2. _____

3. _____

4. _____

5. _____

6. _____

7. _____

8. _____

9. _____

10. _____

11. _____

12. _____

13. _____

14. _____

15. _____

16. _____

17. _____

18. _____

19. _____

20. _____

21. _____

22. _____

23. _____

24. _____

25. _____

26. _____

27. _____

28. _____

29. _____

30. _____

31. _____

November

S	M	T	W	T	F	S
		1	2	3	4	5
6	7	8	9	10	11	12
13	14	15	16	17	18	19
20	21	22	23	24	25	26
27	28	29	30			

GIFTS OF THE SEASON

The Feast

Bountiful table,
nature's gifts shared, grateful hearts
honor our Maker.

*With deep thanksgiving, Lord, we accept all Your
abundance before us. May it nourish us
toward good works in Your name.*

1   *To all the saints in Christ Jesus....*   — Philippians 1:1

TUES

One night, one of our church members, Phoebe Greene, related some of her harrowing experiences of long ago when faith helped her to survive.

Born into one of Boston's privileged families early in this century, Phoebe married Ted Greene, a young Harvard medical student, and they went to war-torn China as missionaries. The Greenes lost their first child Ralph to meningitis when he was twelve years old. Retaining their faith in spite of their tragic loss, Phoebe, Ted and their ten-year-old daughter Joan kept moving just ahead of the invading Japanese armies, tending the sick.

Little by little, their material possessions were destroyed or lost, except some treasured prints of the Madonna and Child. With everything else taken from her, these holy images became a symbol of hope and encouragement. At each temporary dwelling, she would unroll those cherished pictures and tack them carefully to the walls. They were her only beauty, her balance, a tangible touchstone of faith in that dangerous place.

Phoebe recounted the night when enemy soldiers came to their door. She and her daughter fled through a back door into the night, leaving the precious art behind.

This final loss left me breathless. "Oh, Phoebe," I blurted out, "I can't believe you lost your paintings!"

Phoebe answered as if her only thought was to comfort me. "But, my dear, you see, we still had the stars."

The stars.... Of course, Phoebe by now had seen beyond worldly attachments. God could be found wherever one looked, and for Phoebe He was found by looking up.

Today in our church, on All Saints' Day, when we honor those members who have departed, Pheobe Greene's words still sing in my mind. To be like Phoebe, I would have to keep believing in people, even when they disappoint me. I would have to keep loving people, even when they didn't seem to love me. I would have to keep forgiving people, even when they refused to forgive me. And I would have to keep trusting God, no matter what trouble unfolded before me. But, you know, perhaps that's not an impossible task...if I look up and focus on one of Phoebe's stars.

Father, You have sent Your saints to show us the way to You. Oh, that we would follow.
                                                              — Pam Kidd

2

PRAYER CAN CHANGE YOUR LIFE
Pray for Others

Pray one for another....   —James 5:16

"Sometimes...right in the middle of a conversation, I find myself saying a silent prayer for the person I'm talking to," says Ed Smith, a personnel consultant for several national companies. He is one of about twenty people who have gathered to study prayer at our Nashville church. "In fact," Ed continues looking my way, "a few days ago, as I sat across from Pam at lunch, I remember doing just that, pausing mid-sentence to ask God to bless her."

He prayed for me?

Back at home later that evening, my husband David finds a tissue-thin airmail letter waiting. It is from Brian Woods, a South African Presbyterian minister. "I think of you often," Brian writes, "and each Friday I have reserved a special time when I pray for you and Pam and your family." I feel the same warm connection that I felt earlier when Ed mentioned his prayer. *Halfway around the world, someone is praying for me!*

"Pray for others," *Prayer Can Change Your Life* tells us, and I've been trying to make that a daily habit. I pray for those that time and circumstance have taken from my life: *Lord give them happiness.* Of course, I pray for David, Brock and Keri, my mother, and the rest of my family: *Lord watch over them... hold them in Your hand.* And I pray for strangers, like the postal clerk or the service station attendant: *Lord, he looks so tired, let something unexpectedly good come to him today.*

But having someone say, "Pam, I prayed for you" turns this prayer habit inside out. Suddenly, I'm looking at this "pray for others" directive from the other side of the fence. Maybe it wasn't coincidence that I left that lunch with Ed filled with renewed confidence, and that on the way home, I stopped at the local high school "out of the blue" and volunteered for a tutoring program. Did Ed's prayer do that?

And Brian's letter has made Friday more than just the end-of-the-week day, it is a day of expectation. "Someone's praying for me today," I say out loud just to feel the warmth of it.

At that moment, it occurs to me that I, too, should be taking this "praying for others" a step further. Why not dare to share the good news... "I'm praying for you." A week later, after a meeting with the PR director from a large hotel about a church affair, I gather my courage. As he walks me to the door, I say nervously, "Last week, after our phone conversation, I said a prayer for you...I just wanted you to know." By his expression, I think it might have made a difference in his day.

So, playing by this new rule, I must tell you, too, that I have prayed this prayer for you....

Lord, if You would pour an extra measure of Your best blessings into the life of this reader, it would be mighty nice. Thank You and Amen.   — Pam Kidd

---

3 *Whatever your hand finds to do, do it with all your might....*
THURS   — Ecclesiastes 9:10 (NIV)

I read recently about Gerald d'Aboville, the man who single-handedly rowed his boat thousands of miles across the northern Pacific, from Japan to Washington. He persevered through rough water and capsizings (thirty-four of them!), through seasickness and loneliness. But the thing that impressed me most was that during a typhoon, Gerald rowed for eight days against the currents—without moving ahead. *Eight days without moving forward!* Sure, he became discouraged, but the important thing to him was that he did not move *backward.* He was still headed toward his goal.

That's a lesson I'll remember when things aren't progressing quickly enough for me: when my boss doesn't applaud my latest ideas; when the lines of communication with my kids seem knotted. *Keep rowing.* Don't give up. It worked for Gerald d'Aboville, who became the first man ever to row across the northern Pacific. With God's help, it will work for me—and you—too.

In Your earthly ministry, Lord, You did not give in to difficulty and despair. Arm me with the same resolve; keep me rowing in the right direction.   — Mary Lou Carney

---

4 *Let us love one another, for love comes from God....*
FRI   — I John 4:7 (NIV)

During the presidential election campaigns, I used to hear politicians talk about "trickle-down economics," a theory that had something to do with strengthening our economy from the top down. I usually got lost in the rhetoric of the debates, but every time I heard the phrase "trickle-down economics," I thought how God lets His love seep down through His believers to people who seem far away from Him.

To me, God's "Trickle-Down Love" goes like this: I have a neighbor who is difficult to love. I'll call her Jane. Jane seems arrogant, negative and always needs to be right, which irritates me. When I wake up in the morning, I have no feelings of love for Jane. In fact, I could declare bankruptcy when it comes to my supply of love for her. But then I spend time quietly considering God's love for me; how He loved me enough to send His Son to die for me; how He loves me unconditionally, even though He knows how prideful I can be. Soon, the intangible but powerful resource of God's love trickles down and fills me up.

Later that day, Jane calls. She complains about everything from the weather to the amount of work she has to do, and then she asks to borrow my big coffeepot. Jane doesn't know Jesus, but she knows me. Will His love trickle from above to me and then to her? Will the good from the top get through? Does God's "Trickle-Down Love" work? The debate is on. The answer is up to me.

Is the answer ever up to you?

Father, my love for others begins with knowing I am loved by You. Enable me to be part of Your "Trickle-Down Love" today.
— Carol Kuykendall

HOUSE GUEST

5
SAT

He makes me to lie down in green pastures; He leads me beside the still waters. He restores my soul....
—Psalm 23:2–3 (NKJV)

It's only the first week of November, but it's been winter in southeast Minnesota since a blizzard roared through four days ago. Today, at 5:00 A.M., the mercury only reads three degrees below zero, but I still have to deliver the morning paper. I bundle up in snow pants, gloves inside mittens, two pairs of socks, fur-lined boots and a parka with a hood that covers as much of my face as I want.

The dark sky is sparkling clear and perfect for stargazing. After enjoying the beauty for only a few blocks, delivering papers as I go, I notice my body is warm from walking. After a further trek up a wooded hillside, I listen to the wind in the trees. Everything is peaceful up here, including my sleepy little village below. *"Thanks, God,"* I whisper, grateful for this quiet time in His presence. A little farther on, my approach sends white-tailed deer scurrying.

With only a few blocks to go, my reverie breaks when Lydia, one of my customers, remarks through her door, "Nasty out there today, ain't it?"

Startled out of my contemplation, I stutter, "Y-yes...it's an awful morning." But as I resume my walk, I feel bad. After all, I've been having anything *but* a nasty morning. I feel as though I've let God down because I shortchanged this lovely walk with Him and missed an opportunity to encourage Lydia about the day awaiting her.

I turn to God and apologize — and sense His forgiveness restoring my soul. When I see Bernice, another customer, waiting inside her storm door, I bound up the steps. "It's a beautiful day out," I tell her. "God must've added an extra blessing to it."

Help me, Lord, not to be afraid to tell other people what I'm really feeling, even if they don't agree with me. — Ellyn Baumann

6 *Pray without ceasing.*   — I Thessalonians 5:17
SUN

Along with thousands of other New Yorkers, I grieved over the fire that gutted historic St. Agnes Church. Half a block from Grand Central Station, it was a place I often went when waiting for a train. There were always people in the pews, kneeling or simply sitting, and a score of votive candles glowing in their red glass cups. As we left St. Agnes together one day, a woman explained, "I leave a candle burning to say that no matter what else I have to do today, I'll still be praying."

It was an electrical fire in the organ loft that set off a four-alarm blaze. Fire trucks converged from every direction, pumping a million gallons of water into the building. At last, fire fighters were able to enter the sanctuary. Ankle-deep in water, they surveyed the drenched and smoke-blackened ruin. Only in one respect did the sanctuary look familiar; a score of votive candles were still glowing in their red glass cups.

The fire fighters stared. How had these tiny flames remained alight in the cataracts of water that had extinguished an inferno? The shape of the cups was one theory, the chemical components of the wax another. Whatever the physical aspect, for me there's a spiritual one, too. Those unquenchable candles say, no matter what comes our way today, we can still be praying.

Keep my faith alight, Father, when floodwaters come.
— Elizabeth Sherrill

7
MON

A man's heart deviseth his way: but the Lord directeth his steps.
— Proverbs 16:9

Late in my junior year in high school, I was losing the battle with algebra. I couldn't get it. I couldn't balance an equation, and I couldn't untangle the word problems. To me, the subject was an impossible maze!

Finally, Mr. Flinton, our math teacher, said, "Come back after school and I will help you." Without his help, I was sure I wouldn't pass the final exam.

But my troubles were far from over. The first afternoon selected by Mr. Flinton was the afternoon for the football squad picture to be taken. This would appear in the class yearbook forever. I couldn't miss that!

What a tangle. If I attended football practice and had my picture taken, I'd flunk algebra. If I accepted Mr. Flinton's offer, my photo would not be in the yearbook. What should I do? I anguished before finally reporting to Mr. Flinton, who helped me that afternoon and several thereafter. But not having my picture included in the yearbook left me heartbroken.

After an uphill climb, I did learn algebra. And it gave me the boost I needed for college chemistry and physics. Later it was a constant and useful tool during my years as a manager in technical writing.

Now as I look back, I see that making that tough choice not only gave me tools for college and my job, but also set the standard for future decisions. I'm still shortsighted at times, but my algebra lesson gave me a rule of thumb I use to measure the proper response in any situation. When I honestly can't see what's best, I do what I did then — trust God to point me in the right direction.

Understanding Lord, help me to look beyond the moment to a lifetime of Your blessings.
— Oscar Greene

8
TUES
"Now look around among yourselves...and select seven men...."
—Acts 6:3 (TLB)

Sometimes I'm tempted not to vote, especially when my candidate seems to be the underdog. Then I remember the time my elder daughter Teresa ran for student council in the third grade and sent out this flyer:

Dear Voters,
I do not mean to brag about myself. I could be a good council member. I would try to solve your problems. I would work hard, and try to be fair, and I'd look over everyone's side to the problem. If you're nice to me, I'll be nice to you. I'll try to be kind. Please vote for me. I'll do my best.

Teresa Schantz

She lost. And she was devastated for a while, until she began to put her loss into perspective. One day she said to me, "At least I gave my classmates a choice. That's important, isn't it, Dad?"

That started me wondering what it would be like if there were only one candidate on the slate when I went to vote. What if I had no choice?

So when I'm tempted to skip the polls, thinking, *My vote won't make any difference,* I remind myself that my candidate may indeed lose. But by voting — whether or not my candidate gets elected — I am voting for democracy.

Lord, help me to realize what an awesome thing it is to be able to choose our leaders. And let me do my part today — and vote.
—Daniel Schantz

9
WED
Not one sparrow...can fall to the ground without your Father knowing it.
—Matthew 10:29 (TLB)

A little friend left our lives forever this past year: our dog Coco. She died suddenly after a one-week illness. Her death hit me hard because she'd been my companion for almost ten years, starting when I was unmarried and on my own for the first time. How she danced with joy when I walked in the door at the end of a long day. I've become a family of three since then, but Coco was always beside me.

I really struggled in the weeks after her death. Once, my little boy Ross caught me crying. "Are you sad about Coco?" he asked, and I nodded.

"You're all right, Mom. Coco's in heaven," he said. Yes, I told him that when he first asked where she'd gone. But did I really believe it? I did as a child, but now I know the world is a much more complicated place. *Doesn't God have more to be concerned with than my little dog?* I wondered.

My pastor-friend Darrell offered me a most comforting answer from Matthew's Gospel: "Look at the birds of the air; they do not sow or reap or store away in barns, and yet your heavenly Father feeds them" (Matthew 6:26, NIV).

"And then there's the little sparrow who can't fall to the ground without our Father knowing," Darrell added. "I know these verses are supposed to show us *our* value to God, but I can't help thinking they're also meant to assure us that God places a great value on all His creatures."

I'm sure God loved Coco as I did. Maybe she's even in a special place in heaven. But those words from Matthew mean more. How comforting to know that God cares about the smallest concern, if it's large to me. His great love makes no grief too small to bring before Him.

Father, as You hear the sparrow fall, so You hear me cry and welcome me into Your comforting arms.   — Gina Bridgeman

10
THURS

HOUSE GUEST
They shall obtain joy and gladness, and sorrow and sighing shall flee away.   —Isaiah 35:10

It was a perfect day to rake leaves. The sky was bright blue; the air crisp and crackly. As I dragged a bulging leaf bag into the woods, something red, half-buried in the underbrush, caught my eye. Bending down, I discovered an old soccer ball lost by the children years ago. Its red and blue stripes had faded and all of the air had leaked out. It was definitely a goner, so I pitched it into the trash can and continued with the raking.

An hour or so later I relaxed on the porch steps and found myself thinking about the soccer ball. Not long ago, it was bright and shiny, getting a terrific workout by the kids every day. It reminded me of youth—fun, laughter, play, the joy of childhood. And now it was in the bottom of the garbage pail—a sad ending for something that once was so full of bounce and vigor.

A puff of wind scattered red and orange leaves across the lawn. As I got up and walked over to the garage for more leaf bags, I glanced up at the basketball hoop in the driveway. Was it just a few weeks ago that my son Chris asked me to shoot some baskets with him and his friends after school? "C'mon, Mom! It'll be fun!" Afraid of making a fool of myself, I made up an excuse and went inside. Now, I wondered if I was stuck in my rigid "adult" mold — taking life so seriously. Where were those wonderful childlike qualities I once had — spontaneity, delight in the ordinary?

Later, after putting the rake away, I scooped up the basketball lying in a corner of the garage. Giving it a few bounces, I dribbled across the driveway and aimed for the hoop. I jumped and leapt and even made a few baskets. When Chris arrived home from class a few minutes later, I tossed him the ball. He caught it, gave me a big grin, as we played until dark. What a great feeling! I had brushed aside my "adultness" for a little while and found a wonderful surprise — the child in me was still alive and well.

Thank You, Lord, for swings and seesaws, for mud puddles to slosh through and rock piles to climb — they help keep the child in us from being buried under our "maturity."   — Ellen Secrest

11
FRI
I am crucified with Christ: nevertheless I live....
                                                 —Galatians 2:20

Today is Veterans Day, and in appreciation I will bake a chocolate cake for John.

John is a veteran of the Korean War. Although he has been our friend for twenty years, it was only when he was going for the renewal of his driver's license recently and was concerned about his failing eyesight that he told us anything about his war experience. Taken prisoner when his plane was shot down over enemy territory, John's eyes were permanently injured by the near-starvation diet.

When we asked him how he had been able to bear such atrocities and retain his sanity, he told us, "When I was caged and borne through the streets like an animal, I remembered that Jesus hung naked on the cross for me. I knew that the humiliation and degradation that I was suffering was nothing to that of my Lord and Savior Who bore in His body my sins and the sins of the world. In those thirty-four months, I learned the unforgettable lesson that the Apostle Paul wrote of: 'I want to know Christ and the power of his resurrection *and the fellowship of . . . his sufferings*' [Philippians 3:10, NIV, italics added]. I had a sense not only of Christ's presence with me, but of sharing in His pain on my behalf."

Do you know a "soldier of the cross?" Perhaps a retired veteran who can no longer drive and would love to go for a ride to see the beautiful fall color? Someone in the Veterans Hospital who seldom has a visitor? Why not get to know them, find out about their war experience, attend the parade in your town and afterward tell one of the participants that you are thankful for what he or she has done for you.

Without our veterans' sacrifices, we would not have the opportunity to live in a free country.

Dear Lord, today as I remember our veterans, let me remember that You paid the greatest price of all that I might be free from sin. — Dorothy Shellenberger

12
SAT

"But judge your neighbor fairly." — Leviticus 19:15 (NIV)

In my town, there is a man who wanders around in raggedy clothes muttering to himself. For years, I've seen him bending down to collect cigarette butts. Late one evening, I was standing at the train station waiting for my husband Paul, when a family — out-of-towners with bags and carrying cameras — was having trouble figuring out how to buy train tickets from the machine. As I've had trouble figuring out that complicated silver beast myself, I began making my way over, when to my shock I saw the mother tap the raggedy man on the shoulder: "Excuse me, how do I buy a ticket?"

Uh-oh, I thought. I expected him to spew forth a bunch of gibberish, but to my surprise he silently took their money.

Uh-oh, I thought again. *He's going to take their money and run off with it!* So I watched carefully, poised, ready to call for help if (when) he ran off with their cash. But to my amazement the man easily slid their money into the machine, all the while giving the clearest, most lucid explanation of how to buy a train ticket that I had ever heard. He even cleared up a point or two that I had never understood! And when they left, after profusely thanking him, he went right back to muttering and picking up cigarette butts.

A light tap of the horn alerted me that Paul was there. "What were you doing staring like that?" he asked.

"Underestimating someone," I said quietly.

Dear God, let me give every person I run into today the benefit of the doubt. Thanks to You, people can always surprise me.
— Linda Neukrug

13
SUN
PRACTICING THE POWER OF PRAYER
Pass-Along Prayers

I cried unto God with my voice...and he gave ear unto me.
— Psalm 77:1

This past year, I underwent major surgery that turned out to be much more extensive than any of us initially expected. Although my surgeon had warned me in advance, I really didn't expect the severity of pain I experienced afterward. The heavy narcotics that dripped into my IV didn't seem to be doing much good, and as I lay sleepless in my hospital bed the first night, only one thing comforted me: the knowledge that dozens of my friends were part of a "prayer chain" that was holding me before the Lord twenty-four hours a day.

An elderly man in the room next door seemed in even worse agony than I. The nurse told me he'd just had both legs amputated at the hip. As I listened to his cries, I couldn't help wondering who was praying for this poor man? Did he have friends or family, as I did, who were seeking God's healing touch for him? What if he did not?

The idea nearly broke my heart. *Lord,* I thought, *if only there was a way I could pass along some of the prayers being said for me. He needs someone praying for him even more than I do!*

A moment later, it dawned on me that *nobody* was in a better position to be that person than I was. *Could I empathize with his plight? Could I comprehend the urgency of his needs, the desperation he felt?* You bet.

My prayers that night were not eloquent, but they were fervent and frequent. And when the man's cries grew less anguished as dawn approached, I willed myself to focus on him, determined not to stop praying until he was able to sleep. Finally, he was. And so was I.

In a remarkable way, God really *had* allowed me to "pass on" some of the prayers that were being said for me. And in the process, He'd pulled two people through some of the most miserable hours of their lives.

Lord Jesus, help me to see beyond my own pain today so that I may pray for those I know who are also hurting.

— Susan Williams

14
MON
I pray that all may go well with you and that you may be in health; I know that it is well with your soul.
— III John 2 (RSV)

Maryland psychologist John Gartner and his co-workers have reviewed some two hundred studies of religion and mental health, and have found that in several important ways, religious faith bolsters well-being. Here are some of the findings:

- All of the studies reviewed showed lower suicide rates among religious people.

- All but one of the studies indicated that those who had religious values used fewer drugs than the nonreligious people studied.

- Those who attended church had less marital unhappiness and lower divorce rates than the unchurched.

- Those with religious faith were more likely to overcome mental illness once it occurred; schizophrenics who went to church were less likely to be rehospitalized.

- There was less recurrence of depression in those with religious beliefs.

In addition to all the other things our faith means to us, it appears that it's also good mental health insurance!

Today, Lord, I give thanks for my mental and emotional health, and especially for my faith that is so much a part of that.
— Marilyn Morgan Helleberg

15
TUES   *"Trust in the Lord God always, for in the Lord Jehovah is your everlasting strength."*   — Isaiah 26:4 (TLB)

I was settled comfortably into my favorite patio chair early one morning, enjoying the blessed peace and quiet and my first cup of coffee. Suddenly, with a huge explosive burst, the world went crazy. An earthquake, 5.9 on the Richter scale, had struck, its epicenter just eight miles from our home.

Then, suddenly, in one gigantic, terrifying blast, it was over. Water mains were broken. Phone lines had gone dead. Electricity was gone, and sirens screamed throughout the city.

In our home, walls and ceilings had cracked, and cupboards had flown open, spewing out their contents. Mercifully, no one was hurt and neighbors rushed to help one another. During the days it took to put utilities back into service, we were all pioneers, cooking on outdoor grills, sponging down instead of taking baths or showers and, most of all, sharing what we had with those around us—bottled water, cans of food, candles, flashlights, a first-aid kit and a battery-powered radio to get the news.

"What a comfort to have these things," I said to my husband John.

"True," he replied, "and it's good we had stocked up on them in the first place."

His reply got me to thinking about being prepared for other kinds of emergencies. Not just with physical supplies, but with a spiritual reserve from which to draw during "soul" crises—when financial losses, illness or even death strike.

In those dreadful hours after the quake and aftershocks, I drew on my spiritual reserves: the words of the familiar hymn "Great Is Thy Faithfulness"; God's promises, like "Fear not, for I am with you" (Isaiah 43:5, RSV); and more. Our prayers and God's repeated assurances comforted us as we felt His never-failing presence support us.

When our world tumbles down around us, when our hearts are breaking, Lord, be our strength. Let Your presence and the safety of Your ever-loving hands carry us through. —Fay Angus

Quiet Time

O Holy Spirit, descend plentifully into my heart. Enlighten the dark corners of this negative dwelling and scatter there Thy cheerful beams.
                       — *St. Augustine*

16
<u>WED</u>   *Give therefore thy servant an understanding heart... that I may discern between good and bad....* —I Kings 3:9

Agnes is an old friend of mine, I mean ninety-six years old. She has no close relatives, only a few friends who call or drop in like me, and she continues to live alone.

Another thing about Agnes: She *likes* junk mail.

I couldn't believe it either when I first heard her say it. "I've never outgrown the thrill of the postman's ring," she told me. "And these days, who's left to write me a *personal* letter?"

"But all those sales pitches," I protested.

"Love 'em!" she snapped. "Keeps me in touch with the world." She said she knew what was new in magazines, and why. She was up on a number of diseases that no one had heard of back when she was young. She liked reading about the latest rose mutation, enjoyed receiving invitations to join African safaris and lessons in dancing the *salsa;* she left the door open for winning one of those publishing sweepstakes. "On top of that," Agnes said, "when there are so many material things that people want, how nice to see all the things I do *not* want!"

All of these things she told me with a twinkle in her eye. But when it came to requests for donations, she grew serious. "I don't have money to give to starving children or battered wives or all the people in need," she said, "but I never throw a plea for them away. I put each letter I get on the table before me, and *I pray for them.* When the postman comes, he brings me my prayer time."

Something tells me that one day Agnes is going to win one of those sweepstakes. But more importantly, one day, perhaps in the near future, her prayers will help eliminate some of the misfortune that her mail describes. For Agnes and many others, it will be a day of rejoicing.

Father, bless those who find good in unlikely places. —Van Varner

---

17
THURS
For he is our peace, who has made us both one, and has broken down the dividing wall of hostility.
—Ephesians 2:14 (RSV)

I was speaking at a college in Illinois a few years ago when someone came up to me afterward and introduced himself. As soon as he spoke and I heard his Southern drawl, I felt my walls go up. "I'm from Mississippi, too," said the man, who was white. "I'm a Southern Baptist pastor."

Churning inside me were the memories: the white man who stole four acres of my mama's land; the whites who paid us next to nothing for backbreaking labor on their farm; the whites who beat a dear friend to within an inch of his life.

Almost in spite of myself, I kept listening. As I did, I heard the words of a man who was not only a Christian, but who was deeply committed to reconciliation between the races. And I was challenged. All my life I had abhorred racism. Now I was confronted with my own. Here I was judging a man I didn't know by the way he spoke, and not by what he said.

Since then, I've come to see that loving others, *all others*, is a matter of obedience. I may think I have reasons not to love someone because I have been hurt before. Or I may be hanging on to negative things that I learned growing up. But as a Christian, I must be obedient to Christ, Who shows no partiality.

Precious Savior, help me see those walls of my own making, and with Your love, help me tear them down brick by brick. Amen.
— Dolphus Weary

18
FRI   *HOUSE GUEST*
As God's chosen people...clothe yourselves with compassion, kindness, humility, gentleness and patience.
— Colossians 3:12 (NIV)

When I first took up photography, my husband Dick warned me that if I missed a photo opportunity, the image would be lost forever. Only once have I proved him wrong.

A friend told me about a life-sized statue of Christ on the St. Vincent de Paul Downtown Chapel in Portland, Oregon, and I went to photograph it. The figure stood with raised arms reaching out to the city, its face gazing down with compassion on those who wandered in front of the chapel on the sidewalk below. Unfortunately, the lighting was wrong. I'd have to come back another time.

The next week I returned. I parked, walked to a vantage point and inwardly groaned. The chapel had been prepared for painting, and the statue was totally wrapped in opaque plastic to protect it. To me, it seemed as if Christ were hiding His eyes from having to look at the city. The plastic carefully taped around His hands looked like gloves on a surgeon, suggesting that this Christ wanted to avoid direct contact with people. At the time, a photo of such a hidden Christ seemed of no use to me, so I decided to come back later when the statue would be unwrapped.

Since then, however, the memory of the swathed statue has lingered with me and changed my priorities. After seeing how ugly it was to conceal a mere image of Christ, I don't want to conceal the real Christ living in me. I've spent more time just listening to people; I've written "thinking of you" notes to hurting people who can't write back; I've tried harder to be a good neighbor.

That's how the photo I never captured on film was not lost — instead, it captured me.

Lord Jesus Christ, help me to cast aside, as joyously as You threw off Your burial shroud, anything in me that conceals You.

— Elsie Larson

19 Glory to God in the highest.... — Luke 2:14
SAT

The basement is nearly complete: new carpets, new paneling. I was cutting a few last pieces of corner molding when Michael, my seven-year-old son, stepped into the room.

"Can I have those little bits of wood, Daddy?" he asked, watching the extra pieces fall to the ground.

"Sure. How come?"

"I don't know. I want to make something."

Michael gathered up the stray wood and walked out of the basement. I could hear his footsteps going all the way up to his bedroom.

An hour later, my wife Roe called, "Supper!"

I washed my hands in the basement sink, walked up to the kitchen, took my place to my daughter Karen's left. Everyone was seated, except for Michael.

"Michael! Supper!"

We heard Michael's footsteps stomping down the stairs. He stepped into the kitchen with his creation: a cross held together at its intersection with red yarn. Michael placed the cross on the kitchen counter and said, "God helped me make it."

My son took what I considered to be useless bits of wood and made something beautiful...a cross. While I was touched by Michael's creation, I was even more impressed by his *imagination*. It's something I tend to forget, living in this fast-paced, disposable society. Wouldn't it be wonderful if all of us used our imaginations more often to help build a better world? I know Michael would think so.

Lord, may my life always aim to glorify You and to put to good use the marvelous gifts You've given me. — Christopher de Vinck

$\underline{\smash{\overset{\textstyle 20}{}}}$
SUN
For the word of God is living and active....
— Hebrews 4:12 (RSV)

Today is National Bible Sunday, and when I got up to pray this morning, I held my well-worn Bible in my hands and thanked God for His idea of giving the world this Book. As I gently turned my marked-up pages, I thanked Him because His Word is so much more than a collection of words; it is His voice speaking directly to me. I thanked Him because the Bible is *alive*, a truth made real to me every time I find a new meaning in a familiar old passage — a meaning God-tailored to meet my need of the moment. I call these discoveries my "Aha's." I underline and date them, and my Bible is filled with them.

There's one in Matthew dated just last week. That morning I felt burdened by some unkind remarks made by an insensitive friend. "Turn the other cheek," I told myself, assuming that's how Christians keep peace. But as I read the verse again that morning ("If any one strikes you on the right cheek, turn...the other also," Matthew 5:39, RSV), I suddenly saw a whole new meaning. *Aha!* Yes, I'm to turn the other cheek and not seek revenge following an injustice, *but I have only two cheeks.* If this friend's behavior becomes a pattern, happening more than two times, I should say something. God does not intend me to be a doormat, but to give a person a second chance. His words changed the direction of my thinking that morning.

God's words don't change, but they constantly grow and change me as He speaks to me. On this National Bible Sunday, I'm thankful for this Book...the only one on my shelf that is *alive*.

Father, let Your life-changing words fill my every thought, word and deed today and each day. Amen.   — Carol Kuykendall

$\underline{\smash{\overset{\textstyle 21}{}}}$
MON
"Is it not to share your bread with the hungry, and bring the homeless poor into your house; when you see the naked, to cover him, and not to hide yourself from your own flesh?"
— Isaiah 58:7 (RSV)

She seemed to make a lasting impression on everyone she met: my grandmother-in-law Bess Tressler, a feisty, spirited, lifelong Christian, who passed away last year just short of her 101st birthday. I remember one of my last conversations with her during which she enumerated some of the technological changes that had taken place during her life-time. There was the automobile, the airplane, electric lights, radio, the telephone, television, computers—each of which caused life-style changes.

"But the greatest change has been in people," she observed. "They are not as caring or as helpful as they were when I was a girl growing up on a farm in Ohio. There, neighbors were never too busy to lend a hand when a need arose. They believed it was their Christian duty."

I thought of Bess today when I saw how magnificently people in this country responded to the recent hurricane disasters that left thousands homeless and destitute in various parts of the country. Concerned people from all over—government and private agencies, secular and religious bodies, corporations and individuals—rallied to help. Food, water, medicine, supplies were rushed to the affected areas and within a relatively short time hope was restored. Through a great outpouring of love, communities were resurrected. "Thank God for this country, and the caring people in it," replied one grateful survivor.

Such a generous spirit has deep roots in this country, roots that extend back to our pioneer forebears who were dependent upon one another and upon God for their survival. *And, Bess, that generous spirit is not dead.* In my case, I just need to call upon it more often.

God, give me steady eyes that on the needy stay,
Not flitting eyes, forgetting eyes, that sometimes turn away.
—Fred Bauer

22
TUES
What will ye that I shall do unto you? They say unto him, Lord, that our eyes may be opened. —Matthew 20:32–33

Back in the late 1960s, I had to move our household from one city to another while my husband was traveling elsewhere. Because we were on a tight budget, I rented a large moving van that I planned to drive cross-country myself.

On the day of the big move, the rental manager gave me a brief lesson in gear-shifting and maneuvering the huge truck, and by the time I arrived at our apartment's underground garage, I was feeling as confident as a veteran trucker. That is, until I heard the horrible screech as the top of the van wedged itself under the door and brought me to a grinding halt halfway into the garage.

I leaped out of the truck and quickly saw that I could neither back up nor move forward without seriously damaging both the truck and the garage door. In the face of what seemed like my worst nightmare come true, I burst into tears, crying, "Oh, Lord, help! Help! Help!"

A white-haired man appeared through a side door and stopped in his tracks when he saw me and the van. I wiped my eyes. "I'm so sorry for blocking the doorway," I said, "but it might be hours before I can hire someone to bring whatever heavy equipment is needed to dislodge the truck."

The man listened with a puzzled expression and then said, "Maybe it's none of my business, young lady, but why don't you just let some air out of the tires?" Now, I could have run around the truck for hours and that solution never would have occurred to me. It was too simple and obvious! Once I let out some air, of course, I was able to move the van without further problems. And I had a great story to tell after I arrived at my destination.

Now, whenever I'm feeling "stuck" in the midst of seemingly insoluble problems, I try to picture that moving van wedged firmly under the garage door, and I ask myself if it's time to step back and ask the Lord to open my eyes to new ideas and solutions — especially the simple, obvious ones.

Lord Jesus, as I approach the problems of this day, open my eyes to see beyond my own confusion and panic — to Your possibilities and solutions.   — Susan Williams

23
WED
But encourage one another day after day....
                    — Hebrews 3:13 (NAS)

I majored in business in college because my mother wanted me to know how to "do something." I never questioned her decision until I entered freshman English. I could have easily stayed in the class all day. I hung on to every word my professor Dr. George Walker said. When he assigned the first essay of the year, everyone in class moaned, except me. Mine was completed that afternoon. When I got it back, there were thirteen misspelled words circled in red. My grade, however, was an A +. He had scrawled, "You can write — learn to spell!" It was the first bit of encouragement I'd ever received in my lifelong desire to write. Hot tears of joy and relief spilled onto my essay. He continued to circle my misspelled words and give me excellent grades. The microscopic thought of *Maybe I can write after all* grew quickly to enormous proportions because of Dr. Walker's encouragement back in 1954.

In 1974, when my first book was published, I sent a copy to Dr. Walker, now president of a junior college in Georgia, along with a lengthy letter full of details and gratitude to him. I received a prompt thank-you letter from him. He wrote, "It was certainly good of you to take the trouble to write to me after all these years. A letter such as yours makes it all worthwhile, especially after one has been an administrator for years and wonders from time to time whether it has all been worth the effort. I do remember you well...I am glad to know that you have persisted in your writing and that you are having some success. (You had only two misspelled words in your letter; you're improving!) Hang in there!"

The teacher who first nurtured my longing to write was still urging me on. It reminded me how much I needed to receive encouragement — and give it.

Father, quite possibly everyone I meet today will need encouragement. Help me to give it sincerely. Thank You. Amen.

— Marion Bond West

24
THURS   HOUSE GUEST

...*Because he has dealt bountifully with me.*
— Psalm 13:6 (RSV)

I used to think Thanksgiving was about pilgrims and pumpkin pie. My freshman year in college changed my mind.

By mid-November, students were decorating all over campus, and the cafeteria menu offered pumpkin pie. An important final paper was due, and I decided to forego the holiday in favor of research. *I'll just celebrate it up here,* I thought. The right ingredients for Thanksgiving were all around me. Yet I was miserably homesick, and in my head I kept hearing:

> *Over the river and through the woods,*
> *To Grandmother's house we go....*

At the last minute, unable to bear the self-imposed exile, I caught a late-night bus home....

Finally, I'm home. My head is bowed for my father's Thanksgiving prayer. "God, thank You for a full table and a family to share it with…" he begins. I squint one eye half-open and peep around. Uncles, aunts, cousins. *Joy.*

I breathe deeply, savoring the aroma of my grandmother's cornbread dressing browning in the oven. The massive turkey waits on the table. Caramel, apple and pumpkin pie, prune cake, banana pudding are on the sideboard. All the ingredients, just as I had imagined. But the food doesn't seem so important now.

After the prayer, my grandmother squeezes my hand. "Brockwell, we've missed you. We wouldn't be a family without you."

I feel myself growing up a bit as I stand there with my grandmother's arm around me. From now on, Thanksgiving will be a lot less about a table full of turkey and trimmings, and a lot more about giving thanks for the people around the table.

God, bless the precious people in my life, and open me to opportunities to thank them every day.   — Brock Kidd

25
FRI   *HOUSE GUEST*
And he shall make amends for the harm that he hath done….   — Leviticus 5:16

I was surprised when Jennie (not her real name), who'd been friends with my youngest daughter Sandi through elementary school, came to see me. I hadn't seen her for several years. When Jennie got into drugs in high school, she and my daughter had drifted apart. Now Jennie explained that she was a member of AA (Alcoholics Anonymous), and had been "clean" almost a year. "Do you remember the time after I'd graduated from high school that you loaned me some money?" she asked.

"Yes," I said.

"Well, I told you I'd hurt my back and needed to see a doctor. But I have to tell you now that I lied. I used the money to buy drugs. See, I'm up to my ninth step in AA, which is to make amends to people I've harmed. You're my ninth step."

After Jennie left, I began to wonder about the possibility of a "ninth-step person" in my own life. What about my older sister Virginia? We hadn't communicated for five years because of a family disagreement. The situation had bothered me, but as I'd explained to God many times,

"It wasn't my fault." Now I swallowed my pride and wrote her a letter.

By the time I finished the letter, I realized how I'd been stumbling over that ninth step every time I approached God. No wonder He'd seemed so distant.

Has God seemed far away from you lately? Could it be that He's waiting for you to take that ninth step?

Father, thank You for showing me that I don't have to be a recovering addict to need the forgiveness and peace that comes from making amends.   —Bonnie Lukes

P.S. Virginia and I have made a beginning in our now-cordial relationship by exchanging several letters since my first one to her.

Preparing Our Hearts for Christ
HOW SHALL WE ADORE HIM?

The holy and most joyous season of all is upon us — Christmas. As we prepare for the birth of the Baby Jesus, we are filled with wonder and anticipation. This year, while we set aside time for decorating our homes and holiday shopping, let us also make time for worship.

Together, let's raise our voices with the choir, singing that joyful hymn "O Come, All Ye Faithful." But when we come to the familiar words "O come, let us adore *Him," let us stop and ask,* How shall we *adore* Him? How do we ready our hearts to receive Him? *Let's join Phyllis Hobe during this Advent season as she takes us along on a personal journey of adoration.*

May your Christmas be filled with peace and joy, and a reverence for the Child Whose coming we celebrate.   —The Editors

26
SAT
SATURDAY BEFORE ADVENT
Teach Us to Adore Him

And every tongue confess that Jesus Christ is Lord....
—Philippians 2:11 (NIV)

Busy as the holiday season is, I love every moment. Each box of ornaments I carry up from the basement, each card full of good wishes, the hours of work on special programs, the smell of pine needles and cookies in the oven — all of them add to the feeling of anticipation that is a natural part of Advent. God's only Son is coming to earth, and we are preparing to welcome Him!

As I arrived at church for a meeting one evening, our Cherub Choir was rehearsing for Christmas Eve services. The voices of the boys and girls, all under ten, rose uncertainly in the chorus of "Adeste Fideles." In the middle of "O come, let us adore Him!" a boy in front stopped singing and asked, "What does that mean, *adore?*"

Our choir leader smiled patiently and said, "It means to honor someone very important."

The boy wasn't quite satisfied. "But how do we do that to Jesus?"

The choir leader hesitated a moment and then she said, "By telling Him we know who He is—and that we're so happy He's here."

As I drove home after our meeting, I pondered the boy's question: *How shall we adore Him?* It's not enough for us to mark the date of His birth; we need to tell Him that we know Who He is and we're so happy He's here. But how shall we do that? Lovely as the holiday traditions are, they are only symbols of what happened almost two thousand years ago. To experience the miracle of Christ's coming in a life-changing way, we need to prepare ourselves spiritually.

As we approach Christmas, let us become like Christ's first worshipers—those nearby and those who traveled from afar—who awaited His coming. Like them, each day in this Advent season, let us ask, *How shall we adore Him?*—and seek guidance from their example.

Heavenly Father, we humbly await Your leading. Teach us how to adore Your Son.
                                            —Phyllis Hobe

<u>27</u>
SUN

FIRST SUNDAY IN ADVENT
Give Him Our Attention

And they came with haste, and found...the babe....
                                            —Luke 2:16

On that first Christmas, the night sky became brilliant with light. Voices of angels shattered the silence. Something so important was happening that shepherds in the hills around Bethlehem left their flocks— their very livelihood—to pay homage to the Son of God. Perhaps, like them, we need to stop whatever we're doing and give Christ our complete attention.

A group of us were working feverishly to decorate our church for the holidays, and things weren't going well. Some of the lights didn't work, the red ribbon for the wreaths was missing and a bag of sand for the luminarias had burst. Understandably, we were tired, cranky and impatient with one another. No, it didn't feel like Christmas.

Our young pastor's mother arrived late and out of breath. "Hey, everybody, come on out and see the stars!" she insisted. "They're so big!"

"Not now," Pastor Bill said gruffly, brushing sand into a dustpan. Then he saw the disappointment on his mother's face and stood up, taking her hand. "I'm sorry, Mom," he said. "Maybe we all ought to go out and look at the stars. C'mon."

We followed them outside into the darkness. And there, up above us, were more stars than we had ever seen. Like the early shepherds, we could feel God's nearness, and that was what really mattered. Without saying a word, we stood there and joined hands. We had put aside our busyness to be with our Savior, and *now* it felt like Christmas!

On this first Sunday in Advent, we ask, *How shall we adore Him?*

We adore Him by putting Him first in our lives.

Like the shepherds, O Blessed Christ, we put aside our work to be with You.   — Phyllis Hobe

---

28
MON

For the moment all discipline seems painful rather than pleasant; later it yields the peaceful fruit of righteousness to those who have been trained by it.

— Hebrews 12:11 (RSV)

Several years ago, I found myself bumping across the rugged interior of Jamaica in a Jeep. Dr. John Trotter was driving, and we were participating in a medical ministry project. Rounding a narrow corner, we came face to face with a rather complacent cow munching grass in the middle of the road.

Coasting to a stop five feet from her bony flank, John blew the horn. She lifted her head but did not move. Then we began to yell at her. The old bovine seemed to want to beat a retreat but couldn't get herself in gear. Finally, exasperated, John jumped out of the Jeep, intending to be more persuasive. Rounding the front fender, he suddenly looked down and began to laugh. "We could have blown our horn all day and that cow wouldn't have moved! We're parked on her chain!"

Many days since then I have thought of that scene. When I want things to happen in my life, I toot my horn impatiently toward heaven. "Do something, so I can go on to where I want to go!" I bellow at God. But when I finally gain the right perspective on my situation, I usually find that I am "sitting on the chain."

Recently, I have been honking my horn about not having time to work on a book project I've started. It is everybody's fault but my own — the children, my schedule, lack of energy, writer's block, stress and so on. But when I get down to it, the real problem is that I'm sitting on the chain. The culprit is my lack of discipline.

As you pray for change in your life today, look before you honk. Are you sitting on the chain? Can God act without your help?

Dear Lord, help me to help myself. Amen.   — Scott Walker

29
TUES   *HOUSE GUEST*
"Stop judging by mere appearances, and make a right judgment."
                                                — John 7:24 (NIV)

Last night, my husband Alex and I splurged and went to a symphony concert. I eagerly welcomed the evening out, but as the orchestra began tuning I glanced over the program and noticed the main portion was a symphony by Mahler. I began to fear I wouldn't enjoy the concert. From snatches of Mahler's music I had heard on the radio, I had labeled it as too modern and dissonant for my taste.

What a surprise! The beauty of the music swept through me. Images stirred in my mind — I strolled through a woodland, frolicked in a meadow and watched a tumbling waterfall. I whispered to Alex between movements, "I can't believe this is by Mahler."

He answered, "You didn't really know Mahler's music."

After the concert, Alex suggested trying a new café in town.

"I've heard it's loud," I protested and voted for our quiet place where I liked what was on the menu.

He urged, "Let's try this new place. You don't know, you may like it."

The café imitated a 1950s soda shop. We sipped chocolate malts and mingled with college students. Somehow I felt invigorated. As we drove home, I thought, *I must do this again, and not just for an evening out.* I resolved to be more open: to innovations at work; to changes at church; and to that family with "loud" teenagers who had moved in across the street. I want to stop evaluating according to hearsay or stereotypes. I want to make room in my life for welcomed surprises.

Lord, keep me open to new people and opportunities, not judging by mere appearances, but by being adventurous in receiving Your blessings.   — Mary Brown

30 *"Have you entered the storehouses of the snow...?"*
WED   — Job 38:22 (RSV)

I was three, and I was playing on the sidewalk in front of our Cincinnati apartment when it happened.

Suddenly, the air was alive with white confetti. The pieces swirled in circles as they parachuted silently to the ground around me. I stared, my eyes busy trying to interpret this cascade of whiteness. At first, I thought the flakes were some kind of winter butterflies, the way they danced through the cold November air. I chased a flake and caught it. Up close it looked like it was good to eat, like corn flakes or flattened popcorn, but it melted in my warm palm as I raised it to my lips.

The downpour became so thick, it blinded me. All at once I felt I would explode with excitement. "Probably no one else has ever seen anything like this," I said to myself. I turned and ran toward the apartment, shouting, "Mommy, Mommy, come quick! Look what the sky is doing, look what the sky is doing!"

That was in 1945. I'm grown up now. Educated, sophisticated. And I no longer thrill at the sight of the first snowflakes, but it makes me sad to think that I've become such a serious-minded adult. I feel as if I've lost something important.

"Wonder," said Aristotle, "is the first step toward wisdom."

I'm trying to recapture some of that "little boy" perspective on life. Recently, I bought a Big Chief tablet and rediscovered the simple pleasure of writing with a soft pencil on smooth newsprint. And when a big rain left deep puddles on our street, I took off my shoes and socks and joined some children wading in the pools.

Perhaps you, too, can recapture some of that glow which comes from being filled with wonder and appreciation. What could it hurt to try?

Lord, keep the child alive in me forever, that I might enjoy the wonders of everyday life.   — Daniel Schantz

Prayer Diary

My Prayer Requests for November:

1. _____

2. _____

3. _____

4. _____

5. _____

6. _____

7. _____

8. _____

9. _____

10. _____

11. _____

12. _____

13. _____

14. _____

15. _____

16. _____

17. _____

18. _____

19. _____

20. _____

21. _____

22. _____

23. _____

24. _____

25. _____

26. _____

27. _____

28. _____

29. _____

30. _____

December

S	M	T	W	T	F	S
				1	2	3
4	5	6	7	8	9	10
11	12	13	14	15	16	17
18	19	20	21	22	23	24
25	26	27	28	29	30	31

GIFTS OF THE SEASON

The Star

One bright Star shines, and
December's sky awakens
to the mangered Babe.

*Shining Star, faithful Star, I will follow You
into the light of the New Year.*

PRAYER CAN CHANGE YOUR LIFE
1
THURS The Key to Happiness

I make all things new.... —Revelation 21:5

Yesterday, Keri unpacked the nativity and arranged it in the corner of our living room. This has been her exclusive Christmas chore each year since she was a toddler. "Mom," she said as she carefully set the figures amid soft green-cloth hills and plants strung with white light stars, "it's funny how Baby Jesus keeps on being new each year I bring Him out again."

Her words still hang in the air. *New.* Of course, there is something sweet and soft and new about every baby. But when Baby Jesus came, even the "old" became new in Him.

A year ago, feeling very old, I longed for something new. And when the book *Prayer Can Change Your Life* appeared, I took it as a sign. The honest prayer techniques that it offered helped me find solutions to my problems. Today, my mother is happily remarried to a man as dear and loving as was my own father. Keri once again fills our home with friends and laughter. In another year, she will follow her brother Brock to college. And my brother David is settled and at peace in a new life, a new career, a new town. After one year, our small group has experienced its own little miracles, from healing of childhood memories to forgiveness in difficult relationships. We have been so challenged, Diana, Nancy, Gloria, Pam P., Martha Kay and I, that we are continuing our prayer therapy group now into our second year.

In honest, persistent prayer, I found peace, as I took all my troubles to God, trusted Him with the lot and rested in His love from all my failures. Through honest talking and honest listening, I've learned that *new* is an action word. Honest prayer points forward. It tells me that as a child of the living, loving God, there's much left for me to do.

Thanks to Dr. William R. Parker and Elaine St. Johns and their classic book *Prayer Can Change Your Life,* I have been greatly helped in my journey to a new life, changed through prayer. So, I'm going to keep on talking and listening to God, until I'm the best brand-new wife, mother, daughter, friend and child of God I can be.

Come and join me in this journey. Instead of waiting on the "Happy New Year," begin today with "Happy *New You!*"

God, keep listening, keep making me new. I don't ever, ever want to quit talking to You, for You are the kingdom and the power and the glory forever.
—Pam Kidd

2   *"This is how you can show your love...."*
—————————————————————— —Genesis 20:13 (NIV)
FRI

In an adult education class I took years ago, I got a lesson that I didn't expect. For some reason the conversation had turned to the best birthday present we'd ever received. Our small group each told of a favorite gift—from a new (used) car all tied up with a big red bow for a man in his twenties, to an elbow macaroni necklace for a new stepmother from her stepdaughter.

The conversation was full of laughter, but then the teacher surprised us by saying, "My best gift came from myself. One year I was so lonely and depressed. My parents were gone, my sister and I were on the outs, and I had just moved to a new neighborhood where I didn't have any friends who knew it was my birthday. I went out and I bought myself some cologne that I had always wanted. When the clerk asked, 'Would you like it gift wrapped?' I suddenly said, 'Yes! Yes, please, I would! And put in a gift card, too.' And then I took it home, treated myself to a nice dinner and opened my present. And do you know what? It was exactly what I wanted!"

I felt as if that teacher had given me a present. I had been known to sulk when the book I'd hinted for wasn't given to me as a birthday gift. Now, I marched right out to the bookstore myself and bought it—from me to me!

God, let me not wait for someone else to lift my spirits. Is there something I'm waiting for someone else to do for me? Today, let me do or buy or give something nice for myself. —Linda Neukrug

3   *It is a good thing to give thanks unto the Lord....*
—————————————————————— —Psalm 92:1
SAT

I was a bit edgy grocery shopping with my two grandsons. It had been a long time since I'd pushed little ones along in a grocery cart. (How had I ever managed with four?) Alex, age four, was mostly quiet and helpful. Luke, nearly two, was excited, wide-eyed, jabbering constantly and determined to stand up in the cart. I tried to concentrate on my grocery list, but Luke seemed bound and determined to say something to me. I stopped and looked him right in the eyes. "What is it, Luke?" Delighted to have my full attention, he pointed happily over to the bakery section, which we were approaching.

"Thank you," he said to me in obvious anticipation and full trust. He pointed to the chocolate chip cookies.

"A dozen chocolate chip cookies," I said to the clerk. Each time the woman dropped a cookie into the white sack, Luke said loudly, "Thank you!"

There was something about Luke's thank-you's that took away my edginess, and a flush of gratitude swept over me. *Thank You, Father, for this little boy. And for Alex, too,* I prayed silently. *Thank You that I can take care of them today.*

That afternoon as I began the hour-plus drive home, more thank-you's popped into my mind. *Thank You, Lord, for this car that You helped me pick out when I was a widow. Thank You that it didn't rain today. Thank You that a husband who loves me is waiting at home.* What a wonderful feeling it was just to be grateful—and to know what I was grateful for! Why, it even felt good to say, "Thank You, Lord" for things I didn't particularly enjoy: a detour; having to stop and pump gas; red lights. I had forgotten what a remarkable feeling of joy giving thanks triggers somewhere inside us—that is, until two-year-old Luke taught his fifty-four-year-old grandmother a new thing or two.

(A thank-you prayer I'd like to sing:)

> *Thank You, Lord, for saving my soul,*
> *Thank You, Lord, for making me whole....Amen.*
>
> —Marion Bond West

4
SUN
SECOND SUNDAY IN ADVENT
HOW SHALL WE ADORE HIM?
Follow a Star

> *And, lo, the star, which they saw in the east, went before them....*
> —Matthew 2:9

The magi were brilliant scholars, yet they trusted a star to lead them to the Christ Child. Sometimes we, too, have to ignore the wisdom of the world and follow instead the beckoning of God.

One of my best friends in high school was a girl two years ahead of me. Marcia was very popular and extremely bright, and everyone expected her to accomplish great things. Delivering the valedictory at her graduation ceremonies, she stunned us all with the announcement that she was entering a convent to become a nun. "I wasn't known as a 're-ligious' person," she explained with a gentle smile, "so I can under-stand your surprise. I was going to be a lawyer, but God has other plans for me." Like Marcia's other friends, I thought her too lively for a con-templative life.

I lost touch with Marcia until many years later when I visited a friend in a hospital. In the corridor, a nun came toward me, smiling and hold-ing out her arms. It was Marcia or, rather, Sister Veronica, and we hugged each other like two schoolgirls. She was a nurse at the hospital, and as we walked toward my friend's room, she looked in on other pa-tients. She knew each one by name and said something to make them smile. Obviously, God had put her talents to good use. Marcia was still lively, still popular and very much a blessing to many people.

As we said good-bye, I watched her walking away, and even though I couldn't see a star, I knew she was following one.

On this second Sunday in Advent, we ask, *How shall we adore Him?*

> *We adore Him when we seek*
> *His guidance in everything we do.*

Lord Jesus, may the light from Your star illuminate our way.
> — Phyllis Hobe

5
MON

"Call to me and I will answer you...."
> — Jeremiah 33:3 (RSV)

My husband Charles and I are studying a new book, *If Two Shall Agree*, about praying together as a couple. Its premise is that as a husband and wife pray together, not only are their prayers answered (based on Jesus' promise in Matthew 18:19), but they are drawn closer together as they let each other know their needs.

It's a very simple premise, really, and today we had a chance to put it into practice. I woke up early to a "blue Monday." A friend's mother had been in a car accident and wasn't doing well. I had two work assign-ments due and the computer was on the blink. The cedar-pollen count was at an all-time high and Charles was having trouble breathing. Be-sides, it was threatening rain, and a cold, penetrating wind was blowing from the north.

So when we finished our chapters for the day, I told Charles how I was feeling. We followed the suggestions from our study book and asked the Lord to help us find some positive ways to get out of the dumps. Then I went into the kitchen to start broccoli soup for lunch. But the enormous green head of broccoli I'd brought in from the garden two days ago was now a bouquet of little yellow flowers. As I started to throw it in the trash, I took another look. "Wait a minute!" I said to myself. "This is beautiful. I never knew broccoli bloomed like this." So I plunked the head in a pewter tureen and put it in the den. Then, together, Charles and I built a cheery fire in the den fireplace. While he brought in my old, trusty typewriter and placed it on the table, I cut up a big white onion and put it on to boil, to add to leftover carrot soup. Soon a delightful scent was floating through the house.

It's mid-afternoon now. Charles has a praise tape on; he is breathing better. Lunch was pretty good; we've replenished the fire a couple of times and stayed warm, enjoying each other's company in the den. And I'm about finished with my assignments. Outside it is still dreary, but inside my spirits have lifted and the Son is shining.

Thank You, Lord, that we can come to You — anytime — seeking a lightened heart and spirit.

— Dorothy Shellenberger

6
TUES

HOUSE GUEST

Blessed be the Lord, who hath not given us a prey to their teeth.   — Psalm 124:6

Our children's horse Shorty was a patient, obedient cow pony that we could trust with our young, beginning riders. We loved him, but had to watch out for one thing: Shorty liked to nip at people or clothing or whatever came close to his mouth. And sometimes it hurt! We were careful. We learned to work around Shorty's bad habit.

Then I began wondering: *If I find it so easy to accept Shorty, teeth and all, why is it so hard to accept differing habits and traits in people?*

Sometimes I, a speedy person, allow my husband's methodical, orderly manner to frustrate me. (*Why worry if the map is folded correctly so long as it fits in the glove compartment? But I could fold the map correctly instead of making it a federal case with my husband.*) I often permit a sarcastic comment to hurt my feelings. (*Can't I see that Alex is a big tease? I can laugh at Alex and not take myself so seriously.*) When a co-worker is tired and nipping at me, I can often feel like lashing back. (*Is she overworked and nervous about a deadline? Maybe I can offer her a hand.*)

Good actions and a show of understanding put teeth into my faith —

teeth for smiling instead of gnashing, for pronouncing kind words instead of condemnation.

Creator of us all, help me reflect Your patience when dealing with others. — Marjorie Parker

7 *Looking unto Jesus the author and finisher of our faith;*
WED *who for the joy that was set before him endured the cross....* — Hebrews 12:2

When I was seventeen, I took a job as a waitress at a popular dinette. How glad I was when sleek, pretty Pat Churray (an "older woman" of perhaps twenty-three) took pity and showed me the ropes.

I was rattling two cups of coffee past her the first day, watching in woe as about a fourth of the coffee spilled into the saucers. She took me aside. "Don't look at the coffee," she said with patient emphasis. "Look toward where you're taking it."

To my amazement, this tip instantly, magically worked! In no time, I could glide over to customers, my eyes on them, never spilling a drop.

I have since been in situations where I wonder if I haven't concentrated too much on the "spills." For instance, instead of my thinking, *No one appreciates all the hard work I did on the church newsletter,* why don't I say, "Lord, I'm pleased to do this newsletter for Your glory!" Instead of *My concert performance was awful. I can't play at all,* why not say, "Thanks, God, for the gift of my musical talent."

See what I mean? When I try to practice this little spiritual formula, I find I have fewer spills and a lot more cups of joy.

Lord, as I start to work today, may I look beyond the results of my labor to You, the goal of all holy service. Amen.
— Kathie Kania

8 *"You are my beloved Son; you are my Delight."*
THURS — Mark 1:11 (TLB)

My heart is aching tonight because of an angry phone call from my son. As in most families, misunderstandings hurt. And as I sit quietly in the house, our exchange still batters my soul. *Come, Holy Spirit,* I pray. *Heal Paul's heart. Heal mine. Come, Holy Spirit. Come.* I sit at the kitchen table, staring out the window at the softly falling snow, made visible in the darkness only by my neighbor's Christmas lights. In my mind, I begin to compose a letter to Paul, a defensive argument, with a lecture thrown in for good measure.

And then the words come to me again, as they first did that other December night, so many years ago. As I sat alone in the hospital chapel, praying for Paul's life after his serious car accident, God's words to His own Son flooded my heart: "This is my beloved Son, in whom I am well pleased" (Matthew 3:17). What comfort those words brought me that night. What love could equal that between parent and child? Again and again over the years, no matter how rocky at times our relationship, those words have come back to embrace me.

I turn on the light, take a note card and write:

> *Dear Paul,*
> > *You are my beloved son; you are my delight.*
> > > > *I love you.*
> > > > *Mom*

Nothing more is needed. Paul will understand. You see, he loves me, too.

Thank You, Lord, for reminding me that the best way to counter anger is with love.   — Marilyn Morgan Helleberg

9
FRI   *HOUSE GUEST*
"But you, be strong and do not let your hands be weak, for your work shall be rewarded!" — II Chronicles 15:7 (NKJV)

Let me tell you a little Christmas story.

Last night, my husband John and I were invited to join our daughters Kelly and Sandi and their families for "Cookie Night," a tradition of baking Christmas cookies I began when my daughters were young. Watching them as wives and mothers continuing the practice reminded me of those long-ago special nights. With a chuckle, though, I have to tell you a secret about those cookies: *I always hated making them.*

I've never been good with dough, and I found the rolling-cutting-sticking-starting-over-again process a maddening one. Every year I wanted to give up. One such year I was attempting (with gritted teeth) to maneuver a Christmas-shaped tree to the cookie sheet when the girls raced wildly into the kitchen, laughing and pushing and shoving. One of them bounced against me, and the point of the Christmas tree broke off. That was it! My temper flared. "Time out!" I screamed, slamming down the dough. "To the couch right now. And forget about these cookies!" The girls scurried to the couch, and their laughter turned to silence.

Slumped at the kitchen table, staring at my dough-covered fingers, I heard them whispering. "Does she really mean it about the cookies?"

"I don't think so," came the tearful answer. "It wouldn't be Christmas in our house without our cookies!"

The girls were right, I decided. And I scooped up the broken pieces and began kneading the dough into a new ball. What was important became apparent: *"Cookie Night" wasn't about making perfect cookies — it was about preparing for Christmas in our own special way.*

"Girls," I said, "come back and help me. You know I can't make these Christmas cookies without you."

Thus, in our household, an important tradition has continued through the years that is especially poignant. Now each Christmas, as I watch little hands with the help of bigger hands make trees and wreaths and angels and other imaginative shapes out of dough, I say a prayer:

Lord, bless our family with the joy of special nights like these that bring us together in love and gratitude at Christmas. Amen.

—Bonnie Lukes

10
SAT

HOUSE GUEST
PRACTICING THE POWER OF PRAYER
Gift-Wrapped Prayers

Thanks be to God for his indescribable gift!
—II Corinthians 9:15 (NIV)

I poked among toy shelves in a discount store searching for the *perfect* gift, a present for our two-year-old godson Ryan. A fun toy, yet educational. A special one to remind him of his Uncle Alex and Aunt Mary whom he sees only twice a year. Picking up box after box, I grew more discouraged.

Then I caught a few words of the Christmas carols playing in the store:

How silently, how silently,
the wondrous gift is given.

I wheeled my cart down a deserted sporting goods aisle and closed my eyes. "Oh, Jesus," I breathed. "Yes, You are the only perfect gift.

Help Ryan to know You and love You." Then I went back and peacefully chose some building blocks.

Later that week, I spread shopping bags across my bed. As I taped shiny green paper with red rocking horses around Ryan's box of blocks, I found myself praying again for him. Pulling out another parcel, I thought, *Why pray only for Ryan because he's my godchild? Why not pray for Aunt Helen, who's battling Parkinson's disease, as I wrap her candle. And for the new job my husband Alex started. And our dear friends the Richters who are moving away next month.*

As I cut paper, taped, tied ribbon and prayed for each recipient, love for each person swelled in my heart. God's presence filled the room and surrounded me on the bed brimming with gifts.

I plan to wrap up each present with prayer again this year.

Father, I want to give friends and family prayerful support all year long. Please remind me often. Please bless each one.

— Mary Brown

11
SUN

THIRD SUNDAY IN ADVENT
HOW SHALL WE ADORE HIM?
Trust Him to Protect Us

"I am the Lord's servant," Mary answered....
— Luke 1:38 (NIV)

It must have been frightening for young Joseph and Mary to undertake a long journey to a place where they had never been. But they trusted God to protect them. In our uncertain world, we often find ourselves in new situations, and we need their kind of trust.

Just before Christmas several years ago, I moved from a big city to a rural area. I had dreamed of living in the country ever since I was a little girl, and finally I was able to do it. As I drove out to my new home, followed by a moving van, I suddenly realized that I didn't know anyone there. I didn't even know my way to a grocery store without a map. When the movers left, I would be totally alone with my dog and cat in a house on a dark road without street lights. All along I had been convinced that God was helping me fulfill my dream, but suddenly I was frightened. "I'm scared, Lord," I confided. "Are You sure I ought to be here?"

It was dark, all right, when the movers left. As I opened my front door to take my dog out, I couldn't see anything. Then, across the road, a gigantic tree full of Christmas lights was lit up. It was at least three stories high and sparkled in the darkness. Stepping out on the porch and looking around, I saw lights coming on outside houses all around me—distant, but welcoming.

As the months and years have passed, I made deep friendships with many of the families in those houses. I learned, for instance, that the family across the road almost didn't have time to decorate their big tree that year. I told them how it had welcomed me in the darkness on my first night. Now that they know how much it meant to me, they continue to find time for it—and leave it lighted long past the holidays.

Whenever I have to go where I have never been, I remember that Christmas. It tells me that even though I may be frightened when something is new and strange, I can count on God to look after me.

On this third Sunday in Advent, we ask, *How shall we adore Him?*

*We adore Him when we trust Him
to be with us in unfamiliar situations.*

Each new day is a journey, Lord Jesus, and we trust You to lead us safely through it. —Phyllis Hobe

12 *I bring you good tidings....* —Luke 2:10
MON

I'm walking east on 34th Street with my coat buttoned tight against the cold. Christmas is almost here, and I'm thinking about tomorrow's trip west to be with my brother Ham and his family in Illinois. It will be a peaceful time.

"Merry Christmas," say the signs all around me, and yet I can't help recalling some Christmases past that weren't so merry. "Happy Holidays," says the sign at the bank on the corner. Perhaps I really am an old curmudgeon, but not everybody takes such a bright view of this holiday. Only last week, a friend said that going home meant going back to a house full of tensions and old family feuds. "We seldom get through the day without some blowup," he told me.

I turn down Park Avenue South. Another rotund Santa Claus beams at me, another string of letters spells out "M-E-R-R-Y C-H-R-I-S-T-M-A-S." Just before I reach the corner of 32nd Street, I stop to look inside a store window. Talk about merriment! There's a colorful display, and I actually laugh out loud at the antics of a dozen reindeer sitting around a banquet table celebrating, I presume, a successful run across the Christmas skies.

Then I see the words printed quietly on the left corner of the huge window. There are only three of them, but of all the Christmas greetings I've seen splashed across the city, these words on the window of Lane's Floor Coverings & Interiors are the ones that truly promise a joyous celebration of the birth of Jesus. I'll take these words with me to Illinois, but first, I send them to you, and to all close to you: LOVE. UNDERSTANDING. FORGIVENESS.

Lord, I pray that I may give love, strive for understanding and learn to forgive. — Van Varner

---

13
TUES *Children's children are a crown to the aged, and parents are the pride of their children.* — Proverbs 17:6 (NIV)

My mother has been working on the Christmas stockings all year, one for each member of the family. Seventy-two years old, she is still youthful, though her arthritic fingers are beginning to show her age. Now, as her bent fingers hold needle and thread, she is nearing completion of the last beautifully embroidered stocking.

I slip quietly into the room, sliding down into a chair in the recessed shadows. Silently, I watch Mom and my four-year-old daughter Jodi giggle together. The fire by which they bask makes Jodi's hair even redder and her laughter sparkle. It is a tender moment — a picture in time.

Gazing at Jodi, I am surprised to see that she, too, holds needle and thread in her little fingers. Mom has taught her to thread a needle, and she is awkwardly sewing buttons onto a piece of cloth. Smiling, I think, *From now on, every time Jodi threads a needle, every time a button pops loose in her life, she'll remember Mama.*

More than needle and thread are being grasped this night. As a proud grandmother and her granddaughter snuggle close by the fire, the heritage of generations is being passed from old to young. More important, the fabric of love is being sewn together, to be embroidered with beautiful memories. Jodi will never forget this moment. And neither will I.

Dear God, may Your love be the thread that binds our family from generation to generation. Amen. — Scott Walker

14
WED *I will meditate also of all thy work....* — Psalm 77:12

HOUSE GUEST

It was one of those times when life started to slip way off-balance. All sorts of little things were going wrong, and I was uptight and irritable. My sister Nan suggested I schedule a quiet time each day, ten minutes to relax and meditate.

Relax? Meditate? No way. I had trouble just sitting still.

Then our family doctor called with some chilling news. He wanted to schedule our daughter Lauren for a bone scan. The pain in her leg was getting worse, and all the other tests were negative. "We've got to find out what's going on," he said gently. That did it. My anxiety was so bad that I barely slept and had no appetite. I couldn't even find the energy to pray.

Desperate for some relief, I decided to take my sister's advice. Remembering a fitness class I once took years ago, I decided to practice the final cool-down session when, with lights dimmed and music low, we would all lie quietly on our mats. "Breathe in and out slowly as you close your eyes, and picture the tension flowing out of your body. Think of a calming scene — a sunny beach, a sparkling lake," we were told. Slowly, we tensed, then relaxed all of our muscles.

This time I also focused on a Scripture verse. Most calming for me was "Peace I leave with you, my peace I give unto you" (John 14:27). I repeated these words over and over, and pictured God's peace settling deep into my heart.

Each day, until the morning of Lauren's dreaded test, my tension and anxiety eased. I experienced a new calmness and strength. And soon we learned the wonderful news: Lauren was fine, and the mysterious pain eventually disappeared. I also learned that seeking God's peace in relaxation and meditation can help me both physically and spiritually. If you're in pain right now, seek Him.

You are the Prince of Peace, Father, and Your kingdom is in our hearts.   — Ellen Secrest

15
THURS *Thou shalt call me, My father; and shalt not turn away from me.* — Jeremiah 3:19

My friend James is an only child, and he and his mother always get together at Christmas. One Christmas Eve, she came to his house far out in the country. They cooked a fine turkey dinner and dined listening to music by a crackling fire. They had intended going to the midnight church service, but when they looked at the clock, it was too late.

The next morning, they drove to the small, clapboard church down the hill, making fresh tracks in the new-fallen snow. They sat in a pinewood pew and listened to the creaking pipe organ. James looked around, admiring the wreaths and garlands decorating the walls. Suddenly, he realized they were the only parishioners in church.

The pastor walked to the pulpit, welcomed his "congregation" and explained that most of his flock had attended the candlelit service the night before. Then the service began. James and his mother sang the Christmas hymns as loud as they could. They stood, they sat, they knelt. At the end of the prayers, the organist muttered an unusually audible "Amen." The minister preached a beautiful sermon (maybe a bit shorter than usual) and after the final hymn, James greeted him at the door. "Well," James said, grinning, "I suppose wherever two or more are gathered...."

"Actually," the pastor responded, "I was reminded of another quotation, this one from Augustine: 'God loves each one of us as though there were only one of us to love.'"

Thank You, God, for making me always feel special.
                                                           —Rick Hamlin

$\frac{16}{\text{FRI}}$ *To win the contest you must deny yourselves many things that would keep you from doing your best....*
                                                           —I Corinthians 9:25 (TLB)

I guess I'm a one-speed person in a ten-speed world.

All my friends ride bikes that have ten or even twelve speeds, but the gears always seem to be out of adjustment. "How many of those speeds do you really use?" I tease them.

"Oh, one or two," is the usual reply.

A friend of mine has a fancy computer that does everything except fix coffee and carry out the trash, but he needs a college degree to run it, and it seems to be "down" more than it is running. There's a deluxe copy machine in our faculty workroom at the college where I teach. It copies in two colors, reduces, enlarges and collates, among other things. It also sounds like a pile of junk, and it jams at least ten times a day. Too many bells and whistles, if you ask me.

Could it be that technology has made life a little too complex for its own good? Maybe. I know it's too much for *my* good. I've been a one-speed person ever since I first belonged to the Experimental Aircraft Association, a group that helps pilots who want to build their own aircraft. They had a motto that I adopted for my life. They taught us that if you want to make a plane that will fly well, then you must "simplicate and add lightness."

Would you like this day to "fly"? Here's a suggestion. Make a list of everything you have to do today. Now, see if you can delegate some of those items or combine a couple of them into one task. Eliminate where you can, and postpone some of the items to a better day. Lower your ambitions to fit the time and energy you have been given by God.

"Simplicate and add lightness"—it's a great formula for a ten-speed world.

Lord, I have such big ambitions and plans. Keep me from over-reaching myself.   — Daniel Schantz

17 A man who has riches without understanding is like the
SAT beasts that perish.   — Psalm 49:20 (NIV)

I was reading in my local newspaper about a TV and cinema celebrity who when asked what her fantasy was replied, "Living someplace where you can leave the car unlocked, someplace with small-town values."

I laid down the paper and glanced around at my six-year-old sofa and portable TV. I looked outside at my huge yard of freshly cut grass and across the road to the sprouting corn in my neighbor's field. True, I'd never know the fame and riches of TV stars or business tycoons, but at least I was living one of their fantasies. Something I took for granted was their fondest wish!

I'll remember that the next time the list of things I want begins to crowd out the blessings that I already have: children who still need a listening ear now and then; a husband who almost always gives me a good-bye hug; neighbors eager to help in time of need; a church full of Christian friends. I am rich indeed!

Forgive me, Father, when I discount the everyday blessings You have given me. Being Your much-loved child is fame enough!
                           — Mary Lou Carney

18

FOURTH SUNDAY IN ADVENT

HOW SHALL WE ADORE HIM?
Make Room in Our Hearts

There was no room for them in the inn.　　　—Luke 2:7

It is understandable that an inn might be full, especially in Bethlehem at tax collection time. And so Mary and Joseph were turned away. The Bible tells us someone—we don't know who—was touched by their plight and offered them a place to stay. But the innkeeper who initially turned away Joseph and Mary reminds us that we should always find room in our hearts for those in need.

If ever two people had reason to close their hearts, it was my friends Eleanor and Charlie, who lost three of their seven children to illness and accidents within a few years. And for a while, they did. Then one day a friend, a policeman, showed up at their door with a scruffy-looking fifteen-year-old boy. "His folks locked him out," the policeman explained, "and he needs a place to stay for the night. He hasn't done anything wrong. Can you put him up?"

"We didn't know what to do," Eleanor says now. "We had been praying to God to heal our pain, but we didn't expect Him to do it that way."

That was many years ago, and Eleanor and Charlie have been taking in abandoned and homeless youngsters ever since. "It's incredible how many kids are out there," Charlie tells me, "and they seem to know about us. They know they can get a meal, a shower and a bed for the night as long as they obey the rules. They've never caused us any trouble." In the morning, when the young people leave, they go with the couple's love, acceptance and prayers.

And what of Charlie and Eleanor's own pain? "It goes away a little more each time a kid rings our doorbell," Eleanor says.

On this fourth Sunday in Advent, we ask, *How shall we adore Him?*

We adore Him when we care for one another.

Beloved Jesus, as we welcome You, let us also make room in our hearts for those in need of love.　　　—Phyllis Hobe

19

Serving the Lord with all humility....　　　—Acts 20:19

Grandma Hazel is an "adopted" grandma to dozens of us in our church and community. At eighty-eight years old, she's an untiring worker for the Lord. She's either dishing out meals at the Salvation Army dining room, driving a friend to a doctor's appointment, knitting blankets for babies with AIDS or making meat loaf for church suppers. When she has health setbacks or family problems, she keeps moving forward with faith, saying, "To worry is to insult the Lord."

Once I worked hard on presenting a dramatic program for Holy Week at church. I thought I could make a difference for the Lord with that program, but only a handful of people attended. I was discouraged. *Why did I even bother?* I asked myself. When I shared my disappointment with Grandma Hazel, she listened thoughtfully, then told me, "I guess I never think about making a difference. I just try to serve the Lord and let *Him* make the difference."

She was right, of course. When I looked back at my church production, I saw that the people who were there had really enjoyed it. Several even told me how much it had blessed them. And I certainly grew from the prayer and planning I put into it.

So now when I'm inclined to give in to disappointment, I remember the strong working faith of Grandma Hazel and others like her who know how to trust the Lord. I take my eyes off of myself and how I'm doing, and try to please God instead. No project is ever a failure, no opportunity is ever wasted, I'm learning, when we let the Lord make the difference.

Lord, help me serve You joyfully and faithfully, leaving the results to You. Amen. — Gina Bridgeman

20 *For we are unto God a sweet savor of Christ....*
TUES — II Corinthians 2:15

Did you know the red and white striped candy cane is a symbol of Christmas? I learned about the legend of the candy cane at a recent children's worship service at our church, and it goes like this:

In England, when the Puritans came to power under Oliver Cromwell in 1642, celebrations of Christmas were banned as being showy, antireligious, Royalist customs. But a Christian candy-maker wanted to give his friends something symbolic of this holy season, so he made some candy canes shaped like a shepherd's crook for Jesus the Great Shepherd. He then added the red stripes: three thin ones to represent the Trinity, and one thick one to represent the life of Jesus and the blood He shed on the cross to forgive our sins. The candy-maker's finished result became a *sweet* reminder of our Lord.

I don't know for certain that this story is true, but it hardly matters, because now these authentic candy canes are symbolic to me. I'm always on the lookout for them, especially at the shopping mall where the meaning of Christmas often seems buried amid the frantic rush. So when I spot a red and white striped candy cane in a child's hand or on a tree or in a store window, I feel comforted by the sweet reminder of Jesus.

Father, may the world be filled with sweet reminders of You this season.   —Carol Kuykendall

21 PRACTICING THE POWER OF PRAYER
WED Honest Prayers

If you...know how to give good gifts to your children, how much more shall your Father who is in heaven give what is good to those who ask Him!   —Matthew 7:11 (NAS)

When it came to filling out my Christmas wish list, I was always a few years ahead of myself. When I was four, I asked for a BB gun like the one belonging to the older boy I played with next door. Instead, I found a cap gun and holster under the Christmas tree. When I was fourteen, I asked for a motorcycle. I had to settle for a racing bike. They were great gifts, but they weren't exactly what I had requested.

The scenario of these childhood memories is played out into adulthood. I remember as a college student fervently praying that a dating relationship might lead to marriage. I loved this girl and was greatly hurt when things did not work out. But now, in hindsight, I know that God was loving both of us when He led us to different marriage partners.

So, too, have I prayed for vocational opportunities only to have a door closed in my face. I have been stunned by the grief and disappointment, only to realize months later that if I had received my wish, I would not have been happy or fulfilled.

The truth is I believe that God loves to hear our honest desires. I can still see my dad smile and warmly hug me when I asked for a horse when we lived in the middle of a city. And I, too, long to hear what is filling my children's wide-eyed imaginations. It creates a bond between us. But, ultimately, my children can trust me to give them what is good. And so it is with God.

Today, pray openly and honestly with all of your heart. And trust in the goodness of God.

Dear God, You know what is best for me. I recommit myself to trusting Your love and wisdom. Amen.   — Scott Walker

---

22
THURS

Behold, you will conceive in your womb and bear a son....And Mary said... "let it be to me according to your word."...   —Luke 1:31, 38 (RSV)

SAY "YES" AT CHRISTMAS

And Mary said, "Yes" when the angel came,
    not knowing all it would mean.
        For "yes" was only the beginning.
"Yes" to giving birth in a cold, dark stable,
    while cows and sheep looked on.
"Yes" to a sword that pierced her soul, as her
    Son died on a cross, while she looked on.
And Mary said, "Yes, let it be."
But do I? Do I say, "Yes" when God calls to me?
Oh, not through an angel who comes in the night,
But maybe a pastor
    who asks if I'll lead a Sunday school class;
Or a former friend
    who calls to mend our broken relationship;
Or a stranger
    who wonders if I might spare some change for food.
And for a moment as I ponder what to say,
    does God's purpose flicker like a flame
        in a sudden breeze,
      to be snuffed out by "no,"
    or to burn even brighter with the power of "yes"?
For "yes" is only a beginning.
"Yes," I'll give my time to sharing God's Word.
"Yes," I'll end a quarrel by forgiving another, and myself.
"Yes," I'll share what I have with one in need.

For somehow I know that even to the small questions,
    God needs to hear my "yes"
    as much as He needed to hear Mary's.
Perhaps that's why Jesus comes to the world a baby,
    a baby full of questions, needs and desires.
When He asks to come into my heart this Christmas,
    will I say, "Yes"?

Lord, I trust that wherever my "yes" takes me, You will be there.
                       — Gina Bridgeman

23
FRI

For God so loved the world, that he gave his only begotten Son....
                       — John 3:16

On Christmas Eve a couple of years ago, we called our recently widowed friend Jim in the snowy Midwest. He seemed in remarkably good spirits, having spent a quiet evening listening to Christmas music with his cat Purrl. Toward the end of our call, he asked if we'd opened our gifts yet, and we explained that we were waiting for the children to arrive before doing that.

"Good!" he said. "Then I can give you *my* gift first!" Laughing, I asked if he was going to croon a few Christmas carols. "Nope!" he said. "I'm going to tell you a story. A *true* story.

"Once upon a time," he began, "or more specifically, about six hours ago, while I was sitting here feeling depressed and wishing I could sleep through the rest of the holidays, there was a knock on my apartment door. My caller turned out to be a woman I've seen around town for many years. Some time ago, she contracted one of those tragic, withering diseases for which there's no cure and no effective treatment. Everyone marvels at the way she keeps going — especially since she can no longer work, and it's become a real struggle just to exist from month to month.

"We've had brief conversations on the street and in stores," Jim said, "but that's been the extent of our relationship. So I was naturally surprised to find her at my door, especially on Christmas Eve. But when I invited her in, I found she'd come to deliver some cookies. There were five or six altogether — not those fancy cutouts with colored icing and sparkles, but the plain, unadorned, home-baked variety. It seems she hadn't had enough left in her larder to make a bigger batch, but she'd thought of me, knowing I'd be alone this Christmas, and she'd hoped a few cookies might cheer me up. We visited awhile, and I ate them in a few bites, but they didn't do much to improve my mood.

"It was after she left," Jim said, his voice growing thick with emotion, "that it finally dawned on me what I'd just received. Those cookies were *all* that dear woman had in the world to give—and she gave them to *me! Can you imagine* that?" After a pause, he added softly, "I knew then that the Christ Child had truly arrived—and lodged in my heart."

Yes, indeed, Jim. And now, in ours.

On that long-ago night in Bethlehem, Lord God, You gave us all You had to give. How can I pass along Your gift to someone else today?
— Susan Williams

$\frac{24}{SAT}$ *CHRISTMAS EVE*
HOW SHALL WE ADORE HIM?
Expect a Miracle

"If you had faith...you could say to this mountain, 'Move!' and it would go far away. Nothing would be impossible."
— Matthew 17:20 (TLB)

On that first Christmas, the people who awaited the coming of God's Son didn't doubt that such a thing could happen. Shepherds, hearing angel voices in the night sky, knelt in prayer and then ran into town to find a Messiah. Wise men, who had risked their lives to seek a King, were near the end of their journey. Mary and Joseph, far from home and among strangers, sensed that a mystery was about to be explained. They all expected a miracle. Today, we can, too. We can still count on God to do what people cannot do.

St. Augustine's Church in Philadelphia was built in 1796, and President George Washington attended the corner-laying ceremonies. Today, this historic church sits just a stone's throw away from a bridge spanning the Delaware River, connecting New Jersey and Pennsylvania. Looking at the church from the bridge, billboards obscure almost everything but the massive steeple, 196 feet high.

During a hurricane in December 1992, sheets of metal around the steeple came loose and blew onto the bridge roadway, which was crowded with commuters. The steeple itself swayed dangerously, threatening the safety of people on the bridge and in nearby buildings.

Experts called to the scene said nothing could be done until the winds subsided.

As a group of parishioners looked up at the steeple, they knew it couldn't possibly outlast the storm. But together they prayed anyway. "Lord," they pleaded, "please don't let the steeple fall."

Today, when people recall the hurricane, they talk about the steeple of St. Augustine's because it didn't come down. The next day, when it was safe enough for workers to dismantle the steeple, they found that the timbers holding it together had rotted! "I can't understand how it stayed up," an engineer said.

But the parishioners did. "It was a miracle," they said. And they're praying for another miracle: for the enormous financing needed to help them restore the steeple and the damaged roof. Yes, even in our technological world, we can expect such things to happen — when we believe.

On this eve before Christmas, we ask, *How shall we adore Him?*

> *We adore Him when we pray,*
> *believing that all things are possible with God.*

We thank you, Lord, for the miracle of our salvation, for the miracles in each day.   — Phyllis Hobe

25
SUN
CHRISTMAS DAY
HOW SHALL WE ADORE HIM?
Keep Christmas Every Day

They shall call his name Immanuel....God with us.
— Matthew 1:23

It was a glorious morning, the beginning of a glorious day, and today we can share the joy with those who worshiped the Christ Child on that first Christmas Day. But sooner or later, they all had to leave and go back to the lives they knew. So do we. They were not the same as they were before. The coming of Christ had changed their lives. He changes ours, too.

My stepfather, at eighty-three, is beginning to feel useless. Physically, he isn't strong enough to help around our house, and after hip surgery he doesn't walk very well. But he's always been a loner and resents every effort to get him involved with a group. He still loves to read, however, and I drive him to the library every few days for a new book.

When we were there recently, Dad saw another elderly man teaching a younger man how to read. Their heads were bent over an open book, and as the younger man struggled with each word, the older man was patient and encouraging. "That man's older than I am!" my stepfather said. "I think I could do that."

It was something I had always wanted to do, but somehow never did. So this year, as Dad and I celebrate the birth of our Lord Jesus Christ, we're making plans to work with adults who can't read. This is one of the ways Christ is influencing our daily lives. "You work with the younger ones," my dad said. "I'll take the old-timers." His eyes now are full of purpose, and he seems to be standing straighter.

We have come to receive the Christ Child — and as we serve others, we are deeply blessed. On this Christmas Day, we ask, *How shall we adore Him?*

We adore Him when we keep Christmas every day.

Be with us, Jesus, in all we do in the days ahead. — Phyllis Hobe

---

$\frac{26}{\text{MON}}$ *Therefore if any man be in Christ, he is a new creature....* — II Corinthians 5:17

As a civil engineer with a specialty in water conservation, erosion and related problems, my husband has spent a lifetime taming the mountain ranges along our California coastline. Building dams, run-off channels and rainwater catch basins, John is used to kicking a rattlesnake off the trail or clearing out an access with a hatchet.

He is a rugged man. Strong. Silent. Honorable. Given to hard work and a clear, rational response to life that leaves no room for error: "It's either right or wrong. So what's the problem?" But human relations are not that simple or logical, and in the family, John's matter-of-fact manner frequently left a trail of misunderstanding and hurt feelings.

So you can imagine my surprise when John tenderly took our first grandchild Brandon into his arms, sitting down (this face-anything, fearless man) "to have a safer hold." He looked into the baby's small, scrunched-up, just-born face and then turned his eyes to the hills.

"This little fellow has given me a whole *new beginning*," he said quietly in a voice choked in emotion. "He has never seen me angry.

Never seen me lose my temper. Never seen me impatient or frustrated. Never seen me walk out of a room saying, 'I don't have to listen to this!' Never seen me slam a door with irritation...and I hope he never will!"

New beginnings from a newborn babe.

Lord Jesus, You came as a newborn Babe to give us all a new beginning. Thank You that with Your help I, too, can change, to become more the person You'd like me to be. —Fay Angus

27 TUES
Endure hardship as discipline....[Discipline] produces a harvest of righteousness and peace for those who have been trained by it. —Hebrews 12:7, 11 (NIV)

Recently, I was puzzled by the passage above in Hebrews. What exactly did it mean, "being trained by" hardship?

My answer came in the form of a letter last week from a prayer-friend, Mr. Bidwell, who has been undergoing cancer surgery and chemotherapy. "I have dedicated this illness to the Lord, Kathie," he wrote. "Sometimes I get the opportunity to talk about Jesus, my illness being the avenue that causes people to listen where they might not otherwise."

This was it. Here was someone producing a harvest of righteousness, having been trained by hardship most frightening. Such a harvest means quietly trusting God Who never leaves or forsakes His own (Hebrews 13:5), even in the midst of trouble. It's "dedicating" the hardship to God, as Mr. Bidwell put it. It's turning it around and finding ways to use it for His glory, a veritable "weakness...turned to strength" (Hebrews 11:34, NIV).

I am trying to follow Mr. Bidwell's lead. When I was slowed down with flu over Christmas vacation, instead of giving in to just-my-luck frustration, I tried to use it as a time of deep rest, a big time-out to ponder deeply the God-Child in a trough of hay and what it meant to me. Not much baking got done, but I appreciated my family more, and I think my patience increased.

Yes, God can use my off-days, off-weeks, even off-months. It's not wasted under His leadership...*if* I allow myself to be trained by the hardships.

Dear Lord, help me to make my obstacles and hardships into stepping stones of Your training. —Kathie Kania

Quiet Time

O Father, may that holy star
Grow every year more bright,
And send its glorious beams afar
To fill the world with light.
— *William Cullen Bryant*

28
WED

HOUSE GUEST
You comprehend my path...And are acquainted with all my ways. —Psalm 139:3 (NKJV)

I received a check in the mail the other day and hurriedly put it aside, meaning to deposit it as soon as some pressing matters were taken care of.

Later that day, I remembered the check and thought, *Now, where did I put it?* I tried to think of where I was when I opened it — in the car, in the kitchen, or perhaps passing the telephone table where lots of stuff gets stashed for a future time. I looked through my purse and rummaged through my "mail box" on the kitchen table. Maybe I slipped it into a book I'd been carrying that day. But, no, it wasn't there either.

The amount of the check wasn't so large, but my mind kept puzzling over where it could be. I knew the Lord knew exactly where it was, and I tried to give the task of locating it over to Him and continue on with things in a peaceful state of mind. But the missing check nagged at me. The next day, instead of having my usual time with God's Word, I doggedly looked again in all the places I'd looked the day before, still to no avail.

This morning, after another exasperating look for the check, I decided to stop and follow a strong tug to have my morning Bible time instead. Sensing the strain wash off me, I opened the Bible and saturated my heart with it for a while. Then, about to close it, instead I suddenly flipped through its pages, and there was the check, about two pages from where I'd been reading! Right where I'd put it when I opened it in the car the other day. Right where I would have found it if I'd really let go and given the matter over to God.

Are there times in your life when your focus on the All-Knowing One blurs, when you try to take care of things with your own resources and knowledge? Next time, try to spend a few minutes in His Word and quietly listen for the answer. I'll bet the rest of your day will fall into place peacefully, in the way it was meant to.

> *Father, help my focus on You grow clearer each day,*
> *no matter the distractions that come my way.*
>
> — Ellyn Baumann

29
THURS

...And encouraged them with these words.
— II Chronicles 32:6 (NIV)

I've never thought of myself as a funny person ever since I tried to tell a joke at a party years ago and a strange man told me I'd gotten the punch line wrong.

But for one week last year I had the experience of feeling I was a good storyteller. It happened like this: When shopping in an antique store with my mother-in-law, she picked up an old plate with an exorbitant price tag and whispered to me, "The cost is ridiculous! Why, my grandmother had the same thing."

I said, "*Shh!* I once saw a sign in an antique store that said: 'We Charge Fifty Percent Extra If We Have to Listen to What Your Grandmother Had.'"

My mother-in-law thought that was so funny that during my entire visit with her she told practically everyone "the funny sign Linda told me about." Every single time we were in a group, she'd say, "Linda told me the funniest thing today." Then she'd nudge me, "Tell them." I basked in her encouragement, and by the end of the week I felt like a budding Bob Hope. I even got up the courage to tell a small joke back at work.

Since then, I've applied that kind of encouragement to others. When I said to a student, "You used such a vivid example in your writing," I began to see more vivid paragraphs in that young man's work. When I told a sometimes gruff employee, "You have such a pleasant manner on the phone," in just a week I wondered why I had ever considered him to be gruff!

Just as I'd lived up to my mother-in-law's praise so, too, did everyone else around me live up to mine.

Let me congratulate, not correct, someone today, God — a co-worker, a spouse, a child.
— Linda Neukrug

30 *I can do all things through Christ....*   — Philippians 4:13
FRI

I have an idea for a new creative project that I've been thinking about for months. "I'm going to try it one of these days," I keep telling myself. But it doesn't get done. In fact, it doesn't even get started! Lying in bed last night, in the silence that's filled with the mystery of God, I asked why. Immediately, one word flashed through my mind. *Fear.* Of course! Fear of failure. How many of my best ideas are buried beneath that canopy!

This morning, some words in an article I was reading suddenly sprouted wings. They were spoken by that wonderfully creative singer, dancer, poet, writer and storyteller Maya Angelou. She said, "I know that there is no place that God is not. And by knowing that, I can dare things. I can dare to succeed because I can dare to fail."

Oh! I'm going to place those words over my desk, on my bathroom mirror, refrigerator door, on my pillow, wherever I'll see them many times a day. This morning, as soon as these thoughts are printed out, I will begin my new creative project. If I fail, I fall only into the arms of the Spirit of infinite creativity, ready for a new beginning!

*With Your great creative Spirit, Lord, I can risk, I can dare,
I can become all You would have me be!*

— Marilyn Morgan Helleberg

31 *In all these things we are more than conquerors through*
SAT *him that loved us.*   — Romans 8:37

There is a story told about a man who through a tragic auto accident lost his wife and two children. He grieved endlessly. Even time did not ease the pain. Memory of his loss badgered his every waking hour and he slept fitfully. Then one night in a dream, he met God and asked Him if He could wipe away his bad memories. "Yes, I can rid your mind of everything bad that has ever happened in your life," God told him. "But you should know that with it would go all the wonderful memories you have, too." From the sorrowing man's dream of night came the dawn of understanding and the first light of healing.

As you look back on 1994, how do you assess it? Do you have mostly positive memories or mostly negative ones? Did you accomplish the things for which you'd hoped? Did you make new friends? Grow spiritually? Suffer some setbacks? Achieve some victories? If you are like most people, you experienced both pluses and minuses. I wish I'd done better, been more faithful, more helpful, more understanding, more sensitive, more caring. But other than ask God's forgiveness for my sins of omission and commission, and make restitution if possible, I can only go forward praying that He will help me do better in the future.

Predictably, we will all fall short of Christ's high calling many times in the year ahead. Our human nature precludes perfection. Futhermore, we can't control every circumstance that happens in our lives. But we can control our reactions to things that befall us and our attitudes about them, and with God's help become more than conquerors over any contingency—even death. We have His promise, for the new year and all the years of our life.

> *God, we thank You for the year just past,*
> *For the good times and the bad,*
> *We thank You for Your mercy and Your grace,*
> *That temper memories of the sad.*
>
> *Now grant us wisdom for the coming year,*
> *Obedient minds that listen, still,*
> *Trusting hearts that conquer fear,*
> *Steadfast love to do Thy will.*

—Fred Bauer

Prayer Diary

My Prayer Requests for December:

1. _____

2. _____

3. _____

4. _____

5. _____

6. _____

7. _____

8. _____

9. _____

10. _____

11. _____

12. _____

13. _____

14. _____

15. _____

16. _____

17. _____

DECEMBER 1994

18. _____

19. _____

20. _____

21. _____

22. _____

23. _____

24. _____

25. _____

26. _____

27. _____

28. _____

29. _____

30. _____

31. _____

A Gathering of Friends

Welcome! Welcome!
Come and join the merriment! It's time to gather together and have our dear writer-friends share with us what's been going on in their lives this past year. And while they're at it, they'll also tell us what prayer means to them.

"This is the year that life came full circle!" says FAY ANGUS of Sierra Madre, California. *Full circle* as life renewed itself through the wonder of their grandson Brandon, born to son Ian and his wife Melissa. *Full circle* as many of those, such as Fay, who were interned as children in China during World War II met again for the first time at a series of reunions. *Full circle* as husband John kept a honeymoon promise he made 35 years ago and took Fay to Santa Fe, New Mexico. ("Your namesake, after all," he'd say!) And daughter Katrelya decided to enlarge her job options by starting her own medical transcription service. "A few years ago, a friend gave me a little card that said, 'DON'T PANIC—PRAY!' When I'm tempted to panic, I just put my hand on that card, close my eyes and simply pray, 'Help, dear Lord, please help!' I live by prayer."

FRED BAUER of Princeton, New Jersey, returns to *Daily Guideposts* after a year's sabbatical. During that time, he was busy with other writing projects, publishing, editing and consulting. He and his wife Shirley drove their motor home all over the country, but primarily to Hamilton Lake, Indiana, and Englewood Beach, Florida. Fred is happy to report that with the graduation of son Daniel from Penn State, all four of their kids have college degrees. "We are now into grandparenting big time. Our daughter Laraine's kids, Jessica, 10, Ashley, 8, and David, 5, are the apples of our eyes. If we'd known grandparenting was so much fun, we'd have had them first." Fred says that author Frank Laubach was right when he called prayer "the mightiest force in the world." "Someone once asked me if I thought prayer can change things. My answer: 'I know one thing that it changes — me.'"

GINA BRIDGEMAN of Scottsdale, Arizona, began what may become a lifetime project: researching her genealogy. So far she's learned that her family's earliest immigrants came from Darmstadt, Germany, around 1840. She's also discovered a branch of the family from Toronto, Canada, that she never knew existed! Husband Paul satisfied his love of performing when he appeared in a production of *A Christmas Carol* as the ghost of Jacob Marley. Son Ross, who turns 5 this year, began playing soccer and appeared in his first church Christmas pageant as a shepherd. "We've been teaching Ross to pray, but we're the ones who are learning. Listening to Ross ask for God's blessings with a trusting heart, or thank Him for books and dogs and warm, sunny days, I think I know what Jesus meant when He said, 'Anyone who will not receive the kingdom of God like a little child will never enter it' [Luke 18:17, NIV]."

MARY LOU CARNEY of Chesterton, Indiana, has been busy editing the Guideposts award-winning magazine for kids *Faith 'n Stuff.* Daughter Amy Jo entered her senior year at the University of Dayton in Ohio, dividing her time between studying at the library and working as a banquet server at a hotel. Son Brett, 17, expanded his woodcutting service to include tree removal. He even had his own business cards printed! Husband Gary upgraded his equipment and kept busy with new construction, even through the winter months. A new arrival to the family this year was Arkus, a German shepherd puppy who came to the Carneys after their faithful watchdog Susie died. "In the bustle of everyday commitments, prayer provides a haven for me, a place to meditate on the truly important things in life." Mary Lou's best quiet time comes while walking in the nearby Indiana Dunes State Park and along Lake Michigan.

CHRISTOPHER DE VINCK of Pompton Plains, New Jersey, and his wife Roe traveled to Ottawa, Canada, to visit their nephew and niece this past year. Their daughter Karen, 11, endured and recovered from a foot operation. Nine-year-old Michael's soccer team lost every game of the season, and David, 14, built a nifty magazine rack in his technology class. Chris converted the basement into a playroom for the children. "I call that the last frontier. There is nothing else to do to the house now except pay the mortgage!" Between family life and teaching, Chris wrote his third book, a children's novel, *Augusta and Trab* (Macmillan). Chris says a prayer first thing each morning and then asks God for strength. In the semidarkness of his room, he glances at the photos of his three children on the nearby chest, and with that ending to his quiet time, he feels centered, ready to begin his day.

The Pawling, New York, household of ERIC FELLMAN and his wife Joy experienced some major events this year. All three boys officially arrived in adolescence as the youngest, Jonathan, turned 12. Jason, 16, got his driver's permit and promptly wrecked Eric's car. Nathan, 14, went through his first girlfriend breakup and decided to be "just friends" for a while. Joy returned to work as a registered nurse after 17 years at home with the boys. Last year, on their annual March ski trip, they drove through the "Blizzard of '93," until the Vermont Highway Patrol stopped them. After being marooned for 24 hours at a motel, they finally arrived at the slopes and to "the best skiing in ten years." Eric has found a helpful method of practicing prayer: *flash prayers.* "I say short prayers all day through all activities as soon as a prayer thought comes to mind. This keeps my thoughts focused on God's presence and guidance."

OSCAR GREENE of West Medford, Massachusetts, and his wife Ruby reached their 51st wedding anniversary this past September. Each morning they do a 1-mile walk to keep fit, and each Wednesday they dine out to reward themselves. Ruby completed her 19th year as directress of their church altar guild and enlisted Oscar to serve on the previously all-woman association. Oscar also served as master of ceremonies at his 55th high school class reunion in Williamstown. The original graduates numbered 32; 15 attended. "A little more than a year ago, we learned an unexpected lesson in the power of prayer. Within hours, we went from joy over our church fair to sorrow upon learning our cousins were killed in a car crash. We hurried the 1,045 miles to East St. Louis, where mother and grandmother showed amazing strength, courage and faith. Their acceptance was a powerful example to Ruby and me."

RICK HAMLIN of New York City is about to begin his 10th year on staff at *Guideposts* magazine. Son Timothy turns 4 this February, and Willy turns 7. Timothy's great passions are music and food; he's always singing to himself as he cooks gourmet meals out of Play-Doh. Will is deep into Lego, putting together the most complicated contraptions to confuse his parents. Wife Carol has been writing books about Victorian collectibles and how to take photographs of your kids. "One of my favorite prayers has always been this one attributed to the 17th-century English general Lord Astley before going into battle: 'O Lord, thou knowest how busy I must be this day; if I forget Thee, do not Thou forget me.' My days are busy, too, and the only way I can make sure I don't forget God is by setting aside some time, however brief, in prayer every day."

After a couple of years of turning inward, MARILYN MORGAN HELLEBERG of Kearney, Nebraska, has enjoyed a year of more extroverted activity, including swimming, mountain climbing, canoeing, and attending out-of-town events such as concerts and retreats. She and her new friend Curt (who wrote to her after reading one of her books) have been getting acquainted this year by mail, phone calls and frequent visits, even though they live more than 400 miles apart! Marilyn also enjoyed lunchtime chats with daughter Karen and son John, and spent time with son Paul and his wife Cheryl and their five children, ages 3 to 16, during a June trip to Colorado. "For me, the deepest kind of prayer is sitting in silent awareness of God's presence. I pray this way every evening, and it's a spiritual treasure I wouldn't want to be without."

The past year has been a time of spiritual healing for PHYLLIS HOBE of East Greenville, Pennsylvania. "Within a period of six weeks last spring, I lost my dog Kate and my cat Mr. Jones to serious, unexpected illnesses. Like many others with similar experiences, I had to consider whether to bring another animal into my life and expose myself to more sorrow and pain should anything happen to it, or to go on alone. I felt I had to take this up with God, because I trust Him to decide what is best for me. So I prayed in a very focused way, asking Him specifically what to do. The answer came more quickly than I expected when my veterinarian offered me an orphaned kitten he had restored to health. Then another friend offered me a Rottweiler puppy. And a second kitten, quite lost, presented himself on my doorstep and demanded to come in. I'm rebuilding my family with loving creatures who need my care. And I know that God was absolutely right in His decision."

MARJORIE HOLMES moved back to her former home in Manassas, Virginia, after her husband of 10 years, Dr. George Schmieler, passed away. Shortly after George's death, Marjorie broke her hip. "The experience and pleas of my family have convinced me I need to be with my own," says Marjorie. Her house is on a lake, and her daughter and son-in-law live next door. "Talk about the power of prayer. The day before I left McMurray [Pennsylvania] for Virginia, I prayed to God to help me with the move. Wouldn't you know, while packing I found a message from George that night and another the night I arrived in Manassas! George used to write me a love letter every day, and these two were written years ago, but were so appropriate to my departure and arrival. It had to be a miracle to draw them blindly from different sacks!"

DAVID JACOBSEN, the former American hostage held in Beirut, Lebanon, for 18 months, makes a special guest appearance in this year's *Daily Guideposts* (see his series *Faith: Your Daily Survival Kit*, February 5–11). He now lives in Bear Valley, California, a rural area about 100 miles northeast of Los Angeles, and he is the administrator of a small community hospital in Tehachapi. David, 62, jogs daily for an hour on his treadmill. He has three children, Eric, Paul and Diane, and seven grandkids, John, Jakey, Dylan, Joseph, Philip, Stephen and Erika Anne. David says two prayers sustained him while he was in captivity—and even now—the St. Francis Prayer and the 27th Psalm. "When I pray for something, I always pray for knowledge of God and God's will. This is the key to prayer for me, because we don't always start out praying for the right thing."

KATHIE KANIA of The Dalles, Oregon, and her husband Michael went camping this past summer with their two daughters, Breton, 11, and Kristin, 7. One trip was to the mountains of Idaho; the other to the coast, where they camped on Whidbey Island. The day of their 16th wedding anniversary, all of them rode the big ferry over to Victoria, British Columbia, and ate lunch at an outdoor café. Kathie continues to paint, and she entered three art exhibits last year. "This year, I've been seeking *effective* prayer. I look to others whose prayer life I admire. I study the Scriptures and books on the subject. I am coming to see the importance of believing with the heart as I pray—my words aligning with my heart's expectation—if I am to expect results. But this isn't always easy."

PAM KIDD of Brentwood, Tennessee, says her greatest delight is being wife to David, a minister, and mom to Brock, 21, and Keri, 17. She works part-time for a magazine publishing company based in Nashville. A little over a year ago, Pam's mother Arlene Dunn accepted Herbert Hester's proposal of marriage, and they were married in the Kidds' living room in a secret ceremony by David. Though they intended no fanfare, Pam and her family had a miniature reception with lots of pretty flowers, a tiny wedding cake, punch and all the trimmings. "Beyond memorized church prayer and habitual prayers of grace offered at mealtime, my prayers have become less formal and more spontaneous. Still, I have to stop from time to time and remind myself that I don't have to do all the talking...listening is just as important. And I try to give God an occasional day off, praying, 'What can I do for You today?' instead of 'Please do this for me!'"

Flying, floating, fishing and farewells best describe the year for Big Lake, Alaska's CAROL KNAPP. Husband Terry had a dream fishing trip with two friends in the Lake Iliamna area. Carol floated a 100-mile stretch of the Yukon River and flew to Idaho for her mother's 70th birthday. Their student from Okinawa, Japan, rejoined his family. Tamara, 19, graduated from high school and flew off to Whitworth College in Spokane, Washington. Phil, 17, boated to a summer job on Big Lake and performed a lot of airborne stunts on his motorcycle. Kelly, 16, and Brenda, 15, vacationed with their uncle's family in Banff, Canada. "The reverent words of Jesus carved on our Communion table at church, 'Do this in remembrance of me,' have become a sweeping prayer that keeps me living for Him. They help me to say 'no' when I should and say 'yes' when I should. To say, 'I do this, or I do not do this, in remembrance of You' is a prayerful banner that continually lifts my sights toward God."

DIANE KOMP was born in New York City and lives in Guilford, Connecticut. She is a professor of pediatrics at Yale Medical School and a medical doctor who works with young cancer patients at Yale-New Haven Hospital. She tells their stories in her book *A Window to Heaven: When Children See Life in Death* (Zondervan). This past year, she was on sabbatical based out of Marburg, Germany (near the Vogelsberg). When she's not working, Diane enjoys orchiding (she has a greenhouse at home), cross-country skiing and hiking. She is fluent in German, can read French, can deliver a baby in Spanish and can order roller skis in Norwegian. ("It's a great way to meet people!") "I have learned one powerful prayer that always seems to get a 'yes' answer. If I am in a new place or situation and ask God to send me new friends who love Him, I only have to stand back and wait."

For the last couple of years, CAROL KUYKENDALL of Boulder, Colorado, and her husband Lynn have been *downsizing* around their house. Kendall, 17, is the only one left at home, and since she started driving, she's hardly ever there! Still, all five get together on their annual August trek to the West Coast to deliver Derek, 22, to the University of Puget Sound in Tacoma,

Washington, and Lindsay, 20, to Westmont College in Santa Barbara, California. This past year, they added a side trip and took a ferry around the San Juan Islands to Victoria, where they visited the parliament buildings, observed high tea at a fancy hotel and soaked up some local history at the Royal British Columbia Museum—all in 24 hours! "The older I get, the more I cherish and need prayer. Prayer doesn't change God. Usually, it doesn't change my circumstances. But almost always, prayer changes me. I kneel more often when I pray now, not out of obedience or obligation, but desire, because kneeling reminds me Whom I am worshiping."

LINDA NEUKRUG of Walnut Creek, California, has been pretty involved with cats this year. A mother cat and her four tiny tortoiseshell kittens showed up in her backyard, and the mother had a piece of plastic cinched around her waist. Linda spent more than a week trying to catch the cat in order to cut off the plastic, but to no avail. Finally, a local organization made up of caring, cat-loving volunteers lent her a cage and Linda trapped the cat, at which point a volunteer cut off the plastic. Five cats were several too many, but now Linda and husband Paul are the owners of two lovely kittens, Bisto and Marmite. "I once read that Eleanor Roosevelt said this about prayer, and I like it: 'Prayer is a working instrument that does certain things, like a pencil writes or a knife cuts.' To that I would add only, just as you must use a pencil or knife for it to work, so, too, must you use prayer to feel its full power."

NORMAN VINCENT PEALE and RUTH STAFFORD PEALE celebrated their 63rd wedding anniversary and Dr. Peale's 95th birthday last year. They regularly visit the New York editorial offices of Guideposts, of which they are the founders and publishers. They live at the Hill Farm in the foothills of the Berkshire Mountains. From this location, they often spend time at the business office of Guideposts in Carmel, and at the Peale Center for Christian Living in Pawling. Last year, Norman and Ruth, along with their three children, eight grandchildren and one great-grandchild, held a family reunion at the oldest inn in New England. One of their favorite prayers is "I believe I am always divinely guided. I believe I will always take the right turn of the road. I believe God will always make a way where there is no way."

It was a career milestone for ELEANOR SASS of New York City as she celebrated her 30th anniversary with Guideposts. "When I came aboard in the fall of '63, I never dreamed I'd stay in one place this long," Ellie laughs. "And while I'm happy in my work, I must confess that it's fun thinking ahead a few years to retirement." When that time comes, Ellie and her Dandie Dinmont terrier Wally, who are enrolled in therapy dog training, will visit hospitals and nursing homes for the benefit of the patients there. "I grew up on the prayer 'Let the words of my mouth, and the meditation of my heart, be acceptable in thy sight, O Lord, my strength, and my redeemer' [Psalm 19:14]. It was the last prayer I uttered before leaving Sunday school or church each Sunday. Memory led me to carry it over into my daily life. It's a convenient prayer for all hours of the day or night, no matter where I am or what I'm doing."

Last year, DANIEL SCHANTZ of Moberly, Missouri, passed several milestones: 30 years of marriage to Sharon, 25 years of teaching at Central Christian College, his 50th birthday, and his first year as a grandfather to daughter Natalie and son-in-law Matt's daughter Hannah Mae. Dan and Sharon like to relax by taking walks together, especially after dark, and then spending the rest of the evening reading, watching classic videos and talking. On Saturday mornings, they like to have breakfast in bed, followed by a mad race around town to visit rummage sales. Sharon buys knick-knacks, and Dan looks for old books. One of Dan's favorite prayers is "Lord, help me to be all that You intended for me to be when You created me." It expresses Dan's deepest wish to be all that he can be for God. Dan likes to pray aloud while taking his daily walk in the country. "It refreshes me like nothing else."

DOROTHY SHELLENBERGER of Waco, Texas, and her husband Charles made a large deck extending out from their den where they have enjoyed leisurely breakfasts and tea parties in the late afternoon. They also converted a garage apartment into two cozy offices, and Dorothy finally succumbed to the 20th century and got a computer. With eight of their eleven grandchildren now owning driver's licenses, Dorothy says, "I am grateful that Corrie ten Boom gave me the Lord's private telephone number — JE333 [for Jeremiah 33:3, NAS] — and it's available to His children 24 hours of every day. You just have to 'call to Him, and He will answer you, and He will tell you great and mighty things, which you do not know.'" Oftentimes, Dorothy says that her prayers are answered in ways that she never would have imagined, and the answers are much better than the ones she had anticipated.

ELIZABETH (Tib) SHERRILL of Chappaqua, New York, and her husband John were the guests of a friend with ties to the Ritz Hotel in Paris, where she put them up. "There were gold fixtures in the bathroom. If we lay down in the afternoon, that night there'd be fresh sheets on the beds. All of which sent our thoughts back 45 years to when we lived in Paris as students. The bathrooms for our sixth-floor walk-up were two floors below. Actually, there was no bath — that was at the public bathhouse five blocks away. We loved the Ritz! But we loved our walk-up home, too. Our little journey-in-memory pointed up a timeless truth: Joy is not in externals but in the heart." Tib's favorite way to start a day is to sing this prayer on a dawn walk: "Morning has broken/Like the first morning./Blackbird has spoken/Like the first bird./Praise for the singing!/Praise for the morning!/Praise for them springing/Fresh from the Word." *(Photograph © 1990 Helen Marcus)*

With 20-year-old son Timothy off at college, LINDA CHING SLEDGE of Pleasantville, New York, her husband Gary and their 12-year-old son Geoffrey marked the "unbuilding" of their old family unit by "rebuilding" their 65-year-old house. "Renovating was a crazy thing to do," Linda admits in hindsight, "but one that every 'empty nest' parent can sympathize with. Tim's leaving pushed us to shore up our foundations — literally — so this family would keep hold of its moorings." The prayer from Psalm 121:1–4 is printed on a bookmark, which Linda tacked up on the bulletin board above her desk more than 12 years ago. Amid the changing kaleidoscope of faculty announcements and schedules for meetings, it's the one thing that hasn't moved from its place on her wall. "Whenever I am exhausted or blue, I 'lift up mine eyes' and find comfort in the rhythm, the beauty and the promise of these ancient words of King David."

No long trips abroad this past year for august world traveler VAN VARNER of New York City. "Too busy," he says, moving from his post as editor-in-chief of *Guideposts* magazine to his new role as editorial director. One thing unchanged is his overseeing the Guideposts publication for kids *Faith 'n Stuff.* It's a job he clearly loves, especially now that his numerous godchildren seem to be producing numerous *grand*-godchildren. According to Van, "They're all potential subscribers!" After years of collecting — what else? books! — Van was persuaded by a good friend to redecorate his Upper West Side apartment to create a more airy, spacious feel. Would you believe he donated more than 200 books from his treasured collection to various friends and charities. You'll be interested in what Van has learned about the endlessly fascinating subject of prayer. It has to do with dining alone, and you'll find it in his devotional on April 11.

SCOTT WALKER and his wife Beth moved their family to Waco, Texas, this past summer after serving 7 years as pastor of the First Baptist Church of Charleston, South Carolina. Currently, Scott is pastor of the First Baptist Church of Waco, and is also involved in ministry to students at Baylor University and the George W. Truett Theological Seminary. On the family line, Drew, 11, is becoming quite a good tennis player; Luke, 8, is becoming an avid runner; Jodi, 5, is starting kindergarten, and enjoys dolls and T-ball. "There is a keen awareness that I can only be as good personally and professionally as my prayer life is deep and vital. Therefore, as I face the future, I realize that the quality of my life and the realization of my dreams are largely dependent upon the quality of time I spend with God each day. It sounds so simple, but it's the greatest challenge that lies before me."

DOLPHUS WEARY lives in Mendenhall, Mississippi, and is the president of Mendenhall Ministries and associate pastor of Outreach for Mendenhall Bible Church. He and his wife Rosie Camper Weary have three children: Danita Ronique, 19, a sophomore at Rhodes College in Memphis, Tennessee; Reginald Demond, 17, a high school senior; Ryan Donche, 6, a first-grader. Dolphus travels extensively throughout the United

States, speaking in churches, on Christian college campuses, and to various groups that share a message and vision of hope. He wrote his life's story in the book *I Ain't Comin' Back* (Tyndale). "Prayer is a unique and wonderful privilege to commune with the Father. When we pray, we call on God's power to energize us. My desire is to have a prayerful spirit all the time, but generally I seek to pray on a regular basis in the morning and in the evening."

MARION BOND WEST of Watkinsville, Georgia, and her husband Gene Acuff helped to celebrate the 150th year of the church he pastors, Mt. Vernon Christian in Monroe. Gene looked just like a circuit rider in his black, wide-brim hat, string tie and jacket with tails. Marion wore a Scarlett O'Hara dress, complete with hoopskirt. "I'm trying to learn to pray *answers* from Scripture, rather than the problem. *Afraid?* I might pray, 'Thank You, Lord, that You haven't given me a spirit of fear; but of power, and of love, and of a sound mind' (II Timothy 1:7). *Hard times?* 'All right, Lord, I am to consider it all joy when I encounter various trials, knowing that the testing produces endurance' (James 1:2–3). *Need protection?* 'How wonderful, Lord, that You are faithful, and will strengthen and protect me from evil' (II Thessalonians 3:3). *Weak?* 'Help me remember, Father, that in all these things I am more than a conqueror through Him that loved me' (Romans 8:37)."

It's been a year saturated with prayer for SUSAN WILLIAMS of Sacramento, California. "Major surgery and several months of recuperation taught me lessons I never knew I needed to learn. The Lord showed me that even when I could not sit up or feed myself, I could still be vitally involved in His work and in others' lives through prayer. How exciting to discover firsthand that despite my body's limitations, there are no limits to what God can and will do when I pray!" Susan's dog Chewy, a 15-year-old golden lab-German shepherd mix, was her constant companion in the months after surgery. "When I started feeling too sorry for myself, Chewy had a great ploy for snapping me out of it. He'd put his head on my lap, ears drooping, and gaze soulfully into my eyes while whimpering as if his heart were breaking. After a few seconds of this, I couldn't help laughing out loud—while he grinned right along with me. It was the best medicine in the world."

House Guests

Our family circle of writer-friends embraces these old and new faces. They'll be dropping in throughout the year to share their stories with you.

ELLYN BAUMANN lives in Houston, Minnesota, with her son Zeb, 11, whom she's home-schooled for the past 3 years. Ellyn also works for the Houston *Gazette* as a reporter/photographer. "When I awake, I deliberately bring my first thought of the morning to God. 'Good morning, Jesus! Good morning, Father! Good morning, Holy Spirit!' I pray. 'Thank You for this new day.' And I'm much more refreshed than I used to be when I'd just climb out of bed with my eyelids half shut and look at the clock to see if it was really morning already."

This year, MARY BROWN of East Lansing, Michigan, and her husband Alex will celebrate 10 years of marriage. Their children Elizabeth, 6, and Mark, 1, are especially precious to them because Mary struggled with infertility for several years. Those years taught Mary the power of prayer. "Trying to turn to God each day with some praise, thanksgiving or prayer for others drew me out of my consuming emotions and the stress of all the medical procedures. Often I start out asking God to change a situation or remove a trouble, but instead prayer changes me — helps me accept my circumstances and receive grace to handle the problem."

BROCK KIDD, 21, is a senior at the University of Tennessee in Knoxville. He holds the office of secretary with his fraternity Sigma

Chi. "The beautiful outdoors of Tennessee provides a great deal of enjoyment for me. As often as possible, I get out into the woods or in a
clear stream and admire God's work. Whether I'm hunting, fishing or
just soaking in its splendor, God's creation allows me to communicate
with Him in my purest form."

ELSIE LARSON of Beaverton, Oregon, and her husband Dick decided to keep the little farm he inherited from his parents. They spent
several months renovating, and now their grandchildren can enjoy the
creek, the field, the big garden and fruit trees, just as their parents did.
And Elsie has her own quiet place for prayer — she can walk from the
backyard, down a hill to a little stream that has carved a place for itself
at the edge of the property. "Prayer always makes my life go better. I
believe prayer is 'giving God permission' to replace my will with His."

BONNIE LUKES of Canyon Country, California, had a hysterectomy
last August, which the doctors predicted would reveal cancer. But,
ultimately, only a precancerous condition was found. She and husband
John celebrated with a "colorful" autumn vacation in New England,
where in Maine, they bravely tackled the logistics of eating their first
whole lobster. "I pray my 'heavy-duty' prayer during my morning
walk. And since morning is the best part of my day, I want to share the
best with Him."

MARJORIE PARKER of Wichita Falls, Texas, was afraid she would
have a paint can permanently attached to her hand after spending
months repainting the family's new home. But now it's all done, and
husband Joe and daughters Joanna, 13, and Sarah, 10, are happy. They
vacationed in the Colorado mountains this past summer with several
families of friends. "I like to pray by sitting in my rocking chair in the
bedroom by the window. I enjoy addressing God by His various names,
such as the Hebrew name *El Shaddai*, which means 'the Almighty,' because it helps me concentrate on Him in all His roles as Provider, or
Strengthener, or Powerful One, or Father."

ELLEN SECREST of Newport, Rhode Island, and her husband Glenn
flew to Fort Lauderdale, Florida, to celebrate the engagement of their
daughter Lauren to Christopher Howley. Their son Chris is also in
Florida, where he's studying for his commercial pilot's license. "When
I'm praying about a big problem, I try to give a lot of thanks — thanks

for Christ being right with me, thanks for the opportunity to learn from Him, thanks for the chance to get to know Him better. It helps to get my mind off myself and to focus on the Lord."

TIMOTHY SLEDGE, the 21-year-old son of *Daily Guideposts* contributor Linda Ching Sledge, makes his writing debut in this year's devotional. Timothy is a senior at the University of Pennsylvania in Philadelphia, where he is majoring in English and economics. On weekend visits home to Pleasantville, New York, Timothy likes to "jam" on piano and drums with his 12-year-old brother Geoffrey, and make cappuccino with his girlfriend Jennifer.

Editor's Note: This year, as in previous years, we have said good-bye to some of our writers. While we shall miss these dear friends, we wish them well as they move on to seek new challenges and horizons. Meanwhile, some old faces have returned, and we greet them with a hearty "Welcome back to *Daily Guideposts, 1994!*"

MAY WE PRAY FOR YOU?

Every Monday morning at 9:45, Guideposts Prayer Fellowship *gathers to pray for the needs of friends and readers who have sent us their requests. A far-reaching network of pray-ers from all over the country also pray with us at this special time.*

As you learn more about prayer this year in Daily Guideposts, *we invite you to join us in spirit at our Monday morning fellowship. Pray for the needs of family members and friends, and remember, too, the Guideposts family and our work of bringing you helpful Christian literature. Feel free to write us with your own prayer requests, or when you need an extra boost of love and support. Your prayer circle of friends here at Guideposts will gladly pray for you.*

Write to Guideposts Prayer Fellowship, *39 Seminary Hill Road, Carmel, New York 10512. God bless and keep you during the year ahead.*

— The Editors

The Reader's Guide

A handy, three-part index
to all the selections
in Daily Guideposts, 1994

SCRIPTURE REFERENCE INDEX

An alphabetical index of Scripture references to verses appearing either at the top of devotionals or, on occasion, within the text. Chapter and verse numbers are in bold type on the left. Numbers in regular type, on the right, refer to the Daily Guideposts page(s) on which the complete verse or reference can be located.

FIRST FEW WORDS INDEX

An alphabetical index to the first few words of Scripture verses appearing either at the top of the devotionals or within the text, as well as the first few words of poetry, prose quotations and songs appearing in the book. Numbers given refer to the Daily Guideposts *page(s) on which these can be located.*

AUTHORS, TITLES AND SUBJECTS INDEX

An alphabetical index to devotional authors; titles of special series, poems and songs; proper names of people, places and things; holidays and holy days; biblical persons and events appearing in the text; and subjects with subheading breakdowns that will help you find a devotional to meet that special need. Numbers refer to the Daily Guideposts *page(s) on which these can be located.*

----------------- *A Note from the Editors* -----------------

This devotional book was created by the same staff that prepares *Guideposts*, a monthly magazine filled with true stories of people's adventures in faith.

If you have found enjoyment in *Daily Guideposts, 1994*, and would like to order additional copies for yourself or as gifts, the cost is $12.95 for either the regular print edition or Big Print edition. Orders should be sent to Guideposts Associates, Inc., 39 Seminary Hill Road, Carmel, New York 10512.

We also think you'll find monthly enjoyment — and inspiration — in the exciting and faith-filled stories that appear in our magazine as well. *Guideposts* is not sold on the newsstand. It's available by subscription only. And subscribing is easy. All you have to do is write Guideposts Associates, Inc., 39 Seminary Hill Road, Carmel, New York 10512. A year's subscription costs only $9.97 in the United States, and $11.97 in Canada and overseas. Our Big Print edition, for those with special reading needs, is only $9.97 in the United States, Canada and abroad.

When you subscribe, each month you can count on receiving exciting new evidence of God's presence, His guidance and His limitless love for all of us.